Practical Parallel Processing

Practical Parallel Processing

An Introduction to Problem Solving in Parallel

Alan Chalmers
Department of Computer Science
University of Bristol

and

Jonathan Tidmus
University of the West of England

INTERNATIONAL THOMSON COMPUTER PRESS

I ⓣ P   An International Thomson Publishing Company

London • Bonn • Boston • Johannesburg • Madrid • Melbourne • Mexico City • New York • Paris
Singapore • Tokyo • Toronto • Albany, NY • Belmont, CA • Cincinnati, OH • Detroit, MI

Practical Parallel Processing
Copyright © 1996 A. Chalmers and J. Tidmus

I ⓣ P A division of International Thomson Publishing Inc.
The ITP logo is a trademark under licence.

For more information, contact:

International Thomson Computer Press
Berkshire House
168–173 High Holborn
London WC1V 7AA
UK

International Thomson Computer Press
20 Park Plaza
Suite 1001
Boston, MA 02116
USA

Imprints of International Thomson Publishing

International Thomson Publishing GmbH
Königswinterer Straße 418
53227 Bonn
Germany

International Thomson Publishing Asia
221 Henderson Road #05-10
Henderson Building
Singapore

Thomas Nelson Australia
102 Dodds Street
South Melbourne, 3205
Victoria
Australia

International Thomson Publishing Japan
Hirakawacho Kyowa Building, 3F
2-2-1 Hirakawacho
Chiyoda-ku, 102 Tokyo
Japan

Nelson Canada
1120 Birchmount Road
Scarborough, Ontario
Canada M1K 5G4

International Thomson Editores
Campos Eliseos 385, Piso 7
Col. Polenco
11560 Mexico D.F. Mexico

International Thomson Publishing South Africa
PO Box 2459
Halfway House
1685 South Africa

International Thomson Publishing France
1, rue St. Georges
75009 Paris
France

WebExtra is a Service Mark of Thomson Holdings Inc.

Products and services that are referred to in this book may be either trademarks and/or registered trademarks of their respective owners. The Publisher/s and Author/s make no claim to these trademarks.

The programs in this book have been included for their instructional value. While every precaution has been taken with their preparation, the publisher does not offer any warranties or representations, nor does it accept any liabilities with respect to the information contained herein.

British Library Cataloguing-in-Publication Data
A catalogue record for this book is available from the British Library
Library of Congress Cataloguing-in-Publication Data
A catalog record for this book is available from the Library of Congress

First printed 1996

ISBN 1-85032-135-3

Commissioning Editor Samantha Whittaker
Cover Designed by Paragon International
Typeset by Hodgson Williams Associates, Tunbridge Wells and Cambridge
Printed in the UK by Cambridge University Press, Cambridge

Contents

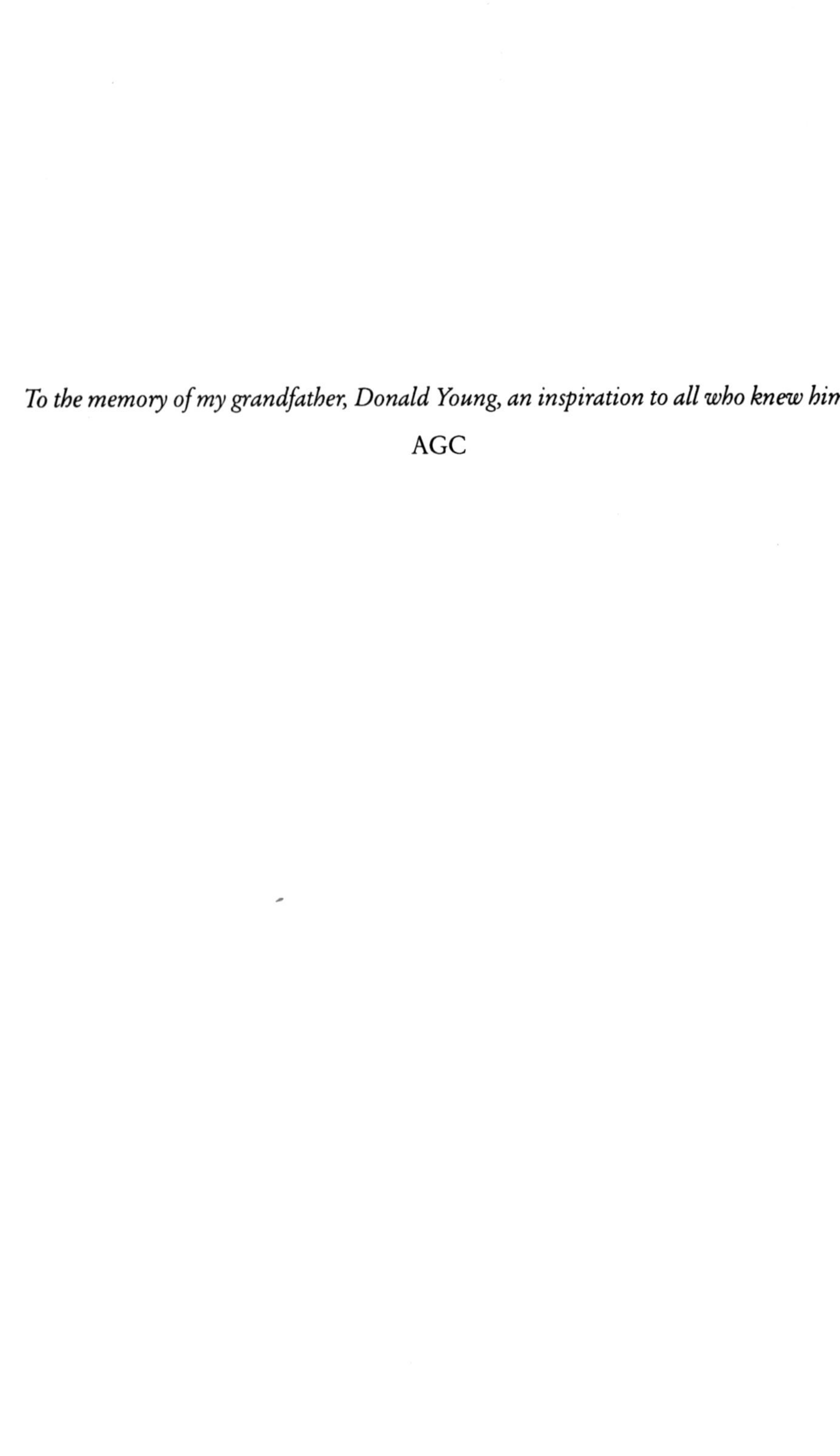

To the memory of my grandfather, Donald Young, an inspiration to all who knew him.

AGC

Foreword

Parallel processing has become pervasive. Parallel instruction execution using pipelining and multiple function units is a major feature of all high-performance processors. Multiprocessor servers and workstations have become commonplace, and experimental use of highly parallel processors has grown. New applications have emerged especially in the creation, storage and communication of multimedia information. Parallel computing continues to have great fascination for computer scientists and computer architects, and for scientists and engineers with large and complex problems.

A major growth in parallel computing occurred during the 1980s when it became clear that microprocessor technology would allow machines with tens, hundreds or even thousands of connected processors to be built. Initial enthusiasm led to the rapid development of a variety of different machines, each with its associated programming tools and techniques. Technological considerations favoured the use of distributed memory architectures, especially for the larger machines. It became clear that communication within these machines was a critical factor for performance, and research in this area has given rise to significant improvements in parallel computer architectures over the last few years.

Over the last decade, there has been much debate about programming languages and tools for parallel machines, but as yet no widespread standards have emerged. Little attention has been paid to issues of software portability and re-use, and general purpose large scale parallelism remains elusive. Nevertheless, many problems have been successfully tackled, and high performance has been achieved. This is especially true when distributed memory machines are programmed using algorithms which take into account their major architectural features.

This book is based on several years experience in the use of distributed memory multiprocessors. It covers the main issues in parallel computer architecture and programming, and shows how to tackle a variety of realistic problems. Conveniently, the algorithms and programs developed for distributed memory machines can be applied to almost any parallel computer. The book will therefore be of interest to anyone wishing to gain an understanding of parallel computer architecture and of the use of parallel computing in science and engineering.

David May   Bristol, January 1996

Preface

The problems facing scientists and engineers today are computationally complex, limiting their solution on computers using traditional approaches. The evolutionary development of the serial computer may finally be reaching its zenith due to fundamental physical limitations. As computational expectations continue to rise, more users are viewing parallel processing as a means to circumvent these restrictions. In this way, a number of processors are able to co-operate in the solution of a single problem, offering almost unlimited possibilities for solving complex problems.

Parallel processing offers the potential of solving real problems in acceptable times. This text is a comprehensive description of the techniques needed to solve complex problems on multiprocessor systems with special emphasis on those with distributed memory. The aim of this book is to provide an understanding of the necessary techniques, present a methodology as to how they may be applied, and demonstrate how their correct usage will improve system performance.

Many of the ideas associated with parallel processing have been developed in the last ten years, and whilst textbooks exist, these have mainly dealt with descriptions of the architectures, been introductions to the field, or dealt with theoretical concepts. These texts provide a useful insight into the intricacies of parallel processing, but provide few guidelines as to how complex problems may be implemented successfully on a given multiprocessor system. Similarly, although the solutions of a number of science and engineering problems on large multiprocessor systems have been reported in the research literature, the details associated with the implementation are often omitted. People with complex problems are not necessarily skilled parallel programmers and will often need to collaborate with computer scientists who may have no understanding of the problems' underlying concepts. These observations point to the need for a comprehensive text which will enable any complex problem to be analysed to determine the criteria necessary for an efficient parallel implementation. This is such a text.

As a wide range of parallel architectures exists, this book concentrates on one particular class of architecture which is arguably the most general purpose and scalable: distributed-memory message-passing systems. The aim of the book is to provide a level of detail suitable for implementors using these parallel systems. In this respect, all the case studies examined have been implemented on such an architecture using the techniques described. Crucial parts of these methods are illustrated using pseudo-code. Appendix B explains the syntax of this pseudo-code.

Distributed computing involves implementing a problem on a network of autonomous computers. While some of the properties of a distributed computing system, such as the computation-to-communication ratio, may be different from those of a dedicated distributed-memory message-passing parallel system, many of the underlying concepts are equivalent. For example, both systems achieve co-operation between computational units by passing messages, and each computational unit has its own distinct memory. So, although this book focuses on parallel processing, the ideas presented here should prove equally useful to the reader faced with implementing his or her complex problem on a distributed system.

Exercises and Project Suggestions

Exercises and suggestions help to illustrate important concepts and thus form an integral part of this text. Some of these are quite lengthy and can be used for course assignments. Outline answers are provided on-line at:

http://www.thomson.com/itcp.html

Also available at this address are the pseudo-code listing for the SAMD system and a set of overhead slides to accompany lectures utilising material covered in this book.

Layout of the Book

Figure 1 illustrates possible pathways through the text. The material can be split into two disciplines:

- Introduction to advanced computer architecture and parallel programming, following Chapters 1–5.

- Advanced parallel computing and practical programming using Chapters 1, 4 and 6–10.

Readers' Guide

The first three chapters provide the background to parallel processing and why it will be vitally important for the future of computers. Chapter 4 introduces the concepts of parallel problem implementation and provides guidelines as to how the parallelism within a given problem may be exploited. The merit of a parallel application may be judged by the resultant solution time. Chapter 5 discusses this, identifies additional metrics and describes their applicability.

Chapters 6 to 9 provide the techniques to overcome the initially daunting prospect of implementing one's own problem on a multiprocessor system. These enable the efficient distribution of work and data to ensure maximum system performance. Case studies are used throughout these chapters to illustrate the application of the techniques within real problems.

Chapter 10 unifies the ideas introduced in the preceding chapters, developing

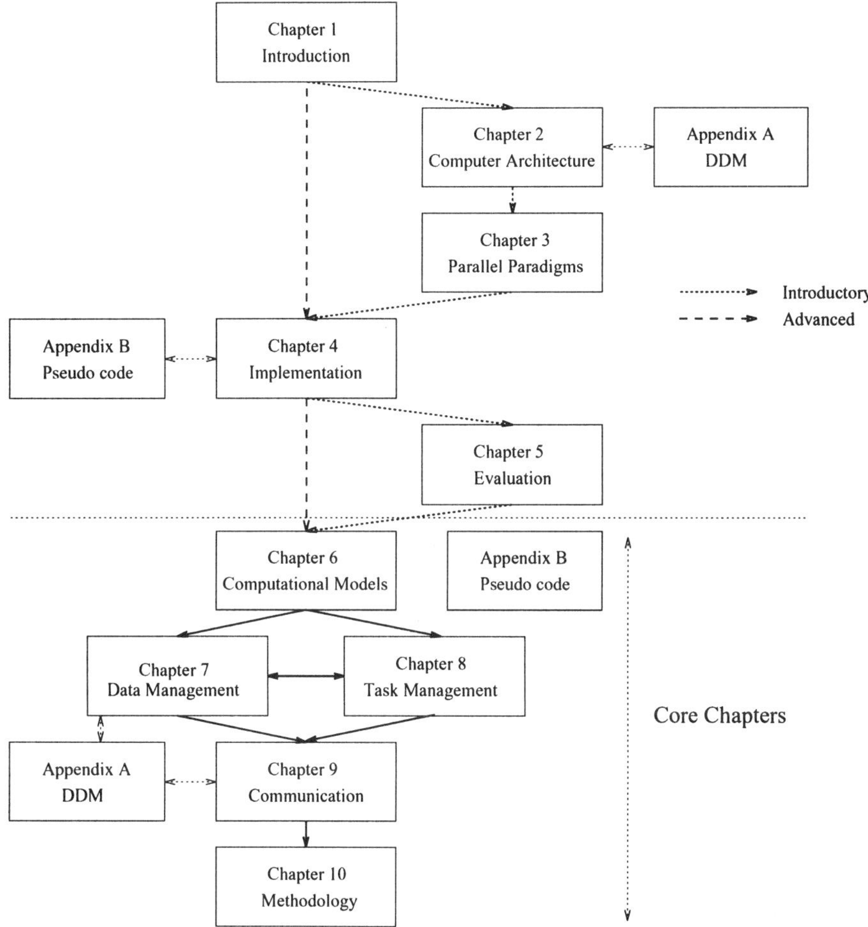

Figure 1 Readers' guide

an approach for solving complex problems and providing the structure of the supporting system software. The solution of a complex problem demonstrating this methodology forms the case study completing this chapter.

Appendix A provides details of a virtual shared memory architecture, the Data Diffusion Machine (DDM). The DDM is a good example of an actual architecture which attempts to address many of the issues associated with efficient data management, discussed in Chapters 8 and 9. The appendix may be used to augment the background on advanced computer architectures given in Chapter 2 and as a case study for Chapters 8 and 9.

Finally, Appendix B helps clarify the pseudo-code used throughout the text. This appendix is useful as an aid when translating the given code segments into actual parallel computer languages.

Acknowledgements

In our experience, a book doesn't just "come about". It has been a slow maturing of material by the input of numerous students and colleagues during lectures and laboratories. We are grateful for the enthusiasm of these people, not only in this country, but also in the Czech Republic, India, Poland, Portugal, Romania and South Africa.

We would like to thank Henk Muller and David Warren of Bristol University who helped with details on virtual shared memory architectures and kindly contributed information about the Data Diffusion Machine. Thank you also to George Wells of Rhodes University, South Africa who assisted with the material on Linda and PVM.

There are many other people to thank for their direct contribution to this book: our editor, Samantha Whittaker, for her patience; the staff of ITP and HWA for their assistance in preparing the manuscript; Doug and Su Smith, John Counsell and Brian Stonebridge and Tabby Davis for the arduous task of proofreading; Peter Welch for his tireless enthusiasm for parallel processing; and Chris Nevison, Janet Edwards and anonymous UK and US reviewers for their helpful comments. Discussions with Stuart Green, Derek Paddon, Steve Fiddes and Luis Paulo dos Santos helped formulate many of these ideas.

Roger Miles and our colleagues and friends at the University of Bristol and the University of the West of England have provided support and a stimulating working environment.

Finally, without the encouragement of our families, and especially Rhona, this book might never have been completed.

Chapter 1

Introduction to Parallel Processing

Death, taxes & parallel processing: nobody's in favour of any of them, but they're inevitable facts of life.

With apologies to Benjamin Franklin

Parallel processing offers the ability to solve complex problems in reasonable times. Despite this, the full potential of large-scale multiprocessor systems is still to be realised. This chapter introduces the concepts of parallel processing, describes its development and considers the difficulties associated with solving problems in parallel.

Parallel processing is an integral part of everyday life. The concept is so ingrained in our existence that we benefit from it without realising. When faced with a taxing problem, we involve others to solve it more easily. This co-operation of more than one agent to facilitate the solution of a particular problem may be termed parallel processing. The goal of parallel processing is thus to solve a given problem more rapidly, or to enable the solution of a problem that would otherwise be impracticable by a single agent.

The practicality of problem solution is often dictated by associated time constraints. The relevance of a 24 hour weather forecast may be questioned if it requires 36 hours to calculate. There are a multitude of real problems which can benefit from completion times that may be deemed 'reasonable' within their given context. These problems may be as diverse as house construction or earthquake prediction.

Contemporary science relies heavily on computer modelling to complement physical experimentation. Numerical simulation reduces overheads such as expense and inherent difficulties associated with the scientific process. Whilst modelling may never exactly mirror physical processes nor obviate the need for exact measurement, it is an increasingly powerful tool. This is particularly true in situations where obtaining a complete data set is impracticable and where numerous factors interact in a complex manner, for example in global climate models. The computational demands of these calculations continue to rise and will always stretch available processing power. Parallel processing is essential if these demands are to be met in the future.

The principles of parallel processing are, however, not new, as evidence suggests that the computational devices used over 2000 years ago by the Greeks recognised and exploited such concepts. In the nineteenth century, Babbage used parallel processing in order to improve the performance of his Analytical Engine [137]. Indeed, the first general purpose electronic digital computer, the ENIAC, was conceived as a highly parallel and decentralised machine with 25 independent computing units, co-operating towards the solution of a single problem [96].

However, the early computer developers rapidly identified two obstacles restricting the widespread acceptance of parallel machines: the complexity of construction; and the seemingly high programming effort required [34]. As a result of these early set-backs, the developmental thrust shifted to computers with a single computing unit, to the detriment of parallel designs. Additionally, the availability of sequential machines resulted in the development of algorithms and techniques optimised for these particular architectures.

The evolution of serial computers may be finally reaching its zenith due to the limitations imposed on the design by its physical implementation and inherent bottlenecks [17]. As users continue to demand improved performance, computer designers have been looking increasingly at parallel approaches to overcome these limitations. All modern computer architectures incorporate a degree of parallelism. Improved hardware design and manufacture coupled with a growing understanding of how to tackle the difficulties of parallel programming has re-established parallel processing at the forefront of computer technology.

1.1 Concepts

Parallel processing is the solution of a single problem by dividing it into a number of sub-problems, each of which may be solved by a separate agent. Co-operation will always be necessary between agents during problem solution, even if this is a simple agreement on the division of labour. These ideas can be illustrated by a simple analogy of tackling the problem of emptying a swimming pool using buckets. This job may be sub-divided into the repeated *task* of removing one bucket of water, as shown in figure 1.1.

A single person will complete all the tasks, and complete the job, in a certain time. This process may be speeded up by utilising additional workers. Ideally, two people should be able to empty the pool in half the time. Extending this argument, a large number of workers should be able to complete the job in a small fraction of the original time. However, practically there are physical limitations preventing this hypothetical situation.

The physical realisation of this solution necessitates a basic level of co-operation between workers. This manifests itself due to the contention for access to the pool, and the need to avoid collision. The time required to achieve this co-operation involves inter-worker communication which detracts from the overall solution time, and as such may be termed an *overhead*.

1.1.1 Dependencies

Another factor preventing an ideal parallel solution is dependencies. Consider the problem of constructing a house. In simple terms, building the roof can only

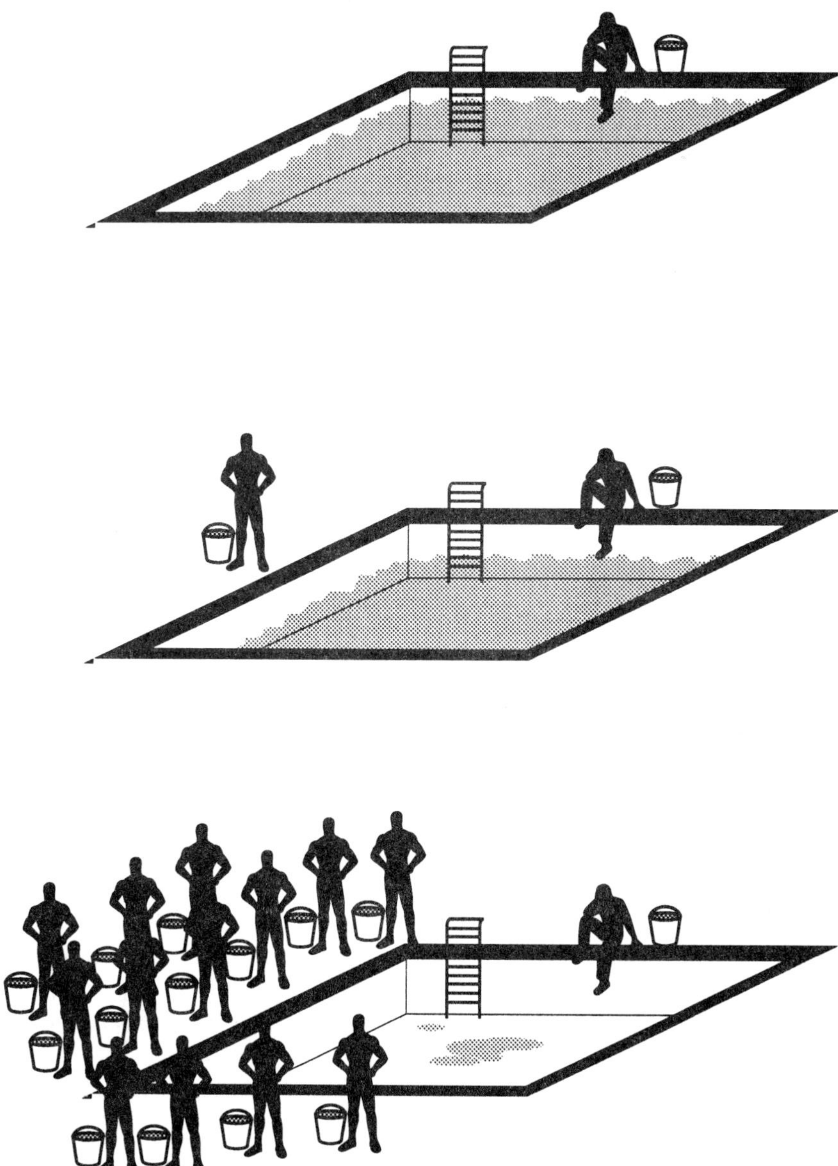

Figure 1.1   Emptying a pool by means of a bucket

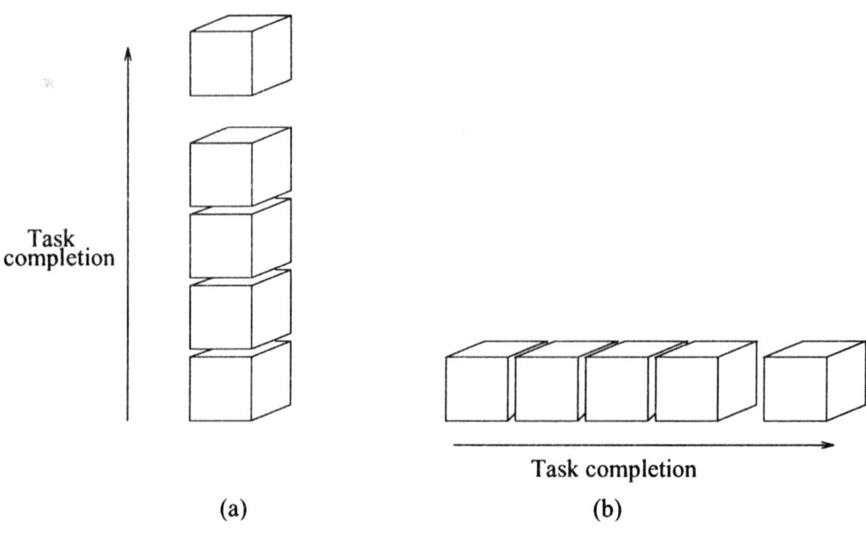

Figure 1.2   Building with blocks: (a) strictly sequential (b) dependency-free

commence after the walls have been completed. Similarly, the walls can only be erected once the foundations are laid. The roof is thus dependent upon the walls, which are in turn dependent on the foundations. These dependencies divide the whole problem into a number of distinct stages. The parallel solution of each stage must be completed before the subsequent stage can start.

The dependencies within a problem may be so severe that it is not amenable to parallel processing. A strictly sequential problem consists of a number of stages, each comprising a single task, and each dependent upon the previous stage. For example, in figure 1.2, building a tower of toy blocks requires a strictly sequential order of task completion. The situation is the antithesis of dependency-free problems, such as placing blocks in a row on the floor. In this case, the order of task completion is unimportant, but the need for co-operation will still exist.

Pipelining is the classic methodology for minimising the effects of dependencies. This technique can only be exploited when a process, consisting of a number of distinct stages, needs to be repeated several times. An automotive assembly line is an example of an efficient pipeline. In a simplistic form, the construction of a car may consist of four linearly dependent stages as shown in figure 1.3: chassis fabrication, body assembly, wheel fitting and windscreen installation. An initial lump of metal is introduced into the pipeline then, as the partially completed car passes each stage, a new section is added until finally the finished car is available outside the factory.

Consider an implementation of this process consisting of four agents, each performing a task in one time unit. Having completed the task, the agent passes the partially completed car on to the next stage. This agent is now free to repeat its task on a new component fed from the previous stage. The completion of the first

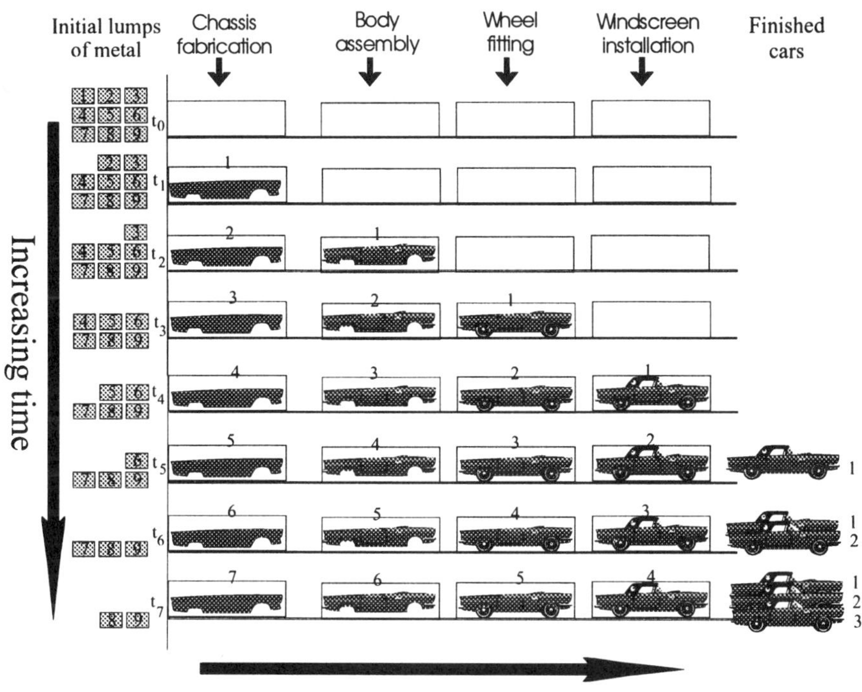

Motion of cars through pipeline

Figure 1.3   Pipeline assembly of a car

car occurs after four time units, but each subsequent car is completed every time unit.

The completion of a car is, of course, sensitive to the time taken by each agent. If one agent were to take longer than one time unit to complete its task then the agents after this difficult task would stand idle awaiting the next component, whilst those before the agent with the difficult task would be unable to move their component on to the next stage of the pipeline. The other agents would thus also be unable to do any further work until the difficult task was completed. Should there be any interruption in the input to the pipeline then the pipeline would once more have to be 'refilled' before it could operate at maximum efficiency.

1.1.2 Scalability

Every problem contains an upper bound on the number of agents which can be meaningfully employed in its solution. Additional agents beyond this number will not improve solution time, and can indeed be detrimental. This upper bound provides an idea as to how suitable a problem is for parallel implementation: a measure of its *scalability*.

A given problem may only be divided into a finite number of sub-problems,

Figure 1.4   Bottleneck caused by doorway

corresponding to the smallest tasks. The availability of more agents than there are tasks will not improve solution time. The problem of clearing a room of 100 chairs may be divided into 100 tasks consisting of removing a single chair. A maximum of 100 workers can be allocated one of these tasks and hence perform useful work.

The optimum solution time for clearing the room may not in fact occur when employing 100 workers due to certain aspects of the problem limiting effective worker utilisation. This phenomenon can be illustrated by adding a constraint to the problem, in the form of a single doorway providing egress from the room. A *bottleneck* will occur as large numbers of workers attempt to move their chairs through the door simultaneously, as shown in figure 1.4.

The delays caused by this bottleneck may be so great that the time taken to empty the room of chairs by this large number of workers may in fact be longer than the original time taken by the single worker. In this case, reducing the number of workers can alleviate the bottleneck and thus reduce solution time.

1.1.3 Control

All parallel solutions of a problem require some form of control. This may be as simple as the control needed to determine what will constitute a task and to ascertain when the problem has been solved satisfactorily. More complex problems may require control at several stages of their solution. For example, solution time could be improved when clearing the room if a controller was placed at the door to schedule its usage. This control would ensure that no time was wasted by two (or more) workers attempting to exit simultaneously and then having to 'reverse' to allow a single worker through. An alternative to this explicit centralised control would be some form of distributed control. Here the workers themselves could have a way of preventing simultaneous access, for example, if two (or more) workers reach the door at the same time then the biggest worker will always go first while the others wait.

Figure 1.5(a) shows the sequential approach to solving a problem. Computation

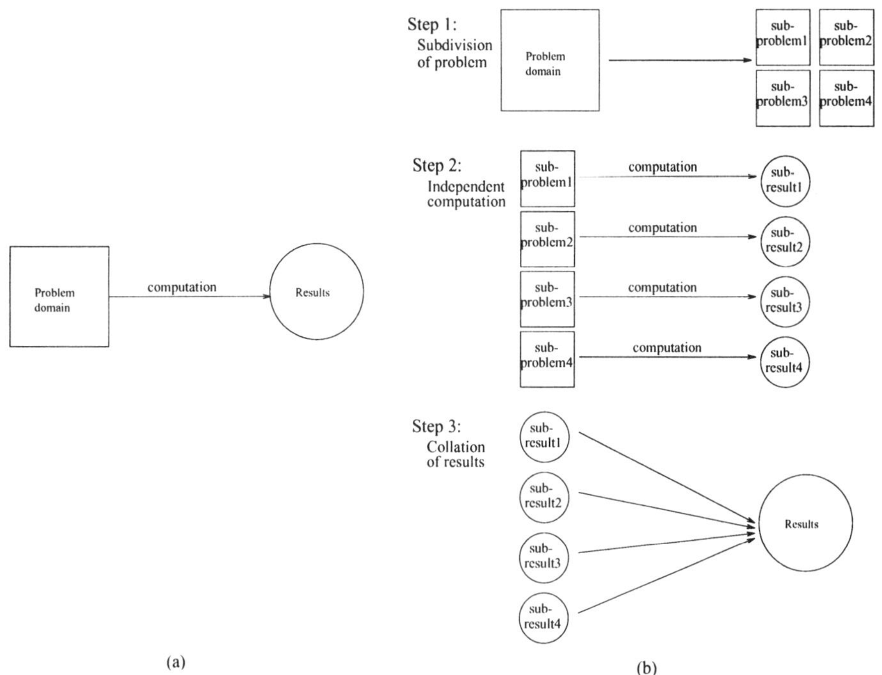

(a)   (b)

Figure 1.5   Control required in (a) sequential versus (b) parallel implementation

is applied to the problem domain to produce the desired results. The controlled parallel approach shown in figure 1.5(b) achieves a parallel implementation of the same problem via three steps. In step 1, the problem domain is divided into a number of sub-problems, in this case four. Parallel processing is introduced in step 2 to enable each of the sub-problems to be computed in parallel to produce sub-results. In step 3, these results must now be collated to achieve the desired final results. Control is necessary in steps 1 and 3 to divide the problem amongst the agents and then to collect and collate the results that the agents have independently produced.

1.2 Technical Parallel Processing Concepts

This section introduces concepts associated with the implementation of problems on multiprocessor architectures. A more technical description of how a problem may be implemented in parallel commences in Chapter 4.

A traditional sequential computer conforms to the von Neumann model. Shown in figure 1.6, this model comprises a processor, an associated memory, an input/output interface and various busses connecting these devices. The processor in the von Neumann model is the single computational unit responsible for the functions of fetching, decoding and executing a program's instructions. Parallel processing may be added to this architecture through pipelining using multiple

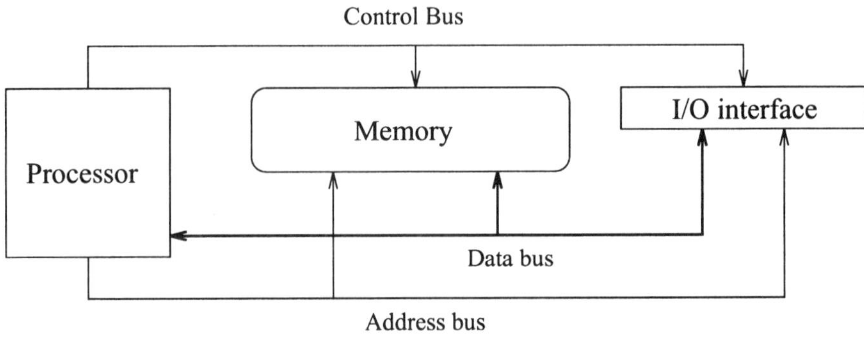

Figure 1.6   Von Neumann model architecture

functional units within a single computational unit or by replicating entire computational units (which may contain pipelining). With pipelining, each functional unit repeatedly performs the same operation on data received from the preceding functional unit. So in the simplest case, a pipeline for a computational unit could consist of three functional units, one to fetch the instructions from memory, one to decode these instructions and one to execute the decoded instructions. As we saw with the automobile assemblage example, a pipeline is only as effective as its slowest component. Any delay in the pipeline has repercussions for the whole system.

Vector processing was introduced to provide efficient execution of program loops on large array data structures. By providing multiple registers as special vector registers to be used alongside the central processing unit, a vector processor is able to perform the same operation on all elements of a vector simultaneously. This simultaneous execution on every element of large arrays can produce significant performance improvements over conventional scalar processing. However, often problems need to be reformulated to benefit from this form of parallelism. A large number of scientific problems, such as weather forecasting, nuclear research and seismic data analysis, are well suited to vector processing.

Replication of the entire computational unit, the processor, allows individual tasks to be executed on different processors. Tasks are thus sometimes referred to as virtual processors which are allocated a physical processor on which to execute. The completion of each task contributes to the solution of the problem.

Tasks which are executing on distinct processors at any point in time are said to be running in parallel. It may also be possible to execute several tasks on a single processor. Over a period of time the impression is given that they are running in parallel, when in fact at any point in time only one task has control of the processor. In this case we say that the tasks are being performed *concurrently*, that is their execution is being shared by the same processor. The conceptual difference between parallel tasks and concurrent tasks is shown in figure 1.7.

The agents which perform the computational work and co-operate to facilitate the solution of a problem on a parallel computer are known as processing elements, often abbreviated to PEs. A PE consists of a processor, one or more tasks, and the

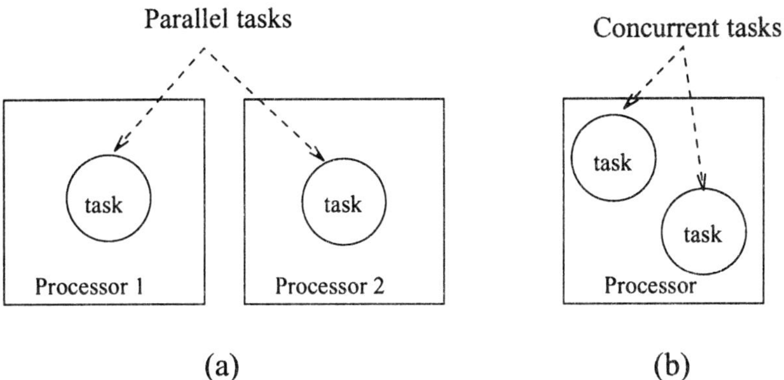

Figure 1.7   (a) Parallel tasks (b) Concurrent tasks

software to enable the co-operation with other PEs. A parallel system comprises more than one PE.

1.3 History

The development of the electronic computer is almost certainly one of the major events in world history [133]. Since the advent of the electronic computer in the 1940s there has been a tremendous surge forward in the performance and usage of computers, coupled with an ever-increasing demand for more computational power from the user community. The computers of the late 1940s and 1950s used vacuum tube technology which was expensive and unreliable. The performance and reliability was dramatically improved with the invention of the transistor in 1948 and the subsequent integration of a number of these transistors into single 'Small Scale Integration' packages. 'Medium Scale Integration' and 'Large Scale Integration' followed, culminating in the present day 'Very Large Scale Integration' (VLSI) computers in which the computing power of the earlier machines, which had occupied several rooms, can now be achieved by a single integrated circuit of a few centimetres in size and at a fraction of the price. The performance of sequential computers has improved in leaps and bounds so that now, after only 50 years, their descendants are capable of many orders of magnitude better performance and are in everyday use throughout the world.

Due to the envisaged design and programming difficulties associated with parallel computers, these machines have been less readily accepted by the commercial world. So, although Babbage's Analytical Engine and ENIAC both had replicated computational units, it was only in 1969 that Control Data Corporation produced their CDC 7600 computer which exploited pipelining to achieve substantial performance improvements over other existing computers. Seven years later in 1976, the Cray-1, arguably the world's first supercomputer, was delivered to Los Alamos National Laboratory. Since then progress on parallel architectures has accelerated rapidly with the rise of new manufacturers. However, the development costs for these advanced machines are high, and with the relatively low volume of current sales, several leading companies have been forced out of business. Until parallel processing is generally accepted in the market place and their sales increase, this trend will continue and novel architectures will disappear.

Table 1.1 lists some of the major developments in parallel computing in the years since the Cray-1 was first delivered. This list is by no means complete, and for a detailed description of the history of parallel computing, the reader is referred to books such as [107, 115].

1976	Cray-1—first pipelined vector computer
1977	C.mmp—16 PDP 11 processors connected via a crossbar switch
1979	ICL DAP—1024 1-bit array processor
1981	BBN Butterfly—256 Motorola 68000 processors connected in a multi-stage network
1982	Cray X/MP—4 Cray-1 processors sharing a common memory
1983	Goodyear MPP—132×128 1-bit array processor
1985	Inmos T414 transputer—32-bit processor including communication links
1986	TMC CM-1—64K 1-bit processors arranged in a 12-D hypercube
1987	TMC CM-2—64K 1-bit processors with FPUs arranged in a 12-D hypercube
1988	Cray Y/MP—16 processors with 2 vector pipes per processor
	Intel iPSC/2—Intel 80386 processors connected in a 7-D hypercube
	Inmos T800 transputer-separate FPU added to T414 design
	Hitachi S-820—1-processor with 18 replicated functional pipelines
1989	Fujitsu VP2000—2-processor multivector multiprocessor
1990	Alliant FX/2800—28 Intel i860 processors connected to memory banks via a crossbar
	MasPar MP1—16K 4-bit processors connected in 8-way mesh
	NEC SX-3—4 processors each with 4 pipelines
1991	Kendall Square Research KSR-1—32-processor virtual shared memory machine
1992	TMC CM-5—1024 SPARC processor connected using fat-tree topology
1993	Cray T3D—2048 DEC Alpha processors arranged in a 3-D torus
	J-Machine—512-processor message-driven multiprocessor arranged in k-ary n-cube
1994	Inmos T9000 transputer—processor includes virtual routing capabilities
1995	Intel announce development of 9000-processor P6-based machine

Table 1.1   Some important architectures in the history of parallel computing

1.4 Summary

Parallel processing is the solution of a single problem by using more than one processing element. This may be achieved by pipelining or replication. To solve the problem the processing elements need to co-operate. This co-operation introduces an overhead into the parallel solution which may restrict the total number of processing elements which can be gainfully employed.

Parallel processing is here to stay! Not only is it now possible to solve existing problems in a fraction of the previous time, but also complex problems, previously thought insoluble, are being tackled by modern computers. These include applications from:

- astrophysics – for example, the simulation of galaxy formation and motion

- pharmacological design – for example, drug construction

- weather and environmental simulation – for example, forecasting by global modelling

- computational fluid dynamics – for example, aircraft structural design

There remain, however, many problems which need even more computational power before they may be solved in reasonable times. The combination of large numbers of powerful computational units offers the potential for achieving this goal.

Parallel processing is conceptually easy: a matter of subdividing a problem into a number of sub-problems. However, the implementation of this concept on a multiprocessor computer is not straightforward. The goal of this book is to show a methodology by which such an implementation can proceed.

Chapter 2

Computer Architectures

The purpose of computers is insight not numbers.

Richard Hamming

Computer architecture describes the internal hardware components and how these are connected and controlled to produce the characteristics of a particular machine. Parallelism in a computer may be achieved either by pipelining or replicating the functional units. In the past few decades there has been an unprecedented explosion in the variety of computer architectures available. In an attempt to classify these diverse architectures Flynn proposed a taxonomy, which although not totally appropriate today, is still widely used. In this chapter we examine a 'classic' example of a high performance architecture from each of Flynn's classes and discuss their suitability for solving complex problems in reasonable times.

Computer architecture is the integration of physical hardware components with a complementary software environment to produce a particular computing resource. Both the hardware and software constituents have evolved considerably since the first generation of electronic computers were built.

The continuous demand by users for increased performance has seen the hardware technology 'leap' from vacuum tubes in the 1940s, to transistors in the 1950s, to integrated circuits with LSI and VSLI in the 1960s and 1970s. Trying to maintain this computational power momentum for single processors led to developments in the 1980s and 1990s, including increasing the packaging density in the hardware devices, investigating new technologies such as gallium arsenide, and the reduction of hardware complexity. This last development gave rise to the remarkable performance improvements brought about by RISC (Reduced Instruction Set Computer) architectures with their philosophy:

Perfection is achieved, not when there is nothing left to add, but when there is nothing left to take away.

Antoine de St. Exupéry

Ultimately, the speed of light places an upper limit on the performance that can be achieved with a sequential architecture. Parallelism offers the potential of

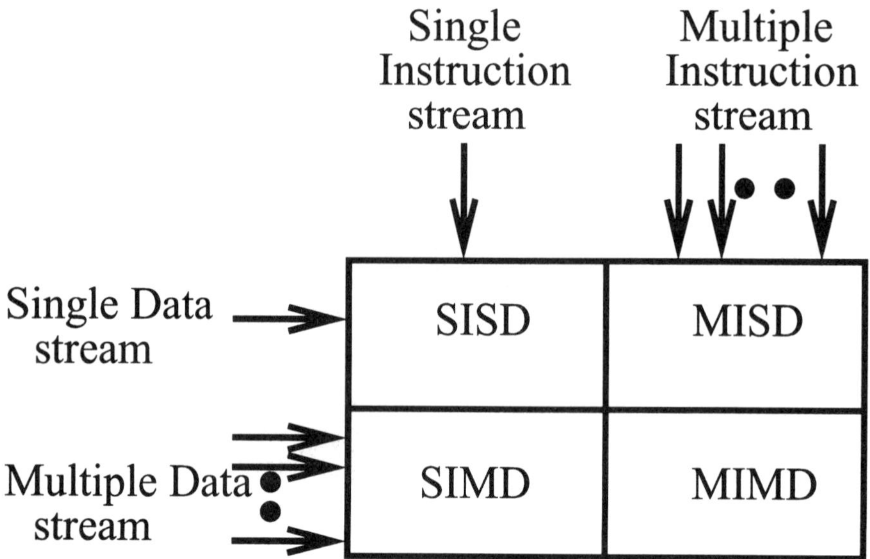

Figure 2.1 Flynn's taxonomy for processors

increasing computer performance indefinitely. However, this still remains very much a dream, and the best we can hope for at the moment is to continue research and developments in this area towards this goal.

2.1 Classification of Architectures

The wide diversity of computer architectures that have been proposed, and in a large number of cases realised, has led to the desire to classify the designs to facilitate evaluation and comparison. Classification requires a means of identifying distinctive architectural or behavioural features of a machine. Early computers, which adopted the model of a single central processing unit (CPU) connected to a memory unit have been described as von Neumann architectures. Within this model a distinct sequence of instructions operates on a single sequence of data. However, as computer designs moved away from this restrictive archetype, other methods of classification were sought.

In 1972 Flynn proposed a classification of processors according to a macroscopic view of their principal interaction patterns relating to instruction and data streams [70]. The term *stream* was used by Flynn to refer to the sequence of instructions to be executed, or data to be operated on, by the processor. What has become known as Flynn's taxonomy thus categorises architectures into the four areas shown in figure 2.1.

Since its inception, Flynn's taxonomy has been criticised as being too broad and has thus been enlarged by several other authors, for example, Shore in 1973 [168], Treleaven, Brownbridge and Hopkins in 1982 [176], Basu in 1984 [19] and perhaps one of the most detailed classifications was given by Hockney and Jesshope in 1988 [108].

Real architectures are, of course, much more complex than Flynn suggested. For example, an architecture may exhibit properties from more than one of his classes. However, if we are not too worried about the minute details of any individual machine then Flynn's taxonomy serves to separate fundamentally different architectures into four broad categories. The classification scheme is simple (which is one of the main reasons for its popularity) and thus useful to show an overview of the concepts of multiprocessor computers. This will allow us to identify the sort of multiprocessor machine that is suitable as the platform for supporting the parallel processing in which we are interested. A number of classic architectures within each of Flynn's categories will be presented to demonstrate the basic principles associated with each type of architecture.

2.1.1 SISD: Single Instruction Single Data

This classification embraces the conventional sequential, or von Neumann, processor. The single processing element executes instructions sequentially on a single data stream. The operations are thus ordered in time and may be easily traced from start to finish. Modern adaptations of this uniprocessor use some form of pipelining technique to improve performance and, as demonstrated by the Cray supercomputers, minimise the length of the component interconnections to reduce signal propagation times [162]. Pipelining introduces temporal parallelism by allowing the sequential execution of instructions to be overlapped in time by a number of functional units within the processor. For example, at the same time that the central processing unit is executing an instruction, the next instruction could be fetched from memory. The idle time of each functional unit is thus kept to a minimum with an obvious improvement in performance. The need for branching instructions can reduce the effectiveness of this strategy, but methods such as very long instruction words can be used to reduce the impact of this branching on throughput by processing several branches at once [68].

The Cray-1 supercomputer

In 1972, Seymour Cray left Control Data Corporation (CDC) to form Cray Research Inc. The Cray-1 computer contained multiple pipelines, which allowed scalar and vector operations to be performed in parallel [162]. The first Cray-1, delivered in 1976, had a performance of 130 MFLOPS (Millions of FLoating point OPerations per Second) on some well-suited matrix problems. This performance was significantly higher than any contemporary machine. The vector processing capability, the compact physical arrangement of its circuit boards, which were designed to minimise the length of interconnections and reduce signal propagation times, and the large scale integration of its circuit components, contributed to achieve such a high performance. These features, coupled with a revolutionary architecture, shown in figure 2.2, enabled the Cray-1 to become, in many people's eyes, the first true 'supercomputer'.

Within the Cray-1 architecture, the single ALU (Arithmetic Logic Unit) of

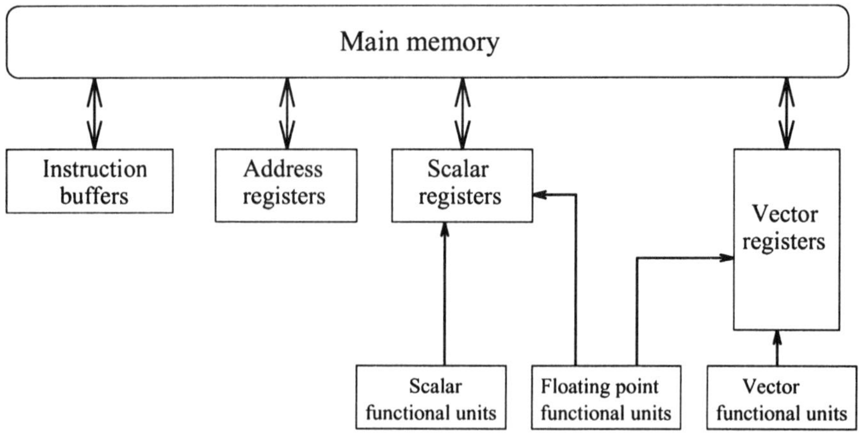

Figure 2.2 An overview of the Cray-1 architecture

conventional uniprocessors was replaced by twelve pipelined functional units, operating with a 12.5 nanosecond clock and 50 nanosecond memory cycle time. These independent functional units fetched operands from a set of scalar and vector registers to perform address, scalar, vector and floating point operations. Each of the functional units was pipelined, accepting a new set of operands in each clock period. The vector functional units were simultaneously able to perform an operation on each of the components of a 64-entry vector. The main memory had a capacity of up to one million 64-bit words. The memory was divided into sixteen banks which could be addressed in parallel.

Specialised software was developed to take full advantage of the novel architecture. A vectorising Fortran compiler was developed which automatically generated the necessary vector code for the 'inner-DO' loops in serial Fortran programs. There were limitations, however, as loops which contained conditional statements, jumps or subroutine calls would not vectorise. In many cases, the restrictions caused by these dependencies could be avoided by reformulating the program.

The Cray X/MP, released in 1983 as the successor to the Cray-1, corrected a memory bandwidth bottleneck within the Cray-1 architecture. The Cray X/MP combined two 'Cray-1 like' processors to form a vector multiprocessor. As well as the improved memory bandwidth, this machine reduced the cycle time to 9.5 nanoseconds. Later advances include the Cray Y/MP, containing up to 16 CPUs and a cycle time of between 4 and 5 nanoseconds, and the Cray T3D with up to 2048 processors and a peak performance of over 300 GFLOPS.

2.1.2 SIMD: Single Instruction Multiple Data

The SIMD class of machine applies a single instruction to a group of data items simultaneously. A master instruction is thus acting over a vector of related operands. A number of processors, therefore, obey the same instruction in the same cycle and may be said to be executing in strict lock-step. Facilities exist to exclude particular

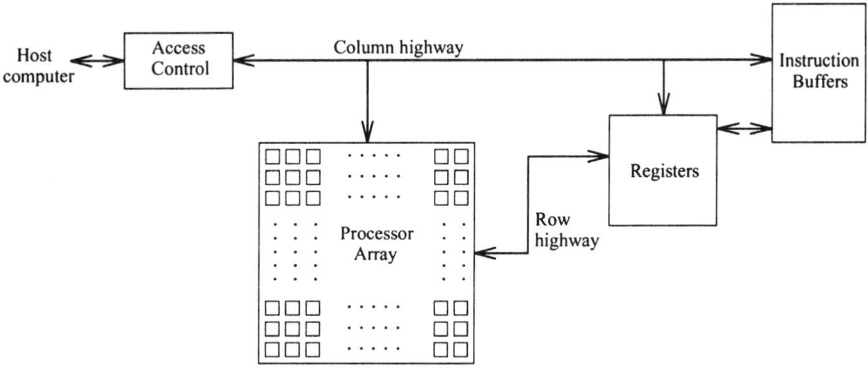

Figure 2.3   Overview of the DAP architecture

processors from participating in a given instruction cycle. Vector processors, as introduced in section 1.2, for example the Cyber 205, Fujitsu FACOM VP-200 and NEC SX1, and array processors, such as the DAP [159], Goodyear MPP (Massively Parallel Processor) [20], or the Connection Machine CM-1 [103], may be grouped in this category. Array processors typically consist of one control unit and a large number of fairly simple bit-serial processing elements. Each processing element is independent, but only operates on command from the control unit.

The Distributed Array Processor

The Distributed Array Processor (DAP) was developed by ICL to enable data to be processed in a highly parallel manner as part of an integrated system. The DAP was, therefore, designed to emulate a memory module of an ICL mainframe computer. The first production machine was delivered in 1979. The DAP consists of an array of 4096 one-bit processing elements arranged in a 64×64 grid. The rows and columns of processing elements are connected by two orthogonal data 'highways'. Each processing element addresses 4 Kbits of memory. A simplified architecture diagram of the DAP is shown in figure 2.3.

The access controller and column highway provide the interface to the host machine. Each bit of the 64-bit word of the mainframe computer corresponds to a row of the DAP memory. The registers are aligned with the row and column highways, and are used to broadcast data to, and collect results from, the array of processing elements. A single instruction stream is decoded by the control unit and the instructions are broadcast to the processing elements via the column highway.

Each processing element is connected to its four nearest neighbours and to its corresponding row and column highway. Instructions are used to define the connections at the edge of the two-dimensional grid. The CPU of each processing element consists of three one-bit registers, two multiplexers and a one-bit full adder which functions in a bit-serial manner.

A limitation of this type of system is that the architecture and the restrictions imposed by the hardware instruction implementations must be considered if performance is to be maximised. Programs which contain operations on arrays of 64×64 elements will be executed most efficiently. However, to tackle arrays with larger dimension, the programmer has to partition the data explicitly to ensure efficient processor utilisation. Another limitation is that the size of the instruction buffer is only 60 words. This means that the number of instructions of each loop to be executed by the array of processing elements is restricted. These architectural features must be considered when software is being developed for the DAP. If not, in the worst case, it is possible for matrix arithmetic instructions, which could potentially be executed by many thousands of processing elements, to be executed in practice by a single processing element.

The Connection Machine CM-1

Hillis conceived the idea of the Connection Machine while doing his doctorate at MIT [103]. This developed into the first prototype, the 16K (16384) processor CM-1, in 1984. The production CM-1 provides up to 64K (65536) processing elements each with 4 Kbits of memory, an interprocessor communications network, one to four sequencers, and one to four front-end computers. The 64K machine consists of 4096 processor integrated circuits and 32 Mbytes of RAM. The processors are arranged at the vertices of a 12-dimensional hypercube. Arithmetic is carried out in a bit-serial fashion, requiring 0.75 microseconds per bit plus instruction decoding and overhead. Hence, a 32-bit *Add* takes about 24 microseconds. With 64K processors computing in parallel this yields an aggregate rate of 2000 MIPS (Million Instructions Per Second).

The concept of virtual processors, called Paris, allows more processes to be used than there are physical processors. If the number of processes specified by the user exceeds the number of physical processors then, transparent to the user, the local memory of each processor is split into as many regions as necessary. The processors then automatically time-slice between the regions. Versions of Lisp, Fortran and C are available on the Connection Machine with extensions to support the data-parallel constructs.

Further development work evolved the CM-2, providing increased memory capacity (64 Kbits per processor), an optional floating point accelerator, a high speed I/O system, called the Data Vault, for peripheral data storage, and display devices. A fully configured 64K-processor system contains 4096 processor chips, 2048 floating point interface chips, 2048 floating point execution chips and 512 Mbyte of RAM. The Data Vault holds up to 10 Gbytes of data stored across an array of 39 disk drives. This data can be transferred at a rate of 40 Mbytes per second. Up to eight of these Data Vaults can operate in parallel.

The Connection Machine has a claimed sustained floating performance of 20 GFLOPS for polynomial evaluation using 32-bit floating point operands. An overview of the system is shown in figure 2.4.

2.1.3 MISD: Multiple Instruction Single Data

Although part of Flynn's taxonomy, no architecture falls obviously into the MISD category. One the closest architectures to this concept is a pipelined computer. In

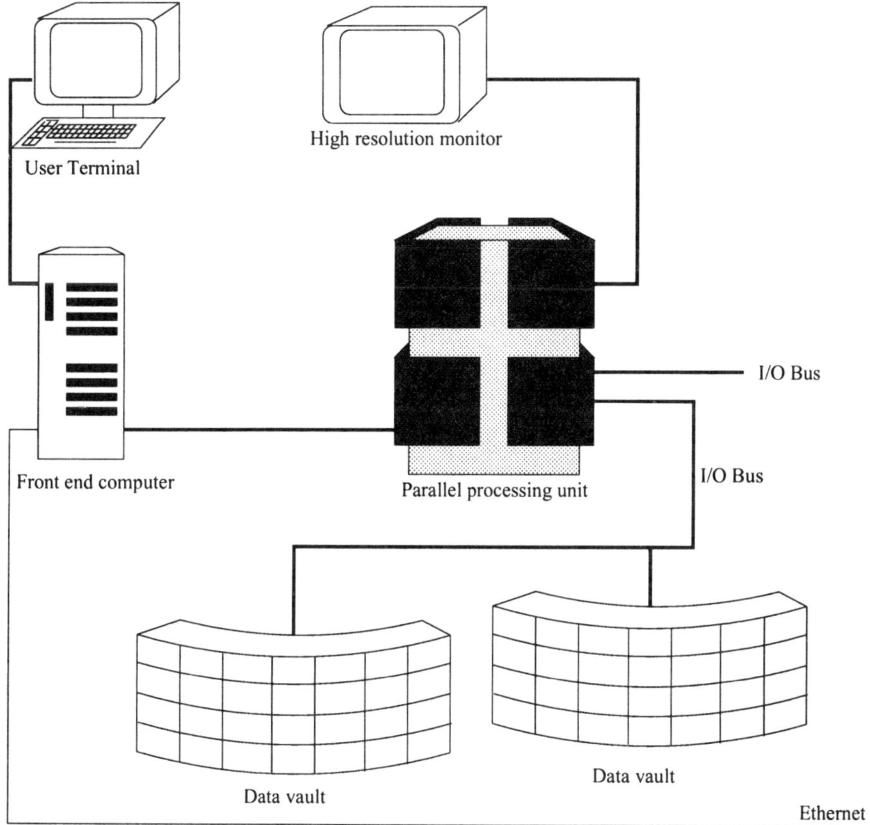

Figure 2.4 An overview of the Connection Machine system

this case, a number of processors pass a stream of data from one processor to the next. Each processor performs a different operation on the data, but only a single stream of results emerges from the system.

Systolic array architectures are also conceptually close to the MISD ideal. The name of this type of architecture derives from the medical term 'systole' used to describe the rhythmic contraction of chambers of the heart. Data arrive from different directions at regular intervals to be combined at the 'cells' of the array. The Intel iWarp system was designed to support systolic computation [11]. Systolic arrays are well suited to specially designed algorithms rather than general purpose computing. As we are interested in solving complex real problems we will not consider these architectures further here. Technical details can be found in [123, 124].

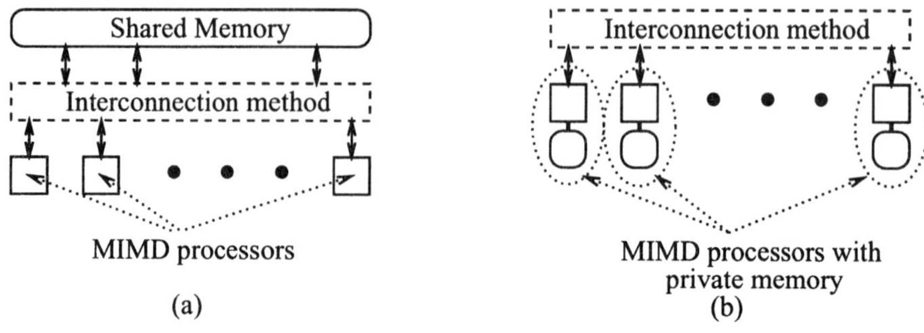

Figure 2.5 Systems of MIMD processors (a) shared memory (b) distributed memory

2.1.4 MIMD: Multiple Instruction Multiple Data

The processors within the MIMD classification autonomously obey their own instruction sequence and apply these instructions to their own data. The processors are, therefore, no longer bound to the synchronous method of the SIMD processors and may choose to operate asynchronously. By providing these processors with the ability to communicate with each other, they may interact and, therefore, co-operate in the solution of a single problem. This interaction has led to MIMD systems sometimes being classified as tightly coupled if the degree of interaction is high, or loosely coupled if the degree of interaction is low.

Two methods are available to facilitate this interprocessor communication. *Shared memory* systems allow the processors to communicate by reading and writing to a common address space. Controls are necessary to prevent processors updating the same portion of the shared memory simultaneously. Examples of such shared memory systems are the Sequent Balance [173] and the Alliant FX/8 [57]. In *distributed memory* systems, on the other hand, processors address only their private memory and communicate by passing messages along some form of communication path. Examples of MIMD processors from which such distributed memory systems can be built are the Intel i860 [154] and the Inmos transputer [110].

The conceptual difference between shared memory and distributed memory systems of MIMD processors is shown in figure 2.5. The interconnection method for the shared memory system, figure 2.5(a), allows all the processors to be connected to the shared memory. If two or more processors wish to access the same portion of this shared memory at the same time then some arbitration mechanism must be used to ensure only one processor accesses that memory portion at a time. This problem of memory contention may restrict the number of processors that can be interconnected using the shared memory model. The interconnection method of the distributed memory system, figure 2.5(b), connects the processors in some fashion and if one or more processors wish to access another processor's private memory, it, or they, can only do so by sending a message to the appropriate processor along this interconnection network. There is thus no memory contention as such. However, the density of the messages that result in distributed memory systems may still limit the number of processors that may be interconnected, although this number is generally larger than that of shared memory systems.

Virtual shared memory systems attempt to provide the simple programming model associated with shared memory systems with the scalability offered by distributed memory architectures. This issue will be examined in some detail in Chapter 8 when data management techniques are investigated.

Busses have been used successfully as an interconnection structure to connect low numbers of processors together. However, if more than one processor wishes to send a message on the bus at the same time, an arbiter must decide which message gets access to the bus first. As the number of processors increases, so the contention for use of the bus grows. Thus, a bus is inappropriate for large multiprocessor systems. An alternative to the bus is to connect processors via dedicated links to form large networks. This removes the bus-contention problem by spreading the communication load across many independent links. Chapter 9 will examine different approaches for connecting large numbers of processors.

The transputer

The name transputer is derived from TRANSistor and comPUTER. The idea behind the design of this device was to combine memory and processor on a single chip and provide an efficient means for directly connecting a number of these devices together. Transputers could, therefore, be used as 'building blocks' to construct distributed memory multiprocessor systems.

A transputer integrates a 32-bit CPU, four communication links, static RAM and an external memory interface onto a single CMOS silicon chip. Some transputers, for example, the IMS T800 transputer, also contain a floating point unit (FPU). This FPU can operate in parallel with the CPU, performing floating point arithmetic on single- and double-length (32- and 64-bit) quantities. The parallel operation of the CPU and FPU allows, for example, address calculations and floating point arithmetic to be fully overlapped [114]. The CPU of the T800 transputer has a peak performance of 30 MIPS at 25 MHz. The four serial communication links each support a bidirectional data transfer rate of up to 2.35 Mbytes per second. The T800 also contains 4 Kbytes of on-chip static RAM, with an access time comparable to that of the CPU registers. An overview of the architecture of the T800 is shown in figure 2.6.

The serial communication links on the transputer provide the key to building distributed memory systems from individual transputers. Each link consists of two unidirectional signal wires which are driven by an autonomous direct memory access (DMA) engine. Transputers use these links to communicate with each other. Once communication has been initiated, the DMA may proceed without further intervention of the CPU. Thus, for example, in the case of the T800, the CPU, FPU and four links can operate truly in parallel. The links of a number of transputers may be joined together to produce a variety of configurations. The advantages and disadvantages of different configurations will be discussed in Chapter 9.

The external memory interface allows, in the case of the T800 transputer, direct access of up to 4 Gbytes of storage. Incorporating this memory interface on the chip itself simplifies the design of a system consisting of a T800 together with some

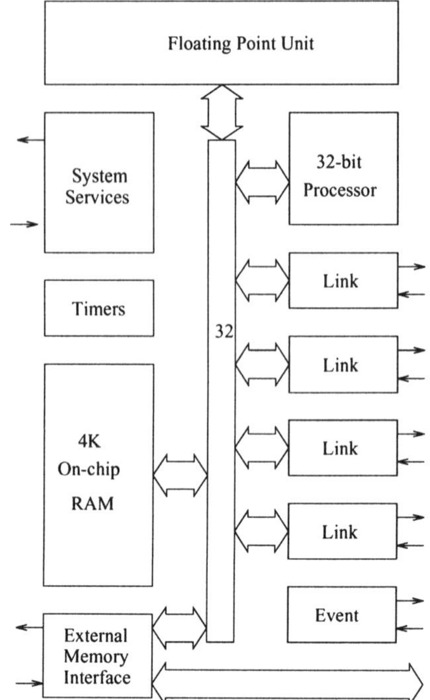

Figure 2.6   The IMS T800 transputer

external memory. Multiprocessor systems based on transputers can be constructed in a highly modular fashion, with each processor and memory 'module' occupying only a small physical area.

Connecting the links of transputers produces a fixed configuration. Any alteration to this configuration will require physically reconnecting these links. Indeed, this was the mechanism employed in most of the early transputer systems, where a number of plugs and sockets were used to enable the connections to be modified. Such a 'hard-wired' topology may be appropriate for embedded systems or other applications where special purpose devices are constructed using transputers. However, a manual reconfiguration strategy is inappropriate for any frequent changes of topology, such as may happen in a multi-user environment. The IMS C004 is a crossbar switch, comprising 32 link inputs and 32 link outputs. The switch can be instructed by software to connect any input link to any output link. These links remain connected in the same configuration for the duration of the computation. Once the problem has completed, the links may be reconfigured using software instructions. Thus, a single C004 could be used to connect the links of eight transputers in any number of topologies. Furthermore, a number of C004s may also be interconnected, increasing the flexibility of any system.

Developments to the T800 led to the production of the T9000 transputer, with improved computational power (a peak performance of 200 MIPS) and faster communications (individual link speed of 100 Mbits/second). The T9000 supports a virtual channel processor, running in parallel with the other components of the chip, and which supports not only faster communication links, but also the concept of a *virtual link*. Virtual links are an attempt to provide the routing requirements of a multiprocessor configuration in the hardware, thereby removing the need for this to be included in the system software. Virtual links (also know as logical links) may be established between any two processes within the system. The hardware router is then responsible for ensuring that messages reach their destinations. Wormhole routing (discussed further in section 9.4) helps reduce communication delays by allowing the 'head' of a message to be sent onward by the router before the 'tail' has been received.

T9000 transputers may be directly connected using their four physical links. Additionally, the IMS C104 router chip, a full 32×32 non-blocking crossbar switch, may be used to provide full connectivity between thirty-two T9000s [3]. A message between two processing elements may consist of one or more packets each with a header, up to 32 data bytes and a tail. The packets from several virtual links which share the same physical link are interleaved on that physical link to ensure a virtual link does not hold on to a path through the network to the exclusion of others. On receipt of the header of a message packet the connection through the crossbar switch is set up for the rest of the packet to pass through. This connection disappears after the tail of the packet has been sent. The connectivity of a network may be further enhanced by joining a number of these router chips together. Multiple levels of header information facilitate the routing between distant processors via several router chips.

2.2 Summary

There is no doubt that sequential computer architectures have improved beyond recognition from the early machines of the 1940s and 1950s. However, physical limitations, such as the speed of light, form a natural barrier to unlimited sequential performance. Parallelism offers the potential of increasing the computational power of computers beyond these barriers.

Flynn's taxonomy provides a broad method for classifying fundamentally different architectures by the manner in which these machines approach parallelism. SISD covers traditional sequential computers, while some pipelined architectures or systolic arrays can be grouped in the MISD category. SIMD computers use large numbers of simple processors to provide a very synchronous form of parallelism with every processor executing the same instruction directly under some central control processor. This type of architecture is suitable for the class of problems whose implementation requires large array data structures. MIMD machines offer the flexibility of autonomous processors working towards the solution of a common problem.

The processors in shared memory MIMD machines communicate through the common shared memory, typically via a bus. The increase in contention for memory and bus access as the number of processors increase is such that shared memory systems are not suitable for large-scale parallel processing. In this case, distributed memory MIMD machines must be used.

Distributed memory MIMD systems consist of a collection of processors, each with its own memory and connected together by some form of network. Processors communicate by passing messages via the interconnection network. Theoretically it is possible to build very large systems, so-called massively parallel processing, to achieve a machine which one industry spokesman imagined contained: 'carpets of processors'. Practically, as we will see throughout this book, the inherent overheads of distributed memory systems will restrict the size of machine we can contemplate to containing perhaps: 'a small welcome-mat of processors'.

The flexibility and potential scalability of distributed memory MIMD architectures make them the most suitable for 'practical parallel processing'. For the remainder of this book we will concentrate on developing the necessary techniques to allow us to solve real problems on these machines.

Chapter 3

Parallel Paradigms

There is no appropriate scale available with which to weigh the merits of alternative paradigms: they are incommensurable.

Thomas Kuhn

A number of methods for solving problems in parallel, both theoretical and practical, have been proposed. These paradigms range from models of theoretical multiprocessor architectures from which indications of parallel performance may be obtained, to practical library routines which can be called from within existing programs to enable these sequential implementations to be moved to multiprocessor environments. This chapter provides an overview of some available paradigms and allows the advantages and limitations of each approach to be appreciated.

The diverse nature of parallel architectures has naturally led to a plethora of approaches for solving problems on multiprocessor systems. These models address the issues of communication, synchronisation and computation in a variety of ways. The theoretical models make certain assumptions about the underlying architecture in an attempt to provide a level of abstraction and thus isolate themselves from any particular machine. Whilst these assumptions cannot be ignored in a real implementation, the theoretical models can provide an 'upper bound' on the efficiency that is possible on a real architecture.

Practical paradigms also distance themselves from any specific multiprocessor system. This ensures portability and thus wider adoption. However, by increasing the 'distance' between themselves and the underlying hardware, these paradigms run the risk of being inefficient on existing machines and may only be practicable on multiprocessor systems of the future.

The following simple problems will be used to illustrate properties of some of the paradigms being discussed:

Matrix multiplication is a fundamental part of many complex science and engineering applications. The algorithm for multiplying together two matrices A and B of dimensions $n \times n$ to form a third matrix C is:

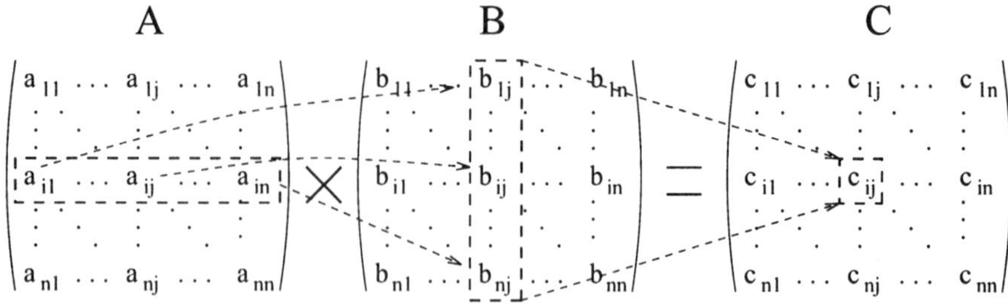

Figure 3.1 Multiplying two matrices of dimension $n \times n$

$$c_{ij} = \sum_{k=1}^{n} (a_{ik} \times b_{kj})$$

where c_{ij} is the element in the ith row and j^{th} column of matrix C, as shown in figure 3.1.

A sequential implementation of this algorithm might be:

```
FOR i = 1 TO n DO
  FOR j = 1 TO n DO
    Begin
      C[i, j] := 0
      FOR k = 1 TO n DO
        C[i, j] := C[i, j] + (A[i, k] * B[k, j])
    End
```

This sequential code for matrix multiplication is obviously very computationally intensive for large values of n. A parallel version is able to exploit the fact that $(a_{ik} \times b_{kj})$ is an independent operation for every i, j and k. However, synchronisation and communication will be necessary to perform the summing operation to compute c_{ij} correctly.

The sieve of Eratosthenes is a well- known algorithm for finding an ascending list of prime numbers [146]. By arranging a pipeline of 'sieves', as shown in figure 3.2, it is possible to extract prime numbers from the input stream of numbers.

A prime number will be the first value a sieve receives from the sieve on its left. The sieve will then be passed the subsequent stream of larger numbers. Any of these numbers which can be exactly divided by the prime value it holds are discarded by the sieve, the other numbers are passed to the sieve on its right. In this way, the first sieve will hold the number 2, the second sieve the number 3, the third sieve the number 5 (with the number 4 being discarded by the first sieve), and so on. N sieves are required to find the first N prime numbers.

The dining philosophers' problem first proposed by Dijkstra, provides a good example of the need to share common resources correctly between independent

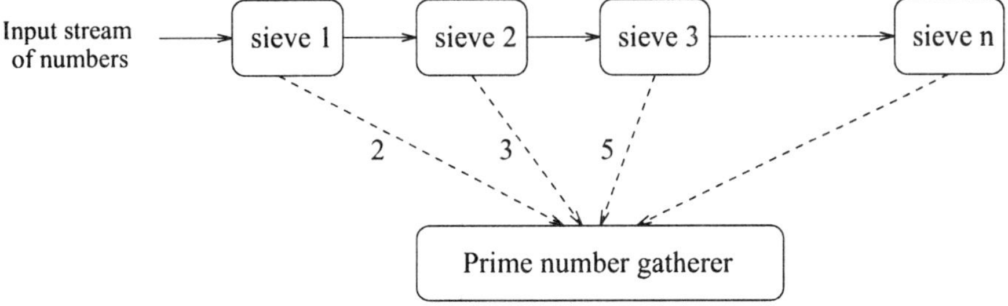

Figure 3.2 The sieve of Eratosthenes

agents. Failure to synchronise the actions of the philosophers can have dire consequences. The problem involves modelling the behaviour of a number (typically five) of philosophers who spend their whole lives thinking and eating. A communal dining room is provided which, as shown in figure 3.3, consists of a table and a reserved chair for each of the philosophers. In the centre of the table is a perennial bowl of spaghetti, and arranged around the table there are five plates and five forks. In order to eat a philosopher must first sit in his seat, pick up the two forks on either side of his plate and then use these two forks to take and eat some spaghetti. Once finished, the philosopher replaces both forks and leaves the room to contemplate further. If both forks are unavailable a philosopher must wait at the table until they are. The issues that must be addressed in the parallel implementation of this problem are:

- preventing two philosophers from attempting to grasp the same fork simultaneously;

- avoiding all the philosophers waiting indefinitely for food if they all pick up one fork at the same time; and

- keeping a single philosopher from starving because the philosophers on either side prevent him from ever acquiring both a left and a right fork.

3.1 PRAMs

The parallel random access machine (PRAM) model was developed in 1978 by Fortune and Wyllie [71]. This is an extension of the work published in 1963 by Sheperdson and Sturgis [167] in which they modelled a conventional sequential processor by a random access machine (RAM). The PRAM simulates a hypothetical shared memory MIMD multiprocessor system in which there is no synchronisation or memory access overhead. While in reality such interaction overheads will exist, this theoretical machine provides a reference point against which actual parallel implementations may be measured and analysed.

Each PRAM consists of a central controller, an unbounded set of processors, each with its own private local memory, and a globally addressable shared memory which all processors may access. Figure 3.4 shows the architecture of a PRAM.

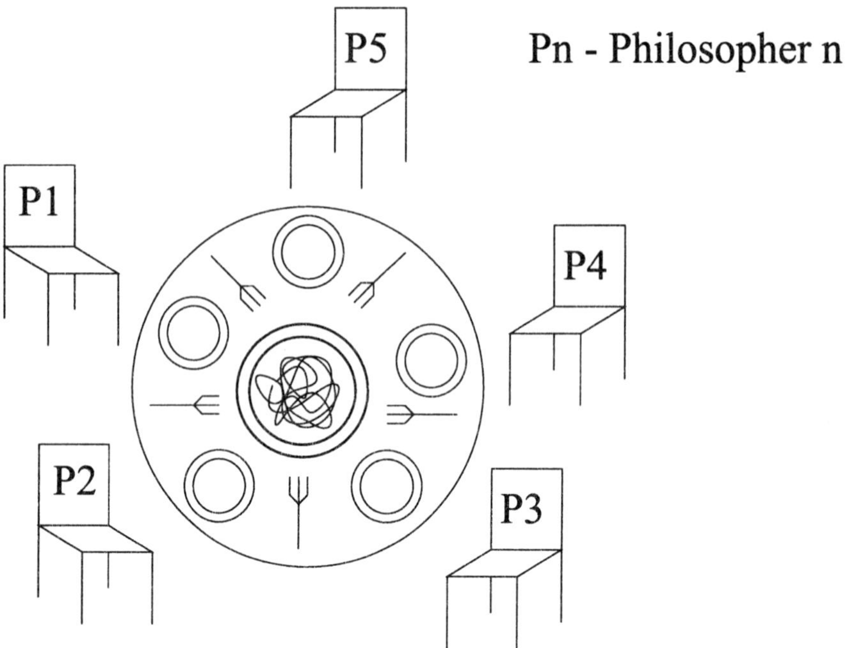

Figure 3.3 The table arrangements for five dining philosophers

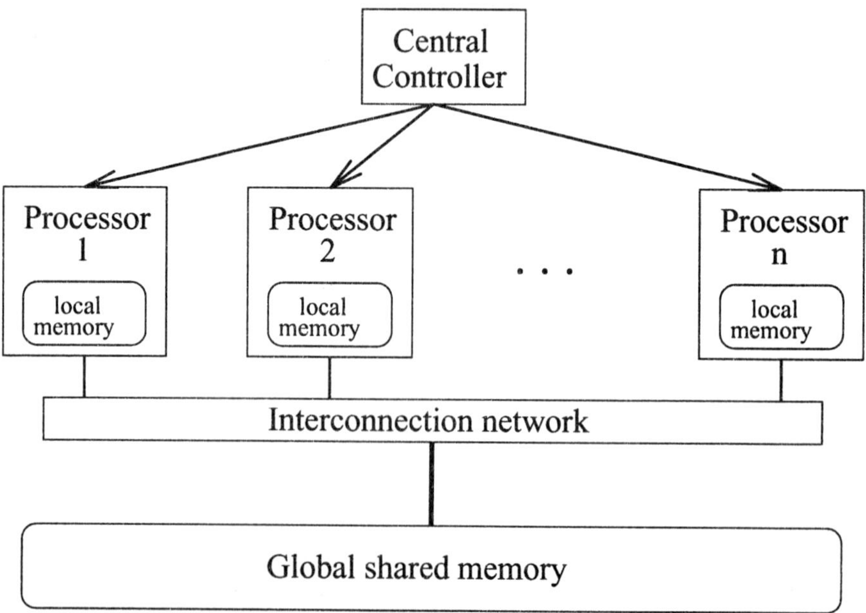

Figure 3.4 The PRAM architecture

Four subclasses of PRAM may be identified depending on the selected method of read and write access to the global memory:

EREW (Exclusive read, exclusive write): Only one processor is permitted to read or write a certain memory location at the same time.

CREW (Concurrent read, exclusive write): Multiple reads of the same memory location may occur, but write access is still exclusive.

ERCW (Exclusive read, concurrent write): At most one processor may read any location, while multiple processors may write to the same location in parallel.

CRCW (Concurrent read, concurrent write): Multiple read and writes of the same memory location are allowed.

Some form of arbitration mechanism is necessary to avoid discrepancies when performing multiple writes to a memory location simultaneously.

All active processors in a PRAM perform the same instruction at each computation step, but this instruction may address different memory locations. An active process may read or write to a single local or global memory address or may activate another processor. When all processors have finished then the computation is complete.

3.2 UMA, NUMA and COMA Models

These three architectural models have been proposed for shared memory multiprocessor systems. They differ in the way in which the shared memory is implemented and thus encompass not only physical shared memory architectures, but also those which support the concept of virtual shared memory. UMA stands for uniform memory access, NUMA non-uniform memory access, while COMA represents a cache-only memory architecture.

Uniform Memory Access: Sharing the memory uniformly amongst all processors, allows each processor equal access to all memory locations. The memory in this class of architecture is typically implemented in a central location with the processors acquiring access across a high-speed interconnection mechanism such as a bus or crossbar switch. Communication and thus co-operation amongst the processors is tightly coupled and occurs within the common memory via shared variables. Some form of arbitration mechanism is necessary to prevent simultaneous updates of these shared variables and to solve contention on the interconnection network.

Non-Uniform Memory Access: In the NUMA model the memory is physically distributed amongst the processors, but maintains a global address space. The memory is still shared, but access time will differ depending on whether the requested memory address is local or remote to the requesting processor. A remote memory access requires a communication across the interconnection network which links the processors and thus the distributed memory.

Hierarchical systems have been built which provide a UMA or NUMA model amongst a small number of processors. These processors form a cluster. Clusters supporting the NUMA model may be arranged hierarchically. Memory access within a cluster will be quick relative to 'off-cluster' requests. A small number of processors arranged in the UMA model within a cluster provides efficient memory access while minimising the contention issues associated with large-scale implementations of this model. Combining such a cluster within the NUMA model provides a powerful means of constructing scalable shared memory architectures.

Cache-Only Memory Architecture: The COMA model is a special case of the NUMA model in which caches at each processor form the distributed memory. As with the NUMA model, all the caches form a global address space. Distributed dictionaries are often used within this model to facilitate locating the data within the physical distributed caches and to assist with problems such as consistency. These issues will be discussed further when virtual shared memory is considered in more detail in section 8.2.

3.3 Bulk-Synchronous Parallel Model

The Bulk-Synchronous Parallel (BSP) model was introduced to provide a bridge between software developed for parallel machines and the architectures on which this software is ultimately implemented [179]. BSP was proposed as a possible standard to facilitate the development of 'general purpose parallel machines' and increase the portability of software between these machines.

The model provides the option of removing from the programmer the problems of memory management, low-level synchronisation and communication. Optimal performance for these facilities is provided 'automatically', as long as there is sufficient parallelism in the program to allow the processor to schedule other processes while waiting for one of these operations to complete. Multiple processes thus exist on each processor and the compiler exploits these threads to ensure minimum processor idle time. BSP terms the availability of these multiple threads *parallel slackness*. To ensure the desired optimal efficiency, the number of processes must typically be much larger than the number of processors.

A 'computer' constructed using this paradigm is made up of a number of components each comprising three parts: parallel threads, known as virtual processors; a point-to-point routing mechanism; and facilities for providing synchronisation between some or all of the threads at a regular time interval, the so-called periodicity parameter. Figure 3.5 shows a number of components arranged in the BSP model. The virtual processors at each component provide the parallel slackness. The communication medium provides the point-to-point communication between the routers of the components. The synchronisation control allows all or a subset of the components to be synchronised at regular time intervals.

The solution of a problem on the BSP computer consists of a number of *supersteps*, at one or more time intervals apart. The threads of each superstep perform the desired combination of computation and communication required to solve the problem. If, at the end of a time interval, all the threads of a superstep have yet to complete, then the superstep proceeds for another interval. The computation proceeds to the next superstep once all the threads of the previous superstep have completed by the time of the next time interval synchronisation point. In addition to the explicit synchronisation of the periodicity parameter, implicit synchroni-

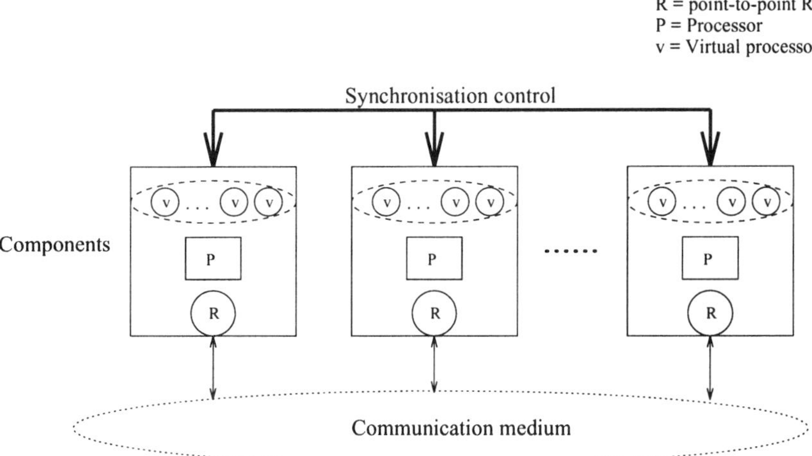

Figure 3.5 The BSP model of parallel processing

sation is also provided between processes by the point-to-point communication strategy.

An important feature of this paradigm is that it allows the computation and communication operations of a parallel machine to be separated and thus overlapped in order to improve overall system performance. To maintain this computation to communication balance it is important that the communication bandwidth is increased as more processors are added.

Efficient distributed memory management must ensure that the computation of a thread is not impeded unnecessarily by unbalanced memory accesses which may result in bottlenecks at overloaded processors. The BSP model provides automatic memory management based on hashing. Random allocation of data items amongst the processors independently of the problem should result in an approximately even spread of memory access across the system provided each data item is accessed an equal number of times. However, to determine the location of a particular data item in this scheme requires the full description of the mapping and thus a pseudo-random hashing function is preferable. With efficient hashing, the periodicity parameter is logarithmic and optimality can be achieved. With sufficient parallel slackness so that the communication delay may be regarded as a constant, the CRCW PRAM model can be simulated optimally using the BSP model. Constant communication time may be achieved by replicating the data items at each processor enabling parallel access of these items.

The BSP model exists between the software and the hardware of the target machine. As such, it is intended to be compatible with a variety of high-level languages and only requires from the hardware a certain level of communication throughput to provide the necessary computation to communication ratio. In 1990 this requisite ratio was not present in contemporary machines and it was proposed that if this were so, 'a machine with a new level of programmability would be obtained' [179].

Matrix multiplication

Matrix multiplication is an inherently parallel algorithm with well-defined points of synchronisation and is thus well suited to implementation on the BSP computer. Figure 3.6 shows the parallel multiplication of two 8×8 matrices on 16 components. A balanced work load is achieved by allocating each component the sub-problem of computing the $(2 \times 8) \times (8 \times 2)$ submatrix of the problem. Each component will perform 32 multiplications and 32 additions. If the data is distributed evenly amongst the components, then each component will hold 8 elements of the initial matrices. In all, 32 elements are required for each component to perform its sub-problem and thus each component will need to receive at most 32 data items and in turn send its 8 elements of the matrices to the four other processors that will require them. These operations may be carried out in parallel. For a computational time of 1 time unit per operation, the optimal solution time for this problem is 64 time units, provided the communication can be completely overlapped with the computation. Only one superstep is required for this problem. For the solution of the multiplication of two $n \times n$ matrices on $p < n^2$ processors, an optimal solution of $O(\frac{n^3}{p})$ is possible provided the computation to communication ratio is $O(\frac{n}{\sqrt{p}})$ and the periodicity parameter is also $O(\frac{n^3}{p})$ [179].

3.4 Synchronisation and Communication Primitives

In the 1970s, rapid advances in hardware design and manufacture led to the increasing availability of inexpensive processors. This made possible the construction of multiprocessor systems which were previously considered economically unfeasible. Accompanying these developments in hardware came new programming notations for the easy and explicit expression of parallel and concurrent process initialisation, communication and synchronisation. Most important amongst these were the low-level construct of the *semaphore* proposed by Dijkstra in 1968 [59] and two high-level constructs, the *monitor* developed independently by Brinch Hansen in 1973 [30, 31, 29] and Hoare in 1974 [104] and the *rendezvous* by Hoare in 1978 [105]. As a result of these developments, parallel programming was no longer restricted to designers of operating systems, but was now available for a far wider range of applications including database management systems, scientific computations and embedded control systems.

In order to co-operate, parallel processes must synchronise and communicate. Communication allows the execution of one process to influence that of another, while synchronisation may be viewed as a set of constraints on the ordering of events. The interleaving in time of the execution of concurrent processes often makes it desirable that the execution of a certain sequence of statements, a so-called critical section, appears to be an indivisible operation. The term mutual exclusion refers to mutually exclusive execution of critical sections. Conditioned synchronisation is required when a resource is in an inappropriate state for performing a particular operation. Any process attempting that operation should be delayed until the state of the resource changes by the action of other processes.

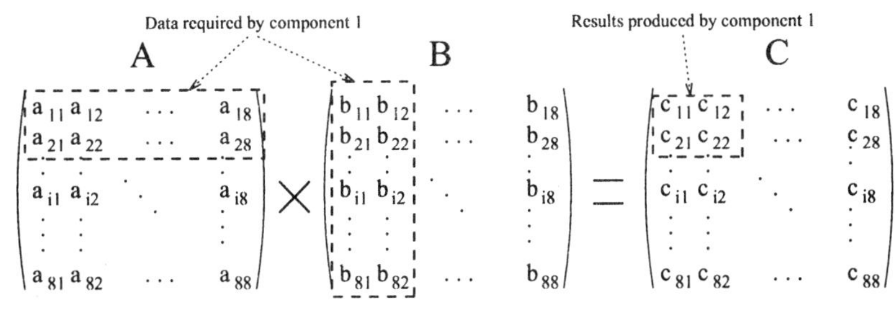

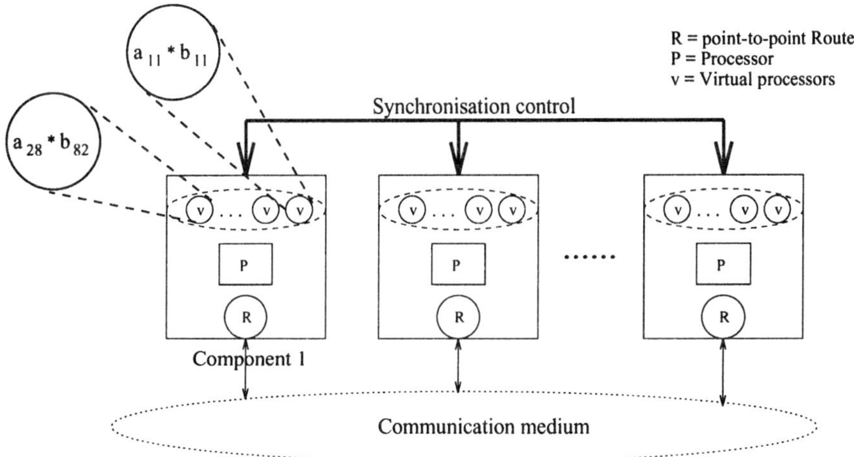

Figure 3.6 Matrix multiplication using the BSP model

3.4.1 Semaphores

Semaphores were proposed by Dijkstra as a means of ensuring mutual exclusion to any resource that is shared by several concurrent processes [59]. A semaphore is conceptually a non-negative integer-valued variable on which two operations, P, which is Dutch for 'Passeren' meaning *wait*, and V, for 'Vrygeven' meaning *signal*, are defined:

- $P(s)$ will delay any process executing this instruction until the value of the semaphore s is greater than 0, whereupon $s := s - 1$ will be executed. The test and decrement are performed as indivisible operations.

- $V(s)$ executes $s := s + 1$ as an indivisible operation.

To implement mutual exclusion each critical section is preceded by a P operation and later followed by a V operation on the same semaphore. The shared variables represent the condition while the semaphores associated with the condition accomplish the synchronisation.

Semaphores have been used as general tools for implementing synchronisation within concurrent systems. However, because the programmer is responsible for the correct placement of the semaphores, constructing such a system solely using these primitives is a complex operation fraught with possible mistakes. Failure to include all the statements which reference shared resources into critical sections could destroy the mutual exclusion required within these sections. Both conditioned synchronisation and mutual exclusion use the same pair of primitives and this makes it difficult to distinguish the purpose of a given wait or signal. The onus is on the programmer to ensure the correct usage of semaphores with no possibility for compile-time error checking. The incorrect placement of wait and signal operations may result in a process waiting indefinitely for access to a critical section.

The code segment below shows a consumer–producer problem using semaphores. For clarity we have used WAIT for P and SIGNAL for V. In this example, the warehouse can only store one item at a time and has to deal with requests from a producer and a consumer which wish continuously to deposit and remove items respectively. The problem is further complicated by the need to prevent the consumer attempting to remove a non-existent item, or the producer trying to deposit an item in the warehouse that might already be full.

```
PROCESS Warehouse()
  Begin
    WAIT(mutex)                 (* wait for mutual exclusion *)
    inside := inside + 1     (* processes in the warehouse *)
    IF operation = deposit THEN
      Begin
        IF warehouse_full THEN  (* cannot deposit yet *)
          Begin
            SIGNAL(mutex)       (* release exclusivity *)
            WAIT(empty)
          End
        ENDIF
        warehouse_full := TRUE  (* only allow 1 item *)
                                (* to be deposited   *)
        SIGNAL(full)
      End
    ELSE
      Begin
        IF NOT warehouse_full THEN
          Begin
            SIGNAL(mutex)
            WAIT(full)
          End
        ENDIF
        warehouse_full := FALSE
        SIGNAL(empty)
      End
    ENDIF
    inside := inside - 1
    IF inside = 0 THEN
      SIGNAL(mutex)     (* release exclusivity *)
    ENDIF
```

```
End (* Warehouse *)

(* initialisations *)
inside := 0
warehouse_full := FALSE
mutex := 1
empty := 0
full := 0
```

The difficulties associated with using semaphores can clearly be seen in this example. Neither the producer nor the consumer would be able to proceed if the two statements in the warehouse process:

```
SIGNAL(mutex)    (* release exclusivity *)
WAIT(empty)
```

had been reversed, that is:

```
WAIT(empty)
SIGNAL(mutex)    (* release exclusivity *)
```

This situation is known as *deadlock*.

3.4.2 Monitors

The monitor was developed independently by Brinch Hansen and Hoare as a mechanism for implicitly ensuring mutual exclusion around a critical section and which could be checked at compile time. A monitor is formed by encapsulating data structures, which may be shared by processes, together with a set of procedures and functions which access those structures. These procedures/functions are typically flagged by some means and accessed by preceding their call with the name of the corresponding monitor, for example `monitor_name.subprogram_name`. A monitor may also incorporate other operations, such as initialisation code, which might be needed on the data structures, but which must be hidden from the processes requiring access. A process has exclusive access to the shared data while it is executing a monitor procedure or function. This exclusivity is provided by the monitor itself. Monitors thus provide a high-level construct for ensuring mutually exclusive access to a shared resource. However, monitors by themselves provide no means of conditioned synchronisation and thus must be augmented by condition variables.

The queueing of processes is an essential factor of the monitor concept. If simultaneous access is requested to a monitor by several processes then some 'fair' queueing must be affected at the 'entrance' to the monitor to ensure that only one process has exclusivity to that monitor. Also, to ensure that another process will gain exclusivity as soon as the monitor becomes available again. Similarly, the queueing of processes is necessary with condition variables if the data structure is not in a required state. Finally, some form of 'polite' queue may be necessary when a process signals another process waiting (suspended) within the same monitor, if this signalling process is to be suspended until the signalled process has completed its activities and left the monitor. The following segment of code shows the warehouse problem encoded by means of a monitor.

```
MONITOR Warehouse()
  (* Procedures Deposit and Remove are exportable.    *)
  (* This is signified by prefixing their declaration *)
  (* with an asterisk.                                *)

  PROCEDURE Deposit(item)
    Begin
      IF warehouse_full THEN
        empty.QWAIT  (* conditional wait *)
      ENDIF
      warehouse_full := TRUE
      full.QSIGNAL   (* conditional signal *)
    End

  PROCEDURE Remove(VAR item)
    Begin
      IF NOT warehouse_full THEN
        full.QWAIT    (* conditional wait *)
      ENDIF
      warehouse_full := FALSE
      empty.QSIGNAL
    End

  Begin (* Warehouse*)
    warehouse_full := FALSE  (* initialisation *)
  End  (* Warehouse *)
```

Monitor constructs are not without their problems. Processes can be suspended 'outside' a monitor waiting for exclusivity or 'inside' the monitor on some condition queue provided by conditioned variables. It may also be possible for a process to call a monitor procedure or function from within another monitor, known as a nested monitor call. Thus a process may be holding exclusivity to several monitors when it is suspended. This can lead to problems of deadlock, loss of parallelism and invariance of monitor variables [38, 93, 117, 132, 150, 184].

If a process which is suspended inside a monitor on a condition queue does not release exclusivity of that monitor then deadlock will result. This is because condition queues are themselves shared data structures and thus totally encapsulated in the monitor. By not releasing exclusivity on a performing QWAIT operation, the process is denying access for another process to perform the corresponding QSIGNAL. Potential deadlock can also occur when a process acquires a set of monitor exclusivities by performing a series of nested monitor calls. Only releasing exclusivity to the current monitor when it is suspended on a condition queue may not prevent deadlock. This occurs if the process which will eventually perform the necessary QSIGNAL operation initially requires some of the exclusivities still held by the suspended process. In addition to the problem of deadlock, failure to release exclusivity to monitors can also result in the loss of parallelism as other processes may be suspended awaiting these exclusivities.

Simply releasing exclusivities on suspension is not without problems either. These released exclusivities will have to be reacquired before a reactivated process is allowed to continue, leading to possible delays. A more significant problem with the release and reacquiring of monitor exclusivity is that of monitor variable invariance. On reacquiring a monitor's exclusivity after being suspended, a process might reasonably expect to find the values of many, if not most, variables in the same state as when exclusivity was released. This, of course, might not always be the case, as once the exclusivity is released, other processes are free to gain access to that monitor and so alter the values of any variables. Furthermore, it is not always desirable to ensure all the monitor variables are invariant. For example, the values of condition variables may need to be altered to enable other processes to have access, or the value of resources supported in the monitor may need to be altered to facilitate communication between processes.

3.4.3 *Communicating Sequential Processes (CSP)*

In his paper of 1978, Hoare suggested that, '... a multiprocessor machine, constructed from a number of similar self- contained processors (each with its own store), may become more powerful, capacious, reliable, and economical than a machine which is disguised as a monoprocessor' [105]. He therefore proposed mechanisms for initiating parallel processes and providing communication and synchronisation between these processes by means of message passing primitives. Unlike previous methods of communication and synchronisation, such as semaphores and monitors, Hoare's Communicating Sequential Processes regards parallelism and communication as a fundamental part of the parallel programming paradigm.

CSP uses a concise pseudo-mathematical notation to specify the desired interaction of processes. The paradigm is intended to be used both on distributed-memory and shared-memory systems, although the concept of shared global variables is strictly excluded from the paradigm. The processes can thus only communicate by sending and receiving messages.

Parallel processes start executing at the same time and the parallel command that initiated them only terminates once they have all finished. The parallel execution of processes is indicated in CSP by the use of the $||$ command. So, for example: [A $||$ B] would launch the two parallel processes A and B.

Communication between the parallel processes is achieved by simple input and output commands, *?* and *!* respectively. These communication commands are primitive constructs of the paradigm. In his original paper [105], Hoare forced processes to name each other explicitly in order to communicate. Thus a process wishing to output a value to another process would have to name this destination process and the destination process would have to name the source process explicitly in order for the value to be transferred:

$$[A!x||B?x]$$

In 1985, Hoare presented a more detailed description of his notion of Communicating Sequential Processes [106]. In this slightly modified version of CSP, processes communicate across named channels. Each channel is only used for communication in a single direction between two processes. The original scheme avoided the need to define explicit channels between communicating processes and ensure that each channel was only used in a uni-directional fashion between

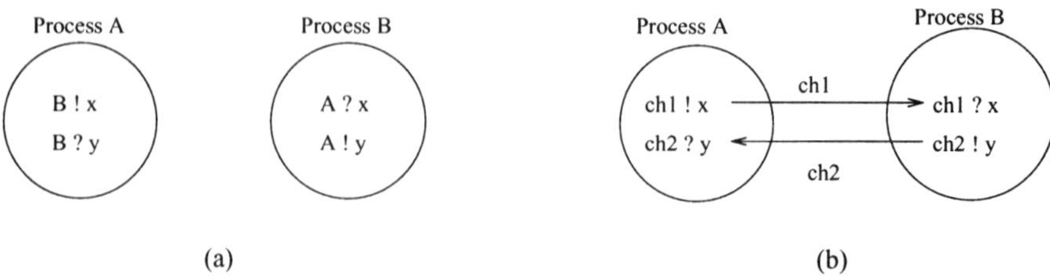

Figure 3.7   (a) Communication between explicitly named processes (b) Communication via a named channel

two processes. However, the explicit naming of processes in the communication commands complicated the development of libraries of processes which could be reused. The difference between the two versions is shown in figure 3.7.

There is no implicit buffering for the transfer of values between processes and thus whichever process performs one of the communication primitives first is delayed until the other process reaches its appropriate communication command. Failure to name a destination (or source) process, or to ever execute the appropriate communication command will result in a process being delayed indefinitely. This will, of course, also prevent the initiating parallel command from terminating.

Guard constructs, first suggested by Dijkstra in 1975, are introduced in CSP to provide a means of controlling the flow of execution of the processes. Preceding a command with a guard ensures that the command is only carried out if the guard succeeds. A guard construct comprises a boolean expression together with any variable declarations which may be necessary within the scope of the guard construct. If the boolean expression evaluates to *false* then the guard fails. Input commands may be included as part of a guard construct, for example:

$$[y \leq 5 \Rightarrow B?x || A!x]$$

In this case if the guard succeeds the input command will only be executed when the corresponding output command has been carried out by the appropriately named process.

The *alternative* command is a powerful means of selecting one of several guard constructs. An alternative command will fail if all its constituent guard commands fail. If one guard command succeeds then this will be selected and if more than one guard could succeed then one of these is arbitrarily selected for execution. So, for example, given the following alternative command:

$$[x < 5 \Rightarrow y := 10 [] x > 7 \Rightarrow y := 11 [] x > 10 \Rightarrow y := 12]$$

if x has the value 6 then the alternative command will fail. If, however, $x = 11$ then either the second or third alternative may be selected.

Alternative commands are particularly useful when used to control the selection of input commands. The first available input command that corresponds to a ready output command can be selected provided its guard commands succeeds.

$$[space < totalspace \Rightarrow producer?item; space := space + 1$$

$$[]space > 0 \Rightarrow consumer1?request; consumer1!item; space := space - 1$$

$$[]space > 0 \Rightarrow consumer2?request; consumer2!item; space := space - 1]$$

CSP also provides the *repetitive* command to allow as many iterations of its constituent alternative commands as required. This is represented by an asterisk preceding the alternative command. The repetitive command terminates when all the guard commands of its alternative commands fail, or in the case of input commands in the guard constructs, when all the named source processes have terminated. In the following example the client process will continue to input values until its server process terminates:

$$*[server?item]$$

We will consider the implementation of two of the simple problems in this paradigm to illustrate the CSP model of parallel processing. The sieve of Eratosthenes produces the list of all prime numbers is ascending order. The following example, which is a slightly modified version of that shown in [105], shows how an elegant solution to this problem can be achieved in CSP by the use of a number of communicating processes (in this case 100), connected in a linear fashion. The stream of odd numbers from 2 until the maximum integer being considered is fed from the leftmost process, as shown in figure 3.8. The first number that a process receives is a prime number and by consuming any subsequent numbers that are a multiple of this first prime number, the algorithm ensures that the first number that a process passes on to the process to its right is also a prime number. Sending the first number a process receives to the print process produces the desired ascending list of prime numbers.

The dining philosophers' problem serves to illustrate how a potentially disastrous problem, that of the philosophers starving should each one pick up a single fork, can be overcome by correctly controlling the shared resources, in this case the forks. In the example shown in figure 3.9, the problem with five philosophers and five forks is again considered. The problem may be represented in CSP by eleven processes, one process for each of the philosophers and forks, and a process to represent the room.

One of most important applications of CSP has been the design and specification of concurrent computer systems. CSP provides a secure mathematical foundation which allows systems to have provable correctness and thus problems of parallel systems, such as non- termination, can be avoided. Despite these desirable properties, CSP is more an expressive way of describing a parallel system, rather than a practical programming language. In the 1980s, Inmos Ltd. used the insight that CSP provided into parallel systems to design and develop the transputer as a practical architecture for constructing multiprocessor systems, and occam as a practical computer language for programming the transputers and developing parallel software.

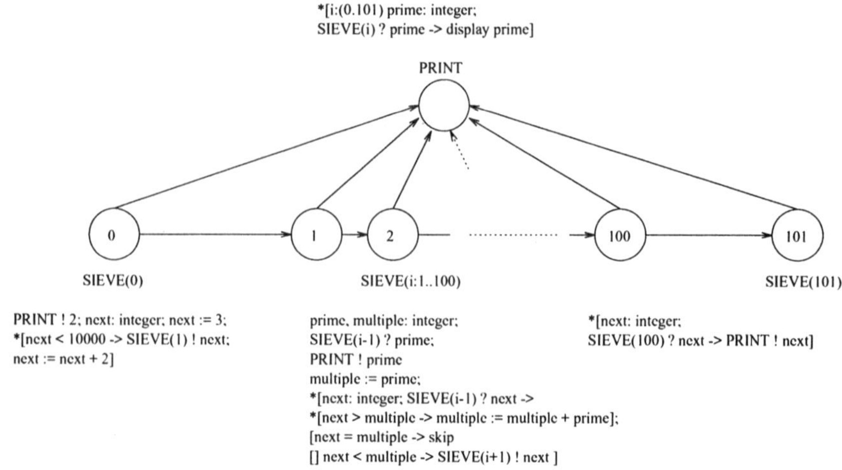

Figure 3.8   The sieve of Eratosthenes implemented as a linear configuration of communicating sequential processes

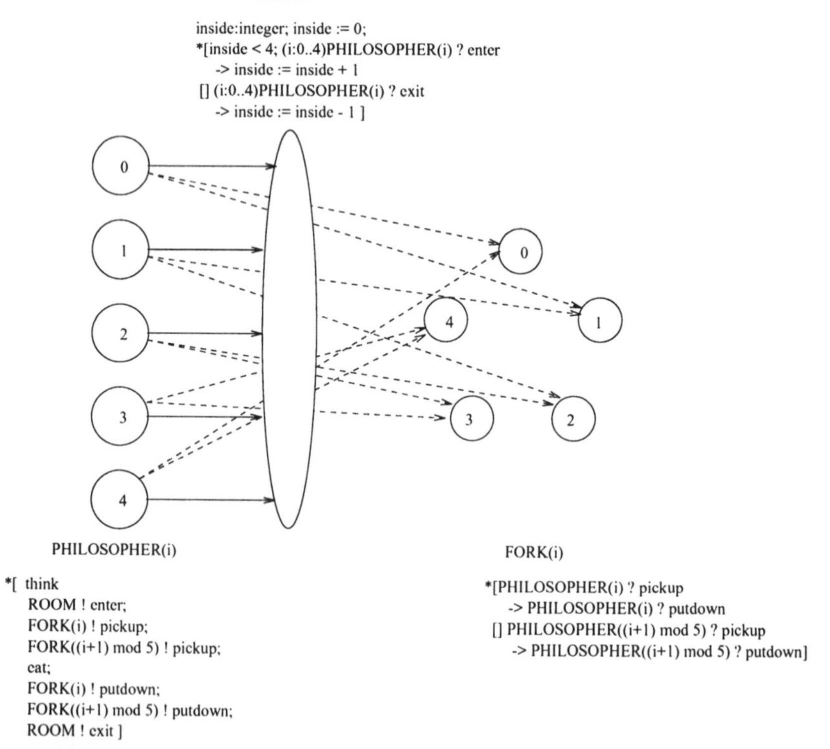

Figure 3.9   The dining philosophers problem in CSP

3.4.4 *The rendezvous*

Message passing, such as that introduced in CSP, is based on the belief that data transmission and synchronisation are two inseparable activities. In its basic form it can be viewed as extending semaphores to convey data as well as to implement synchronisation. The rendezvous is one form of message passing between two processes. The processes accomplish communication by the destination process receiving values from the source while synchronisation is achieved because a message can only be received after it has been sent, thus constraining the order in which the two events can occur. During the rendezvous, both processes remain synchronised and the message is transferred, subsequently resuming their respective activities independently. The rendezvous model as subsequently introduced in languages including Ada, differed from the original concept that Hoare proposed as part of CSP in 1978 [105]. In CSP the message transfer is symmetric as each process has to explicitly name the other in order to enter a rendezvous. An alternative asymmetric approach was adopted by Brinch Hansen in 1978 [32] (and later by Hoare in his revised version of CSP in 1985 [106]).

An asymmetric rendezvous involves one process, the so-called *client* process, naming the other process, the *server* process. The rendezvous can be represented at the language level by including an *accept* statement in the server process which takes the form:

```
ACCEPT Request(parameter_list) THEN
  begin
    (* accept statement body *)
  end
```

The actual data transfer is performed in the same way as in an ordinary procedure call, that is, the actual parameters supplied by the request for rendezvous are bound to the formal parameters supplied in the specification of the accept statement. This form of rendezvous is often referred to as a remote procedure call.

3.5 Linda

Linda is a co-ordination language providing a communication mechanism based on a shared memory space called 'tuple space'. The tuple space is accessed using associative addressing to specify the required objects or 'tuples'. The tuple space may be implemented using a physically shared memory. More usually it is distributed over the separate memories of a distributed memory multi-processor computer, as shown in figure 3.10, or even a network of autonomous computers. One of the main benefits of the tuple space mechanism for communication is that it provides both temporal and spatial decoupling of the processes co- operating in the execution of a problem. Temporal decoupling is provided by the tuple space in that a process may place a tuple into the tuple space for retrieval by another process without any concern as to whether the other process is ready to receive the tuple or whether it is even executing yet. The tuple space acts as a buffer between the processes. Spatial decoupling refers to the fact that processes communicating using the tuple space need not know each others' identity or location in a multiprocessor network. This decoupling provides a great deal of freedom and simplicity.

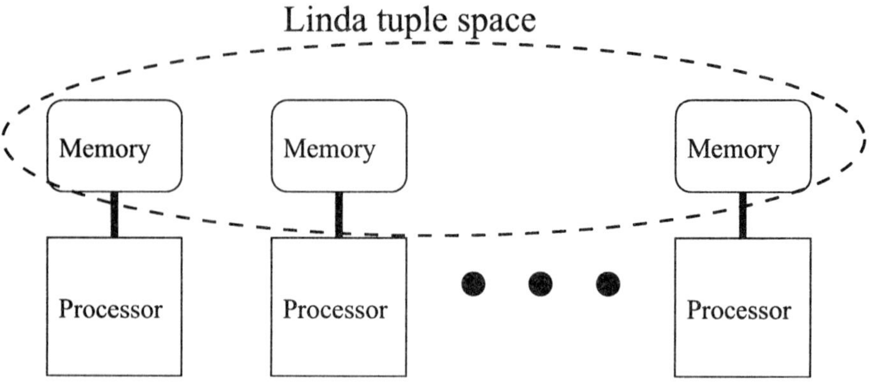

Figure 3.10 The Linda tuple space

It should be noted that Linda, as a co-ordination language, is designed to be coupled with a sequential programming language (referred to in this discussion as the 'host language'). In practice Linda is usually implemented as a library of routines that are used to access the tuple space, together with a preprocessor for the analysis and optimisation of the Linda operations. In this section, we will assume that the host language being used is C.

There are two classes of tuples in Linda: active and passive tuples. We will consider passive tuples first and return to the subject of active tuples later. Note that the term 'tuple' on its own generally refers to a passive tuple. A passive tuple is an ordered collection of data values. An example of a tuple with four fields is ("Pat", 34, 'm', 1.83). The fields may be made up of any of the basic types of the host language, and possibly compound data structures such as arrays or records (such details are implementation specific). Additionally, a field may not be defined, but may be a 'formal'. Formals are generally used when retrieving tuples from the tuple space and allow a variable to be bound to the corresponding value in the retrieved tuple.

Fields with defined values, called 'actuals', are used to perform the associative retrieval of the tuple. For example, assuming that i is an integer variable and r is a real variable, then the tuple ("Pat", ?i, 'm', ?r) could match the previous example tuple, in which case the variables i and r would be bound to the values 34 and 1.83 respectively. Note that the associative matching mechanism could also match this tuple with any other tuple with corresponding actual fields, for example ("Pat", 19, 'm', 1.63) or ("Pat", -35, 'm', 0.25).

The operations provided by Linda for accessing the tuple space are out, used to place passive tuples into tuple space, in and inp, used to remove tuples from tuple space, and rd and rdp, used to access tuples without removing them from tuple space. Whereas in and rd provide blocking communication, that is, they will suspend execution until a matching tuple is placed into tuple space, if necessary, the predicate forms, inp and rdp, will return an indication of failure if no matching tuple is found and any formal values will remain unbound. Using the previous example, the tuple would be placed in tuple space as follows: `out("Pat", 34, 'm', 1.83)`. Using `in("Pat", ?i, 'm', ?r)` to access the data would remove the tuple from tuple space and bind the variables `i` and `r`, whereas using `rd("Pat", ?i, 'm', ?r)` would simply bind the variables while leaving the tuple in tuple space.

The matching mechanism performs a field by field comparison of the tuples in tuple space and the tuple specified by the input operation (`in`, etc.), which is sometimes referred to as an 'anti-tuple'. The first criterion for a match to succeed is that the number of fields in the tuple and the anti-tuple must agree. Secondly, the types of corresponding fields must be the same. If these two criteria are met then the matching proceeds by examining the values of the individual fields. If all the fields match then the tuples are matched. If corresponding fields are actuals then their values must be identical for the matching to succeed.

Active tuples are the mechanism used by Linda to create new processes dynamically. An active tuple is placed into tuple space using the `eval` command. Among the fields of an active tuple will be unevaluated function calls which are then executed in parallel. Again it should be noted that this mechanism provides temporal and spatial decoupling; there is no mechanism for specifying when the evaluation of the active tuple should take place or where in the processor network the execution should occur. Following the evaluation of the active tuple it becomes a passive tuple with the previously unevaluated fields taking on the values resulting from the execution of the specified functions. This passive tuple may then be retrieved using any of the usual operations, such as `in`. Note that the active tuple mechanism is one of the more 'difficult' areas in implementing a Linda system and the exact semantics may differ considerably on different systems. An example of the use of the `eval` operation is: `eval("result", x, f(x))`. This will result in a separate process being created to evaluate `f(x)`. On termination the resulting passive tuple could be retrieved by the operation `in("result", x, ?r)`, assuming that the type of the variable `r` was the same as the result type of the function `f`.

Let us consider the example of the dining philosophers' problem in Linda. As we have seen, it is clear that if the number of philosophers attempting to eat at any time is restricted to four, then at least one of them will be able to access two forks. In this way deadlock is prevented. In the Linda solution below, eating access is restricted to four processes using the tuples labelled `"meal ticket"`. The forks are represented by tuples labelled `"fork"` and numbered such that process i requires the forks numbered i and $(i + 1)$ *MOD* 5. The first part of the program is the controlling process which places the tuples in tuple space, creates the philosopher processes and then waits for the user to press a key, whereupon the program is terminated. This makes use of the 'poison pill' mechanism, whereby termination is signalled to all the processes in a system by placing a tuple in tuple space. The processes can check for the presence of this tuple using `rdp` and terminate themselves when it is present.

```
#define NPHIL 5

void main ()
{ int i;
```

```
  for (i = 0; i < NPHIL; i++)
    out("fork", i);
  for (i = 0; i < (NPHIL - 1); i++)
    out("meal ticket", i);
  for (i = 0; i < NPHIL; i++)
    eval(phil(i));

  getchar();
  out("end");

  /* At this point a series of in operations could be
     carried out to retrieve the tuples from tuple space
     if necessary */
}
```

The philosopher processes are separate instances of the following function.

```
void phil (int i)
{ int pos;

  while (! rdp("end"))  /* Termination signal */
    { think();

      in("meal ticket", ?pos);
      in("fork", i);
      in("fork", (i + 1) % NPHIL);

      eat();

      out("fork", i);
      out("fork", (i + 1) % NPHIL);
      out("meal ticket", pos);
    }
}
```

In this example the tuples are really being used as simple semaphores. Notice how the meal ticket tuple is retrieved without consideration for which tuple (of the four) will be retrieved, while the fork tuples are specified precisely.

As another example, we will use Linda to implement the sieve of Eratosthenes algorithm. (Our implementation is similar to the one shown in [36].) To implement this algorithm in parallel we will construct a pipeline of processes where each process is responsible for 'sieving' the multiples of one prime number. The pipe segments are represented by tuples of the form ("pipe", p, i, n) where p is the prime being sieved by the process reading the tuple, i is the index (position) of the tuple in the stream and n is the number being transmitted. Consider the process responsible for sieving the multiples of 5. It would input tuples of the form ("pipe", 5, i, ?n) where i is a counter which is incremented for every number received. If a particular value of n is not a multiple of 5 then it is a potential prime number (as far as this process is concerned) and it would be passed on to the next process in the pipeline as the tuple ("pipe", 7, o, n) where o is the output index number. If n is a multiple of five then it is discarded. The end of the calculation is signalled by passing a value of zero down the pipeline. The function which implements a pipeline stage is as follows.

```
int sieve (int p, int next_stage, int index)
/* Sieve multiples of p, passing non-multiples to next_stage,
   given the current input index. */
{ int n, out_index;

  out_index = 0;

  do
    { in("pipe", p, index++, ?n);
      if ((n == 0) || ((n % p) != 0))
        out("pipe", next_stage, out_index++, n);
    }
  while (n != 0);

  return p;
}
```

At the end of the pipeline is a process which sieves the highest current prime number. It dynamically creates new processes as new primes are discovered. This function is as follows.

```
int sink ()
/* Monitor end of pipeline and add new pipe stages as required */
{ int p, index, n;

  p = 2;
  index = 0;

  for (;;)
    { in("pipe", p, index++, ?n);
      if (n == 0)  /* Finished */
        break;
      if ((n % p) != 0) /* New prime */
        if (n * n < MAX) /* Create a new process to sieve p */
          { eval("result", sieve(p, n, index));
            index = 0;
            p = n;
          }
        else /* Simply output result */
          out("result", n);
    }
  return p;
}
```

Note how the `eval` mechanism is used to create the `sieve` processes which, on termination, form passive tuples of the form (`"result"`, `p`).

The last part of the program is the main process which starts the sink and then sends the stream of integers down the pipeline. After this it waits for the sink process to terminate and then prints the prime numbers.

```
#define MAX 1000

void main ()
{ int i, index;

  eval("sink", sink());

  for (i = 3; i < MAX; i++)
    out("pipe", 2, index++, i);

  out("pipe", 2, index, 0);  /* Termination signal */

  in("sink", ?i);  /* Wait for sink to terminate */
  printf("Primes: %d ", i);

  while (inp("result", ?i))
    printf("%d ", i);
}
```

The results will be printed in no particular order. If the answers were required in ascending order then the 'result' tuples would require an additional field to specify an index value. This could be done by adding an 'output index' in the `sink` process.

This solution is not particularly efficient in practice as the grain-size of the problem is very fine. In addition, the amount of work performed by each process depends on its position along the pipeline. The processes at the head of the pipeline have more work to do than those at the end of the pipeline.

3.6 Dataflow

Dataflow considers the fundamental issues of parallelism at the operation level. Using this model, a problem is structured in terms of the flow of information through the algorithm. Instructions are executed as soon as the necessary data inputs are available. These data inputs are then no longer available for reuse. There is thus no need for a shared memory or even a program counter. The order of computation is only constrained by the presence of data dependencies, that is, where the output of one operation is required as the input of another operation.

Problems are represented in the dataflow model as a graph comprising operators connected by arcs. Arcs carry *tokens* which have values. An operator is only enabled if tokens are available on input arcs and no token is present on its output arc. Once enabled, an operator *fires* by removing the tokens on the input arcs, performing the operation on these values and then placing the result on the output arc. Figure 3.11 shows the dataflow graph for computing a simple expression.

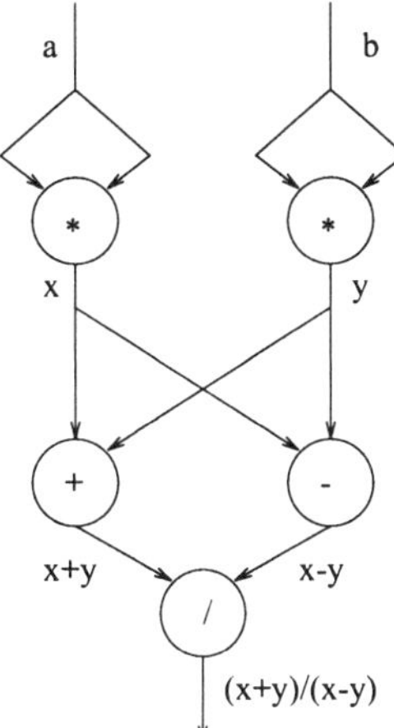

Figure 3.11   Dataflow graph to compute $\frac{a^2+b^2}{a^2-b^2}$

As well as traditional operators, other operators may be introduced to increase the functionality of dataflow graphs [158]. Figure 3.12 shows the diagrammatic representation of the following operators:

Fork: An input token is copied onto each of the output arcs.

Gates: True or false gates provide control over the flow of data within the graph. The presence of a TRUE token on the control arc of a true gate allows the token on the input arc to be transmitted to the output arc. However, should a FALSE token be present on the control arc, then the input token is destroyed and no token appears on the output arc.

Merge: The merge operator allows one input token to be selected from the input arcs based on the token on the control arc. The selected token is transmitted on the output arc. The remaining token on the other input arc is not destroyed.

Predicate: The values of the input arcs are compared with the predicate operator. If the predicate succeeds then a TRUE token appears on the output arc, and if not, a FALSE token is transmitted on the output arc.

Switch: A switch is simply a combination of a true and a false gate. This operation allows the input token to be 'switched' to the appropriate output arc depending on the value on the control arc.

There have been a number of attempts to design computer architectures based on the dataflow model, for example [15, 16, 91]. Operands in data flow machines are forwarded directly to instructions which need them rather than being stored in memory as in von Neumann computers. There is also no program counter giving the address of the next instruction to be executed. Figures 3.13(a) and (b) illustrates this difference.

A dataflow instruction is activated as soon as all its input operand slots are filled and can fire if the input operand slots of the instruction(s) to which the result is to be sent are empty. The operand slots of the receiving instruction will be free if

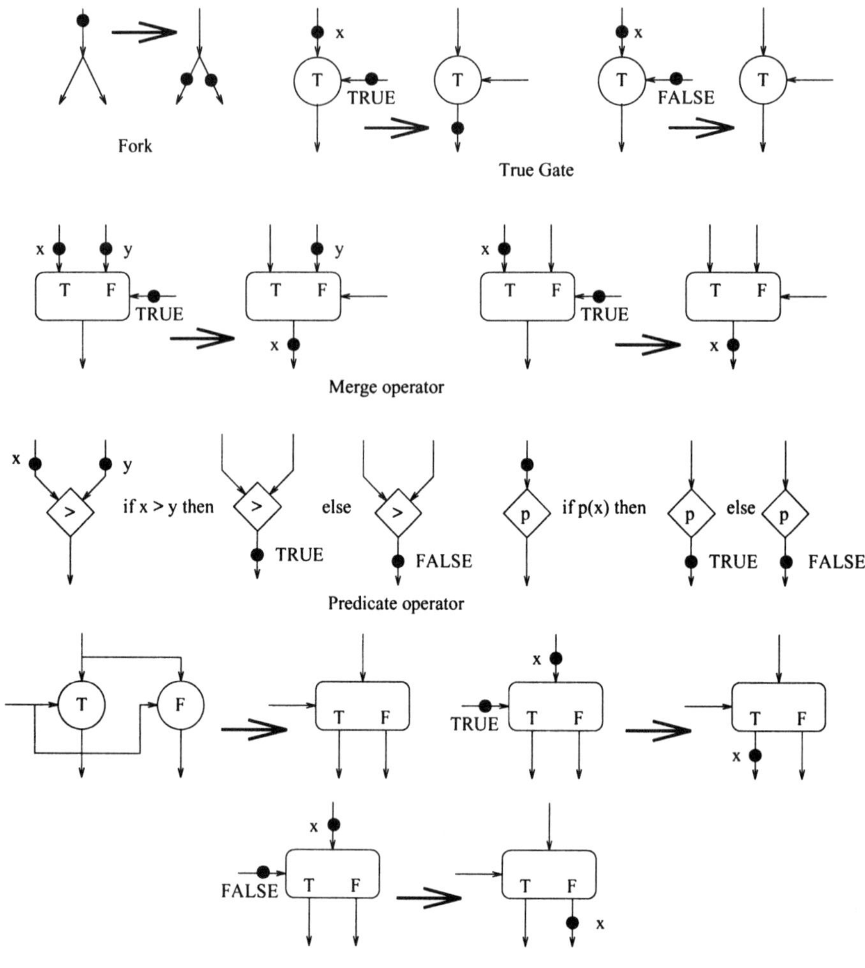

Figure 3.12 Pictorial representation of the dataflow operators

it has used up whatever operands came to it earlier. Thus as soon as a receiving instruction consumes its input operands, it sends an acknowledgement to all sending instructions. An enabled instruction fires after it receives acknowledgements from all the destination addresses of its results. A dataflow instruction format should thus provide slots for acknowledgements, as shown in figure 3.13(c).

Figure 3.14 shows the dataflow graph to computer element c_{ij} in the matrix multiplication example. Note that dataflow has no concept of variables. The traditional procedural manner of accumulating the value of c_{ij}, `C[i, j] := C[i, j] + (A[i, k] * B[k, j])`, is implicit in the dataflow graph so that the value that eventually 'flows' out of the graph for this portion of the matrix multiplication implementation will be c_{ij}.

Operation to be performed	Slot for operand from left arc	Slot for operand from right arc	Address of machine instruction(s) and in which slots in it the results should be stored

(a)

Operation to be performed	Address(es) in main memory of operand	Address in main memory of result	Address of the next instruction to be carried out. Normally provided by program counter

(b)

Operation code	Left operand slot	Right operand slot	Result destination addresses	Address to which acknowledgements are sent	No. of input operands and acks. needed to fire

(c)

Figure 3.13   Computer instructions (a) simple dataflow (b) von Neumann (c) modified dataflow

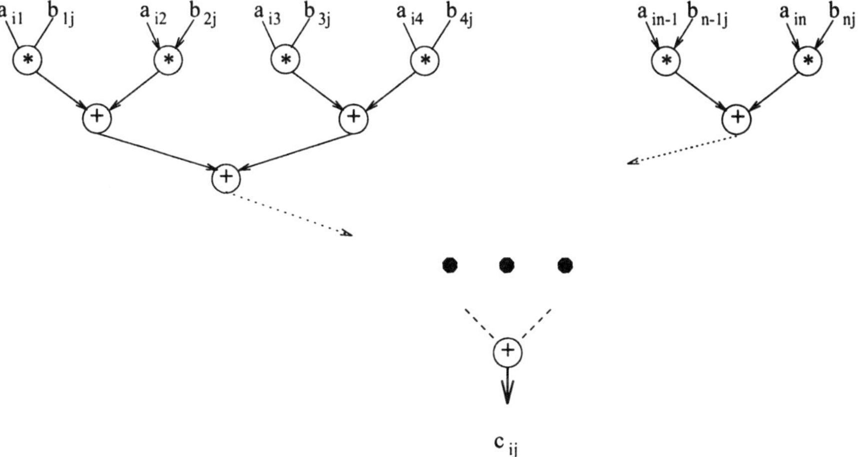

Figure 3.14   Dataflow graph to compute c_{ij}

3.7 Parallel Virtual Machine (PVM)

Parallel Virtual Machine, known generally as PVM, is a message- passing library for use with networks of heterogeneous computers. While strictly not a model for parallel computing, PVM provides an easy framework for implementing both parallel and distributed systems. The heterogeneous computers supporting PVM may be workstations, supercomputers or multiprocessors. Libraries are currently available for C, C++ and Fortran (the examples below all make use of C).

The PVM run-time system makes use of a dæmon process running on each machine that forms a part of the virtual machine to handle message passing and co-ordination. A front-end 'console' program is also provided to allow the user to examine the status of the machines and tasks running under the PVM system. The libraries provide facilities for packing and sending messages, receiving and unpacking messages, for constructing groups of tasks, simple database manipulation and various housekeeping operations, such as starting PVM on a new host or setting options which govern some aspects of the system.

A process running under PVM is called a task, and is identified by a task identifier which is an integer value. Messages are constructed by building up the message in a number of steps, referred to as 'packing' the message, and then sending it to the recipient(s). The message also has an associated message type: an integer value, which may be used to identify a particular class of messages. In the following simple example of the use of these routines the message to be sent is a record with an integer field and an array of ten floating point fields:

```
struct
  { int label;
    float data[10];
  } record;
```

The sending task needs to initiate the sending process, pack the data to form the message and then send it to the recipient:

```
pvm_initsend(PvmDataDefault);
pvm_pkint(&record.label, 1, 1);
pvm_pkfloat(record.data, 10, 1);
pvm_send(task2, 99); /* Send the message to the task specified
                        by the variable task2, with message
                        type 99 */
```

The packing routines, `pvm_pkint` and `pvm_pkfloat`, take a pointer to the data to be packed, the number of items to be packed and the array stride to be used. This allows arrays or slices of arrays to be packed in a single operation. Packing routines are also provided for complex, double, short integers, long integers, unsigned integer values and character strings. If it is known that the message is being sent to a machine of the same architecture then it may be packed as an untyped array of bytes and sent using 'raw' format, as shown here:

```
pvm_initsend(PvmDataRaw);
pvm_pKbyte(&record, sizeof(record), 1);
pvm_send(task2, 99);
```

Communication is asynchronous so that the sending task continues as soon as the message has been sent.

The PVM library provides a number of functions for receiving messages:

- `pvm_recv`: block and wait until a message is received
- `pvm_trecv`: block and wait until a specified time-out period elapses or a message is received
- `pvm_nrecv`: check for a waiting message, receiving it if there is one

In addition, a check can be made to see if a message has arrived without receiving it. When receiving a message, the sending task and the message type may both be specified if desired. As an example, the following code will wait for a message of the type in the previous example and then unpack it:

```
pvm_recv(-1, 99); /* Receive a message with type 99
                      from ANY task */
/* Unpack the message into the record structure */
pvm_upkint(&record.label, 1, 1);
pvm_upkfloat(record.data, 10, 1);
```

The parameters for the unpacking routines are analogous to those for the packing routines described above. Similarly, where the machines involved are of the same architecture, the unpacking may be simplified by treating the message as a byte array.

As a full example, consider the matrix multiplication problem. In our parallel implementation, rows of the matrix are sent to three 'worker' tasks which produce rows of the result. The main program begins by 'spawning' the worker tasks which are to perform the row multiplications. The PVM spawn operation allows the user to select a particular host or architecture for the child task or, as here, to leave the choice of processor to the PVM system. The main program then uses the `pvm_barrier` operation, together with the PVM task group facilities to synchronise with the worker tasks. Once this is achieved, the main program leaves the group and broadcasts the entire matrix to the worker tasks. Each worker is then sent a number of rows to deal with.

```
#include <pvm3.h>

#define MSIZE 10
#define NWORKERS 3

double A[MSIZE][MSIZE], B[MSIZE][MSIZE];

void fill_matrix(double A[MSIZE][MSIZE])
/* Fill matrix with values */
{ int i,j;

    for (i = 0; i < MSIZE; i++)
      for (j = 0; j < MSIZE; j++)
        A[i][j] = (i+j) % 2;
}
```

```c
void collect_rows (double B[MSIZE][MSIZE])
{ int i, j, row;

  for (i = 0; i < MSIZE; i++)
    { pvm_recv(-1, -1); /* Receive any message from any task */
      pvm_upkint(&row, 1, 1);
      pvm_upkdouble(B[row], MSIZE, 1);
    }

  printf("Rows collected = \n");
  for (i = 0; i < MSIZE; i++)
    { for (j = 0; j < MSIZE; j++)
        printf("%6.2f", B[i][j]);
      printf("\n");
    }
}

void main (void)
{ int i, j;
  int my_tid, worker_tid[NWORKERS];

  printf("PVM matrix multiplication demonstration, by rows\r\n");
  printf("\nSize of matrix: %d\n", MSIZE);

  my_tid = pvm_mytid();
  pvm_joingroup("matrix");

  /* Start worker tasks */
  pvm_spawn("matwrkr", NULL, PvmTaskDefault, 0, NWORKERS,
            worker_tid);

  /* Synchronise with workers */
  pvm_barrier("matrix", NWORKERS+1);

  pvm_lvgroup("matrix");

  fill_matrix(A);

  pvm_initsend(PvmDataDefault);
  pvm_pkdouble(A, MSIZE * MSIZE, 1);
  /* Broadcast first matrix to all workers */
  pvm_bcast("matrix", 1);

  /* Distribute rows to workers */
  for (i = j = 0; i < MSIZE; i++, j = ++j % NWORKERS)
    { pvm_initsend(PvmDataDefault);
      pvm_pkint(&i, 1, 1);              /* Row number */
      pvm_pkdouble(A[i], MSIZE, 1); /* Row data */
      pvm_send(worker_tid[j], 1);
    }
```

```
collect_rows(A);

/* Terminate workers */
i = -1;
for (j = 0; j < NWORKERS; j++)
  { pvm_initsend(PvmDataDefault);
    pvm_pkint(&i, 1, 1);
    pvm_send(worker_tid[j], 1);
  }

}
```

The worker tasks, after using the barrier synchronisation operation to synchronise with the main program, read in the entire first matrix. They then read a series of individual rows which are used to produce the rows of the result matrix, sending these results back to the main program.

```
#include <pvm3.h>

#define MSIZE 10
#define NWORKERS 3

double A[MSIZE][MSIZE], B[MSIZE][MSIZE];

void main (void)
/* Row worker which caches matrix. */
{ double R1[MSIZE], R2[MSIZE][MSIZE], R3[MSIZE];
  int i, row, col;
  double sum;
  int parent_tid;

  parent_tid = pvm_parent();
  pvm_joingroup("matrix");

  /* Wait for all tasks to synchronise */
  pvm_barrier("matrix", NWORKERS+1);

  /* Get first matrix */
  pvm_recv(parent_tid, -1);
  pvm_upkdouble(R2, MSIZE * MSIZE, 1);

  /* Get first row */
  pvm_recv(parent_tid, -1);
  pvm_upkint(&row, 1, 1);
  while (row != -1)
    { pvm_upkdouble(R1, MSIZE, 1);
      for (col = 0; col < MSIZE; col++)
        { sum = 0.0;
          for (i = 0; i < MSIZE; i++)
            sum += R1[i] * R2[i][col];
          R3[col] = sum;
        }
```

```
        /* Send result */
        pvm_initsend(PvmDataDefault);
        pvm_pkint(&row, 1, 1);
        pvm_pkdouble(R3, MSIZE, 1);
        pvm_send(parent_tid, 1);

        /* Get next row */
        pvm_recv(parent_tid, -1);
        pvm_upkint(&row, 1, 1);
    }
}
```

It should be noted that, for clarity, these examples do not do any error checking. In fact, the PVM library routines all make provision for error checking, and there are routines for formatting standard error messages.

There are a number of similar models to support parallel processing via message-passing libraries including, for example, p4 and Express. In an attempt to provide some coherence to this form of parallel processing, a de facto standard MPI, standing for Message Passing Interface, was proposed. In the MPI environment, a fixed number of processes communicate by calling library routines. In general, one process is created per processor and these processes may execute different programs. Communication may be point-to-point between one named process and another. Library routines also exist to support broadcasting and asynchronous communication. More details of MPI can be found in, for example, the technical description of the standard [138] or books such as [72].

3.8 Summary

This chapter has discussed some of the important paradigms from the plethora that have been proposed over the years. The goal of these paradigms is to try to make parallel processing easier to use and thus to facilitate a more general acceptance of parallel solutions to problems.

By abstracting away from the underlying architectures, some of the paradigms attempt to insulate the user from the complexities of the hardware. An additional advantage of this abstraction is the portability it offers to programs developed in this way. However, too much abstraction incurs an efficiency penalty as discovered, for example, by the early implementors of Linda.

Library based communication assistance, such as that provided by PVM, offers a straightforward message passing environment for both parallel and distributed systems. These models, however, provide no support for fundamental parallel processing issues, such as load balancing and the management of data. These will have to be provided explicitly by the user.

For 'practical parallel processing' we need an environment which has:

- sufficient abstraction to provide portability, but enough understanding of the underlying architecture to ensure efficiency; and,

- a simple communication strategy, which also includes system software to provide data and task management.

3.9 Exercises and Project Suggestions

1. Show how the addition of an 'output index' in the sink process of the Linda implementation of Eratosthenes' sieve can be used to print the results in ascending order.

2. Discuss the difficulties likely to be encountered if the Linda model were to be implemented on a distributed memory MIMD multiprocessor system.

3. Construct the dataflow graph for the following statements such that only one branch of the IF statement will be executed:

```
IF x < z THEN
   result := x + (z * y)
ELSE
   result := (x * y) - z
ENDIF
```

4. The dataflow model is often described as exhibiting the 'finest grain of parallelism'. Discuss what is meant by this statement and describe the problems inherent in this type of parallelism and why this may prevent an efficient simulation of a dataflow architecture on a large distributed memory MIMD multiprocessor system.

5. Design an implementation for the multiplication of two 8×8 matrices using a systolic array (described in section 2.1.3) consisting of 64 processing elements. Each processing element should be responsible for one element of the result matrix, $C = AB$. The processing elements are connected by two channels (*top, bottom*) running vertically and two (*left, right*) running horizontally. The elements of matrix A are passed along the rows of the array from the left, and the elements of matrix B are passed down the columns from the top.

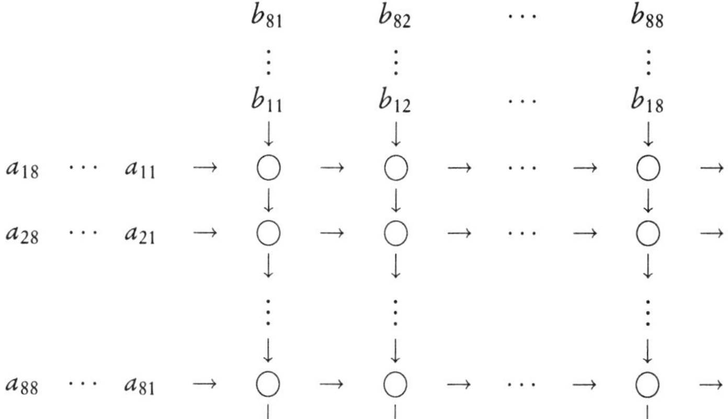

Hint: Each processing element takes a pair of values, one from the *top* channel and one from the *left* channel, multiplies them together, and adds this result to a running total. The value read from the *top* channel is output on the channel *bottom*, and the value from the *left* channel is output on the channel *right*. These may then be processed by the adjacent processing elements.

Once a processing element has received all eight pairs of numbers it is finished and may return the total it has calculated. These results may either be gathered by a process below, or to the right, of the systolic array.

(a) Why is it necessary to have two 'consumer' processes, one below and one to the right of the systolic array?

(b) The natural way to process this problem in parallel would be to assign one processor to each processing element with four additional processors, two to feed in the data, and two to collect the outputs from the systolic array. If the total number of processors are not available how easy would it be to implement this systolic array on fewer processors?

(c) If the desired 64 + 4 processors were available, can it be expected that the problem will be solved 64 times quicker?

Chapter 4

Implementing Problems in Parallel

Parallel processing is like a dog's walking on its hind legs. It is not done well, but you are surprised to find it done at all.

Steve Fiddes (University of Bristol) with apologies to Samuel Johnson

---

A purely sequential problem may be defined as one in which all operations on data items must be carried out in a strictly sequential order, and the data must also be handled in some strict sequential manner. Fortunately for parallel programmers, such pure sequential applications do not abound, and so the parallelism inherent in the algorithm or data of a problem may be exploited. This chapter discusses methods of problem decomposition that facilitate efficient parallel implementation, and introduces the Sequential-Algorithm Multiple-Data approach.

The implementation of any problem on a computer comprises two components:

- the algorithm chosen to solve the problem; and
- the domain of the problem which encompasses all the data requirements for that problem.

The algorithm interacts with the domain to produce the result for the problem, as shown diagrammatically in figure 4.1.

A sequential implementation of the problem means that the entire algorithm and domain reside on a single processor. To achieve a parallel implementation it is necessary to divide the problem's components in some manner amongst the parallel processors. Now no longer resident on a single processor, the components will have to interact within the multiprocessor system in order to obtain the final result. This co-operation requirement introduces a number of novel difficulties into any parallel implementation which are not present in the sequential version of the same problem.

4.1 Inherent Difficulties

User confidence in any computer implementation of a problem is bolstered by the successful termination of the computation and the fact that the results meet design

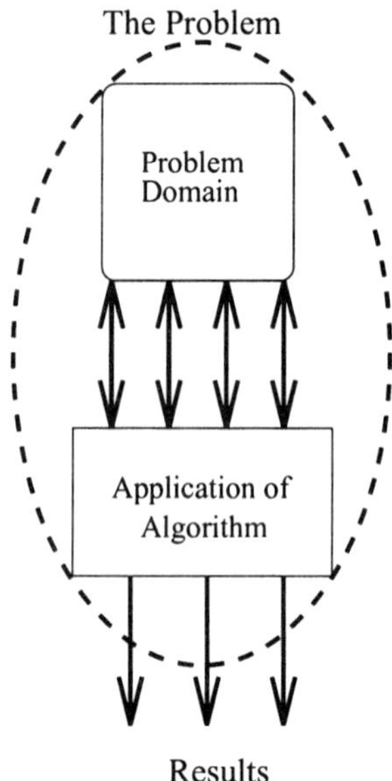

Figure 4.1 The components of a problem

specifications. The reliability of modern computer architectures and languages is such that any failure of a sequential implementation to complete successfully will point automatically to deficiencies in either the algorithm used or data supplied to the program. In addition to these possibilities of failure, a parallel implementation may also be affected by a number of other factors which arise from the manner of the implementation:

Deadlock: An active parallel processor is said to be deadlocked if it is waiting indefinitely for an event which will never occur. A simple example of deadlock is when two processors, using synchronised communication, attempt to send a message to each other at the same time. Each process will then wait for the other process to perform the corresponding receive operation which will never occur.

Data consistency: In a parallel implementation, the problem's data may be distributed across several processors. Care has to be taken to ensure:

- if multiple copies of the same data item exist then the value of this item is kept consistent,
- mutual exclusion is maintained to avoid several processors accessing a shared resource simultaneously, and
- the data items are fetched from remote locations efficiently in order to avoid processor idle time.

While there is meaningful computation to be performed, a sequential computer is able to devote 100% of its time for this purpose. In a parallel system it may happen that some of the processors become idle, not because there is no more work to be done, but because current circumstances prevent those processors being able to perform any computation.

Parallel processing introduces communication overheads. The effect of these overheads is to introduce latency into the multiprocessor system. Unless some way is found to minimise communication delays, the percentage of time that a processor can spend on useful computation may be significantly affected. So, as well as the factors affecting the successful termination of the parallel implementation, one of the fundamental considerations also facing parallel programmers is the *computation to communication ratio*.

Subdividing a single problem amongst many processors introduces the notion of a task. In its most general sense, a task is a unit of computation which is assigned to a processor within the parallel system. In any parallel implementation a decision has to be taken as to what exactly constitutes a task. The *task granularity* of a problem is a measure of the amount of computational effort associated with any task. The choice of granularity has a direct bearing on the computation to communication ratio. Selection of too large a granularity may prevent the solution of the problem on a large parallel system, while too fine a granularity may result in significant processor idle time while the system attempts to keep processors supplied with fresh tasks.

On completion of a sequential implementation of a problem, any statistics that may have been gathered during the course of the computation may now be displayed in a straightforward manner. Furthermore, the computer is in a state ready to commence the next sequential program. In a multiprocessor system, the statistics would have been gathered at each processor, so after the solution of the problem the programmer is still faced with the task of collecting and collating these statistics. To ensure that the multiprocessor system is in the correct state for the next parallel program, the programmer must also ensure that all the processors have terminated gracefully.

Bearing all these difficulties in mind, a programmer is now in a position to begin the parallel implementation process. The first job is to identify the parallelism that exists within the problem and to decide how this may be best exploited.

4.2 Problem Decomposition

A problem may be solved on a parallel system either by exploiting the parallelism inherent in the algorithm, known as *algorithmic decomposition*, or by making use of the fact that the algorithm can be applied to different parts of the problem domain in parallel, which is termed *domain decomposition*. These two decomposition methods can be further categorised as shown in figure 4.2.

To illustrate the differences between algorithmic and data decomposition and to highlight the underlying concepts of each of these methods we will introduce a simple example: that of a teacher faced with the daunting job of marking a large number of exam scripts. The domain of this problem consists of the piles of exam scripts together with a copy of the model solutions to all the questions. The algorithm used to solve the problem involves comparing the model solution for

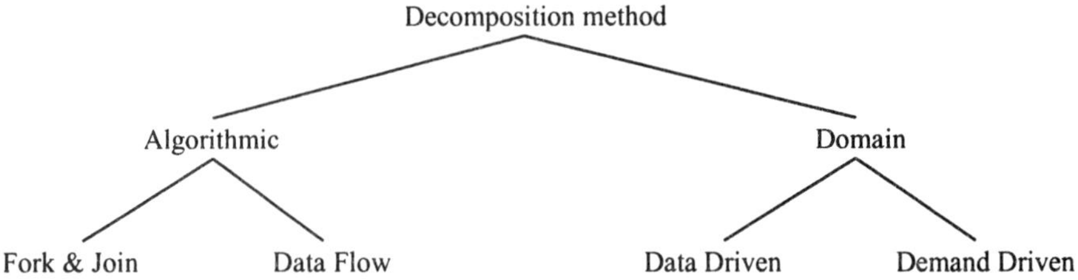

Figure 4.2 Methods of decomposing a problem to exploit parallelism

a question with the answer supplied by a student and assigning a mark for that answer. This has to be repeated for every answer.

Each individual exam script can be thought of as one data item of the problem. (Indeed, as we will see in Chapter 7, we could consider each key point in the student's answer as a data item. For now we will restrict ourselves to assuming the exam scripts are the data items.) The model solutions can be thought of as additional data required to solve the problem. The algorithm will not be applied to this additional data, but its presence is essential for solving the problem. If each exam script contains four questions that have been answered, a simple sequential algorithm for marking all the scripts may be:

```
FOR i = 1 TO total_number_of_scripts DO
  Begin
    Compare(Model_Solution[1], Script[i].Question[1])
    Assign_Mark(Script[i].Question[1])

    Compare(Model_Solution[2], Script[i].Question[2])
    Assign_Mark(Script[i].Question[2])

    Compare(Model_Solution[3], Script[i].Question[3])
    Assign_Mark(Script[i].Question[3])

    Compare(Model_Solution[4], Script[i].Question[4])
    Assign_Mark(Script[i].Question[4])
  End
```

If we assume that each question takes approximately 5 minutes to mark and there are four questions per script and 100 scripts, then the teacher will be occupied for about 2000 minutes, that is over 30 hours! A possible way of reducing this enormous completion time is to enlist the help of several colleagues (parallel processing) as shown in figure 4.3.

The reason for introducing a parallel implementation to this problem is to reduce significantly the time to mark all the exam scripts. An algorithmic or domain decomposition can be used to achieve this parallel implementation.

Figure 4.3 Marking exam scripts (a) sequential (b) parallel implementation

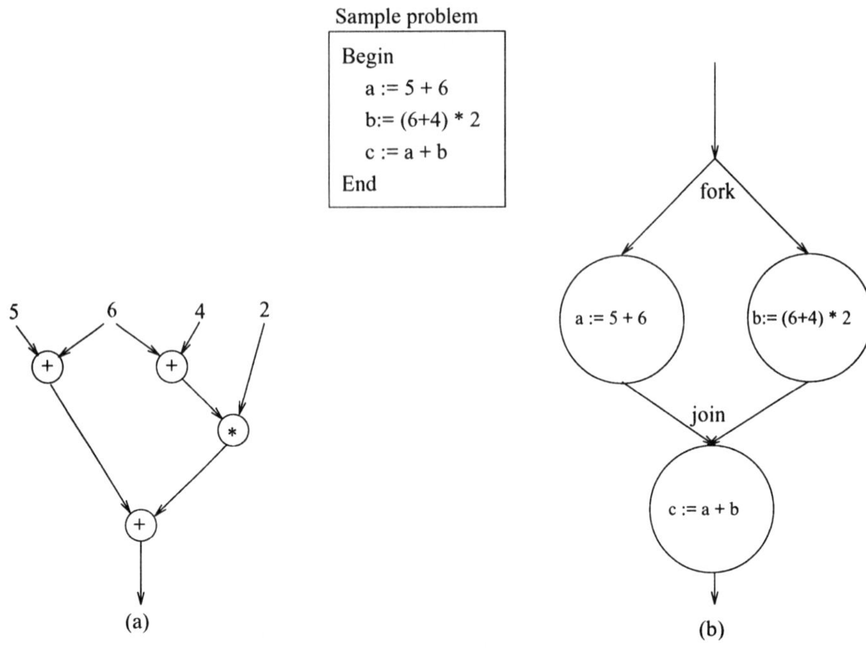

Figure 4.4   Algorithmic decomposition (a) dataflow (b) fork & join

4.2.1 Algorithmic decomposition

In algorithmic decomposition the algorithm itself is analysed to identify which of its features are capable of being executed in parallel. The finest granularity of parallelism is achievable at the operation level. Known as *dataflow*, at this level of parallelism the data 'flows' between individual operands which are being executed in parallel [5]. An advantage of this type of decomposition is that little data space is required per processor [102], however, the communication overheads may be very large due to the very poor computation to communication ratio. This approach has already been discussed in detail in section 3.6.

Fork & join parallelism, on the other hand, allocates portions of the algorithm to separate processors as the computation proceeds. These portions are typically several statements or complete procedures. The difference between the two algorithmic forms of decomposition is shown for a simple case in figure 4.4.

The algorithmic decomposition approach to our script marking example would be to divide the marking algorithm amongst the teachers, for example as shown in figure 4.5. In this approach, each teacher needs to know the procedure for marking a subset of the questions from each script. In figure 4.5, teacher 1 knows how questions 1 and 2 should be marked, while teachers 2 and 3 are aware of the procedure for marking questions 3 and 4 respectively. Note that each teacher does not require a complete copy of the model solutions, but only those parts pertaining to the subset of questions that he or she is marking. Each exam script, that is each data item, will thus be dealt with by every teacher, but obviously not at the same

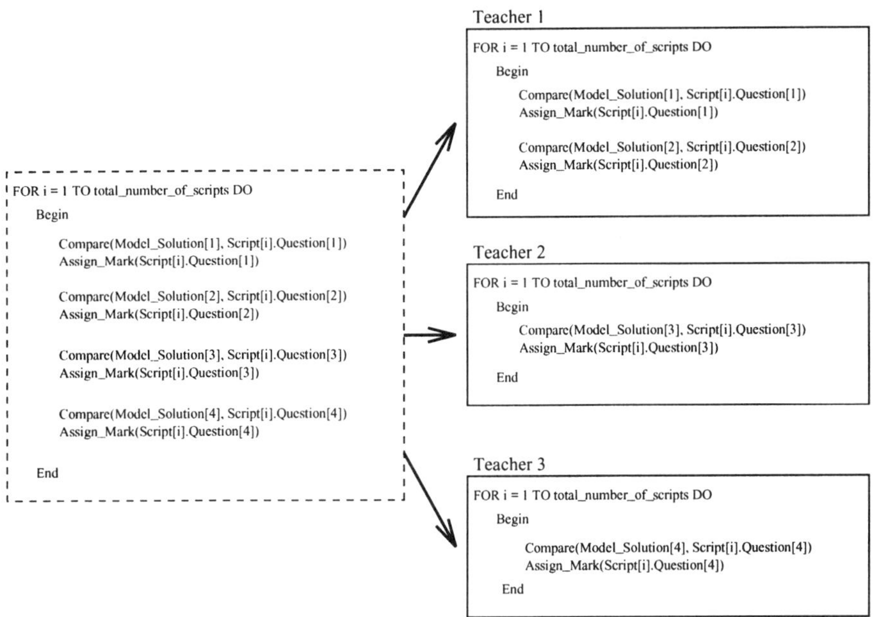

Figure 4.5   Algorithmic decomposition of exam marking problem

time. Having marked his or her subset of questions for one script, the teacher must return the script to a common pile, from which it can be accessed by the other teachers. A mechanism, such as separate piles of partially marked scripts, will be needed to avoid each teacher inadvertently selecting a script which he or she has previously marked.

4.2.2 Domain decomposition

Instead of determining the parallelism inherent in the algorithm, domain decomposition examines the problem domain to ascertain the parallelism that may be exploited by solving the algorithm on distinct data items in parallel. Each parallel processor in this approach will, therefore, have a complete copy of the algorithm and it is the problem domain that is divided amongst the processors.

Returning to the problem of marking exam scripts, we note that each script may be marked independently of all other scripts. So, provided each teacher is supplied with a complete copy of the model solutions, he or she is able to be given a script and mark it in parallel with the other teachers. Now it is no longer necessary for each teacher to see every script, and so each teacher need only be assigned a subset of the total number of the scripts. After a script has been marked it may be placed onto a common 'completed' pile. The only co-operation required between the teachers is to ensure that different teachers do not attempt to mark the same script. To solve the problem we need, therefore, to divide the problem domain,

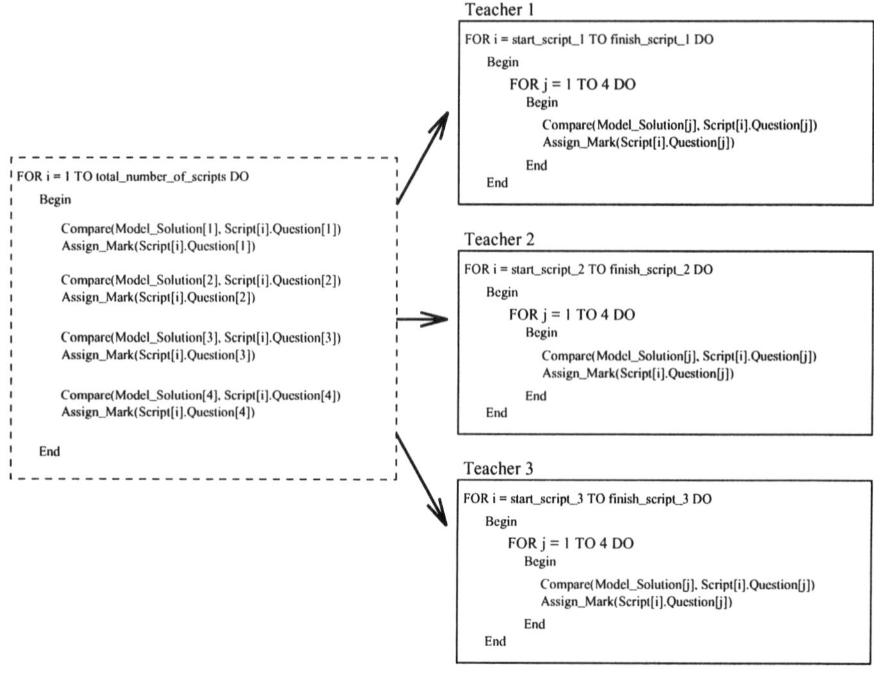

Figure 4.6   Data driven method to solve exam marking problem

the pile of unmarked scripts, amongst the teachers. Domain decomposition can be accomplished using either a data driven or demand driven approach.

The *data driven* method divides the total number of scripts into separate piles, one of which is then given to each teacher. In figure 4.6, all three teachers are aware of how all the four questions are to be marked. Marking the individual piles of scripts is indicated by the loops `FOR i = start_script_n TO finish_script_n DO`.

A *demand driven* method is in place when work allocation is performed dynamically as solution to the problem proceeds. In our marking example, a demand driven model would exist if a single central pile of unmarked scripts is used. The teachers now take a script from this pile, mark it and then take (demand) another from the central pile. This process continues until there are no more scripts to be marked, as shown in figure 4.7. These methods of work division are explained in detail in Chapter 6.

4.3 The Sequential-Algorithm Multiple-Data Model

The Sequential-Algorithm Multiple-Data (SAMD) approach to parallelism is a domain decomposition method which, as its name suggests, applies the same sequential algorithm to different data items within the problem domain in parallel. When implemented on a multiprocessor system, every processor is provided with a copy of the same sequential algorithm which it then executes on different data items

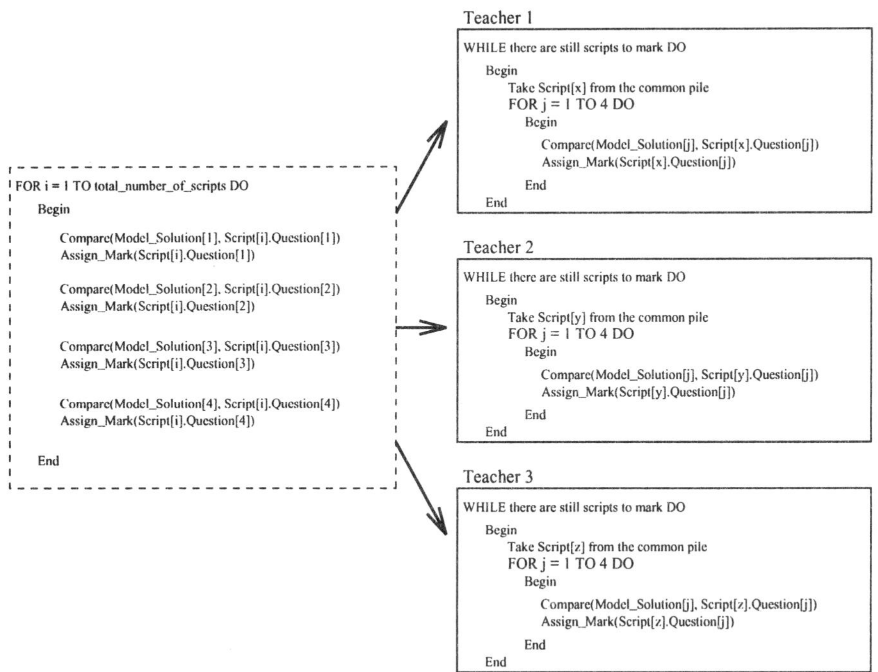

Figure 4.7 Demand driven method to solve exam marking problem

in parallel. The SAMD model of parallelism may be implemented on SIMD machines, in which case the processors perform the instructions synchronously, or on a MIMD multiprocessor architecture, on which the processors may execute their own instruction stream asynchronously, communicating when co-operation is necessary.[1]

Over the years, an abundance of algorithms have been developed to solve a multitude of problems on sequential machines. A great deal of time and effort has been invested in the production of these sequential algorithms. Users are thus loath to undertake the development of novel parallel algorithms, and yet still demand the performance that multiprocessor machines have to offer.

Algorithmic decomposition approaches to this dilemma have led to the development of compilers, such as those for High Performance Fortran, which attempt to parallelise automatically these existing algorithms. Not only do these compilers have to identify the parallelism hidden in the algorithm, but they also need to decide upon an effective strategy to place the identified segments of code within the multiprocessor system so that they can interact efficiently. This has proved to be an extremely hard goal to accomplish.

The SAMD approach, on the other hand, requires little or no modification to

---

[1] This model of parallelism has sometimes been referred to as the Single-Program Multiple-Data, or SPMD, model. However, in reality it is only the algorithm that is executed sequentially by each processor and not the whole program and thus the term SAMD is more appropriate.

the existing sequential algorithm. There is thus no need for sophisticated compiler technology to analyse the algorithm. However, there will be a need for a parallel framework in the form of system software to support the division of the problem domain amongst the parallel processors. As we shall see, given this framework, the SAMD approach is applicable to a wide range of problems. Adoption of this approach to solve a particular problem in parallel, consists of two steps:

1. **Choosing the appropriate sequential algorithm.**

   Over the years, algorithms have been selected and honed for implementation on sequential machines. The data dependencies that these highly sequential algorithms exhibit may substantially inhibit their use in a parallel system. In this case, alternative sequential algorithms which are more suitable to the SAMD approach will need to be considered. This is discussed further in Chapter 7.

2. **Analysis of the problem in order to extract the criteria necessary to determine the optimum system software.**

   The system software provides the framework in which the sequential algorithm can execute. This system software takes care of ensuring each processor is kept busy, the data is correctly managed, and any communication within the parallel system is performed rapidly. To provide maximum efficiency, the system software needs to be tailored to the requirements of the problem. There is thus no general purpose parallel solution using the SAMD approach, but, as we shall see, a straightforward analysis of any problem's parallel requirements will determine the correct construction of the system software and lead to an efficient parallel implementation.

The means of analysing a problem's parallel requirements form the basis for the remainder of this book and a simple methodology is presented. The analysis proceeds by the user determining which of the choices offered at each step of the methodology is correct for the problem being considered. The correct system software composition will be apparent at the conclusion of this process.

4.4 Problem Solving Methodology

The system software necessary for the SAMD approach is made up of four distinct aspects:

- computational models
- task management
- data management, and
- system communication.

Despite being identifiable components of the system software, the correct choice of approach within each of these is dependent on previous decisions, as shown in figure 4.8. The methodology examines each of the four constituents in turn in the chapters shown in figure 4.8. Finally in Chapter 10, the manner in which the system software is combined is described and illustrated by a detailed case study.

Before commencing the detailed description of how we intend to tackle the solution of problems in parallel, it might be useful to clarify some of the terminology we shall be using.

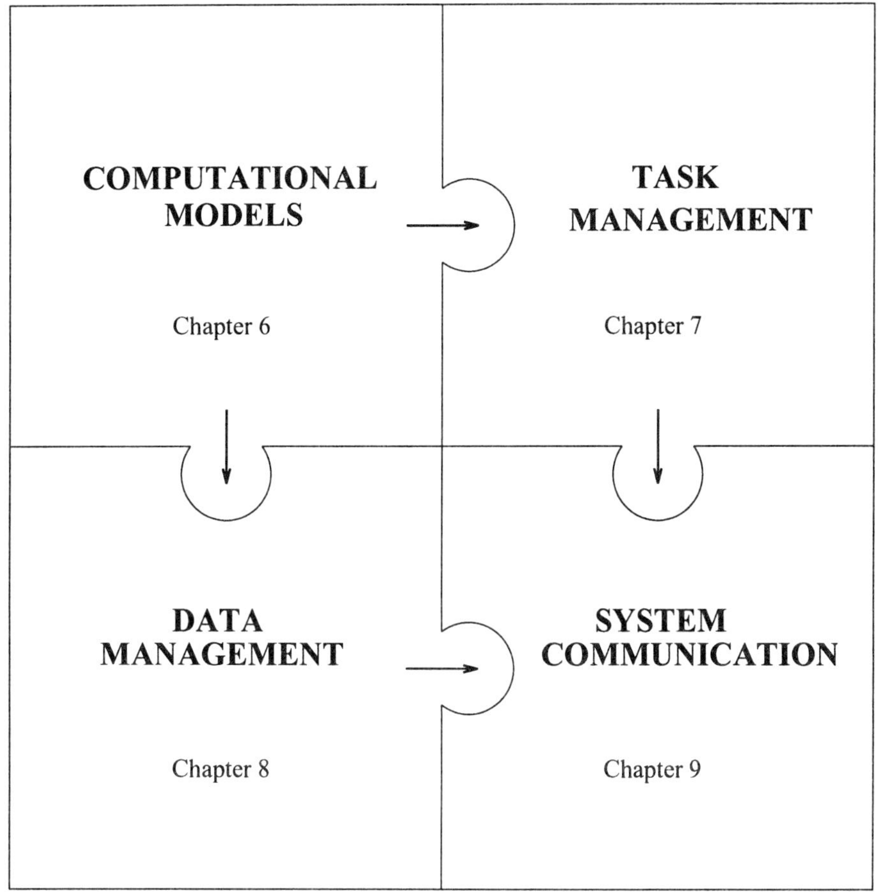

Figure 4.8   The interaction of elements of the methodology

4.4.1 Abstract definition of a task

The SAMD model solves a single problem in parallel by having multiple processors apply the same sequential algorithm to different data items from the problem domain in parallel. The lowest unit of computation within the parallel system is thus the application of the algorithm to one data item within the problem domain.

The data required to solve this unit of computation consists of two parts:

1. the *principal data items* (or PDIs) on which the algorithm is to be applied, and

2. *additional data items* (or ADIs) that may be needed to complete this computation on the PDIs.

Returning to our simple example of the domain decomposition solution to the problem of marking exam scripts, as discussed in section 4.2.2, the exam scripts would be the PDIs, while the set of model solutions would constitute the ADIs. The problem domain is the 100 exam scripts *plus* the model solutions.

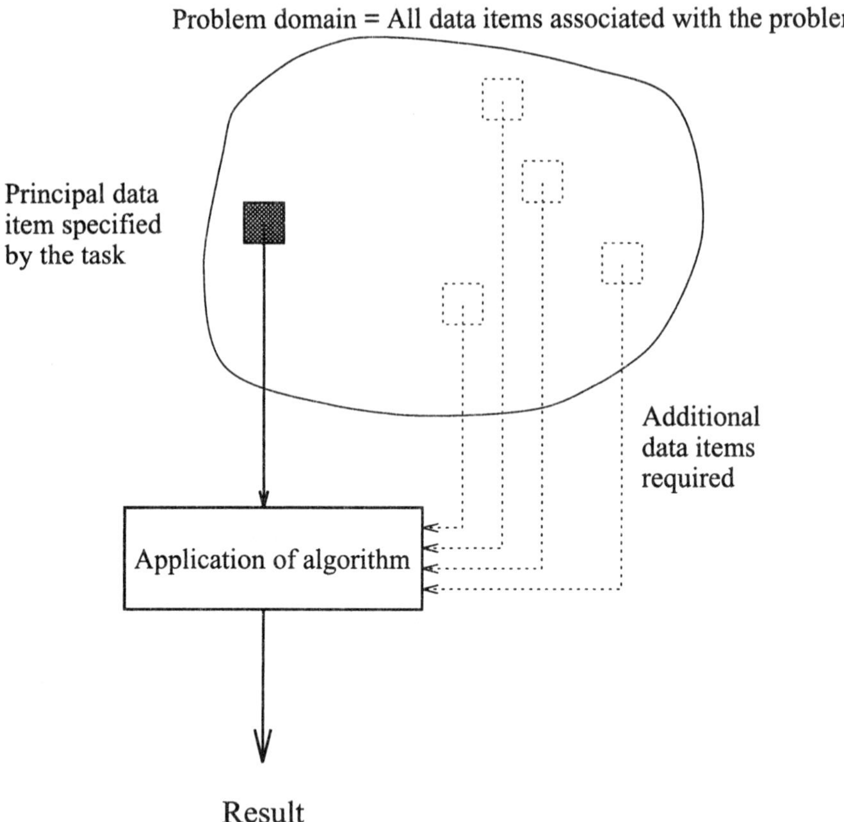

Figure 4.9   A task: the processing of a principal data item

The application of the algorithm to a specified principal data item may be regarded as performing a single *task*. The task forms the elemental unit of computation within the parallel implementation. This is shown diagrammatically in figure 4.9.

4.4.2 System architecture

In section 2.2 we identified the type of system that we are concentrating on as one consisting of distributed memory MIMD processors. These processors may be connected together in some manner to form a configuration. We shall use the term *interconnection network* or *topology* to describe a number of processors connected in some configuration. A *process* is a segment of code that runs concurrently with other processes on a single processor. Several processes will be needed at each processor to implement the desired application and provide the necessary system software support. A *processing element* consists of a single processor together with these application and system processes and is thus the building block of the *multiprocessor system*. (We shall sometimes use the abbreviation PE for

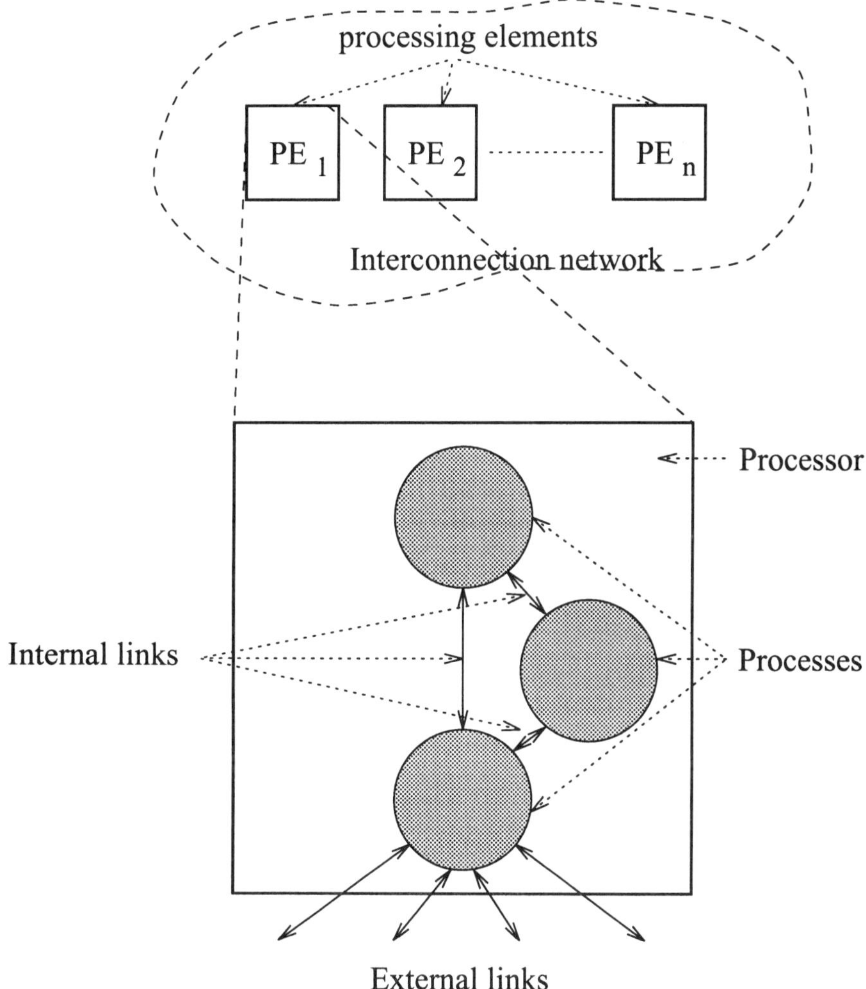

Figure 4.10   System terminology

processing element in the figures and code segments.) *Internal links* provide the communication medium between processes on the same processing element and *external links* provide the communication medium between processes on different processing elements. When discussing the configurations of processing elements, we shall simply use the term *links* to mean the external links associated with that processing element. The relationship between the terms we have chosen is shown in figure 4.10.

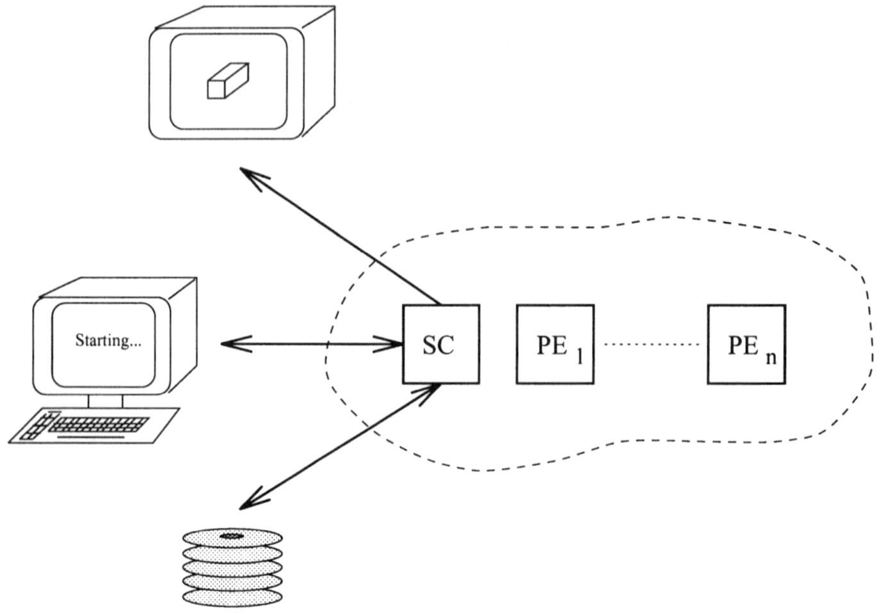

Figure 4.11 The system controller as part of a parallel system

Structure of the system controller

In order to realise our system software on systems of distributed memory MIMD processors we must engineer the structure of each processing element to be able to cope with the computational model, management of data, tasks and communication as required. To provide a useful parallel processing platform, a multiprocessor system must have access to input/output facilities. Most systems achieve this by designating at least one processing element as the *system controller* (SC) with the responsibilities of providing this input/output interface, as shown in figure 4.11. If the need for input/output facilities becomes a serious bottleneck then more than one system controller may be required. Other processing elements perform the actual computation associated with the problem.

In addition to providing the input/output facilities, the system controller may also be used to collect and collate results computed by the processing elements. In this case the system controller is in the useful position of being able to determine when the computation is complete and gracefully terminate the concurrent processes at every processing element.

If we implement the different functions required from the system controller as a number of concurrent processes we get a structure as shown in figure 4.12. In this case we have identified five distinct functions. The User Manager (UM) is responsible for interaction with the user. This includes input via the keyboard and displaying textual information such as how the work is progressing, results obtained so far and statistics. The Graphics Manager (GM) is responsible for overseeing the correct display of any graphical results on any specialised graphics

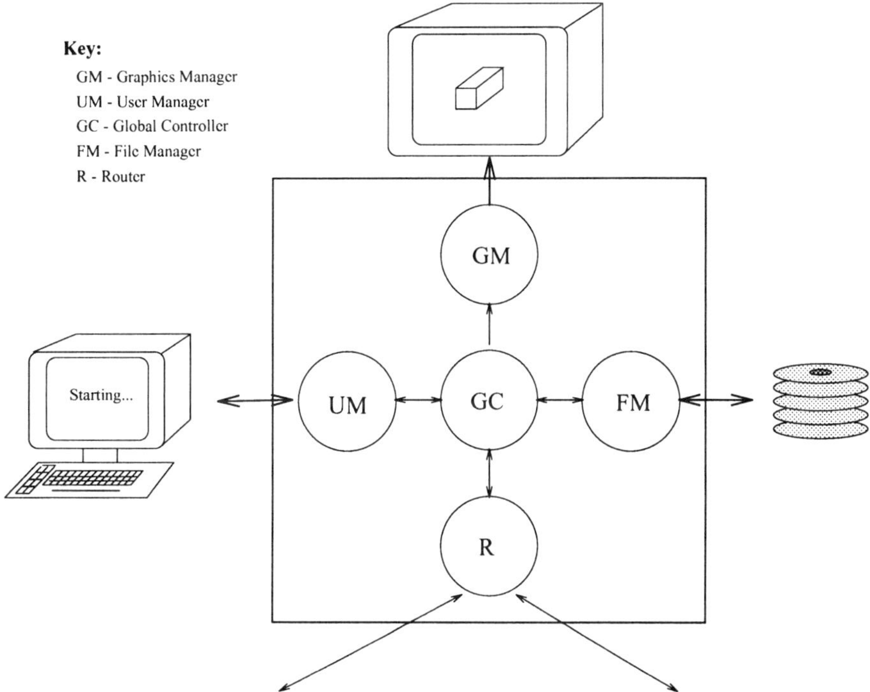

Figure 4.12 A system controller

devices (if appropriate). This may entail such actions as colour table lookup and the necessary transformations for rendering. The File Manager (FM) controls the reading of data from, and writing of data to, secondary storage devices, such as hard disk units.

The Router process (R) provides communication with the processing elements of the parallel system. The activities of these processes are co-ordinated by the Global Controller (GC) process which ensures the processing elements are initially provided with the correct configuration information and application parameters. The global controller process may also be responsible for terminating the processing elements either when the computation is complete, or when the user wishes to abort processing. The control loop for the global controller process of the system controller looks as follows:

```
PROCESS Global_Controller()
  Begin
    (* Get initialisation information and pass it on to the *)
    (* processing elements in the system.                   *)
    RECEIVE application specific parameters FROM user via UM
    SEND which configuration and routing files required TO FM
    RECEIVE routing information and initial data FROM FM
    SEND this information TO all PEs
```

```
abort := FALSE
results_received := 0

(* Start the computation *)
WHILE (NOT abort) AND (results_received < required) DO
   PRIORITISED INPUT ALTERNATIVES
      1. RECEIVE inputs or abort FROM UM

      2. RECEIVE result FROM PE
            Begin
               results_received := results_received + 1
               Handle(result)
            End

      3. RECEIVE other_inputs FROM PEs
            Handle(other_inputs)

   (* Computation is complete so gather statistics *)
   (* and terminate gracefully                     *)
   SEND terminate TO all PEs
   RECEIVE statistics FROM all PEs
   SEND statistics TO UM
   SEND terminate TO GM, FM and UM
End (* Global Controller *)
```

Structure of a processing element

The construction of a processing element is fundamental to providing the necessary
system software that the SAMD approach requires. As we shall see in the following
chapters, to provide the necessary parallel framework we will develop a processing
element such as that shown in figure 4.13. All processing elements within the
multiprocessor system will have this same structure.

The Application Process (AP) has a copy of the sequential algorithm and applies
this to tasks supplied by the Task Manager (TM) to produce results. To improve
system performance it may be necessary to introduce more than one application
process at each processing element controlled by an Application Process Controller
(APC). We term this concurrent execution of more than one application process,
multi-threading. A Data Manager (DM) process is responsible for keeping the
application processes supplied with data items. The Router process (R) handles
communication of messages that originate at, are destined for, or pass through the
processing element. All local activities are controlled by the Local Controller (LC)
process.

4.5 Summary

The parallel implementation of a problem may be achieved by dividing either the
algorithm or the domain amongst the processing elements. Such a division introduces difficulties not encountered in a sequential implementation. Pitfalls, such as

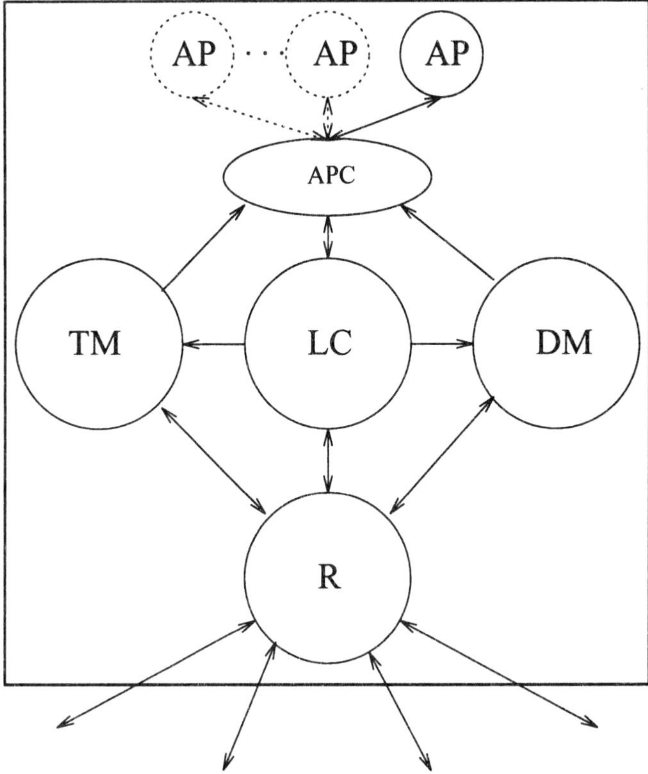

Key:

AP - Application Process

APC - Application Process Controller

TM - Task Manager

LC - Local Controller

DM - Data Manager

R - Router

Figure 4.13   Structure of a processing element

deadlock and data consistency, will have to be addressed to ensure the successful solution of the problem.

Any parallel implementation introduces communication overheads. These overheads have to be tackled effectively to maintain a balanced computation to communication ratio and ensure processing elements are never idle while work remains to be done.

The Sequential-Algorithm Multiple-Data model provides each processing element with a copy of the sequential algorithm and exploits the parallelism that exists within the problem domain. This approach allows existing sequential algorithms to be used directly with little or no modification within a multiprocessor environment. System software is necessary to support the computational model, data and task management, and communication required within the framework to ensure an efficient parallel implementation.

The next chapter investigates how a parallel implementation may be evaluated, whilst the following chapters show how the different elements of the system software may be constructed. As we will see, in answer to Fiddes' quote at the start of this chapter, people should not be surprised to see parallel processing being used, and if we are to be successful in implementing our problems in parallel then it must be done well.

4.6 Exercises and Project Suggestions

1. Use the fork & join method of algorithmic decomposition to achieve the maximum possible parallelism from the following segment of code:

```
Begin
  a := 4 + 5
  b := 6 * 3
  c := a * b
  d := 2 + 4
  e := 7 * 3 * 5
  f := d + e
  g := c + f
End
```

   If an addition takes 2 time units and a multiplication 4 time units to perform on your parallel machine, how much faster is your parallel implementation compared with the sequential version? (You may assume negligible communication overheads when calculating your answer.)

2. Construct the control loop for the user manager of the system controller. How can a user decision to abort the system be detected and then passed on to the global controller to ensure the immediate graceful termination of the system?

3. Numerical integration is often used to evaluate definite integrals of the form $\int_a^b f(x)dx$ [112]. The definite integral may be interpreted as the area under the curve $y = f(x)$ for $a \leq x \leq b$. The trapezoidal rule for solving this problem divides the interval $a \leq x \leq b$ into N equal strips of width h by the points:

$$x_j = a + jh \quad j = 0, 1, 2, \ldots, N$$

   such that $b = a + Nh$. The integration is now approximated as the sum of the areas of N trapezoids of width h and average height $\frac{1}{2}(f(x_j) + f(x_{j+1}))$, as shown in figure 4.14.

   Design a sequential algorithm for the trapezoidal rule and describe how it may be implemented using the SAMD approach on a ten-processor system. Is it possible to implement your algorithm using an algorithmic decomposition approach efficiently on the ten-processor system?

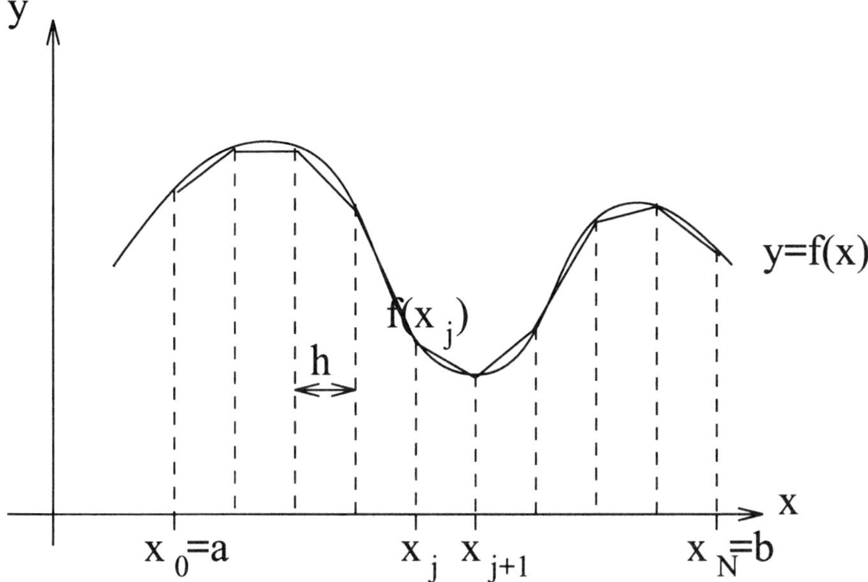

Figure 4.14 The trapezoidal rule

4. The z-co-ordinate on the surface of a sphere may be calculated given the centre points (x_c, y_c, z_c), the radius r, and the x, y points on the surface of sphere, for all cases except for $z_c = 0$.

Draw the dataflow diagram for this problem. Now implement the problem on your parallel system using the fork & join and data driven methods. Use your implementations to calculate the z-co-ordinate on the sphere for each of some given x_c, y_c, z_c, r, x and y points. Compare and contrast the efficiency of the algorithmic and domain decomposition implementations.

Hint: The equation for a sphere is:

$$(x - x_c)^2 + (y - y_c)^2 + (z - z_c)^2 = r^2$$

So we have:

$$x^2 - 2x_c x + x_c^2 + y^2 - 2y_c y + y_c^2 + z^2 - 2z_c z + z_c^2 - r^2 = 0$$

Now the centre points (x_c, y_c, z_c), and the radius r are known and thus we need to solve the equation for each of the given pairs of x, y points on the surface of the sphere.

So we have to solve:

$$az^2 + bz + c = 0$$

where

$a = 1,$
$b = -2z,$ and

$$c = x^2 + y^2 - 2x_c x - 2y_c y + x_c^2 + y_c^2 - r^2$$

5. Genetic algorithms, developed by Goldberg [80] and also by Holland [109], are a powerful directed search technique which are loosely based on biological models of evolution. They are extremely robust in the face of conflicting information. Genetic algorithms may be used to optimise members of a population of structures, where the structures are encoded in a 'gene string'. The population of structures is evolved in a manner which is analogous to a naive view of biological evolution using 'survival of the fittest'. In this case, the determinant of evolution is the 'fitness' of each structure as measured by an appropriate fitness function. During the evolution of the population, genes which do well in terms of the fitness function are more likely to be selected for the 'breeding' process which creates new, more 'fit' populations [56]. The process may be summarised as:

(a) Randomly generate a large population of genes.
(b) For each gene, calculate its utility in terms of the fitness function.
(c) For each gene, calculate a selection probability based on its fitness.
(d) Create a new population by selecting genes, based on the selection probability, and applying genetic operators.
(e) Repeat from (b) until a specified stop condition.

How could a genetic algorithm be implemented in parallel using the SAMD approach? What constitutes the problem domain? A dependency is inherent in the algorithm by the need to select the new population from the 'best' out of all the previous populations. Investigate ways in which this 'rigid' synchronisation point can be relaxed and the implications this has for the time required to achieve the stop condition in the parallel implementation and how the solution obtained from this parallel genetic algorithm may be affected.

Chapter 5

Evaluating Parallel Implementations

It doesn't matter if the answers from the parallel implementation are right, as long as they are achieved faster.

Doug Smith (University of Bristol)

Before attempting to solve a problem on a multiprocessor system it is useful to establish one or more metrics by which the relative merits of the eventual parallel implementation may be measured. The time taken to solve the problem is one sure means of comparison, however, other measurements, such as speed-up and efficiency, may provide useful insight on the maximum scalability of the implementation.

Doug Smith's comment on the attitude of some parallel programmers is not quite true. Obviously, we do want the correct answer, but the comment does accurately reflect the reasons why we have opted for a parallel implementation: to obtain the answers faster. The time that the parallel implementation takes to compute the results is perhaps the most natural way of determining the benefits of the approach that has been taken. If the parallel solution takes longer than any sequential implementation then the decision to use parallel processing needs to be re-examined.

Of course, there are many issues that need to be considered when comparing parallel and sequential implementations of the same problem, for example:

- Was the same processor used in each case?
- If not, what is the price of the sequential machine compared with that of the multiprocessor system?
- Was the algorithm chosen already optimised for sequential use, that is, did the data dependencies present preclude an efficient parallel implementation?

5.1 Realisation Penalties

If we assume that the same processor was used in both the sequential and parallel implementation, then we should expect, as discussed in Chapter 1, that the time to solve the problem decreases as more processing elements are added. The best we

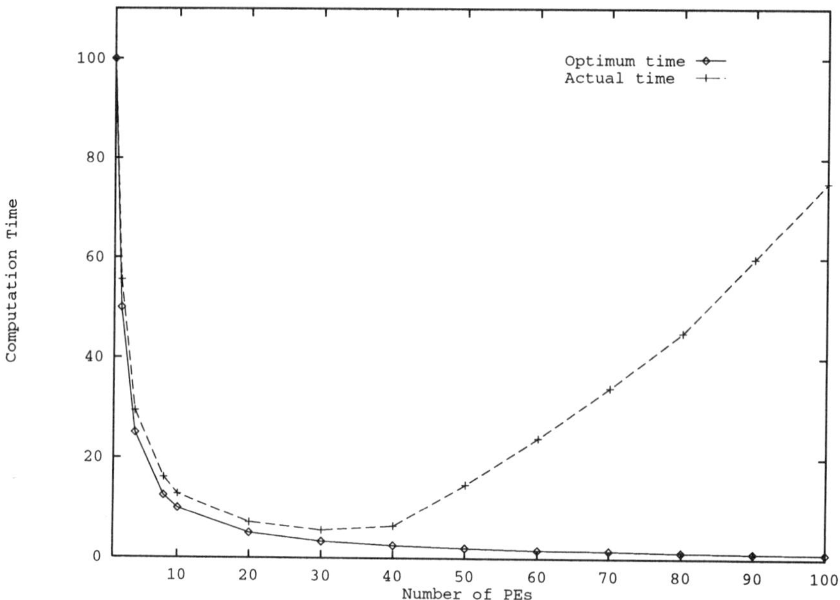

Figure 5.1   Optimum and actual parallel implementation times

can reasonably hope for is that two processing elements will solve the problem twice as quickly, three processing elements three times faster, and n processing elements n times faster. If n is sufficiently large then by this process we should expect our large scale parallel implementation to produce the answer in a tiny fraction of the sequential computation, as shown by the 'optimum time' curve in the graph in figure 5.1.

However, in reality we are unlikely to achieve these optimised times as the number of processors is increased. A more realistic scenario is that shown by the curve 'actual time' in figure 5.1. This curve shows an initial decrease in time taken to solve the example problem on the parallel system up to a certain number of processing elements. Beyond this point, adding more processors actually leads to an increase in computation time.

Failure to achieve the optimum solution time means that the parallel solution has suffered some form of *realisation penalty*. A realisation penalty can arise from two sources:

- an *algorithmic* penalty, and

- an *implementation* penalty.

The algorithmic penalty stems from the very nature of the algorithm selected for parallel processing. The more inherently sequential the algorithm, the less likely it is that the algorithm will be a good candidate for parallel processing.[1]

---

[1] It has also been shown, albeit not conclusively, that the more experience the writer of the parallel algorithm has in sequential algorithms, the less parallelism that algorithm is likely to exhibit [39].

This sequential nature of an algorithm and its implicit data dependencies will translate, in the SAMD approach, to a requirement to synchronise the processing elements at certain points in the algorithm. This can result in processing elements standing idle awaiting messages from other processing elements. A further algorithmic penalty may also come about from the need to reconstruct sequentially the results generated by the individual processors into an overall result for the computation.

Solving the same problem twice as fast on two processing elements implies that those two processing elements must spend 100% of their time on computation. We know that a parallel implementation requires some form of communication. The time a processing element is forced to spend on communication will naturally impinge on the time a processor has for computation. Any time that a processor cannot spend doing useful computation is an implementation penalty. Implementation penalties are thus caused by:

- **The need to communicate**

  As mentioned above, in a multiprocessor system, processing elements need to communicate. This communication may not only be that which is necessary for a processing element's own actions, but, as we will see in Chapter 9, a processing element may also have to act as a intermediate for other processing elements' communication.

- **Idle time**

  Idle time is any period of time when an application process is available to perform some useful computation, but is unable to do so because either there is no work locally available, or its current task is suspended awaiting a synchronisation signal, or a data item which has yet to arrive.

  It is the job of the local task manager to ensure that an application process is kept supplied with work. The computation to communication ratio within the system will determine how much time a task manager has to fetch a task before the current one is completed. A *load imbalance* is said to exist if some processing elements still have tasks to complete, while the others do not.

  While synchronisation points are introduced by the algorithm, the management of data items for a processing element is the job for the local data manager. The SAMD approach means that the problem domain is divided amongst the processing elements in some fashion. If an application process requires a data item that is not available locally, then this must be fetched from some other processing element within the system. If the processing element is unable to perform other useful computation while this fetch is being performed, for example by means of multi-threading as discussed in section 8.5.2, then the processing element is said to be idle.

- **Concurrent communication, data management and task management activity**

  Implementing each of a processing element's activities as a separate concurrent process, as discussed in section 4.4.2, means that the physical processor has to be shared. When another process other than the application process is scheduled then the processing element is not performing useful computation even though its current activity is necessary for the parallel implementation.

The fundamental goal of the system software is to minimise the implementation penalty. While this penalty can never be removed, intelligent communication, data management and task management strategies can avoid idle time and significantly reduce the impact of the need to communicate.

5.2 Performance Metrics

Solution time provides a simple way of evaluating a parallel implementation. However, if we wish to investigate the relative merits of our implementation then further insight can be gained by additional metrics. A range of metrics will allow us to compare aspects of different implementations and perhaps provide clues as to how overall system performance may be improved.

5.2.1 Speed-up

A useful measure of any multiprocessor implementation of a problem is *speed-up*. This relates the time taken to solve the problem on a single processor machine to the time taken to solve the same problem using the parallel implementation. We will define the speed-up of a multiprocessor system in terms of the elapsed time that is taken to complete a given problem, as follows:

$$\text{speed-up} \;=\; \frac{\text{elapsed time of a uniprocessor}}{\text{elapsed time of the multiprocessors}} \qquad (5.1)$$

The term *linear speed-up* is used when the solution time on an n processor system is n times faster than the solution time on the uniprocessor. This linear speed-up is thus equivalent to the optimum time shown in section 5.1. The optimum and actual computation times in figure 5.1 are represented as a graph of linear and actual speed-ups in figure 5.2. Note that the actual speed-up curve increases until a certain point and then decreases. Beyond this point we say that the parallel implementation has suffered a *speed-down*.

The third curve in figure 5.2 represents so-called *super-linear speed-up*. In this example, the implementation on 20 processors has achieved a computation time which is approximately 32 times faster than the uniprocessor solution. It has been argued, see [66], that it is not possible to achieve a speed-up greater than the number of processors used. While in practice it certainly is possible to achieve super-linear speed-up, such implementation may have exploited 'unfair' circumstances to obtain such timings. For example, most modern processors have a limited amount of cache memory with an access time significantly faster compared with a standard memory access. Two processors would have double the amount of this cache memory. Given that we are investigating a fixed size problem, this means that a larger proportion of the problem domain is in the cache in the parallel implementation than in the sequential implementation. It is not unreasonable, therefore, to imagine a situation where the two-processor solution time is more than twice as fast as the uniprocessor time.

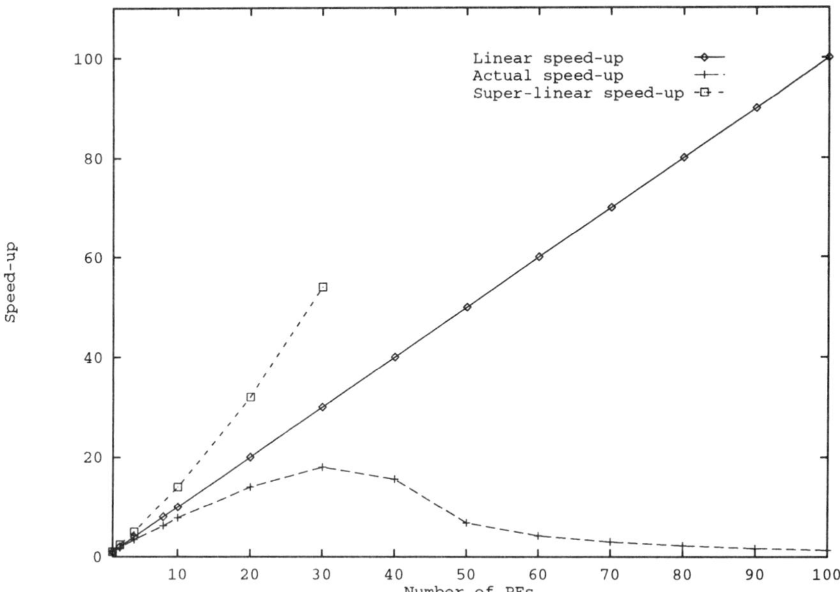

Figure 5.2 Linear and actual speed-ups

Although super-linear speed-up is desirable, in this book we will assume a 'fair' comparison between uniprocessor and multiprocessor implementations. The results that are presented in the case studies thus make no attempt to exploit any hardware advantages offered by the increasing number of processors. This will enable the performance improvements offered by the proposed system software extensions to be highlighted without being masked by any variations in underlying hardware. In practice, of course, it would be foolish to ignore these benefits and readers are encouraged to 'squeeze every last ounce of performance' out of their parallel implementation.

Two possibilities exist for determining the 'elapsed time of a uniprocessor'. This could be the time obtained when executing:

1. an optimised sequential algorithm on a single processor, T_s, or

2. the parallel implementation on one processing element, T_1.

The time taken to solve the problem on n processing elements we will term T_n. The difference between how the two sequential times are obtained is shown in figure 5.3. There are advantages in acquiring both these sequential times. Comparing the parallel with the optimised sequential implementation highlights any algorithmic efficiencies that had to be sacrificed to achieve the parallel version. In addition, none of the parallel implementation penalties are hidden by this comparison and thus the speed-up is not exaggerated. One of these penalties is the time taken simply to supply the data to the processing element and collect the results.

The comparison of the single processing element with the multiple processing

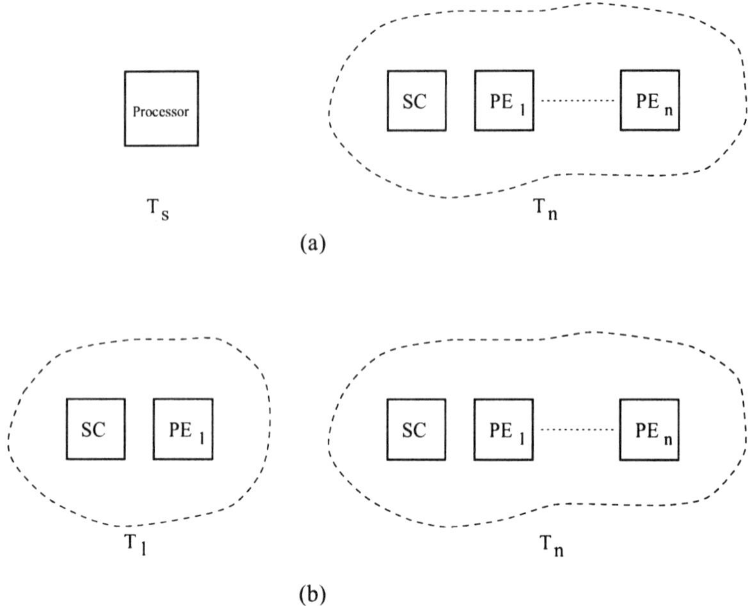

Figure 5.3 Systems used to obtain T_n and (a) T_s (b) T_1

element implementation shows how well the problem is 'coping' with an increasing number of processing elements. Speed-up calculated as $\frac{T_1}{T_n}$, therefore, provides an indication as to the scalability of the parallel implementation. Unless otherwise stated, we will use this alternative for speed-up in the case studies in this book as it better emphasizes the performance improvements brought about by the system software we shall be introducing.

As we can see from the curve for 'actual speed-up' in figure 5.2, the speed-up obtained for that problem increased to a maximum value and subsequently decreased as more processing elements were added. In 1967 Amdahl presented what has become known as 'Amdahl's law' [8]. This law attempts to give a maximum bound for speed-up from the nature of the algorithm chosen for the parallel implementation. We are given an algorithm in which the proportion of time that needs to be spent on the purely sequential parts is s, and the proportion of time that might be done in parallel is p, by definition. The total time for the algorithm on a single processor is $s + p = 1$ (where the 1 is for algebraic simplicity), and the maximum speed-up that can be achieved on n processors is:

$$\text{maximum speed-up} = \frac{(s + p)}{s + \frac{p}{n}}$$

$$= \frac{1}{s + \frac{p}{n}} \tag{5.2}$$

Figure 5.4 shows the maximum speed-up predicted by Amdahl's law for a se-

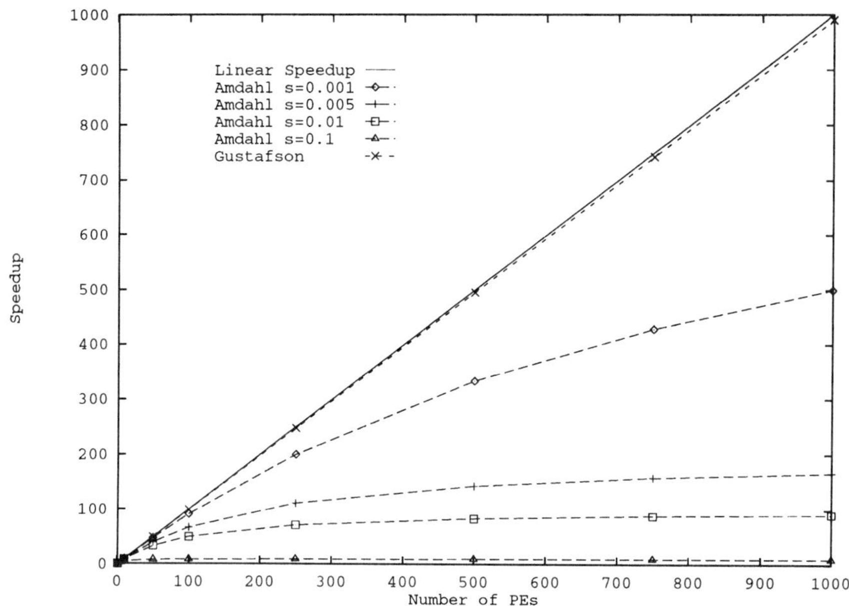

Figure 5.4 Example maximum speed-up from Amdahl and Gustafson's laws

quential portion of an algorithm requiring 0.1%, 0.5%, 1% and 10% of the total algorithm time, that is $s = 0.001$, 0.005, 0.01 and 0.1 respectively. For 1000 processors the maximum speed-up that can be achieved for a sequential portion of only 1% is less than 91. This rather depressing forecast put a serious damper on the possibilities of massive parallel implementations of algorithms and led Gustafson in 1988 to issue a counter claim [92]. Gustafson stated that a problem size is virtually never independent of the number of processors, as it appears in equation (5.2), but rather '... in practice, the problem size scales with the number of processors'.

Gustafson thus derives a maximum speed-up of:

$$\text{maximum speed-up} \quad = \quad \frac{(s + (p \times n))}{s + p}$$

$$= \quad n + (1 - n) \times s \qquad (5.3)$$

The maximum speed-up according to Gustafson is also shown in figure 5.4. As the curve shows, the maximum achievable speed-up is nearly linear when the problem size is increased as more processing elements are added. Despite this optimistic forecast, Gustafson's premise is not applicable in a large number of cases. Most scientists and engineers have a particular problem they want to solve in as short a time as possible. Typically, the application already has a specified size for the problem domain. For example, in the case study we will be considering in Chapter 10, aerospace engineers wish to determine the flow of air about a particular three-dimensional surface, say an aircraft. In this example it would be inappropriate for the engineers to follow Gustafson's advice and increase the problem size as more processing elements were added to their parallel implementation, because to do so would mean either:

- the physical size of the three-dimensional object being considered would have to be increased, which is of course not possible; or

- the size of the panels used to approximate the surface would have to be reduced, thereby increasing the number of panels and thus the size of the problem domain.

This latter case is also not an option, because the computational method is sensitive to the size of the panels relative to their distances apart. Artificially decreasing the size of the panels introduces numerical instabilities into the method. Furthermore, artificially increasing the size of the problem domain may improve speed-up, but it will not improve the time taken to solve the problem.

For fixed sized problems it appears that we are left with Amdahl's gloomy prediction of the maximum speed-up that is possible for our parallel implementation. However, all is not lost, as Amdahl's assumption that an algorithm can be separated into a component which has to be executed sequentially and a part which can be performed in parallel may not be totally appropriate for the SAMD approach. Remember, in this model we are retaining the complete sequential algorithm and exploiting the parallelism that exists in the problem domain. So, in this case, an equivalent to Amdahl's law would imply that the data can be divided into two parts, that which must be dealt with in a strictly sequential manner and that which can executed in parallel. Any data dependencies will certainly imply some form of sequential ordering when dealing with the data, however, for a large number of problems such data dependencies may not exist. It may also be possible to reduce the effect of dependencies by clever scheduling.

The achievable speed-up for a problem using the SAMD approach is, however, bounded by the number of tasks that make up the problem. Solving a problem comprising a maximum of 20 tasks on more than 20 processors makes no sense. In practice, of course, any parallel implementation suffers from realisation penalties which increase as more processing elements are added. The actual speed-up obtained will thus be less than the maximum possible speed-up.

5.2.2 Efficiency

The relative efficiency, based on the performance of the problem on one processor, can be a useful measure as to what percentage of a processor's time is being spent in useful computation. This, therefore, determines what the system overheads are. We will measure the relative efficiency as:

$$\text{efficiency} = \frac{\text{speed-up} \times 100}{\text{number of processors}} \tag{5.4}$$

Figure 5.5 shows the optimum and actual computation times given in figure 5.1 represented as processing element efficiency. The graph shows that optimum computation time, and therefore linear speed-up, equates to an efficiency of 100% for each processing element. This again shows that to achieve this level of efficiency

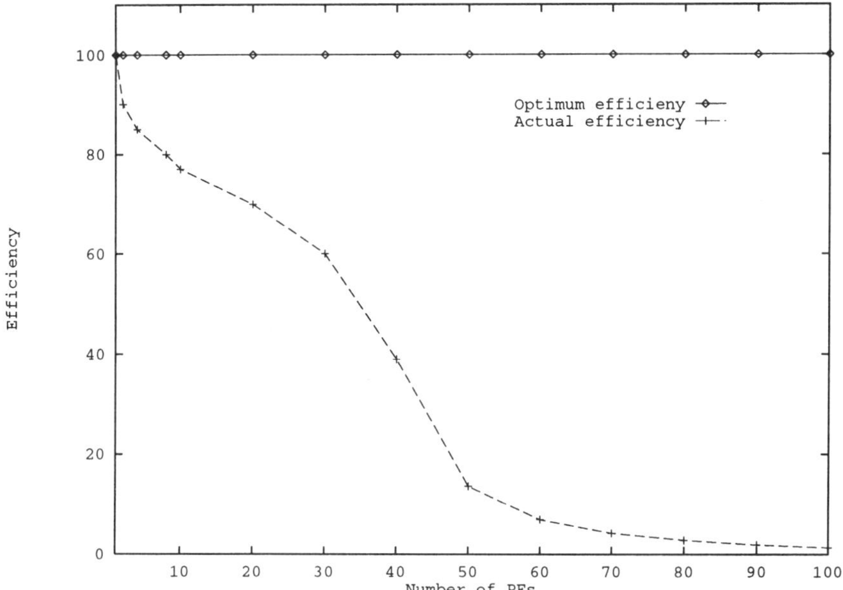

Figure 5.5   Optimum and actual processing element efficiency

every processing element must spend 100% of its time performing useful computation. Any implementation penalty would be immediately reflected by a decrease in efficiency. This is clearly shown in the curve for the actual computation times. Here the efficiency of each processing element decreases steadily as more are added until by the time 100 processing elements are incorporated, the realisation penalties are so high that each processing element is only able to devote just over 1% of its time to useful computation.

5.2.3 Optimum number of processing elements

Faced with implementing a fixed size problem on a parallel system, it may be useful to know the optimum number of processing elements on which this particular problem should be implemented in order to achieve the best possible performance. We term this optimum number n_{opt}. We shall judge the *maximum performance* for a particular problem with a fixed problem domain size, as the shortest possible time required to produce the desired results for a certain parallel implementation. This optimum number of processing elements may be derived directly from the 'computation time' graph. In figure 5.1 the minimum actual computation time occurred when the problem was implemented on 30 processing elements. As figure 5.6 shows, this optimum number of processing elements is also the point on the horizontal axis in figure 5.2 at which the maximum speed-up was obtained.

The optimum number of processing elements is also the upper bound for the scalability of the problem for that parallel implementation. To improve the scal-

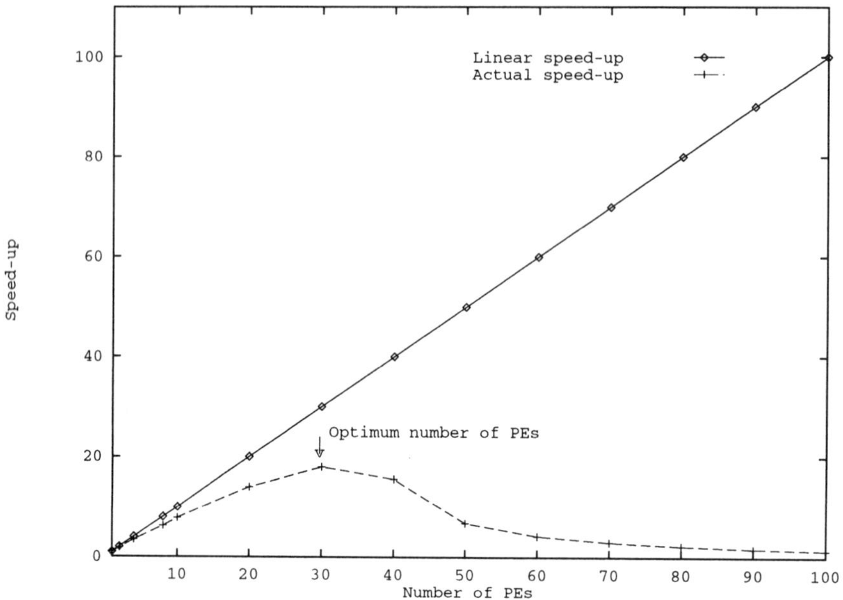

Figure 5.6   Optimum number of processing elements related to speed-up

ability of the problem it is necessary to re-examine the decisions concerning the algorithm chosen and the make-up of the system software that has been adopted for supporting the parallel implementation. As we will see in subsequent chapters, the correct choice of system software can have a significant effect on the performance of a parallel implementation.

Figure 5.7 shows the speed-up graphs for different system software decisions for the same problem. The goal of a parallel implementation may be restated as 'to ensure that the optimum number of processing elements for your problem is greater than the number of processing elements physically available to solve the problem!'

5.2.4 Other metrics

Computation time, speed-up and efficiency provide insight into how successful a parallel implementation of a problem has been. As figure 5.7 shows, different implementations of the same algorithm on the same multiprocessor system may produce very different performances. A multitude of other metrics have been proposed over the years as a means of comparing the relative merits of different architectures and to provide a way of assessing their suitability as the chosen multiprocessor machine.

The performance of a computer is frequently measured as the rate of some number of events per second. Within a multi-user environment the elapsed time to solve a problem will comprise the user's CPU time plus the system's CPU time.

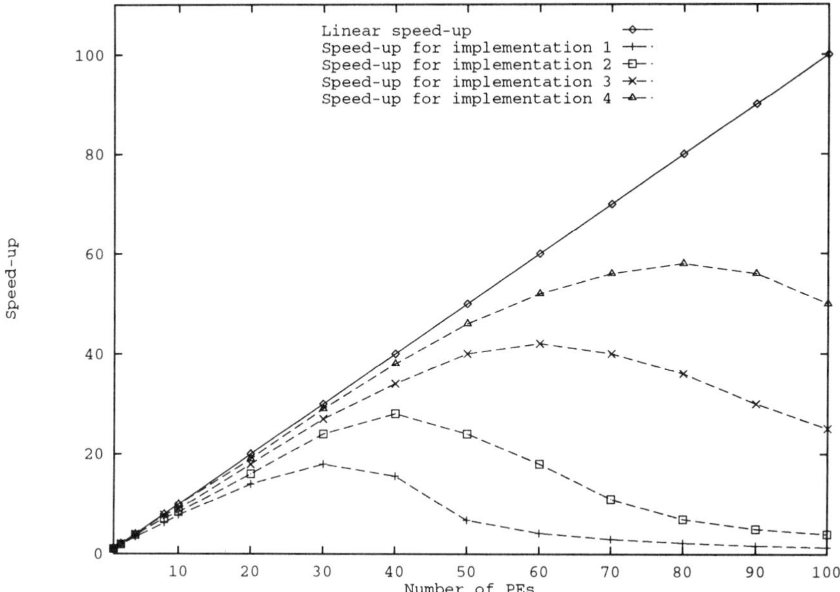

Figure 5.7   Speed-up graphs for different system software for the same problem

Assuming that the computer's clock is running at a constant rate, the user's CPU performance may be measured as:

$$\text{CPU time} = \frac{\text{CPU clock cycles for a program}}{\text{clock rate (e.g. 100 MHz)}}$$

The average clock cycles per instruction (CPI) may be calculated as:

$$\text{CPI} = \frac{\text{CPU clock cycles for a program}}{\text{instruction count}}$$

We can also compute the CPU time from the time a program took to run:

$$\text{CPU time} = \frac{\text{seconds}}{\text{program}}$$

$$= \frac{\text{seconds}}{\text{clock cycles}} \times \frac{\text{clock cycles}}{\text{instructions}} \times \frac{\text{instructions}}{\text{program}}$$

Such a performance metric is dependent on:

Clock rate: this is determined by the hardware technology and the organisation of the architecture,

CPI: a function of the system organisation and the instruction set architecture, and

Instruction count: this is affected by the instruction set architecture and the compiler technology utilised.

One of the most frequently used performance metrics is the MIPS rating of a computer, that is how many Million Instructions Per Second the computer is capable of performing:

$$\text{MIPS} = \frac{\text{instruction count}}{\text{execution time} \times 10^6} = \frac{\text{clock rate}}{\text{CPI} \times 10^6}$$

However, the MIPS value is dependent on the instruction set used and thus any comparison between computers with different instruction sets is not valid. The MIPS value may even vary between programs running on the same computer. Furthermore, a program which makes use of hardware floating point routines may take less time to complete than a similar program which uses a software floating point implementation, but the first program will have a lower MIPS rating than the second [98]. These anomalies have led to MIPS sometimes being referred to as 'Meaningless Indication of Processor Speed'.

Similar to MIPS is the 'Mega-FLOPS' (MFLOPS) rating for computers, where MFLOPS represents Million FLoating point Operations Per Second:

$$\text{MFLOPS} = \frac{\text{no. of floating point operations in a program}}{\text{execution time} \times 10^6}$$

MFLOPS is not universally applicable, for example a word processor utilising no floating point operations would register no MFLOPS rating. However, the same program executing on different machines should be comparable, because, although the computers may execute a different number of instructions, they should perform the same number of operations, provided the set of floating point operations is consistent across both architectures. The MFLOPS value will vary for programs running on the same computer which have different mixtures of integer and floating point instructions as well as a different blend of 'fast' and 'slow' floating point instructions. For example, the *add* instruction often executes in less time than a *divide* instruction.

An MFLOPS rating for a single program cannot, therefore, be generalised to provide a single performance metric for a computer. A suite of benchmark programs, such as the LINPACK or Livermore Loops routines, have been developed to allow a more meaningful method of comparison between machines. When examining the relative performance of computers using such benchmarks it is important to discover the sustained MFLOPS performance as a more accurate indication of the machines' potential rather than merely the peak MFLOPS rating, a figure that 'can be guaranteed never to be exceeded'.

Other metrics for comparing computers include:

Dhrystone: A CPU intensive benchmark used to measure the integer performance especially as it pertains to system programming,

Whetstone: A synthetic benchmark without any vectorisable code for evaluating floating point performance,

TPS: Transactions Per Second measure for applications, such as airline reservation systems, which require on-line database transactions,

KLIPS: Kilo Logic Inferences Per Second is used to measure the relative inference performance of artificial intelligence machines.

Tables showing the comparison of the results of these metrics for a number of architectures can be found in several books, for example [107, 115].

Cost is seldom an issue that can be ignored when purchasing a high performance computer. The desirability of a particular computer or even the number of processors within a system may be offset by the extraordinarily high costs associated with many high performance architectures. This prompted an early 'law' by Grosch that the speed of a computer is proportional to its cost [90, 89]. Fortunately, although this is no longer completely true, multiprocessor machines are nevertheless typically more expensive than their general purpose counterparts. The parallel computer eventually purchased should provide acceptable computation times for an affordable price, that is maximise 'the bangs per buck' (performance per unit price).

5.2.5 Performance modelling

There have been many attempts to model the performance of parallel systems and thus predict the performance of any algorithm implemented on these systems, for example [12, 48, 72, 139, 163]. Of these, Mohan's thesis [139], is a particularly detailed description. However, modelling all the interdependencies of different components of a parallel implementation of a complex problem on a large multiprocessor system may be simply not possible. Some form of simplification will be necessary to make the model computationally tractable. A common simplification is to assume a constant communication time between any two processing elements. Such a simplification ignores the presence of different levels of message density on the path between the processing elements. In the real implementation these densities may have a major effect on communication throughput and thus significantly affect overall system performance.

The case studies described in this book will use empirical evidence to show system performance. From this evidence and given an understanding of the realisation penalties for a particular problem it may be possible to predict likely performance of the problem when implemented on different numbers of processing elements.

5.3 Summary

Comparing the performance of a sequential and a parallel implementation of the same problem provides an indication as to how significantly realisation penalties have affected the parallel version. Using an optimised sequential algorithm for the sequential implementation highlights algorithmic penalties. Measuring the parallel implementation on a single processing element shows how the implementation penalties increase as more processing elements are used to solve the problem.

If processing elements could spend 100% of their time performing useful computation then we would achieve linear speed-up and each processing element we added would give us an improvement in solution time. In reality, processing elements must communicate and so unless we can exploit 'unfair' architectural improvements with the addition of more processing elements, linear speed-up is an unobtainable goal. However, for a fixed size problem, we need not be discouraged by Amdahl's gloomy prediction of maximum speed-up. The SAMD approach we are following is not inhibited by algorithmic dependencies, but rather by possible data dependencies, which may impose far less of a restriction on our parallel implementation.

The optimum number of processing elements, n_{opt}, shows the scalability of our parallel implementation, that is the maximum number of processing elements we can use to solve the problem and still get a performance improvement. For practical parallel processing we must strive to ensure that this optimum number is greater than the maximum number of processing elements we have available in our multiprocessor system. The correct choice of the computational model, data and task management and communication strategy will help us achieve this objective.

5.4 Exercises and Project Suggestions

1. A problem implementation executing on one processing element takes 5 seconds to solve. We wish to solve the same problem in 0.4 second on a multiprocessor system containing 20 processing elements. What percentage of their time must each of the 20 processing elements spend performing useful computation?

2. Derive an expression that can be used to determine the amount of time each of the optimum number of processing elements for a problem is spending doing useful computation.

3. Amdahl's law states that any parallel computation is necessarily limited by its sequential portion. Furthermore, independent of the number of processors, the speed-up is always limited to the inverse of the sequential fraction of the algorithm. Gustafson provided an answer for this law, saying that the purpose of parallel computers is to attack larger and larger problems, where the inherently sequential part shrinks as a percentage of the total computation. Illustrate the difference in these two approaches using the prime number sieve example given in Chapter 3.

4. Using the SAMD approach, the time to solve a problem consisting of x tasks on n processors is $T_n(x)$. Let us assume that this time is equal to the start up and result correlation time, $T_{s\&r}$, plus x times the time to complete a single task, T_{task} (where this time includes both the computation and communication overheads), that is:

$$T_n(x) = T_{s\&r} + x(T_{task})$$

Now derive an expression that shows the conditions under which the speed-up achieved when solving this same problem now comprising more tasks, $y > x$, on the same n processors, $S_n(y)$ is greater than $S_n(x)$ while the time to solve the smaller problem $T_n(x)$ is less than that required for this larger problem, $T_n(y)$.

5. Assume we have a problem consisting of 100 tasks, each of which takes 1 second to compute. Using the SAMD approach and ignoring communication overheads, answer the following questions:

   (a) What is the fastest time this problem can be solved in parallel and on how many processing element is this optimal time achieved?

   (b) If only three processing elements were available, how quickly could the problem be solved?

   (c) If dependencies existed in the problem domain such that the first 20 tasks had to be completed before the next 20 could be started and these had to be completed before the next 20, and so on, what would be the optimal solution time? What would be the relative efficiency of this solution?

   (d) If the only dependencies in the problem domain were such that tasks 18, 19, 20 and 21 had to be completed in sequence, how would this affect the optimal solution time for the problem on three processing elements?

   (e) In light of the above simple calculations, discuss how we may use task scheduling to reduce the impact of data dependencies when using the SAMD approach.

Chapter 6

Computational Models

Work expands so as to fill the time available for its completion.

C. Northcote Parkinson

The computational model chosen to solve a particular problem determines the manner in which work is distributed across the processors of the multiprocessor system. In our quest for an efficient parallel implementation we must maximise the proportion of time the processors spend performing necessary computation. Any imbalance may result in processors standing idle while others struggle to complete their allocated work, thus limiting potential performance. Load balancing techniques aim to provide an even division of computational effort to all processors.

The Sequential-Algorithm Multiple-Data paradigm exploits the parallelism that exists by simultaneously applying the algorithm to different data items. Two approaches may be identified: the data driven and the demand driven models of computation. The former corresponds to a predetermined work division scheme, while the latter performs work allocation dynamically as computation proceeds. A hybrid scheme may also be defined, utilising the appropriate choice of technique as the problem demands.

In this chapter we highlight the differences between these approaches and discuss their application.

The solution of a problem using the SAMD model involves each processing element applying the specified algorithm to a set of principal data items. The computational model ensures that every principal data item is acted upon and determines how the tasks are allocated amongst the processing elements. A choice of computational model exists for each problem. To achieve maximum system performance, the model chosen must see that the total work-load is distributed evenly amongst the processing elements. This balances the overheads associated with communicating principal data items to processing elements with the need to avoid processing element idle time.

The problem of calculating the air flow through a simple two-dimensional duct will be used to illustrate the differences between the computational models. Figure 6.1 shows the physical situation being simulated.

A sequential solution to this problem may be achieved by dividing the duct into

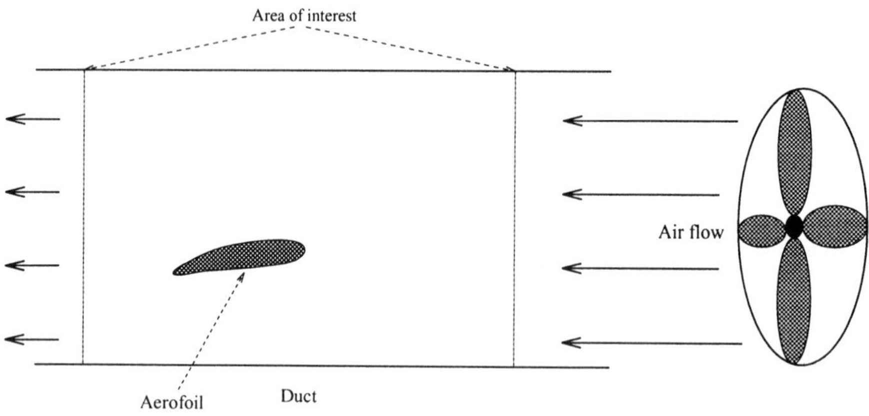

Figure 6.1   Air flow through a duct containing an obstruction

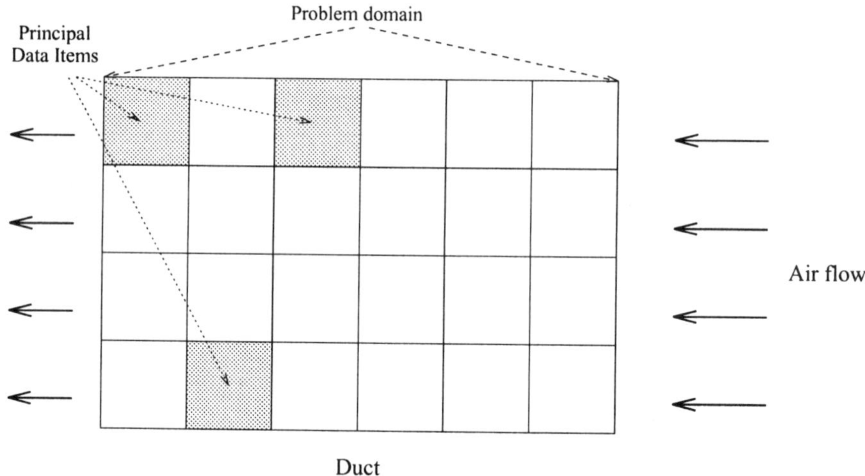

Figure 6.2   Principal data items for calculating the flow in a two-dimensional duct

24 distinct regions, with each region constituting a single principal data item, as shown in figure 6.2, and then applying the flow calculation algorithm at each of these regions in turn. There are thus 24 tasks to be performed for this problem where each task is the computation of the flow at one area of the duct. To understand the computational models, it is not necessary to know the details of the algorithm; suffice it to say that each principal data item represents an area of the duct on which the algorithm can be applied to determine the flow at that position. We will assume that no additional data items are required to complete any task.

6.1 The Data Driven Model

The data driven model allocates all the principal data items to specific processing elements before computation commences. Each processing element thus knows in advance the principal data items to which they are required to apply the algorithm. Providing there is sufficient memory to hold the allocated set at each processing element, then, apart from the initial distribution, there is no further communication of principal data items. If there is insufficient local memory, then the extra items must be fetched as soon as memory space allows. This fetching of remote data items will be discussed further when data management is examined in Chapter 8.

6.1.1 Balanced data driven model

In balanced data driven systems (also known as geometric decompositions), an equal number of principal data items is allocated to each processing element. This portion is determined simply by dividing the total number of principal data items by the number of processing elements:

$$\text{portion at each PE} = \frac{\text{number of principal data items}}{\text{number of PEs}}$$

If the number of principal data items is not an exact multiple of the number of processing elements, then *(number of principal data items) MOD (number of PEs)* will each have one extra principal data item, and thus perform one extra task. The required start task and the number of tasks is communicated by the system controller to each processing element and these can then apply the required algorithm to their allotted principal data items. This is similar to the way in which problems are solved on arrays of SIMD processors.

In this example, consider the simple two-dimensional flow calculation for an empty duct. The principal data items may be allocated equally to three processing elements, labelled PE_1, PE_2 and PE_3, as shown in figure 6.3. In this case, each processing element is allotted eight principal data items.

As no further principal data item allocation takes place after the initial distribution, a balanced work load is only achieved for the balanced data driven computational model if the computational effort associated with each portion of principal data items is identical. If not, some processing elements will have finished their portions while others still have work to do. With the balanced data driven model the division of principal data items amongst processing elements is geometric in nature, that is each processing element simply may be allocated an equal number of principal data items irrespective of their position within the problem domain. Thus, to ensure a balanced work load, this model should only be used if the computational effort associated with each principal data item is the same, and preferably where the number of principal data items is an exact multiple of the number of processing elements. This implies *a priori* knowledge, but given this, the balanced data driven approach is the simplest of the computational models to implement.

Using figure 6.3, if each task of the air flow computation takes 1 time unit to complete, then the sequential solution of this problem would take 24 time units. The parallel implementation of this problem using the three processing elements each allocated eight tasks should take approximately 8 time units, a third of the

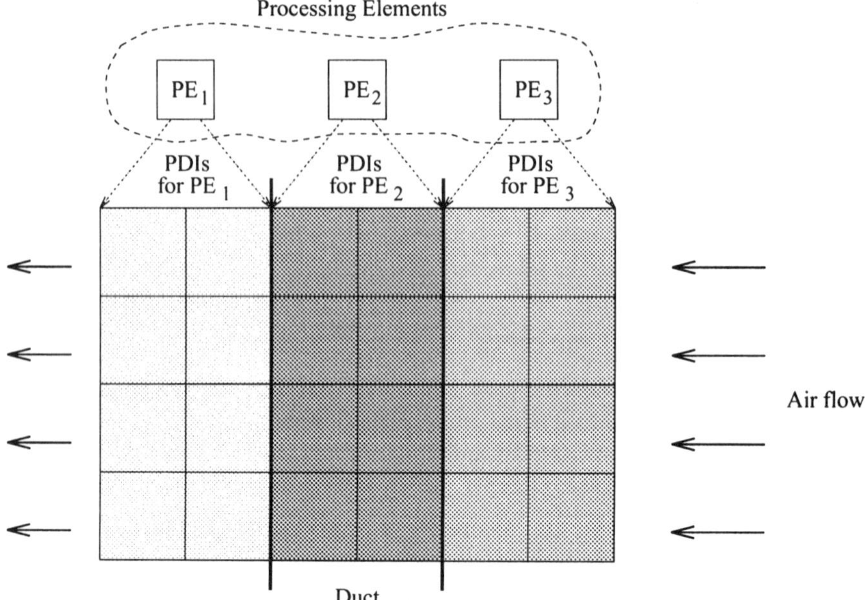

Figure 6.3   Equal allocation of data items to processing elements

time required by the sequential implementation. Note, however, that the parallel solution will not be exactly one third of the sequential time as this would ignore the time required to communicate the portions from the system controller to the processing elements. This would also ignore the time required to receive the results back from the processing elements and for the system controller to collate the solution. A balanced data driven version of this problem on the three processing elements would more accurately take:

$$\text{solution time} = \text{initial distribution} + \lceil \frac{24}{3} \rceil + \text{result collation}$$

Assuming low communication times, this model gives the solution in approximately one third of the time of the sequential solution, close to the maximum possible linear speed-up. Solution of the same problem on five processing elements would give:

$$\text{solution time} = \text{initial distribution} + \lceil \frac{24}{5} \rceil + \text{result collation}$$

This will be solved in even longer than the expected 4.8 time units as, in this case, one processing element is allocated 4 principal data items while the other four have to be apportioned 5. As computation draws to a close, one processing element will be idle while the four others complete their extra work. The solution time will thus be slightly more than 5 time units.

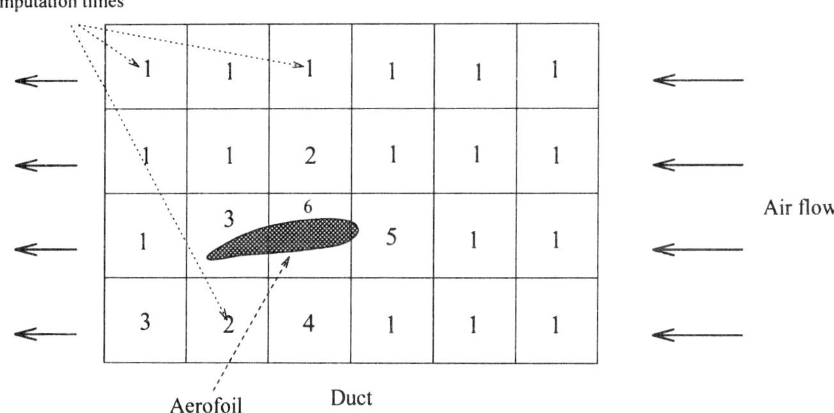

Figure 6.4   Unequal computational effort due to presence of aerofoil

6.1.2 Unbalanced data driven model

Differences in the computational effort associated with the principal data items will increase the probability of substantial processing element idle time if the simplistic balanced data driven approach is adopted. If the individual computation efforts differ, and are known *a priori*, then this can be exploited to achieve optimum load balancing.

The unbalanced data driven computational model allocates principal data items to processing elements based on their computational requirements. Rather than simply apportioning an equal number of tasks to each processing element, the principal data items are allocated to ensure that each processing element will complete its portion at approximately the same time.

For example, the complexity introduced into the air flow calculations by placing an aerofoil into the duct, as shown in figure 6.4, will cause an increased computational effort to be required to solve the portions allocated to PE_1 and PE_2 in the balanced data driven model. This will result in these two processing elements still being busy with their computations long after the other processing element, PE_3, has completed its less computationally complex portion.

Should *a priori* knowledge be available regarding the computational effort associated with each principal data item then they may be allocated unequally amongst the processing elements, as shown in figure 6.5. The computational effort now required to process each of these geometrically unequal portions will be approximately the same, minimising any processing element idle time.

The sequential time required to solve the air flow in the duct with the aerofoil in position is now 42 time units. To balance the workload amongst the three processing elements, each processing element should compute for 14 time units. Allocation of the portions to each processing element in the unbalanced data driven model involves a preprocessing step to determine precisely the best way to subdivide the principal data items. The optimum computation time for each processing element

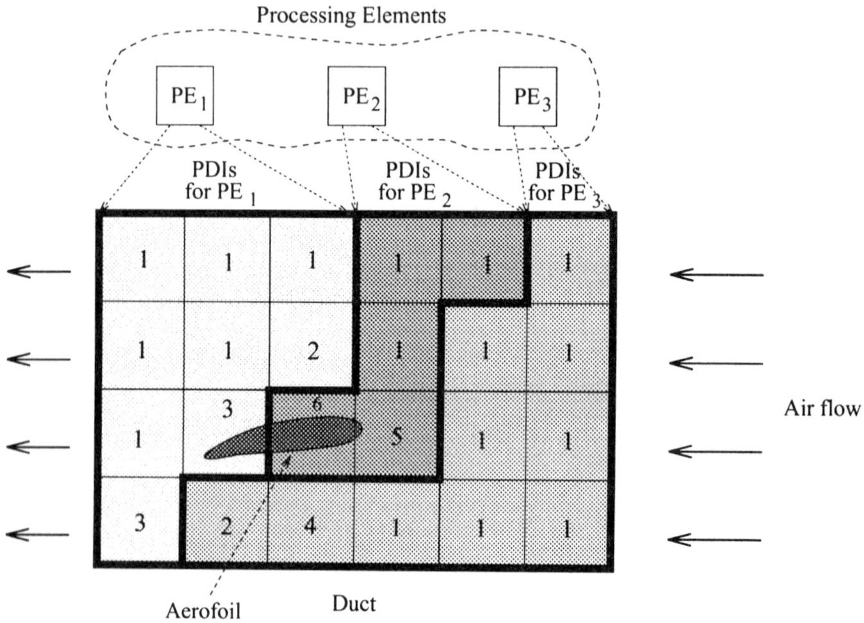

Figure 6.5   Unequal allocation of data items to processing elements to assist with load balancing

can be obtained by simply dividing the total computation time by the number of processing elements. If possible, no processing element should be allocated principal data items whose combined computation time exceeds this optimum amount. Sorting the principal data items in descending computation times can facilitate the subdivision.

The total solution time for a problem using the unbalanced data driven model is thus:

solution time =

    preprocessing + distribution + longest portion time + result collation

So comparing the naive balanced distribution from section 6.1.1

balanced time   =   distribution + 21 + result collation

unbalanced time = preprocessing + distribution + 14 + result collation

The preprocessing stage is a simple sort requiring far less time than the air flow calculations. Thus, in this example, the unbalanced data driven model would be significantly faster than the balanced model due to the large variations in task computational complexity.

The necessity for the preprocessing stage means that this model will take more time to use than the balanced data driven approach should the tasks have the same

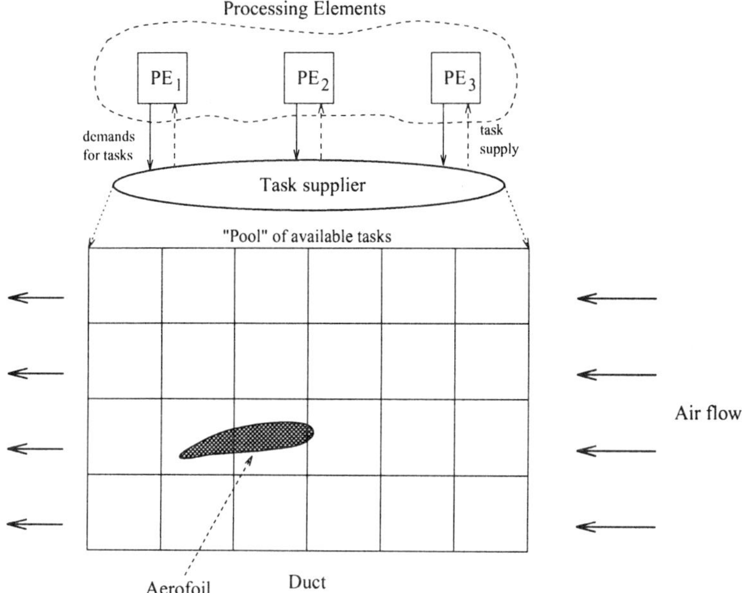

Figure 6.6 A demand driven model for a two-dimensional flow calculation

computational requirement. However, if there are variations in computational complexity and they are known, then the unbalanced data driven model is the most efficient way of implementing the problem in parallel.

6.2 The Demand Driven Model

The data driven computational models are dependent on the computational requirements of the principal data items being known, or at least being predictable, before actual computation starts. Only with this knowledge can these data items be allocated in the correct manner to ensure an even load balance. Should the computational effort of the principal data items be unknown or unpredictable, then serious load balancing problems can occur if the data driven models are used. In this situation the demand driven computational model should be adopted to allocate work to processing elements evenly and thus optimise system performance.

In the demand driven computational model, work is allocated to processing elements dynamically as they become idle, with processing elements no longer bound to any particular portion of the principal data items. Having produced the result from one principal data item, the processing elements demand the next principal data item from some work supplier process. This is shown diagrammatically in figure 6.6 for the simple two-dimensional flow calculation.

Unlike the data driven models, there is no initial communication of work to the processing elements, however, there is now the need to send requests for individual principal data items to the supplier and for the supplier to communicate with the processing elements in order to satisfy these requests. To avoid unnecessary communication it may be possible to combine the return of the results from one computation with the request for the next principal data item.

The optimum time for solving a problem using this simple demand driven model is thus:

$$\text{solution time} = 2 \times \text{total comms time} + \frac{\text{total computation time for all PDIs}}{\text{number of PEs}}$$

This optimum computation time, $\dfrac{\text{total computation time for all PDIs}}{\text{number of PEs}}$, will only be possible if the work can be allocated so that all processing elements complete the last of their tasks at exactly the same time. If this is not so then some processing elements will still be busy with their final task while the others have completed. It may also be possible to reduce the communication overheads of the demand driven model by overlapping the communication with the computation in some manner. This possibility will be discussed further when task management is considered in Chapter 7.

On receipt of a request, if there is still work to be done, the work supplier responds with the next available task for processing. If there are no more tasks which need to be computed then the work supplier may safely ignore the request. The problem will be solved when all principal data items have been requested and all the results of the computations on these items have been returned and collated. The dynamic allocation of work by the demand driven model will ensure that while some processing elements are busy with more computationally demanding principal data items, other processing elements are available to compute the less complex parts of the problem. The following segment of code shows how this simple demand driven task supply could occur.

```
PROCESS Task_Supplier()
  Begin
    remaining_tasks := total_number_of_tasks
    (* Initialise all processors with one task *)
    FOR p = 1 TO number_of_PEs
      Begin
        SEND task TO PE[p]
        remaining_tasks := remaining_tasks - 1
      End
    WHILE results_outstanding DO
      Begin
        RECEIVE result FROM PE[i]
        IF remaining_tasks > 0 THEN
          Begin
            SEND task TO PE[i]
            remaining_tasks := remaining_tasks - 1
          End
        ENDIF
      End
  End (* Task_Supplier *)
```

Using the computational times for the presence of the aerofoil as shown in figure 6.5, figure 6.7 shows how the principal data items may be allocated by the task

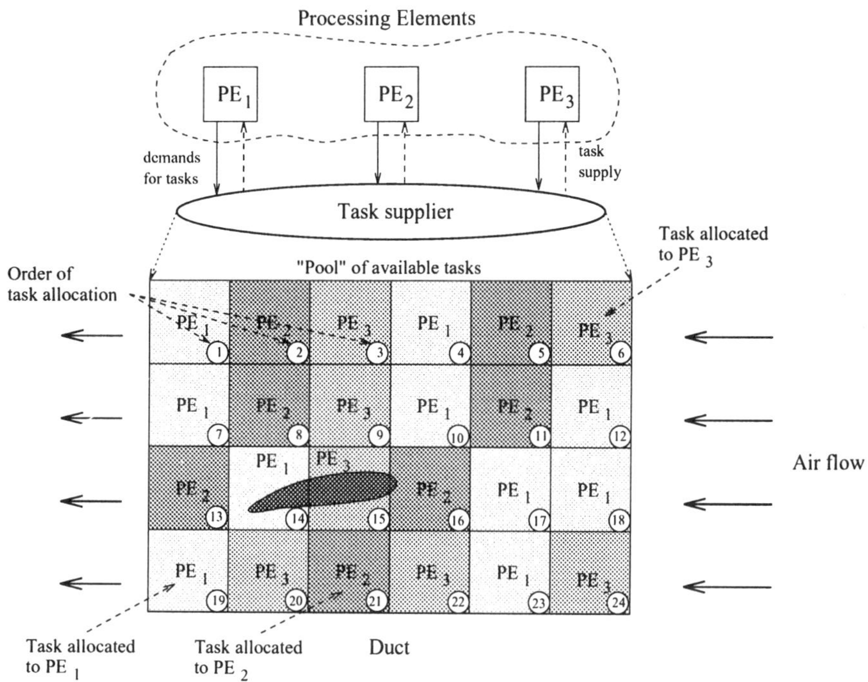

Figure 6.7 Allocation of principal data items using a demand driven model

supplier to the processing elements using a simple serial allocation scheme. Note that the processing elements do not complete the same number of tasks. So, for example, while processing elements 2 and 3 are busy completing the computationally complex work associated with principal data items 15 and 16, processing element 1 can compute the less computationally taxing tasks of principal data items 17, 18 and 19.

The demand driven computational model facilitates dynamic load balancing when there is no prior knowledge as to the complexity of the different parts of the problem domain. Optimum load balancing is still dependent on all the processing elements completing the last of the work at the same time. An unbalanced solution may still result if a processing element is allocated a complex part of the domain towards the end of the solution. This processing element may then still be busy well after the other processing elements have completed computation on the remainder of the principal data items and are now idle as there is no further work to do. To reduce the likelihood of this situation it is important that the computationally complex portions of the domain, the so called *hot spots*, are allocated to processing elements early on in the solution process. Although there is no *a priori* knowledge as to the exact computational effort associated with any principal data item (if there were, an unbalanced data driven approach would have been adopted), nevertheless, any insight as to possible hot spot areas should be exploited. The task supplier would thus assign principal data items from these areas first.

In the example of the two-dimensional flow calculation, while the exact computational requirement associated with the principal data items in the proximity of the aerofoil may be unknown, it is highly likely that the solution of the principal items in that area will more complex than those elsewhere in the duct. In this problem, these principal data items should be allocated first.

If no insight is possible then a simple serial allocation, as shown in figure 6.7, or spiral allocation, as shown in figure 6.8, or even a random allocation of principal data items will have to suffice. While a random allocation offers perhaps a higher probability of avoiding late allocation of principal data items from hot spots, additional effort is required when choosing the next principal data item to allocate to ensure that no principal data item is allocated more than once, as shown in the following code segment:

```
PROCEDURE Select_Task(VAR task)
  Begin
    (* first select a random number from 1 to remaining_tasks *)
    index_position := Generate_Random_Number(1, remaining_tasks)
    task := task_index[index_position]
    (* now replace chosen tasks position with *)
    (* last task in the list.                  *)
    task_index[index_position] := task_index[remaining_tasks]
    (* one less task to compute *)
    remaining_tasks := remaining_tasks - 1
  End  (* Select_Task *)


(* The initialisation for this would have been *)
Begin
  FOR i = 1 TO total_number_of_tasks DO
    task_index[i] := task[i]
  remaining_tasks := total_number_of_tasks
End


(* And the request for a task is dealt with as follows: *)
WHILE results_outstanding DO
  Begin
    RECEIVE results from PE[i]
    IF remaining_tasks > 0 THEN
      Begin
        Select_Task(task)
        SEND task TO demanding_PE
      End
    ENDIF
  End
```

As with all aspects of parallel processing, extra levels of sophistication can be added in order to exploit any information that becomes available as the parallel solution proceeds. Identifying possible hot spots in the problem domain may be possible from the computation time associated with each principal data item as these become known. If this time is returned along with the result for that principal data item, the work supplier can build a dynamic profile of the computational requirements associated with areas of the domain. This information can be used

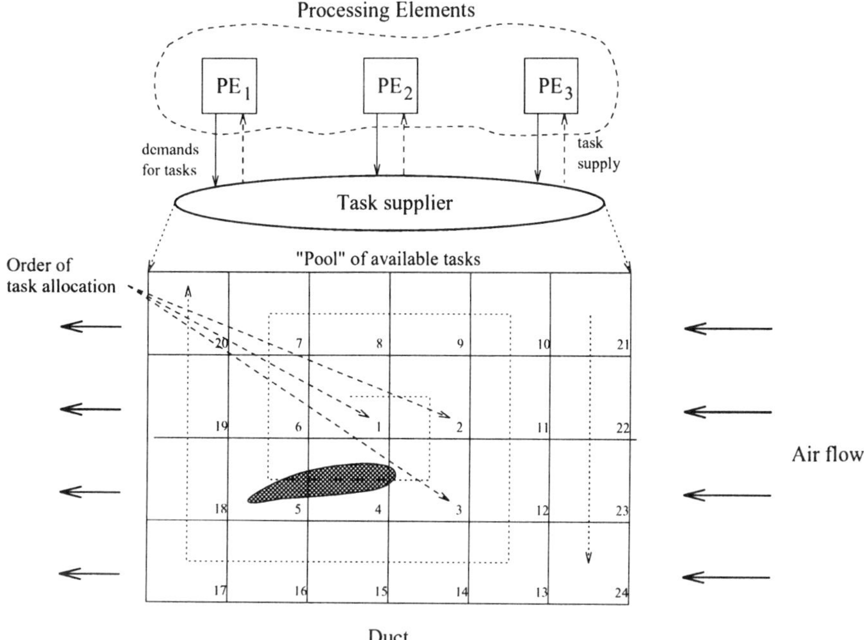

Figure 6.8 Allocation of principal data items in a spiral manner

to adapt the allocation scheme to send principal data items from the possible hot spot regions. There is, of course, a trade-off here between the possible benefits to load balancing in the early allocation of principal data items from hot spots, and the overhead that is introduced by the need to:

- time each computation at the processing elements,
- return this time to the work supplier,
- develop the time profile at the work supplier, and
- adapt the allocation strategy to take this profile into account.

The benefits gained by such an adaptive scheme are difficult to predict as they are dependent on the problem being considered and the efficiency of the scheme implementation. The advice in these matters is always, 'implement a simple scheme initially and then add extra sophistication should resultant low system performance justify it'.

6.3 The Hybrid Computational Model

For most problems, the correct choice of computational model will either be one of the data driven strategies or the demand driven approach. However, for a number of problems, a hybrid computational model, exhibiting properties of both data and demand driven models, can be adopted to achieve improved efficiency. The class of problem that can benefit from the hybrid model is one in which an initial set of principal data items of known computational complexity may spawn an unknown quantity of further work.

In this case, the total number of principal data items required to solve the problem is unknown at the start of the computation, however, there are at least a known number of principal data items that must be processed first. If the computational complexity associated with these initial principal data items is unknown then a demand driven model will suffice for the whole problem, but if the computational complexity is known then one of the data driven models, with their lower communication overheads, should at least be used for these initial principal data items. Use of the hybrid model thus requires the computational model to be switched from data driven to demand driven mode as required.

The use of the hybrid model will become clearer in the case study presented in section 6.5.

6.4 Summary

Any computational model can be selected to solve a problem using the SAMD approach. However, only the correct choice of model will ensure optimum system performance for that problem. Figure 6.9 shows the questions that should be answered for every problem in order to select the appropriate model. At the top level of the hierarchy is the number of principal data items that make up the problem domain. If this number remains constant for the duration of the problem solution then the choice is simply one of data or demand driven, but if the number of principal data items changes as computation progresses, then a hybrid model may have to be considered.

Assuming a fixed number of principal data items, the overriding criterion for the choice of computational model is whether there are any computational complexity variations associated with the principal data items. That is, does the time taken to apply the algorithm to one principal data item differ from the time taken for a different principal data item. If the answer is no, then the balanced data driven model is the most efficient computational model that can, and should, be chosen. This model requires no preprocessing step to sort the principal data items into descending computational time order, nor does it have the communication overheads associated with having to request every single principal data item from a work supplier process.

If there are variations in computational complexity, then the balanced data driven model will be inappropriate as the simple geometric allocation of principal data items to processing elements may lead to a substantial work load imbalance within the system. If the computational complexity variations are known, then the unbalanced data driven model should be chosen. Despite the preprocessing stage to allocate the principal data items amongst the processing elements fairly based on their computation times, this computational model avoids the need to communicate a request and a reply for every principal data item. Rather, all the principal data items are allocated prior to the computation commencing.

Only the demand driven computational model is able to cope effectively with unknown variations in computational complexity. By demanding work as they

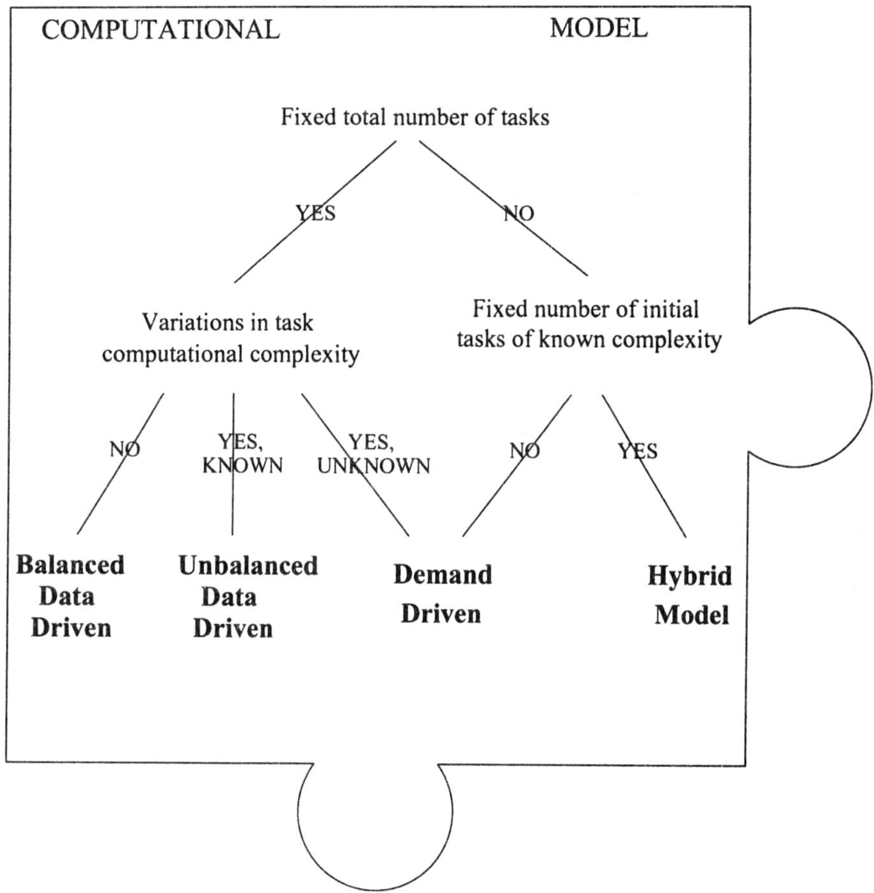

Figure 6.9   Factors affecting choice of computational model

proceed, the processing elements ensure they are kept busy while there is still work that needs completing. With an appropriate allocation strategy the demand driven model is able to dynamically load balance the system and counter any hot spots in the problem domain should they arise. In this way, the demand driven model minimises processing element idle time, but pays the price for this by the increased communication overheads that must be introduced. Chapter 7 will examine ways in which these overheads can be kept to a minimum.

Data driven models are inappropriate for problems for which the total number of principal data items required to solve the problem is initially unknown. If an initial number of principal data items is fixed and these are of known computational complexity then the hybrid computational model should be used. This model exploits the lower communication overheads of the data driven models when it can and otherwise resorts to the flexibility of the demand driven model to ensure the processing elements are always kept busy.

6.5 Case Study: Feature Recognition in X-Ray Images

The correct choice of computational model is an important criterion for reducing the processing time of a parallel implementation. This case study will demonstrate how the choice of model affects system performance. This problem involves detecting and, if necessary, tracking features of interest in a sequence of X-ray images. As we shall see, the optimum computational model is different for a problem in which the features are stationary and one where the features move an unknown distance between each image. We shall thus consider each case separately.

6.5.1 Problem description

With the increase in sophistication of aircraft engines, it is important that reliable information is available to enable designers to verify and improve engines. The use of temperature probes and other intrusive sensors, by their very nature, affect any results obtained. A technique of X-ray imaging has recently been introduced to allow non-intrusive testing. In this method, a high energy X-ray source passing through a small section of a running aircraft engine is imaged by a specialised camera. Important information may be derived by analysing the differences within a sequence of images. One typical use is to track the thermal expansion and vibration of engine parts such as turbine blades.

Detection and tracking of features has become one of the most important fields in computer vision. Applications include intruder detection, traffic monitoring and motion analysis. Although other techniques are available, one widely used method is template matching [164]. A template is a subimage which defines the feature of interest, for example the tip of the turbine blade. The template is specified in the initial image and then used in subsequent images to detect the feature. This method has the advantage that it is simple to implement, the template can be of a variable size dependent upon the feature complexity and the technique is robust in the presence of noise. This latter characteristic is especially important in this application since the imaging of the X-ray source is noisy due to a lack of synchronisation between source and camera. Template matching is, however, computationally expensive since every picture element (known as a *pixel*) in the template needs to be matched with many pixels in the image. Figure 6.10 shows a template of 3×7 pixels defining a feature of interest in an image.

6.5.2 Feature detection

Having defined the template around the feature of interest in the initial image, an associated reference point is identified to allow a subsequent match between template and feature. Movement of a feature can be identified by a corresponding movement of this reference point in the new images. Figure 6.11 illustrates this movement.

Feature detection is accomplished using a correlation function to quantify the degree of match between the template and image at a given pixel location. A variety of functions may be used; one of the simplest involves calculating the total squared

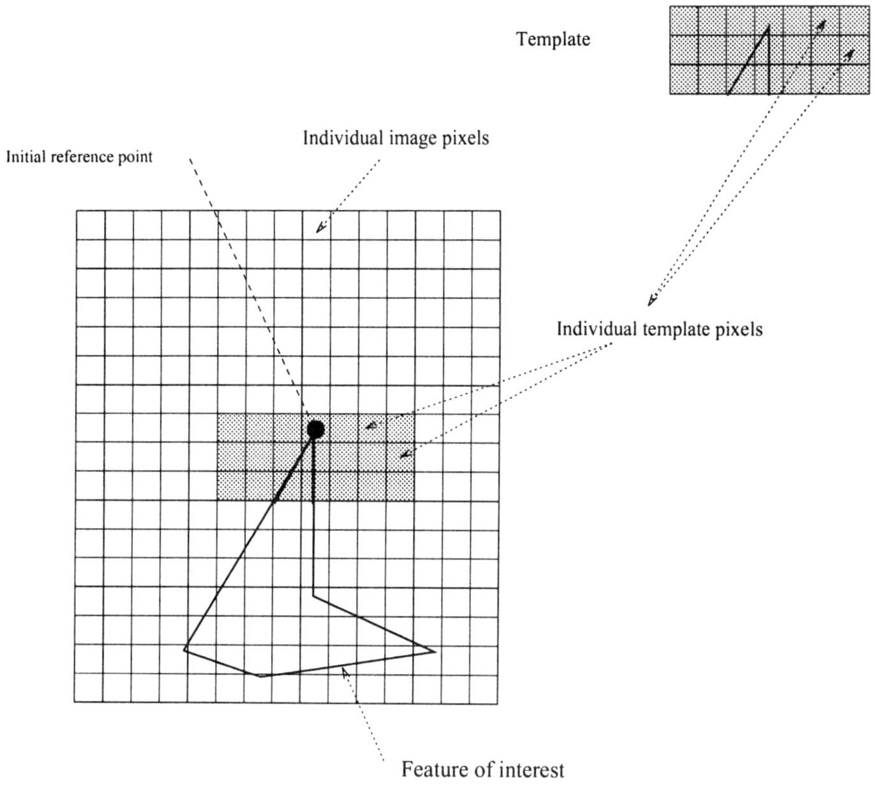

Template

Initial reference point

Individual image pixels

Individual template pixels

Feature of interest

Figure 6.10 Template defining a feature of interest in an image

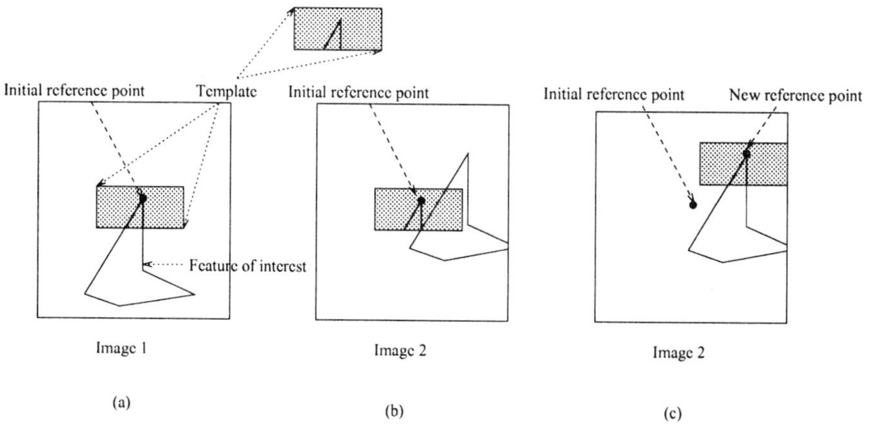

Figure 6.11 (a) Template and reference point specification (b) New image showing feature movement (c) Match of template to feature producing new reference point

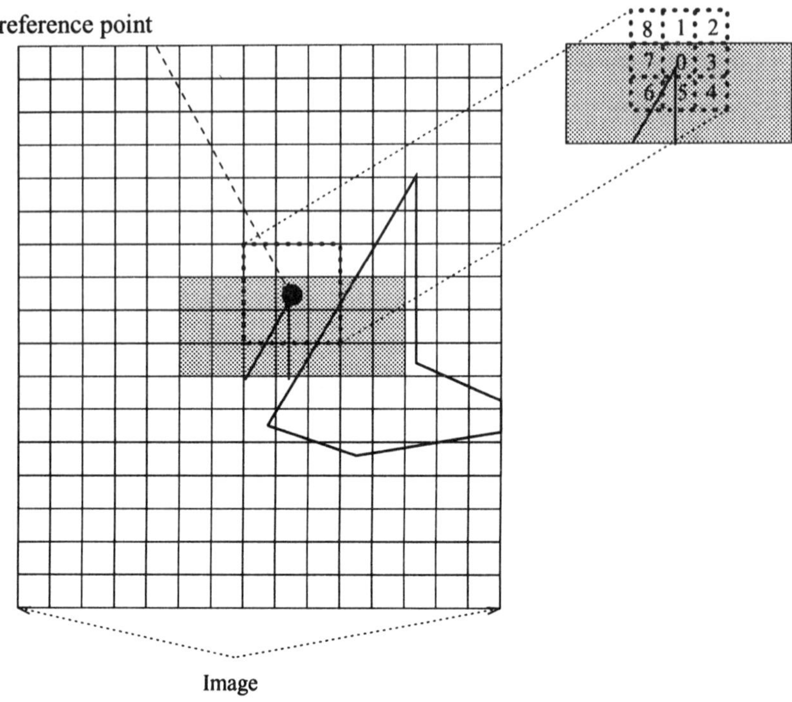

Figure 6.12   The nine pixels at which the correlation function is initially applied

error distance between template, t, and image, I. In this case, a lower value indicates a better fit. The total squared error distance is defined as:

$$d^2(i,j) = \sum_{x=x_{min}}^{x_{max}} \sum_{y=y_{min}}^{y_{max}} (I(x,y) - t(x-i,y-i))^2$$

where (i,j) is the reference point and the corners of the template are defined by the coordinates (x_{min}, y_{min}) and (x_{max}, y_{max}).

The gradient descent method can be used to track movement of the reference point from one image to the next. In this technique, the correlation function is applied at the current reference point (identified in figure 6.12 as pixel 0) and its eight neighbouring pixels. If the correlation value at a neighbour is lower, representing a better match, then the feature has moved. Further searching is then initiated with this pixel as the updated reference point. This process is continued until the minimum occurs at the new reference point, corresponding to the feature's current location.

Figure 6.13 illustrates how this searching procedure creates new work. In this example, correlation at the pixel designated 2 results in a minimum value, thus becoming the new reference point. Note that some of the correlation values for this new position have already been calculated so only five new values (numbered

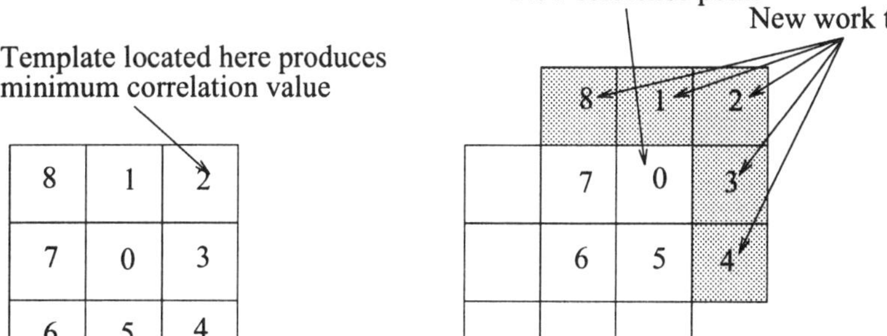

Figure 6.13   (a) Initial work at nine locations around reference point (b) Gradient descent creates five new (shaded) locations as reference point moves

1, 2, 3, 4 and 8 in figure 6.13(b) need to be tested to ascertain if the feature has moved still further.

The following section of pseudo-code highlights how the gradient descent continues until a new reference point with a lower correlation value cannot be found:

```
PROCEDURE Locate_Feature()
  (* Use gradient descent to locate a single feature in image *)
  Begin
    reference_point := initial_reference_point
    feature_located := FALSE
    REPEAT
      Begin
        (* Find pixel around reference point with lowest *)
        (* correlation value.                           *)
        lowest_point := Calculate_Correlations(reference_point)
        IF lowest_point = reference_point THEN
          feature_located := TRUE    (* new reference point *)
        ELSE
          reference_point := lowest_point (* Move point *)
        ENDIF
      End
    UNTIL feature_located
  End (* Locate_Feature *)
```

The following procedure is used to determine the correlation values at and around the current reference point. This returns the pixel location corresponding to the lowest correlation value:

```
PROCEDURE Calculate_Correlations(reference_point)
  (* Calculate template correlations at pixels around current *)
  (* reference point. Return position corresponding to        *)
  (* lowest value (best fit).                                 *)
  Begin
```

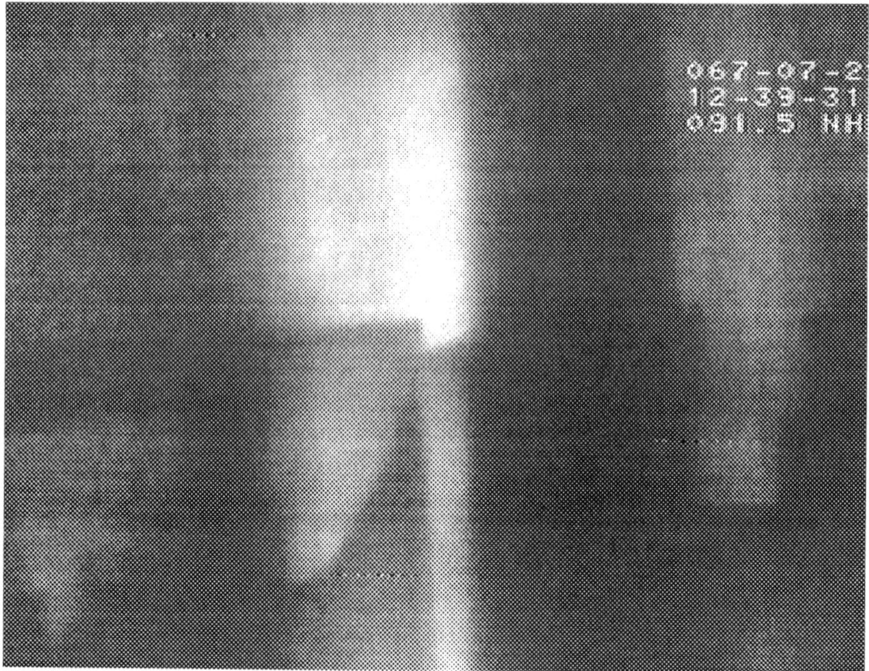

Figure 6.14 Typical X-ray image of an aircraft engine

```
FOR point = reference_point_and_eight_surrounding_pixels DO
   IF NOT previously_calculated THEN
     error := Calculate_Total_Squared_Error(point)
   ELSE
     error := stored_value(point)
   ENDIF
  RETURN point_with_lowest_error
End (* Calculate_Correlations *)
```

6.5.3 The production system

The system considered in this case study is from the VIMS2 (Visual Image Measurement System) project of the University of Bristol [42]. This was a joint project with a leading aircraft engine manufacturer to process a stream of X-ray images in order to examine the behaviour of a variety of components in an operational aircraft engine. Figure 6.14 shows a typical X-ray image of an aircraft engine. The low contrast and high noise component of these images makes analysis difficult.

It was important to the manufacturer to ascertain that some features of the engine remain stationary throughout testing, and to determine the movement of others. Several components are monitored simultaneously in a test, each requiring its own template definition. The dimensions of these templates may vary in size from 20 × 10 to 60 × 20 pixels.

One fundamental requirement of this system was the ability to analyse the engine in real-time, that is to be able to process 25 images per second. The principal goal of VIMS2 thus required a speed increase of at least two orders of magnitude over the existing system by the use of parallel processing. The configuration of VIMS2 is shown in figure 6.15. The system is controlled by an operator interacting with an X-Windows front-end running on a Sun microcomputer. The Sun's processing power is not utilised further except to communicate directly with a transputer network across a VME interface.

The transputer network carries out all image processing functions as well as other housekeeping services. A digitiser board receives the analogue signal from an X-ray imaging camera and broadcasts it to transputer frame-stores along a high-bandwidth dedicated digital video bus. On-board circuitry enables each frame-store to capture the required portion of this information stream into local memory for processing. This ensures that all processing elements have access to image data without any communication across the transputer serial links, often a serious bottleneck in image processing applications.

The other boards in the system are:

- Disk Controller: allowing images to be stored to a SCSI disk at several frames per second, enabling processing results to be verified or reworked off-line;

- Smoothing board: used to temporally smooth a sequence of images to remove the types of noise associated with X-ray imaging.

6.5.4 Parallel requirements

Calculation of the correlation function at a given location is independent of similar calculations at all other locations. The computational requirement for each correlation function is solely dependent on the template size. In the production system the template size was such that each correlation could be treated as an individual task in the parallel implementation.

Case 1: Stationary features

As the features do not move, a correlation, that is a task, needs to be performed for each pixel around the reference point of each feature. This includes the reference point and eight neighbouring pixels. The total number of tasks for all the features is thus:

$$\text{total number of tasks} = 9 \text{ times number of features} \tag{6.1}$$

This process must be repeated for each image in the sequence.

The balanced data driven approach for this problem would be to divide the total number of tasks for all templates evenly amongst the available processing elements. Each processing element thus performs at most:

$$\left\lceil \frac{\text{total number of tasks}}{\text{number of PEs}} \right\rceil \text{ tasks} \tag{6.2}$$

Obviously if the total number of tasks is not exactly divisible by the number of processing elements then some processors will have one less task than others.

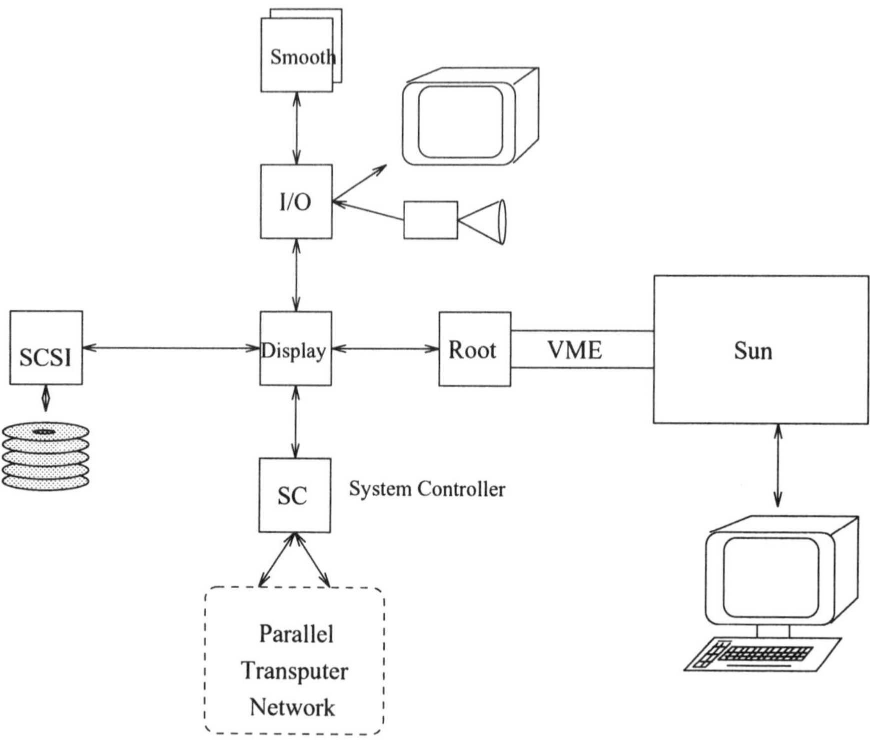

Figure 6.15 The VIMS2 production system

An unbalanced data driven model can only be used if the time to perform each task, T_{task}, is known *a priori*. In this application, because the size of the templates are defined by the user, we know how long it will take to calculate the correlation function at any pixel. This is the time taken to compute the total squared error of one point, T_{tse} (which is a constant value for all pixels), multiplied by the size of the template:

$$T_{task}(n) = (\text{size of template } n) \times T_{tse}$$

The features do not move and so for a balanced work load, ideally the tasks should be distributed such that each processing element spends:

$$\frac{\sum_{f=1}^{\text{no. of features}} T_{task}(f) \times 9}{\text{number of PEs}} \tag{6.3}$$

computational time per image. The tasks can now be allocated in a way that most closely matches this situation.

In a demand driven system the processing elements demand the next task to be performed on completion of their current task. These tasks are allocated from a 'pool of tasks' by a task supplier. The hybrid model will be equivalent to the balanced data driven approach for the case of stationary features, because the total amount of work is known in advance.

Case 2: Moving features

In order to locate moving features, the correlation function is applied repeatedly until the minimum value is detected at the current reference point. The total amount of computational work involved in this process is thus not known in advance. However, the first nine tasks must always be completed for every feature at the initial reference point in each image.

The balanced data driven approach for these initial tasks is the same as for stationary features. Movement of the features will generate additional work at each stage of the gradient descent method. Therefore, although the total number of subsequent tasks cannot be predicted, allocation may occur after the work for each stage has been identified. This creates a synchronisation point as each stage of the gradient descent is completed and results are collated prior to allocation of new work.

The procedure for the unbalanced data driven model is the same as above except it is the time taken to perform the tasks that is divided evenly amongst the processing elements.

The demand driven model has the advantage that as soon as the nine initial tasks have been calculated for a feature, new tasks that are generated may be added immediately to the 'task pool'. They are thus available for distribution upon demand. In this way, a synchronisation point at the end of each stage of the gradient descent method is avoided, increasing system performance.

The hybrid approach benefits both from the efficiency of the data driven allocation scheme for initial tasks, and the elimination of synchronisation points using the demand driven model. The initial tasks are, therefore, allocated using a balanced or unbalanced method, as appropriate, with any additional tasks entering the task pool for subsequent distribution upon demand.

Worked example

The following worked example demonstrates the operation of the four task allocation strategies during the solution of a simple problem. This problem consists of analysing an image with two features of interest, defined by two different sized templates, A and B. For purposes of illustration we will assume that it takes 4 time units to compute the correlation of template A at a single pixel location, and 1 time unit for template B. In the image under consideration the feature defined by template A has moved one pixel rightward, generating three new tasks, whilst the feature defined by B has moved diagonally rightward (as illustrated in figure 6.13) requiring five extra tasks to determine its new location. This problem is to be solved on a system with four processing elements, labelled $PE_1, \ldots, PE_4$. Figure 6.16 shows the allocation of tasks to processing elements during problem solution for each of the four models.

In the balanced data driven approach the number of initial tasks is divided evenly, resulting in processing elements PE_1 and PE_2 being allocated five consecutive tasks

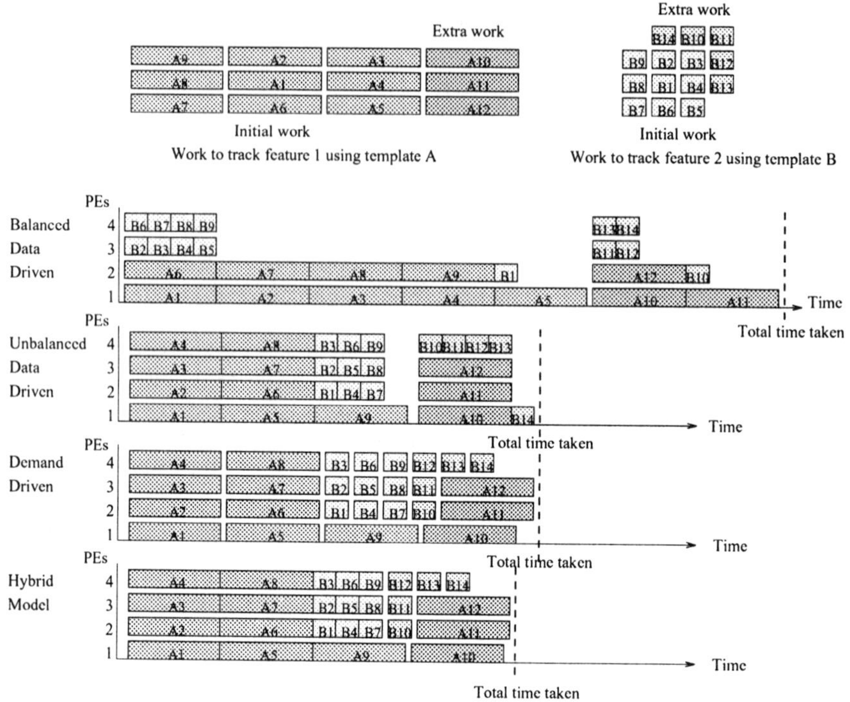

Figure 6.16   Task allocation for each of the four computational models

$(A1, \ldots, A5$ for PE_1, and $A6, \ldots, A9, B1$ for PE_2). This contrasts with PE_3 and PE_4 which can only be allocated four. The computation and communication required by this allocation procedure incurs the small delay shown in the figure. In this strategy, the extra work $(A10, \ldots, A12$ and $B10, \ldots, B15)$ can only be allocated on completion of all 18 initial tasks. Once more, consecutive tasks are divided evenly, resulting in two new tasks for each processing element.

An additional sorting stage is required in the unbalanced data driven model, prior to the even distribution of tasks based upon predicted completion times. As with the balanced data driven model, assignment of new tasks cannot occur until all initial tasks are completed. As shown in the figure, division of labour based upon predicted computation time rather than number of tasks can significantly reduce the time required to solve the problem.

In the demand driven model, processing elements are not apportioned work specifically, but dynamically request tasks. However, this introduces extra communication overheads, illustrated in the figure. The demand driven strategy of allocating the more computationally complex tasks (if known) first in the task pool requires an initial sorting process similar to that of the unbalanced data driven method. As soon as extra work is identified, these tasks can be introduced to the task pool. Note therefore, that it is not possible to allocate the more complex extra work generated by template A $(A10, \ldots, A12)$ until all tasks $A1, \ldots, A9$ have been completed. Prior to this, tasks $B10, \ldots, B12$, which are available, are allocated.

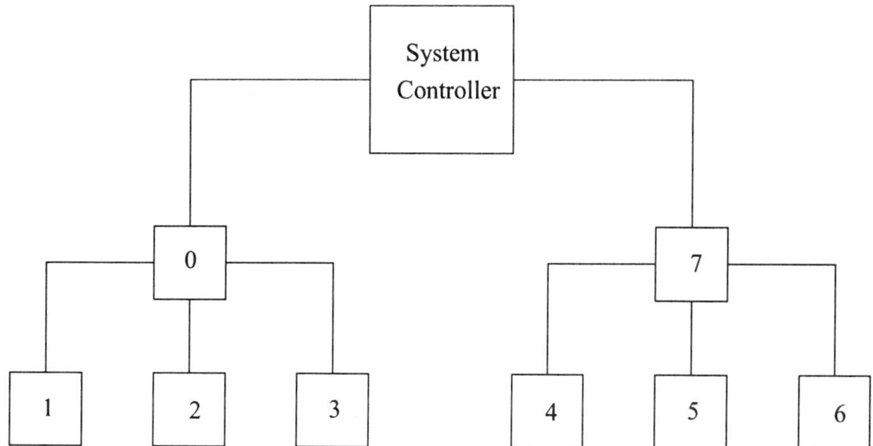

Figure 6.17   8-processing element tree

The hybrid model has the benefits of reduced communication overheads due to initial specific task allocation, and later the advantage of extra work being distributed to waiting processing elements when known. Even in this simple problem, these advantages means the hybrid model outperforms the three alternative strategies. For more complex problems, involving greater variation in size and number of templates, the performance benefits will be even more pronounced.

6.5.5 Results

The effect of the choice of computational model for a simulated application is shown here. The system was implemented on a simple tree configuration consisting of eight processing elements, as shown in figure 6.17. The choice of system configuration is explained more fully in Chapter 9. The graphs show the solution times for each of the four approaches using varying numbers of moving and stationary features with different template sizes.

Figure 6.18 shows the time to solve the problem consisting of differing numbers of stationary features using constant template sizes of 400 pixels. In all cases the balanced data driven model (and the hybrid model which in this case is equivalent to the balanced data driven model) performs the best followed by the unbalanced data driven system. The demand driven system was the least efficient. The unbalanced data driven model is marginally less efficient than the balanced data driven approach due to the extra complexity associated with calculating the even distribution of task times.

If the features remain stationary, but the template sizes defined for each feature differ markedly then the results shown in figure 6.19 are obtained. As is clearly shown, the balanced data driven approach is no longer appropriate due to the imbalance associated with the large variations in template sizes. The unbalanced

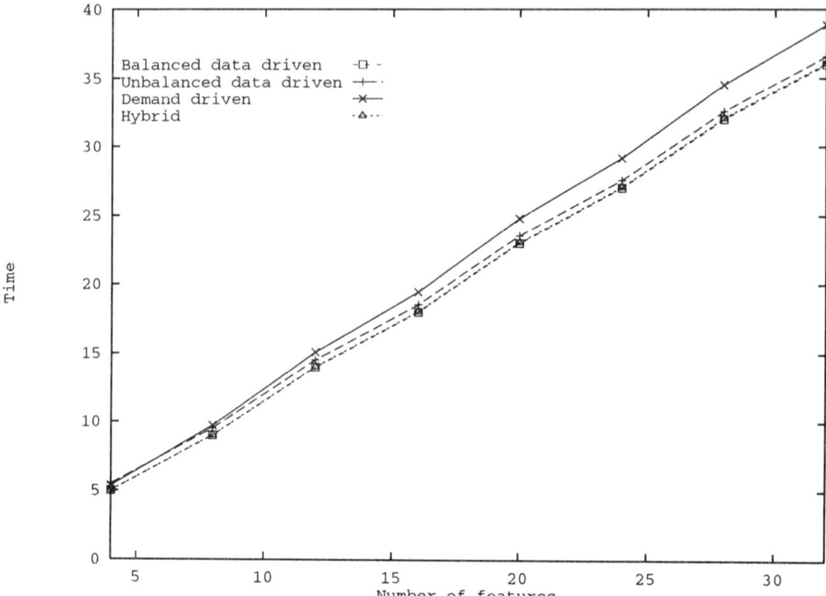

Figure 6.18 Stationary features, constant template sizes

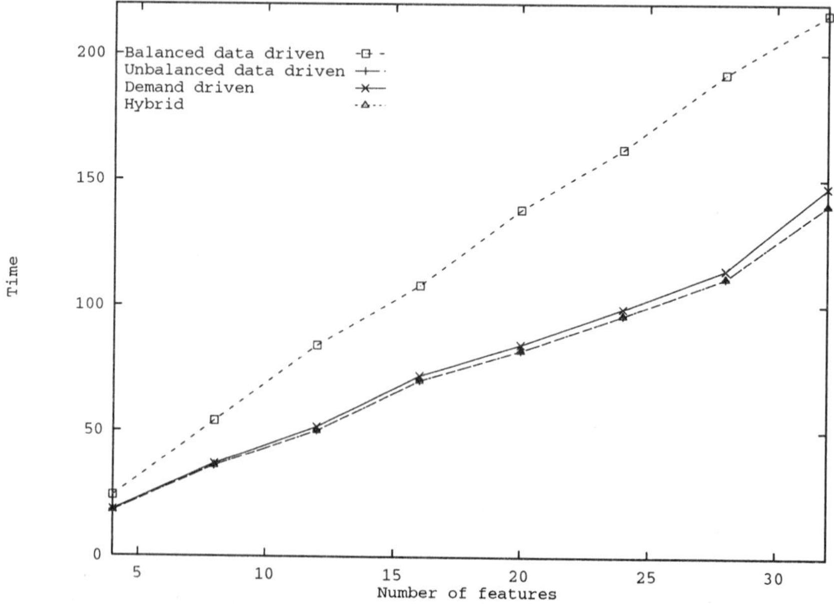

Figure 6.19 Stationary features, variable template sizes

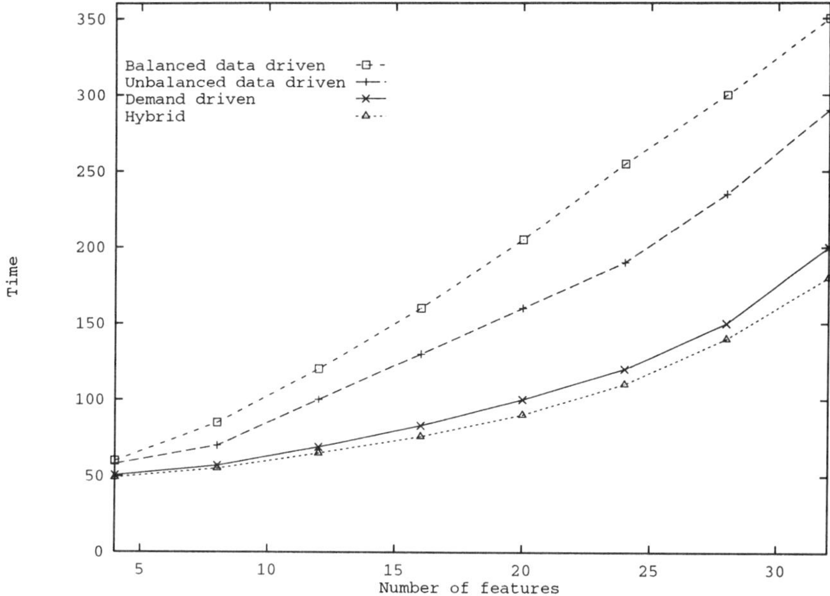

Figure 6.20   Moving features, variable template sizes

data driven and hybrid methods are now suitable, while the demand driven system is still penalised by inherent communication overheads.

Figure 6.20 shows results for each of the four computational models for varying template sizes and moving features. The necessary synchronisation point in the balanced and unbalanced data driven models is a major impediment to the efficient solution of this problem. The hybrid approach outperforms even the demand driven system due to lack of communication overheads associated with the initial tasks.

6.5.6 Conclusions

The above simulation has investigated the performance improvements that can be achieved within a parallel implementation by the correct choice of computational model. The results show that no computational model should be chosen without first analysing the nature of the problem. The reasoning for the choice for this model is shown in figure 6.21. As we have seen, an incorrect choice can result in a substantial increase in problem solution time.

The results of the simulation highlighted the significant performance improvements of the demand driven and hybrid models when the different template sizes were used to track moving features. The correct choice of computational model allowed the VIMS2 project to meet its design goals. The system is capable of tracking features of interest in an image at video frame rates on eight processing elements. Evaluation has shown that, for the current system, real-time tracking is

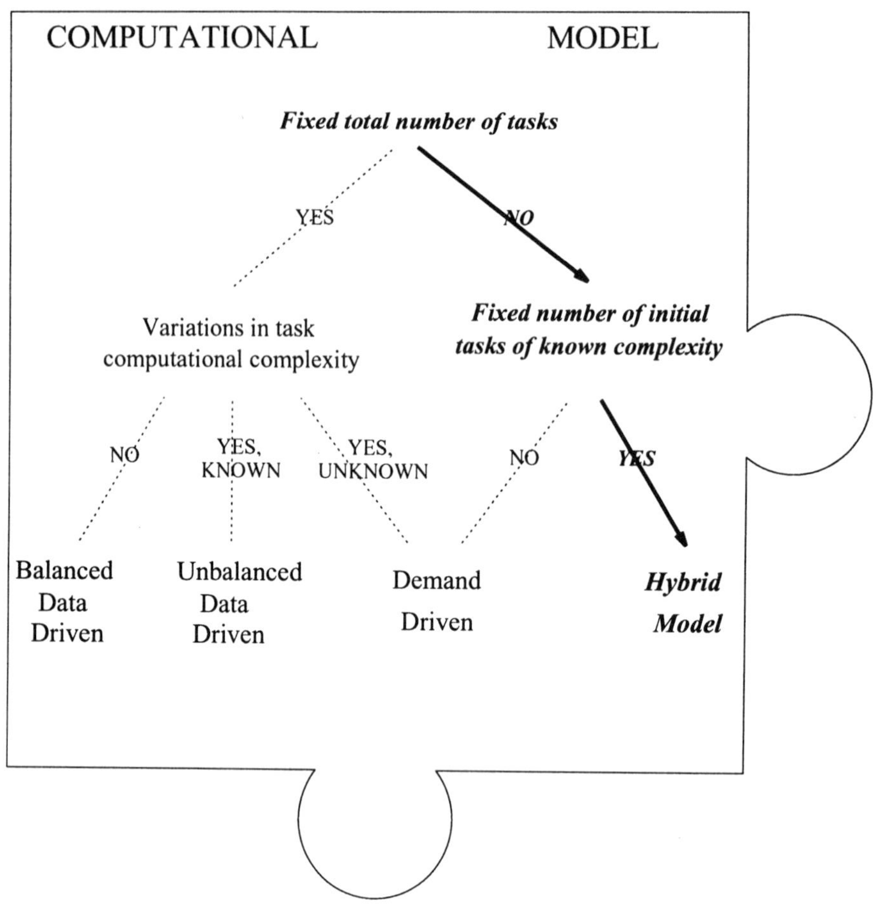

Figure 6.21   Choice of the correct computational model for the VIMS2 case-study

possible for a large number of features provided the total number of pixels in the templates does not exceed 5600.

If the features are moving it is important that they are tracked quickly in the production system. The hybrid computational model was thus recommended as it was shown by the simulator to be the most efficient on eight processing elements for this scenario.

6.6 Exercises and Project Suggestions

1. In the feature-recognition case study, if the time to compute a correlation at each pixel varied according to its grey-scale value, how would this affect the choice of computational model?

2. Sorting is a common procedure of everyday life. Once sorted, large amounts

of data can be searched rapidly to acquire a desired item. The 'bubble sort' is a classic example of an exchange sort algorithm [118]. A sequential bubble sort algorithm to sort a large list A containing `number_of_items` into ascending order is as follows:

```
PROCEDURE Bubble_Sort()
  Begin
    bound := number_of_items
    change := 0
    REPEAT
      Begin
        FOR j = 1 TO (bound-1) DO
          IF A[j] > A[j+1] THEN
            Begin
              Swap(A[j], A[j+1])   (* Swap elements j and j+1 *)
              change := j
            End
          ENDIF
        bound := change
      End
    UNTIL change = 0
  End (* Bubble_Sort *)
```

The bubble sort gets its colourful name by the fact that the items being sorted 'bubble' up to their proper position in the list.

Consider how you could use this algorithm to sort a large list of numbers using (a) the balanced data driven, (b) the unbalanced data driven, and (c) the demand driven approach. Issues you need to consider are: the principal data items, additional data items, what constitutes a task, dependencies and what will the overhead be when collating the results?

3. Discuss one way in which a data driven model can be simulated by the way in which tasks are supplied in a demand driven approach. Use pseudo-code to illustrate your answer.

4. The trapezoidal rule of numerical integration described in section 4.6, corresponds to a rather crude straight line approximation between successive points, x_j and x_{j+1}. The method is only accurate for sufficiently small values of h. This value of h may be varied from interval to interval. In general, to improve the accuracy of the method, an interval should be subdivided until the difference in the integral value for the interval between successive subdivisions is below a specified tolerance. How will this subdivision of the intervals affect your parallel implementation? With the aid of pseudo-code, design the control loop to implement the correct computational model for this problem.

5. Assume an unbalanced data driven computational model has been chosen for a problem with a fixed number of tasks. The task computation times are known *a priori* and we wish to minimise the load balancing problems by allocating each processor an (approximately) equal proportion of the total computation time. Write a pseudo-code algorithm for allocating the tasks to the processors.

Hint: You may use the routine `Bubble_Sort`, shown above to sort the list of tasks into descending order of computational time.

Now derive an expression to provide an approximate indication of the overhead that the unbalanced data driven model incurs by this task allocation scheme.

Chapter 7

Task Management

There is no substitute for hard work.

Thomas Edison

In the Sequential-Algorithm Multiple-Data model, the application of the algorithm to a specified principal data item may be regarded as performing a single task. For distribution within the system, tasks may be grouped into packets. To avoid processing elements standing idle, performing no useful computation, care should be taken to ensure that the next task to be performed is available when required by the proceeding computation. The task management strategies described in this chapter attempt to minimise these potential performance limitations.

The efficient solution of a problem on a parallel system requires the computational performance of the processing elements to be fully utilised. Any processing element that is not busy performing useful computations is degrading overall system performance. As explained in section 5.1, some of a processing element's computational idle time will result from the need to communicate or while performing concurrent task or data management functions.

A more serious problem is the unavailability of work at the processing element. This can result from a delay in fetching the next task to be performed or by poor load balancing. This occurs when the tasks have not been allocated amongst processing elements properly to ensure an even distribution of work. The aim of the task manager is to ensure that a processing element is never lacking work while a portion of the problem remains to be solved.

The task management strategy is closely linked to the computational model chosen to solve the problem, as shown in figure 7.1. Data driven computational models have *implicit* load balancing in which all the principal data items are allocated to specific processing elements before any computation proceeds. A demand driven model requires *explicit* load balancing. In this case, the onus falls upon the work supplier process and the processing elements themselves to ensure they never run out of work until the entire problem has been solved.

Task management encompasses the following functions:

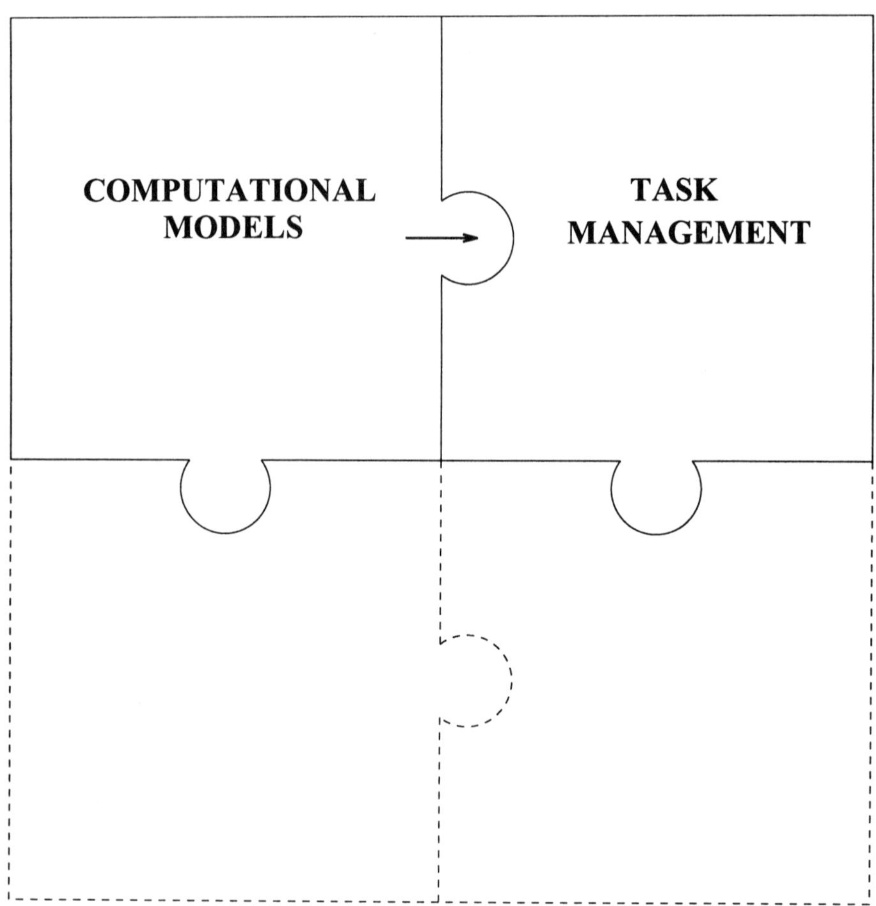

Figure 7.1 The choice of computational model influences the task management strategy

- the definition of a task,
- controlling the allocation of tasks,
- distribution of the tasks to the processing elements, and
- collation of the results, especially in the case of a problem with multiple stages.

7.1 Task Definition and Granularity

An *atomic element* may be thought of as a problem's lowest computational element within the sequential algorithm adopted to solve the problem. As introduced in Chapter 4, in the SAMD model a single task is the application of this sequential algorithm to a principal data item to produce a result for the subparts of the problem domain. The task is thus the smallest element of computation for the problem within the parallel system. The *task granularity* (or grain size) of a problem is the

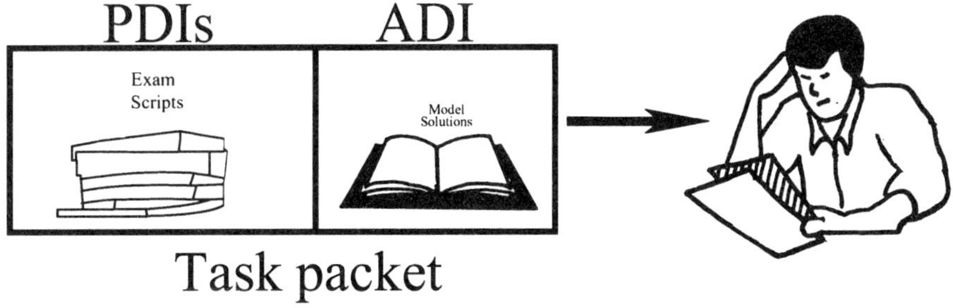

Figure 7.2 Illustrating the terminology for task management

number of atomic elements which are included in one task. Generally, the task granularity remains constant for all tasks, but in some cases it may be desirable to alter dynamically this granularity as the computation proceeds. A task which includes only one atomic element is said to have the *finest granularity*, while a task which contains many is *coarser grained*, or has a coarser granularity. The actual definition of what constitutes a principal data item is determined by the granularity of the tasks.

A parallel system solves a problem by its constituent processing elements executing tasks in parallel. A *task packet* is used to inform a processing element which task, or tasks, to perform. This task packet may simply indicate which tasks require processing by that processing element, thus forming the lowest level of distributed work. The packet may include additional information, such as additional data items, which the tasks require in order to be completed.

To illustrate the differences in this terminology, consider again the problem introduced in Chapter 4, of marking a large number of exam scripts. The algorithm chosen is marking and the atomic element of a sequential solution of this problem could be to mark a single question. (The atomic element could be reduced to the placing of a single 'tick' or 'cross' on the script, but it is not necessary to subdivide the problem to this level to illustrate the point.) The principal data item is thus each question in a script and the additional data items required will be the model answers for each question. A sequential solution of this problem would be for a single teacher to mark each question in turn. The help of several teachers could substantially improve the time taken to mark a large number of scripts.

The finest task granularity for the parallel implementation of this problem is for each task to complete one atomic element, that is mark one question. For practical considerations, it is perhaps more appropriate that each task should instead be the marking of a complete exam script. The granularity of each task is now the number of questions per script and each exam script is a principal data item. A sensible task packet to distribute the work to the teachers would include one or more exam scripts together with the necessary model answers, as shown in figure 7.2.

To summarise our choices for this problem:

- **atomic element:** to mark one question,
- **task:** to mark one script (consisting of four atomic elements),

- **PDI:** one student's exam script,

- **ADI:** the model answers, and

- **task packet:** one or more scripts together with the model answers.

Choosing the task granularity for the parallel implementation of a problem is not straightforward. Although it may be fairly easy to identify the atomic element for the sequential version of the problem, such a fine grain may not be appropriate when using many processing elements. Although the atomic element for marking the exam scripts was specified as marking a single question in the above example, the task granularity for the parallel solution was chosen as marking an entire script. If one atomic element had been used as the task granularity then additional problems would have been introduced for the parallel solution, namely, the need for the teachers to exchange exam scripts. This difficulty would have been exacerbated if, instead, the atomic element had been chosen as the placing of a single tick or cross on the script. Indeed, apart from the higher communication overhead this would have introduced, the issue of dependencies would also have to be checked to ensure, for example, that part of a student's question was not marked more than once.

As well as introducing additional communication and dependency overheads, the incorrect choice of granularity may also increase computational complexity variations and hinder efficient load balancing. Consider once again the problem of marking the exam scripts. A granularity of individual question marking may result in those teachers assigned to mark the easy questions, for example a multiple choice question, sitting idle while the others struggle with their complex essay questions. Even a granularity of one or more exam scripts is not without its problems. Some scripts may be easy to mark, while others, thanks to poor student handwriting etc., may require far more time.

The choice of granularity is seldom easy; however, a number of parameters of the parallel system can provide an indication as to the desirable granularity. The computation to communication ratio of the architecture will suggest whether additional communication is acceptable to avoid dependency or load balancing problems. As a general rule, where possible, data dependencies should be avoided in the choice of granularity as these imply unnecessary synchronisation points within the parallel solution which can have a significant effect on overall system performance.

7.1.1 Task distribution and control

The task management strategy controls the distribution of packets throughout the system. Upon receipt, a processing element performs the tasks specified by a packet. The composition of the task packet is thus an important issue that must be decided before distribution of the tasks can begin. To complete a task a processing element needs a copy of the algorithm, the principal data item(s), and any additional data items that the algorithm may require for that principal data item. The SAMD paradigm provides each processing element with a copy of the algorithm, and so the responsibility of the task packet is to provide the other information[1].

---

[1] A more general form of this paradigm could include the (executable) code for the required algorithm as part of the task packet

The principal data items form part of the problem domain. If there is sufficient memory, it may be possible to store the entire problem domain as well as the algorithm at each processing element. In this case, the inclusion of the principal data item as part of the task packet is unnecessary. A better method would be simply to include the identification of the principal data item within the task packet. Typically, the identification of a principal data item is considerably smaller, in terms of actual storage capacity, than the item itself. The communication overheads associated with sending this smaller packet will be significantly less than sending the principal data item with the packet. On receipt of the packet the processing element could use the identification simply to fetch the principal data item from its local storage. The identification of the principal data item is, of course, also essential to enable the results of the entire parallel computation to be collated.

If the additional data items required by the task are known then they, or if possible, their identities, may also be included in the task packet. In this case the task packet would form an integral unit of computation which could be directly handled by a processing element. However, in reality, it may not be possible to store the whole problem domain at every processing element. Similarly, numerous additional data items may be required which would make their inclusion in the task packet impossible. Furthermore, for a large number of problems, the additional data items which are required for a particular principal data item may not be known in advance and will only become apparent as the computation proceeds.

A task packet should contain as a minimum either the identity, or the identity and actual principal data items of the task. The inability to include the other required information in the packet means that the parallel system will have to resort to some form of *data management*. This topic is described fully in Chapter 8.

7.2 Algorithmic Dependencies

The algorithm of the problem may specify an order in which the work must be undertaken. This implies that certain tasks must be completed before others can commence. These dependencies must be preserved in the parallel implementation. In the worst case, algorithmic dependencies can prevent an efficient parallel implementation, as shown with the tower of toy blocks in figure 1.2. Amdahl's law, described in Chapter 5, shows the implications to the algorithmic decomposition model of parallel processing of the presence of even a small percentage of purely sequential code. In the SAMD approach, algorithmic dependencies may introduce two phenomena which will have to be tackled:

- *synchronisation points* which have the effect of dividing the parallel implementation into a number of distinct stages, and

- *data dependencies* which will require careful data management to ensure a consistent view of the data to all processing elements.

7.2.1 Multi-stage algorithms

Many problems can be solved by a single stage of computation, utilising known principal data items to produce the desired results. However, the dependencies inherent in other algorithms may divide computation into a number of distinct stages. The *partial results* produced by one stage become the principal data items for the following stage of the algorithm, as shown in figure 7.3. For example, many scientific problems involve the construction of a set of simultaneous equations, a distinct stage, and the subsequent solution of these equations for the unknowns. The partial results, in this case elements of the simultaneous equations, become the principal data for the tasks of the next stage.

Even a single stage of a problem may contain a number of distinct substages which must first be completed before the next substage can proceed. An example of this is the use of an iterative solver, such as the Jacobi method [77, 112], to solve a set of simultaneous equations. An iterative method starts with an approximate solution and uses it in a recurrence formula to provide another approximate solution. By repeatedly applying this process a sequence of solutions is obtained which, under suitable conditions, converges towards the exact solution.

Consider the problem of solving a set of six equations for six unknowns, $\mathbf{A}x = \mathbf{b}$. The Jacobi method will solve this set of equations by calculating, at each iteration, a new approximation from the values of the previous iteration. So the value for the x_i at the nth iteration are calculated as:

$$x_1^n = \frac{b_1 - a_{12}x_2^{n-1} - \ldots - a_{16}x_6^{n-1}}{a_{11}}$$

$$x_2^n = \frac{b_2 - a_{21}x_1^{n-1} - \ldots - a_{26}x_6^{n-1}}{a_{22}}$$

$$\vdots$$

$$x_6^n = \frac{b_6 - a_{61}x_1^{n-1} - \ldots - a_{65}x_6^{n-1}}{a_{66}}$$

A parallel solution to this problem on two processing elements could allocate three rows to be solved to each processing element as shown in figure 7.4. Now PE_1 can solve the nth iteration values x_1^n, x_2^n and x_3^n in parallel with PE_2 computing the values of x_4^n, x_5^n and x_6^n. However, neither processing element can proceed onto the $(n+1)^{\text{th}}$ iteration until both have finished the nth iteration and exchanged their new approximations for the x_i^n. Each iteration is, therefore, a substage which must be completed before the next substage can commence. This point is illustrated by the following code segment from PE_1:

```
PROCEDURE Jacobi()    (* Executing on PE 1 *)
  Begin
    Estimate x[1] ... x[6]
    n := 0                        (* Iteration number *)
    WHILE solution_not_converged DO
      Begin
        n := n + 1
        Calculate new x[1], x[2] & x[3] using old x[1] ... x[6]
        PARALLEL
          SEND    new x[1], x[2] & x[3] TO   PE_2
          RECEIVE new x[4], x[5] & x[6] FROM PE_2
```

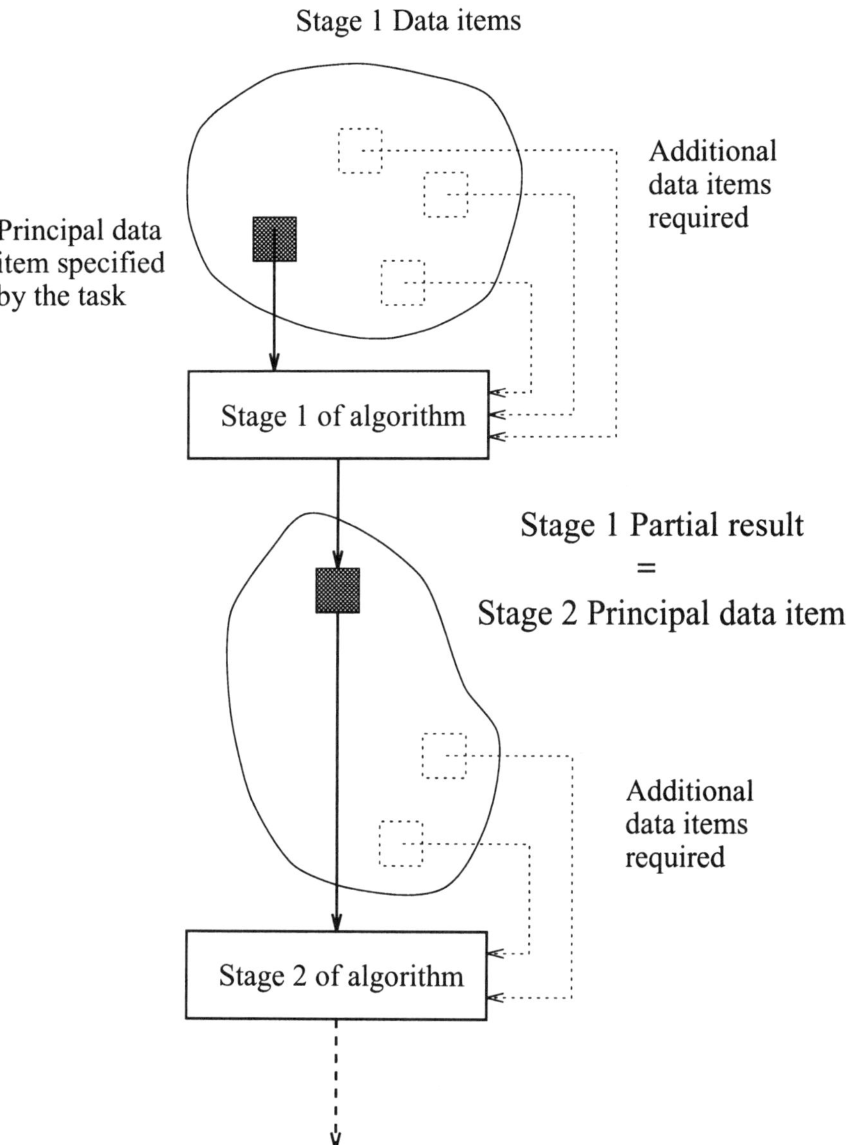

Figure 7.3 The introduction of partial results due to algorithmic dependencies

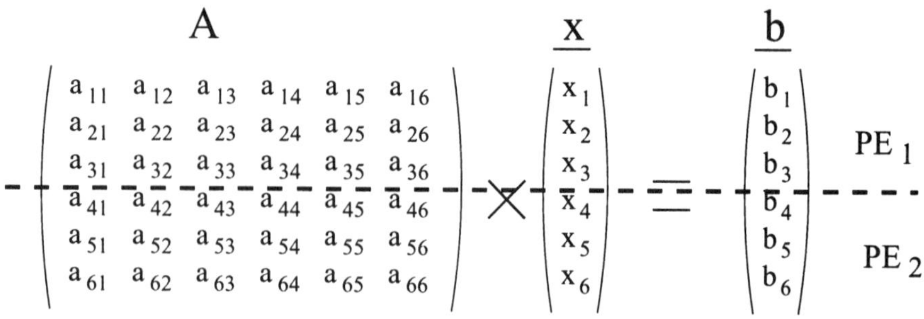

$$\text{A} \qquad\qquad \text{x} \qquad \text{b}$$

$$-\begin{pmatrix} a_{11} & a_{12} & a_{13} & a_{14} & a_{15} & a_{16} \\ a_{21} & a_{22} & a_{23} & a_{24} & a_{25} & a_{26} \\ a_{31} & a_{32} & a_{33} & a_{34} & a_{35} & a_{36} \\ a_{41} & a_{42} & a_{43} & a_{44} & a_{45} & a_{46} \\ a_{51} & a_{52} & a_{53} & a_{54} & a_{55} & a_{56} \\ a_{61} & a_{62} & a_{63} & a_{64} & a_{65} & a_{66} \end{pmatrix} \times \begin{pmatrix} x_1 \\ x_2 \\ x_3 \\ x_4 \\ x_5 \\ x_6 \end{pmatrix} = \begin{pmatrix} b_1 \\ b_2 \\ b_3 \\ b_4 \\ b_5 \\ b_6 \end{pmatrix} \quad \begin{array}{l} \text{PE}_1 \\[1.5em] \text{PE}_2 \end{array}$$

Figure 7.4   Solving an iterative matrix solution method on two processing elements

```
      End
End (* Jacobi *)
```

7.2.2 Data dependencies

The concept of dependencies was introduced in section 1.1.1 when we were unable to construct a tower of blocks in parallel as this required a strictly sequential order of task completion. In the SAMD model, data dependencies exist when a task may not be performed on some principal data item until another task has been completed. There is thus an implicit ordering on the way in which the task packets may be allocated to the processing elements. This ordering will prevent certain tasks being allocated, even if there are processing elements idle, until the tasks on which they are dependent have completed.

A linear dependency exists between each of the iterations of the Jacobi method discussed above. However, no dependency exists for the calculation of each x_i^n, for all i, as all the values they require, x_j^{n-1}, $\forall j \neq i$, will already have been exchanged and thus be available at every processing element.

The Gauss–Seidel iterative method has long be preferred in the sequential computing community as an alternative to Jacobi. The Gauss–Seidel method makes use of new approximations for the x_i as soon as they are available rather than waiting for the next iteration. Provided the methods converge, Gauss–Seidel will converge more rapidly than the Jacobi method. So, in the example of six unknowns above, in the nth the value of x_1^n would still be calculated as:

$$x_1^n = \frac{b_1 - a_{12}x_2^{n-1} - \ldots - a_{16}x_6^{n-1}}{a_{11}},$$

but the x_2^n value would now be calculated by:

$$x_2^n = \frac{b_2 - a_{21}x_1^n - a_{23}x_3^{n-1} - \ldots - a_{26}x_6^{n-1}}{a_{22}}$$

Although well suited to sequential programming, the strong linear dependency that has been introduced makes the Gauss–Seidel method poorly suited for parallel implementation. Now within each iteration no value of x_i^n can be calculated until all the values for x_j^n, $j < i$ are available; a strict sequential ordering of the tasks. The less severe data dependencies within the Jacobi method thus make it a more suitable candidate for parallel processing than the Gauss–Seidel method which is more efficient on a sequential machine.

It is possible to implement a hybrid of these two methods in parallel, the so-called 'Block Gauss–Seidel–Global Jacobi' method [45]. A processing element which is computing several rows of the equations, may use the Gauss–Seidel method for these rows as they will be computed sequentially within the processing element. Any values for x_i^n not computed locally will assume the values of the previous iteration, as in the Jacobi method. All new approximations will be exchanged at each iteration. So, in the example, PE_2 would calculate the values of x_4^n, x_5^n and x_6^n as follows:

$$x_4^n = \frac{b_4 - a_{11}x_1^{n-1} - a_{12}x_2^{n-1} - a_{13}x_3^{n-1} - a_{15}x_5^{n-1} - a_{16}x_6^{n-1}}{a_{44}}$$

$$x_5^n = \frac{b_5 - a_{11}x_1^{n-1} - a_{12}x_2^{n-1} - a_{13}x_3^{n-1} - a_{14}\mathbf{x}_4^{\mathbf{n}} - a_{16}x_6^{n-1}}{a_{55}}$$

$$x_6^n = \frac{b_6 - a_{11}x_1^{n-1} - a_{12}x_2^{n-1} - a_{13}x_3^{n-1} - a_{14}\mathbf{x}_4^{\mathbf{n}} - a_{15}\mathbf{x}_5^{\mathbf{n}}}{a_{66}}$$

7.3 Elementary Management Strategies

7.3.1 Data driven task management strategies

In a data driven approach, the system controller determines the allocation of tasks prior to computation proceeding. With the unbalanced strategy, this may entail an initial sorting stage based on the known computational complexity, as described in section 6.1.2. A single task-packet detailing the tasks to be performed is sent to each processing element. The structure of a suitable processing element is shown in figure 7.5. The application processes may return the results upon completion of their allocated portion, or return individual results as each task is performed, as shown in this code segment:

```
PROCESS Application_Process()
  Begin
    RECEIVE task_packet FROM SC via R
    FOR i = start_task_id TO finish_task_id DO
      Begin
        result[i] := Perform_Algorithm(task[i])
        SEND result[i] TO SC via R
      End
  End (* Application_Process *)
```

In a data driven model of computation a processing element may initially be supplied with as many of its allocated principal data items as its local memory will allow. Should there be insufficient storage capacity a simple data management strategy may be necessary to prefetch the missing principal data items as computation

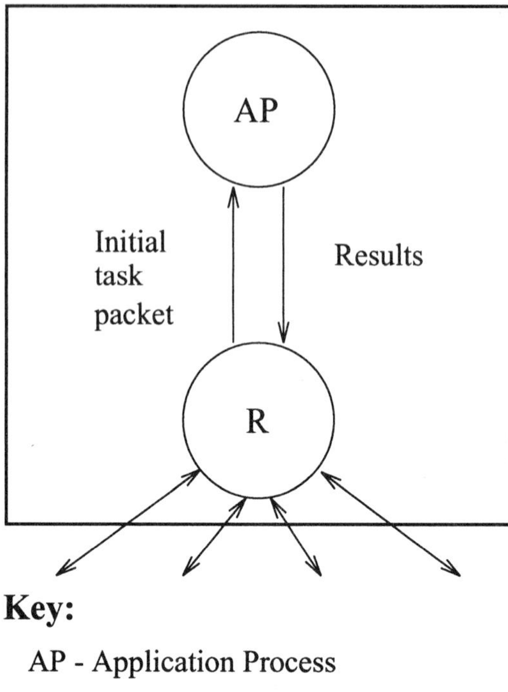

Key:

AP - Application Process

R - Router

Figure 7.5   A processing element for balanced data driven model

proceeds and local storage allows. This is discussed further when considering the management of data in Chapter 8.

7.3.2 Demand driven task management strategies

Task management within the demand driven computational model is explicit. The work supplier process, which forms part of the system controller, is responsible for placing the tasks into packets and sending these packets to requesting processing elements. To facilitate this process, the system controller maintains a *pool* of already constituted task packets. On receipt of a request, the work supplier simply dispatches the next available task packet from this task pool, as can be seen in figure 7.6.

The advantage of a task pool is that the packets can be inserted into it in advance, or concurrently as the solution proceeds, according to the allocation strategy adopted. This is especially useful for problems that create work dynamically, such as those using the hybrid approach as described in section 6.3. Another advantage of the task pool is that if a hot spot in the problem domain is identified, then the ordering within the task pool can be changed dynamically to reflect this and thus ensure that potentially computationally complex tasks are allocated first.

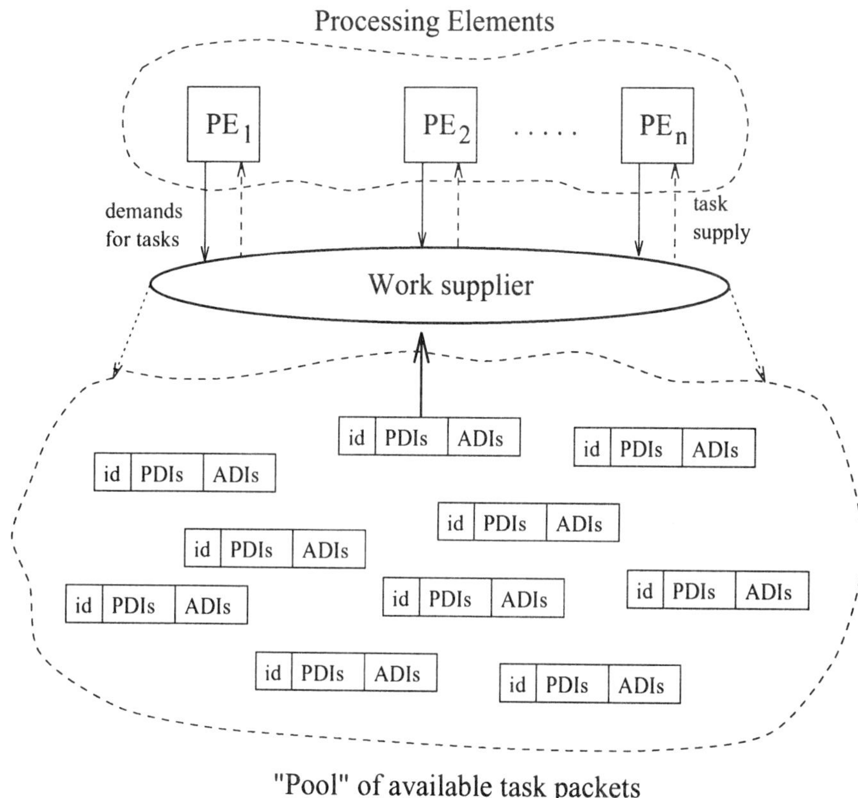

Figure 7.6 Supplying task packets from a task pool at the system controller

More than one task pool may be used to reflect different levels of task priority. High priority tasks contained in the appropriate task pool will always be sent to a requesting processing element first. Only once this high priority task pool is (temporarily) empty will tasks from lower priority pools be sent. The multiple pool approach ensures that high priority tasks are not ignored as other tasks are allocated.

In the demand driven computational model, the processing elements demand the next task as soon as they have completed their current task. This demand is translated into sending a request to the work supplier, and the demand is only satisfied when the work supplier has delivered the next task. There is thus a definite delay period from the time the request is issued until the next task is received. During this period the processing element will be computationally idle. To avoid this idle time, it may be useful to include a buffer at each processing element capable of holding at least one task packet. This buffer may be considered as the processing element's own private task pool. Now, rather than waiting for a request to be satisfied from the remote system controller, the processing element may proceed with the computation on the task packet already present locally. When the remote request has been satisfied and a new task packet delivered, this can be stored in the buffer waiting for the processing element to complete the current task.

Whilst avoiding delays in fetching tasks from a remote task pool, the use of a buffer at each processing element may have serious implications for load balancing, especially towards the end of the problem solution. We will examine these issues in more detail after we have considered the realisation of task management for a simple demand driven system – the processor farm.

A first approach: The processor farm

Simple demand driven models of computation have been implemented and used for a wide range of applications. One realisation of such a model, often referred to in the literature, is that implemented by May and Shepherd [134]. This simple demand driven model, which they term a *processor farm*, has been used for solving problems with high computation to communication ratios. The model proposes a single system controller and one or more processing elements connected in a linear configuration, or chain. The structure of a processing element in this model is shown in figure 7.7.

The application process performs the desired computation, while the communication within the system saceis dealt with by two router processes, the Task Router (TR) and the Result Router (RR). As their names suggest, the task router is responsible for distributing the tasks to the application process, while the result router returns the results from the completed tasks back to the system controller. The system controller contains the initial pool of tasks to be performed and collates the results. Such a communication strategy is simple to implement and largely problem independent.

To reduce possible processing element idle time, each task router process contains a single buffer in which to store a task so that a new task can be passed to the application process as soon as it becomes idle. When a task has been completed the results are sent to the system controller. On receipt of a result, the system controller releases a new task into the system. This synchronised releasing of tasks ensures that there are never more tasks in the system than there is space available.

On receipt of a new task, the task router process either:

1. passes the task directly to the application process if it is waiting for a task; or

2. places the task into its buffer if the buffer is empty; or, otherwise

3. passes the task onto the next processing element in the chain.

The processor farm is initialised by loading sufficient tasks into the system so that the buffer at each task router is full and each application process has a task with which to commence processing.

Figure 7.8 shows the manner in which task requests are satisfied within a simple system consisting of two processing elements configured as a chain. The overall structure of a processor farm consisting of a single system controller and a number of processing elements running in parallel is:

```
PROCESS Processor_Farm()
  Begin
```

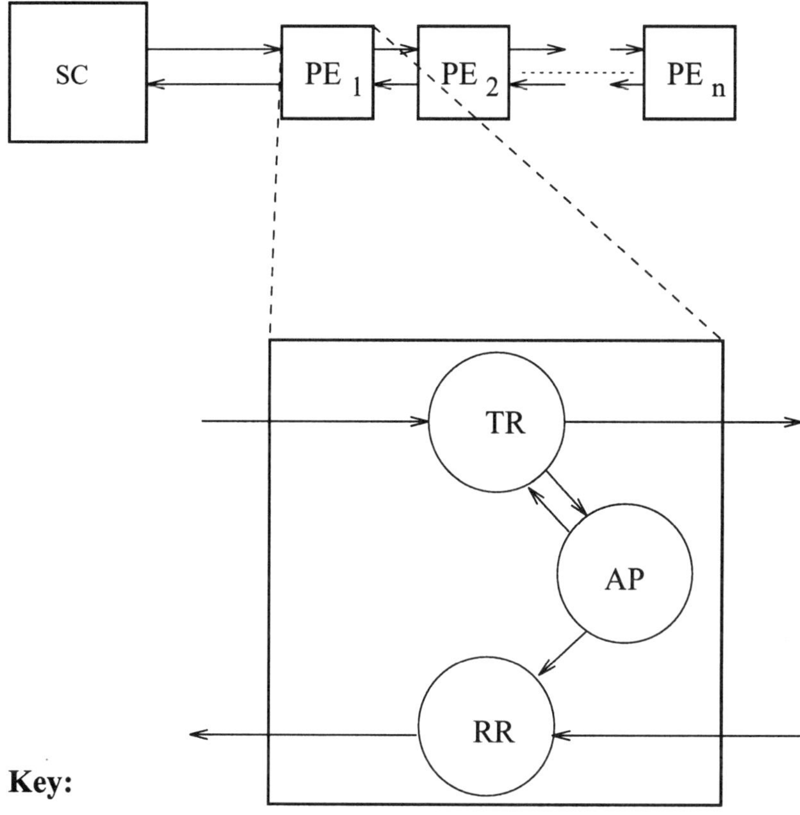

Key:

SC - System Controller

AP - Application Process

TR - Task Router

RR - Result Router

Figure 7.7   A processing element for the processor farm model

```
    PARALLEL
      System_Controller()
      PARALLEL FOR id_number = 1 TO number_of_PEs
        Processing_Element(id_number)
  End (* Processor_Farm *)
```

Each processing element contains the three processes running concurrently:

```
PROCESS Processing_Element(id_number)
  Begin
    PARALLEL
      Application_Process()
      Task_Router()
```

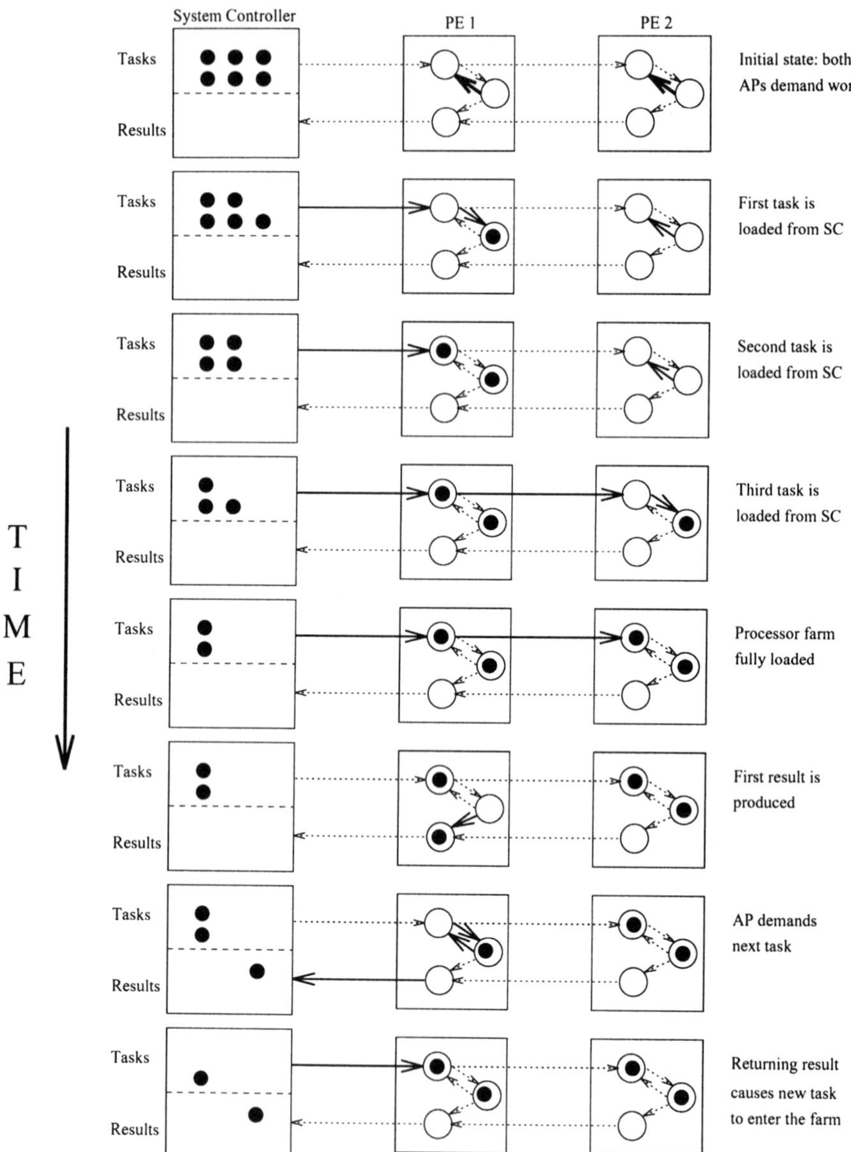

Figure 7.8 Task movement within a two-PE processor farm

```
            Results_Router()
    End (* Processing_Element *)
```

A description of the application process, result router and task router are shown in the following code segments:

```
PROCESS Application_Process()
  Begin
    busy := TRUE
    WHILE busy DO (* continue whilst tasks remain *)
      Begin
        SEND request_for_task TO TR (* the DEMAND for tasks *)
        PRIORITISED INPUT ALTERNATIVES
          1. RECEIVE closedown_command FROM TR (*problem solved*)
              Begin
                SEND closedown_command TO RR
                busy := FALSE
              End
          2. RECEIVE task FROM TR       (* get next task *)
              Begin
                Perform_Algorithm(task)
                SEND result TO RR
              End
      End
  End (* Application_Process *)

PROCESS Result_Router()
  Begin
    busy := TRUE
    WHILE busy DO
      PRIORITISED INPUT ALTERNATIVES
        1. RECEIVE closedown_command FROM AP  (*no more results*)
            busy := FALSE
        2. RECEIVE result FROM AP         (*result from local AP*)
            SEND result TO processor to the left
        3. RECEIVE result FROM processor to the right
            SEND result TO processor to the left
  End (* Result_Router *)

PROCESS Task_Router()
  Begin
    busy := TRUE  (* continue whilst tasks remain *)
    buffer_empty := TRUE
    AP_ready_for_task := FALSE (* AP has yet to make its *)
                              (* first request.        *)
    WHILE busy DO
      PRIORITISED INPUT ALTERNATIVES
        1. RECEIVE closedown_command FROM SC  (* no more tasks *)
            Begin
              IF (NOT last PE in chain) THEN
                SEND closedown_command TO processor on the right
              ENDIF
              SEND closedown_command TO AP
```

```
                    busy := FALSE
                 End
      2. RECEIVE request_for_task FROM AP (* local request *)
            IF (NOT buffer_empty) THEN
               Begin
                 SEND buffer TO AP
                 buffer_empty := TRUE
               End
            ELSE
               AP_ready_for_task := TRUE
            ENDIF
      3. RECEIVE task FROM processor to the left (* remote request *)
            IF AP_ready_for_task THEN
               Begin
                 SEND task TO AP
                 AP_ready_for_task := FALSE
               End
            ELSEIF (buffer_empty) THEN
               Begin
                 buffer := task
                 buffer_empty := FALSE
               End
            ELSE
               SEND task TO processor on the right
            ENDIF
End (* Task_Router *)
```

A general purpose system controller for a processor farm for the chain configuration is shown in this code segment:

```
PROCESS System_Controller()
  Begin
    Initialise_Task_Pool()
    (* A task to each AP and TR buffer *)
    (* Assume there are enough tasks   *)
    FOR i = 1 to number_of_PEs * 2 DO
      SEND next_task TO farm
    results_received := 0
    WHILE (results_received < total_tasks) DO
      Begin
        RECEIVE result FROM farm
        results_received := results_received + 1
        IF more_tasks_to_process THEN
          SEND next_task TO farm
      ENDIF
    SEND closedown_command TO farm
  End (* System_Controller *)
```

The simplicity of this realisation of a demand driven model has contributed largely to its popularity. Note that because of the balance maintained within the system, the only instance at which the last processing element is different from any other processing element in the chain is to ensure the `closedown_command` does not get passed any further. However, such a model does have disadvantages which may limit its use for more complex problems.

The computation to communication ratio of the desired application is critical in order to ensure an adequate performance of a processor farm. If this ratio is too low then significant processing element idle time will occur. This idle time occurs because the computation time for the application process to complete its current task and the task buffered at the task router may be lower than the combined communication time required for the results to reach the system controller plus the time for the new tasks released into the system to reach the processing element. This problem may be partially alleviated by the inclusion of several buffers at each task router instead of just one. However, without *a priori* knowledge as to the computation to communication ratio of the application, it may be impossible to determine precisely what the optimum number of buffers should be. This analysis is particularly difficult if the computational complexity of the tasks vary; precisely the type of problem demand driven models are more apt at solving. The problem independence of the system will also be compromised by the use of any *a priori* knowledge.

If the number of buffers chosen is too small, then the possibility of application process idle time will not be avoided. Provision of too many buffers will certainly remove any immediate application process idle time, but will re-introduce the predicament as the processing draws to a close. This occurs once the system controller has no further tasks to introduce into the system and now processing must only continue until all tasks still buffered at the processing elements have been completed. Obviously, significant idle time may occur as some processing elements struggle to complete their large number of buffered tasks.

Chapter 9 explains why the computation to communication ratio of the processor farm is severely exacerbated by the choice of the chain topology. The distance between the furthest processing element in the chain and the system controller grows linearly as more processing elements are added. This means that the combined communication time to return a result and receive a new task also increases. Furthermore, this communication time will also be adversely affected by the message traffic of all the intermediate processing elements which are closer to the system controller.

One possibility is to use a tree configuration instead of a chain, as shown in figure 7.9. In a tree configuration, the average distance from any processing element to the system controller is smaller. Thus we can expect a lower communication time and hence a better computation to communication ratio for a given application. However, the simplicity of the implementation is lost in the tree version as we now have to distinguish between branch nodes, which may have to route messages further and the leaf nodes which do not. In order to implement a processor farm on a tree configuration, it is now necessary for each task to be sent to a *specified* processor. Each task packet must thus contain the identity of the destination processor. Failure to do so may result in a message overflow within the system. On receipt of a result, the system controller should ensure that the next task that is sent out (if any) is sent to the processor that has just returned the result. The task routers on the branches of the trees have to check the destination of the task

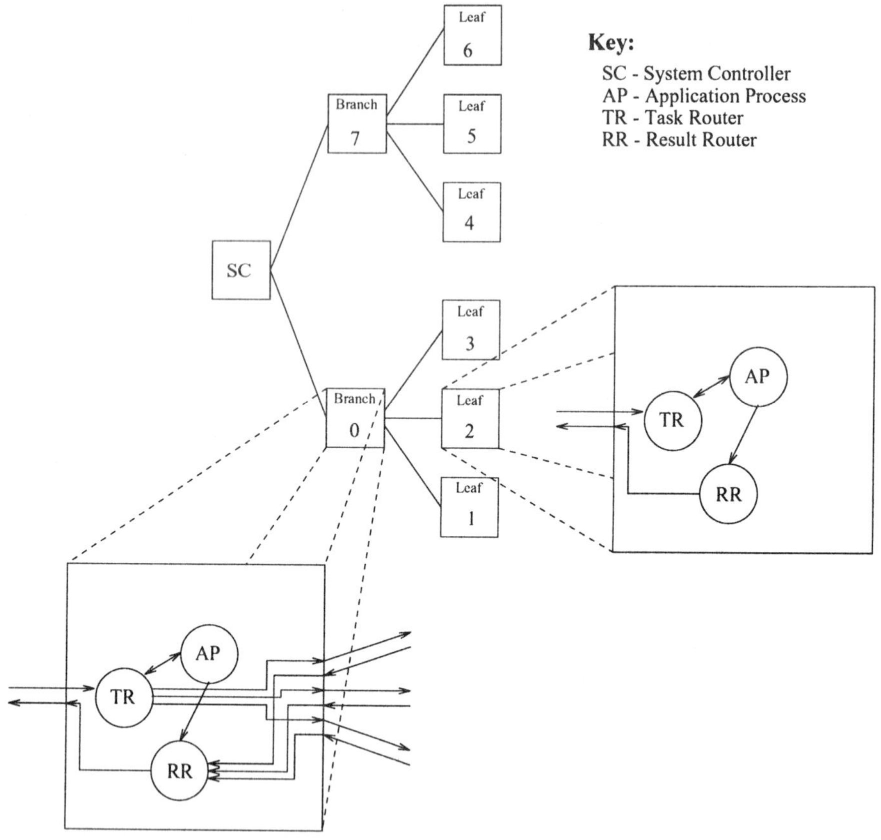

Figure 7.9 Processor farm implemented using a tree configuration

and either deal with the task themselves if they are the destination, or route it on the appropriate link.

7.4 The Task Manager Process

The aim of task management within a parallel system is to ensure the efficient supply of tasks to the processing elements. A Task Manager process (TM) is introduced at each processing element, as shown in figure 7.10, to assist in maintaining a continuous supply of tasks to the application process. The application process no longer deals with task requests directly, but rather indirectly using the facilities of the task manager. The task manager process assumes the responsibility for ensuring that every request for additional tasks from the application process will be satisfied immediately. The task manager attempts to achieve this by maintaining a local task pool.

In the processor farm, the task router process contains a single buffered task in order to satisfy the next local task request. As long as this buffer is full, task supply

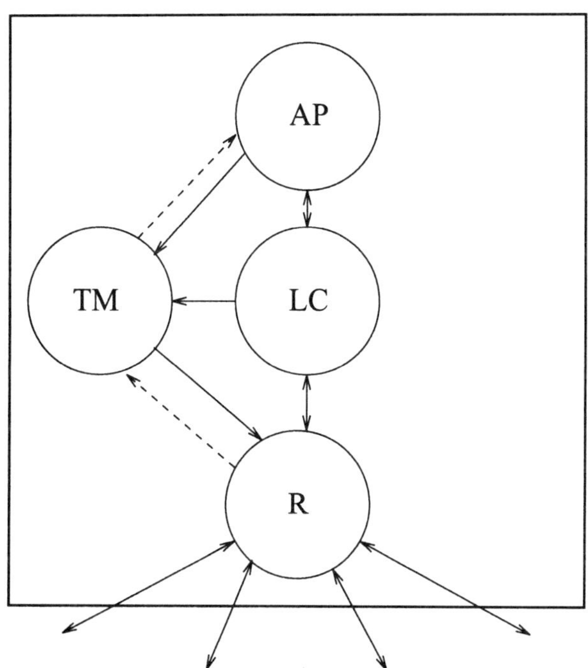

Figure 7.10 Processing element structure with task manager process

is immediate as far as the application process is concerned. The buffer is refilled by a new task from the system controller triggered on receipt of a result. The task router acts in a *passive* manner, awaiting replenishment by a new task within the farm. However, if the buffer is empty when the application process requests a task then this application must remain idle until a new task arrives. This idle time is wasted computation time and so to improve system performance the passive task router should be replaced by a 'intelligent' task manager process more capable of ensuring new tasks are always available locally.

The task management strategies implemented by the task manager and outlined in the following sections are *active*, dynamically requesting and acquiring tasks during computation. The task manager thus assumes the responsibility of ensuring local availability of tasks. This means that an application process should always have its request for a task satisfied immediately by the task manager unless:

- at the start of the problem the application processes make a request before the initial tasks have been provided by the system controller,

- there are no more tasks which need to be solved for a particular stage of the parallel implementation, or

- the task manager's replenishment strategy has failed in some way.

7.4.1 A local task pool

To avoid any processing element idle time, it is essential that the task manager has at least one task available locally at the moment the application process issues a task request. This desirable situation was achieved in the processor farm by the provision of a single buffer at each task router. As we saw, the single buffer approach is vulnerable to the computation to communication ratio within the system. Adding more buffer space to the task router led to the possibility of serious load imbalances towards the end of the computation.

The task manager process maintains a local task pool of tasks awaiting computation by the application process. This pool is similar to the task pool at the system controller, as shown in figure 7.6. However, not only will this local pool be much smaller than the system controller's task pool, but also it may be desirable to introduce some form of 'status' to the number of available tasks at any point in time.

Satisfying a task request will free some space in the local task pool. A simple replenishment strategy would be for the task manager immediately to request a new task packet from the system controller. This request has obvious communication implications for the system. If the current message densities within the system are high and as long as there are still tasks available in the local task pool, this request will place an unnecessary additional burden on the already overloaded communication network.

As an active process, it is quite possible for the task manager to delay its replenishment request until message densities have diminished. However, this delay must not be so large that subsequent application process demands will deplete the local task pool before any new tasks can be fetched, causing processor idle time to occur. There are a number of indicators which the task manager can use to determine a suitable delay. Firstly, this delay is only necessary if current message densities are high. Such information will be available for the router, as discussed further in Chapter 9. Given a need for delay, the number of tasks in the task pool, the approximate computation time each of these tasks requires, and the probable communication latency in replenishing the tasks should all contribute to determining the request delay.

In a demand driven system, the computational complexity variations of the tasks are not known. However, the task manager will be aware of how long previous tasks have taken to compute (the time between application process requests). Assuming some form of preferred biased allocation of tasks in which tasks from similar regions of the problem domain are allocated to the same processing element, as discussed in section 7.5, the task manager will be able to build up a profile of task completion time which can be used to predict approximate completion times for tasks in the task pool. The times required to satisfy previous replenishment requests will provide the task manager with an idea of likely future communication responses. These values are, of course, mere approximations, but they can be used to assist in determining reasonable tolerance levels for the issuing of replenishment requests.

The task manager's task pool is divided into three regions: green, orange and red. The number of tasks available in the pool will determine the current status

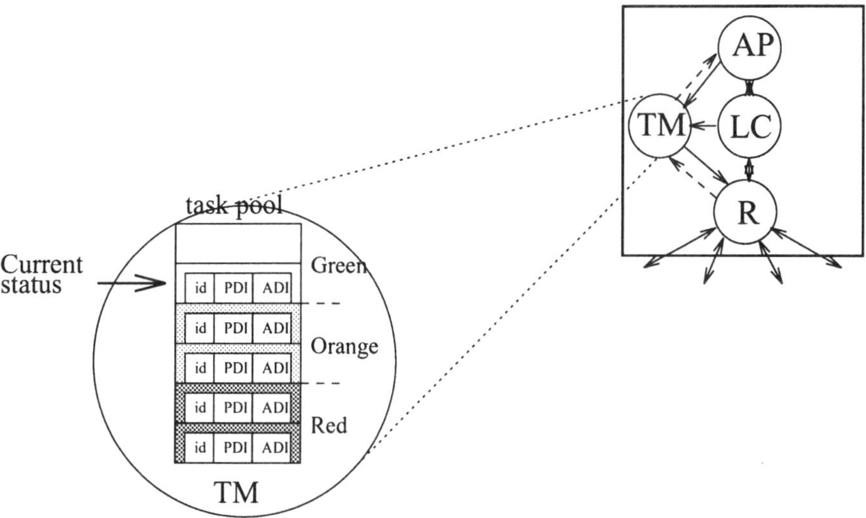

Figure 7.11   Status of task manager's task pool

level, as shown in figure 7.11. When faced with the need to replenish the task pool the decision can be taken based on the current status of the pool:

- **green:** only issue the replenishment request if current message traffic density is low,
- **orange:** issue the replenishment request unless the message density is very high, and
- **red:** always issue the replenishment request.

The boundaries of these regions may be altered dynamically as the task manager acquires more information. At the start of the computation the task pool will be all red. The computation to communication ratio is critical in determining the boundaries of the regions of the task pool. The better this ratio, that is when computation times are high relative to the time taken to replenish a task packet, the smaller the red region of the task pool need be. This will provide the task manager with greater flexibility and the opportunity to contribute to minimising communication densities.

7.4.2 Distributed task management

One handicap of the centralised task pool system is that all replenishment task requests from the task managers must reach the system controller before the new tasks can be allocated. The associated communication delay in satisfying these requests can be significant. The communication problems can be exacerbated by the bottleneck arising near the system controller. Distributed task management allows task requests to be handled at a number of locations remote from the system controller. Although all the tasks originate from the system controller, requests from processing elements no longer have to reach there in order to be satisfied.

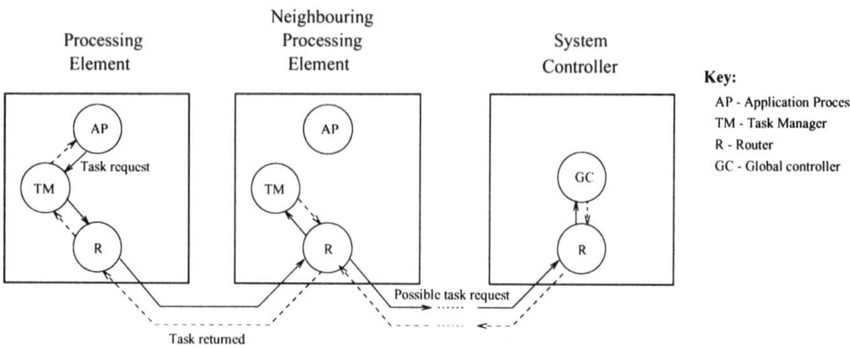

Figure 7.12 Task request propagating towards the system controller

The closest location for a task manager to replenish a task packet is from the task pool located at the task manager of one of its nearest neighbours. In this case, a replenishment request no longer proceeds directly to the system controller, but simply via the appropriate routers to the neighbouring task manager. If this neighbouring task manager is able to satisfy the replenishment request then it does so from its task pool. This task manager may now, in turn, decide to replenish its task pool, depending on its current status and so it will also request another task from one of its neighbouring task managers, but obviously not the same neighbour to which it has just supplied the task. One sensible strategy is to propagate these requests in a 'chain like' fashion in the direction towards the system controller, as shown in figure 7.12.

This distributed task management strategy is referred to as a *producer–consumer* model. The application process is the initial consumer and its local task manager the producer. If a replenishment request is issued then this task manager becomes the consumer and the neighbouring task manager the producer, and so on. The global controller process of the system controller is the overall producer for the system. If no further tasks exist at the system controller then the last requesting task manager may change the direction of the search. This situation may occur towards the end of a stage of processing and facilitates load balancing of any tasks remaining in task manager buffers. As well as reducing the communication distances for task replenishment, an additional advantage of this 'chain reaction' strategy is that the number of request messages in the system is reduced. This will play a major rôle helping maintain a lower overall message density within the system.

If a task manager is unable to satisfy a replenishment request as its task pool is empty, then to avoid 'starvation' at the requesting processing element, this task manager must ensure that the request is passed on to another processing element. The structure for the task manager is shown in the following segment of code:

```
PROCESS Task_Manager()
   Begin
      busy := TRUE
      RECEIVE initial_task_allocation FROM System Controller
      WHILE busy DO
```

```
      PRIORITISED INPUT ALTERNATIVES
        1. RECEIVE closedown_command FROM Local Controller
              busy := FALSE (* LC terminates local processes *)
        2. RECEIVE request_for_task FROM AP (* local request *)
            IF task available in local_taskpool THEN
              Begin
                SEND task TO AP
                IF available_tasks < tolerance THEN
                  (* assume initiative *)
                  (* based on some strategy *)
                  REQUEST task FROM another_PE
                ENDIF
              End
            ELSE
              (* occurs when no work left or *)
              (* replenishment has failed    *)
              AP_ready_for_task := TRUE
            ENDIF
        3. RECEIVE task FROM another_PE
            IF (AP_ready_for_task) THEN (*replenishment failed*)
              Begin
                SEND task TO AP
                AP_ready_for_task := FALSE
              End
            ELSE
              Add_To_Local_Taskpool(task)
            ENDIF
        4. RECEIVE task_request FROM PE  (* remote request *)
            IF task_available in local_taskpool THEN
              Begin
                SEND task TO PE
                IF available_tasks < tolerance THEN
                  (* Assume initiative and request *)
                  (* based on chosen strategy      *)
                  REQUEST task FROM another_PE
                ENDIF
              End
            ELSE (* local task pool is empty *)
              SEND task_request TO another_PE
            ENDIF
End (* Task_Manager *)
```

A number of variants of the producer–consumer model are also possible:

- Instead of following a path towards the system controller, the 'chain reaction' could follow a predetermined Hamiltonian path[2] (the system controller could be one of the processors on this path). Such a path would ensure that a processing element would be assured of replenishing a task if there was one available and

---

[2] A Hamiltonian path is a circuit starting and finishing at one processing element. This circuit passes through each processor in the network once only.

there would be no need to keep track of the progress of the 'chain reaction' to ensure no task manager was queried more than once per chain.

- In the course of its through-routing activities a router may handle a task packet destined for a distant task manager. If that router's local task manager has an outstanding 'red request' for a task then it is possible for the router to *poach* the 'en route task' by diverting it, so satisfying its local task manager immediately. Care must be taken to ensure that the task manager for whom the task was intended is informed that the task has been poached, so it may issue another request. In general, tasks should only be poached from 'red replenishment' if to do so would avoid local application process idle time.

7.5 Preferred Bias Task Allocation

The preferred bias method of task management is a way of allocating tasks to processing elements which combines the simplicity of the balanced data driven model with the flexibility of the demand driven approach. To reiterate the difference in these two computational models as they pertain to task management:

- Tasks are allocated to processing elements in a predetermined manner in the balanced data driven approach.

- In the demand driven model, tasks are allocated to processing elements on demand. The requesting processing element will be assigned the next available task packet from the task pool, and thus no processing element is bound to any area of the problem domain.

Provided no data dependencies exist, the order of task completion is unimportant. Once all tasks have been computed, the problem is solved. In the preferred bias method the problem domain is divided into equal regions with each region being assigned to a particular processing element, as is done in the balanced data driven approach. However, in this method, these regions are purely *conceptual* in nature. A demand driven model of computation is still used, but the tasks are not now allocated in an arbitrary fashion to the processing elements. Rather, a task is dispatched to a processing element from its conceptual portion. Once all tasks from a processing element's conceptual portion have been completed, only then will that processing element be allocated its next task from the portion of another processing element which has yet to complete its conceptual portion of tasks. Generally this task should be allocated from the portion of the processing element that has completed the least number of tasks. So, for example, from figure 7.13, on completion of the tasks in its own conceptual region, PE_3 may get allocated task number 22 from PE_2's conceptual region. Preferred bias allocation is sometimes also referred to as *conceptual task allocation*.

The implications of preferred bias allocation are substantial. The demand driven model's ability to deal with variations in computational complexity is retained, but now the system controller and the processing elements themselves know to whom a task that they have been allocated conceptually belongs. As we will see in section 8.6, this can greatly facilitate the even distribution of partial results at the end of any stage of a multi-stage problem.

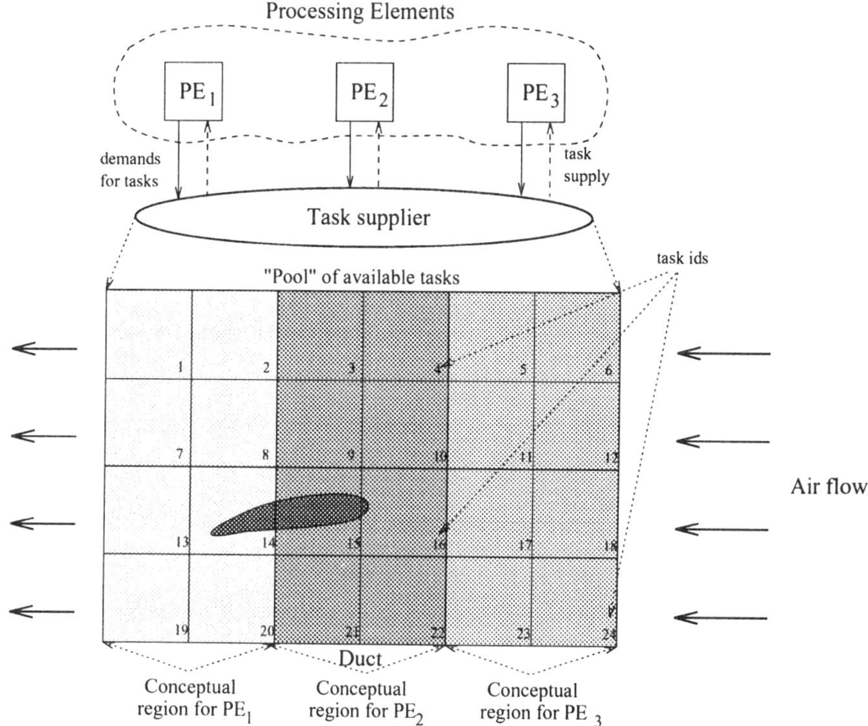

Figure 7.13   Partial result storage balancing by means of conceptual regions

The exploitation of data coherence is a vital ploy in reducing idle time due to remote data fetches. Preferred bias allocation of tasks can ensure that tasks from the same region of the problem are allocated to the same processing element. This can greatly improve the cache hit ratio at that processing element. This topic will be expanded in section 8.5.3.

7.6 Summary

The choice of task granularity must be made before the parallel implementation can commence. This granularity is determined as the 'most reasonable' computational unit for the problem. This is, of course, very problem dependent, but the choice should always be made to minimise any data dependencies that may exist in the problem domain. The task granularity will determine the principal data items as well as the number of tasks into which the problem may be subdivided. The solution of the problem now becomes the parallel solution of these tasks.

The task manager process must try to ensure that the next task is available at a processing element when the application process completes its current task. This prevents unnecessary processing element idle time. Figure 7.14 shows how the correct task management strategy can be chosen to achieve this goal.

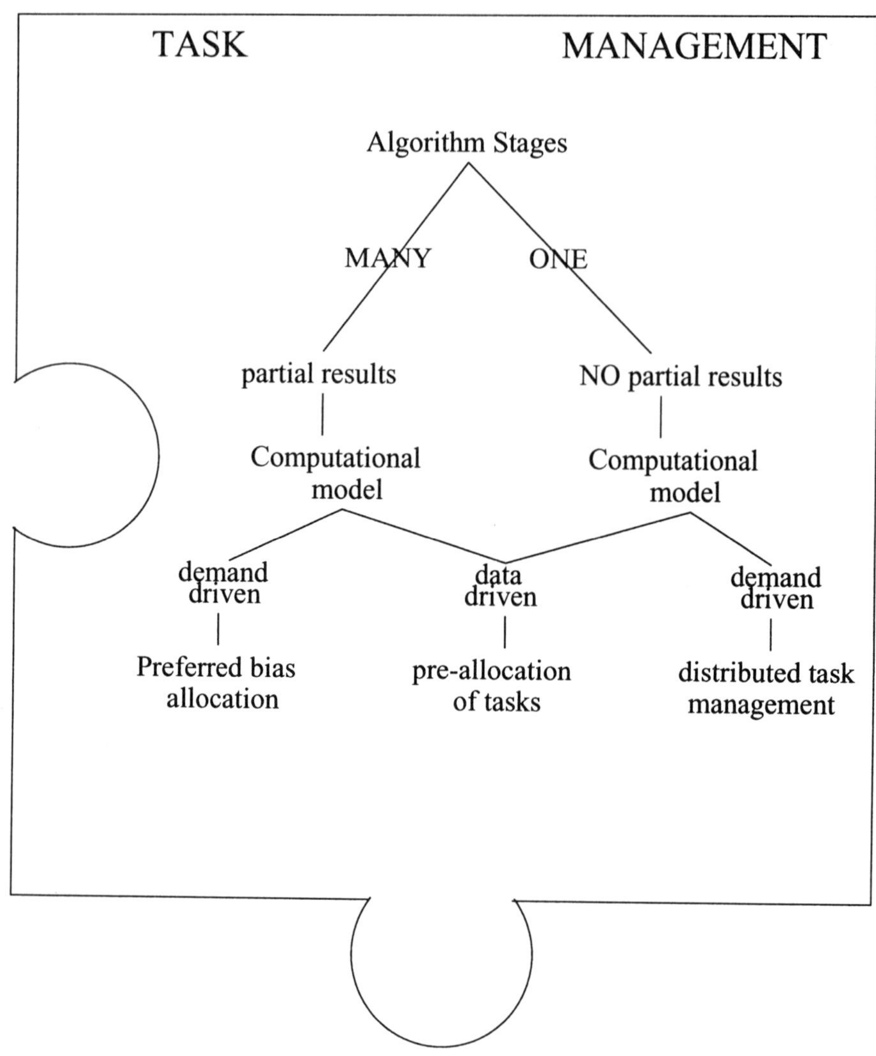

Figure 7.14   Selecting the appropriate task management strategy

The algorithm selected to solve the problem must be analysed to identify whether it contains any distinct stages. Multi-stage algorithms contain the possibility of partial results in which the results from one stage become the principal data items for the next.

The selection of a data driven computational model to solve the problem certainly simplifies the task management requirements. In both the balanced and unbalanced data driven approaches, the system controller decides before the computation which processing elements are to perform which tasks. This pre-allocation of tasks requires no further task management other than the initial distribution of the allotted tasks to each processing element

A demand driven computational model, on the other hand, requires that the task manager provides tasks to its application process dynamically as the computation proceeds. The task manager thus assumes the responsibility of fetching additional tasks from the task pool at the system controller. A better strategy which helps reduce communication overheads is for the task manager to maintain its own local task pool: distributed task management. In this approach, additional tasks are fetched, when the need arises, from the task pools of neighbouring task managers. In a multi-stage algorithm there is the added complication of ensuring that the partial results are in the correct locations for the start of the next stage. A preferred bias allocation strategy can achieve this by enabling the task managers to be aware of which processing elements are responsible for different portions of the problem domain.

Some of the issues of task management will be highlighted in the following case study which calculates the thermal radiation in a room.

7.7 Case Study: Thermal Radiation in a Room

Many scientific problems involve more than one distinct stage of computation. Task management must ensure that the preliminary results from one stage are correctly distributed in anticipation of the following stages. Thermal radiation is the electromagnetic radiation emitted by a body as a result of its temperature. The radiant heat transfer method was developed to calculate the transmission of heat between surfaces of objects within an environment, for example between elements in a furnace [169]. The technique described in this case study naturally divides into two stages:

1. The formulation of a set of simultaneous equations to describe the interaction of surfaces within the environment under consideration; and,

2. The solution of these equations for the intensity of each surface's radiation.

7.7.1 Problem description

Thermal engineering uses the term *radiosity* of a surface to indicate the rate at which radiant energy streams away from a surface per unit area [74, 171]. This radiant energy consists of the energy that the surface itself emits as well as the fraction of energy impinging on the surface and which is reflected back into the environment. The radiosity of a surface i, B_i, is defined as:

$$B_i = E_i + \rho_i H_i, \tag{7.1}$$

where:

E_i is the radiation emitted by the surface,

ρ_i is the reflectance of the surface, and

H_i is the incident radiant energy arriving at the surface per unit time and unit area.

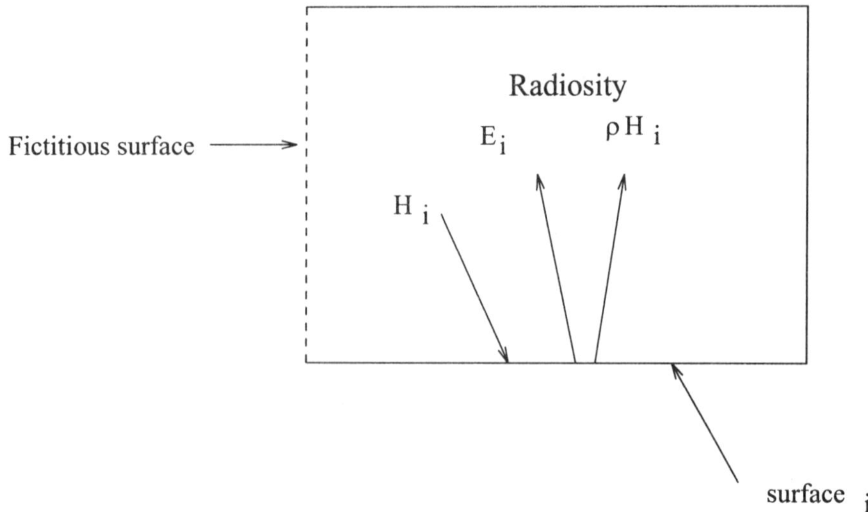

Figure 7.15   An enclosure of four surfaces including a fictitious surface

The exchange of thermal radiation between surfaces is a function of the surface emission, absorption, reflection and transmission properties and the properties of the medium that lies within the path of the thermal radiation [174]. To calculate the radiant energy interchange at any surface, it is necessary to include radiant energy arriving at that surface from all directions in space. To account fully for all the radiation a hypothetical enclosure may need to be constructed that completely defines the environment under consideration [74, 82, 171]. Some of these surfaces may not be material, for example an open window, in which case fictitious surfaces may be created. These fictitious surfaces are assigned the radiant energy properties that correspond to the energy that may pass through them. An enclosure of four surfaces is shown in figure 7.15. To solve this problem we will make the further assumption that all surfaces are isothermal and diffuse reflectors, scattering radiation equally in all directions. The intensity of this diffuse reflection is given by Lambert's law [174]:

$$I_d = I_l k_d \cos\theta \text{ where } 0 \leq \theta \leq \frac{\pi}{2},$$

where:

I_l is the intensity of the energy source,

θ is the angle between the surface normal and a line from the surface point to the point light source, and

k_d is an approximation to the diffuse reflectivity. This depends on the nature of the material and the wavelength of the incident energy.

As we are dealing with only diffuse surfaces, both the emitted and reflected radiant energies are directionally indistinguishable and can, therefore, be treated as a single entity. This single entity is the radiosity of the surface. The incident radiant energy that arrives at surface i, H_i, consists of the fraction of all other surfaces' radiosity that arrives at the surface and if surface i is concave, also the fraction of B_i that impinges on itself. So for an enclosure of N surfaces:

$$H_i = \sum_{j=1}^{N} B_j F_{A_i A_j}, \tag{7.2}$$

where:

$F_{A_i A_j}$ designates the fraction of radiant energy leaving surface i that arrives at surface j.

Thus from equation 7.1 the radiosity of surface i is:

$$B_i = E_i + \rho_i \sum_{j=1}^{n} B_j F_{A_i A_j}. \tag{7.3}$$

The term $F_{A_i A_j}$ in equation (7.3) is known as the *form factor*, and is used to indicate the fraction of the diffusely distributed radiant energy leaving one surface that arrives at a second surface. For diffuse surfaces with a constant radiosity across any surface, the form factors are geometrical in nature. The form factor for differential area dA_i to differential area dA_j, as shown in figure 7.16, may be calculated as:

$$F_{dA_i dA_j} = \frac{\cos \Phi_i \cos \Phi_j}{\pi r^2}. \tag{7.4}$$

The form factors may be calculated by subdividing the environment into a number of finite areas, known as patches. Each patch is chosen such that its surface characteristics can be assumed to be constant. The hemi-cube method may now be used to approximate the form factor from a patch i to a patch j [51, 87].

The hemi-cube method uses a discrete cube constructed round the centre of the receiving patch so that the patch normal always coincides with the centre of the hemi-cube's top face. All other patches are now projected onto this hemi-cube, as shown for a single projection in figure 7.17. The form factor can then be calculated as the proportion of the hemi-cube surface covered by this projection. The projection of patch j onto the hemi-cube positioned at the centre of patch i produces the form factor, which we will now write as F_{ij}. Projection of all patches onto the hemi-cube positioned at patch i will produce a complete row of form factors, $F_{ij} \; \forall j \neq i$.

If one patch projects onto the same portion of the hemi-cube as another then only the projection of the nearer patch is selected. The other patch is hidden from the receiving patch (occluded) and thus does not have a form factor value for the overlapped portion of the hemi-cube. Furthermore, many surfaces in an environment may be facing away from the receiving patch. This can be easily determined from the normals of any patch. Patches that face away will have no form factor for that receiving patch and do not need to be considered.

Hemi-cubes positioned around the centres of all patches generate the set of simultaneous equations shown in (7.5). This set of equations can now be solved for the unknown patch radiosities for each of the energy wavelengths required.

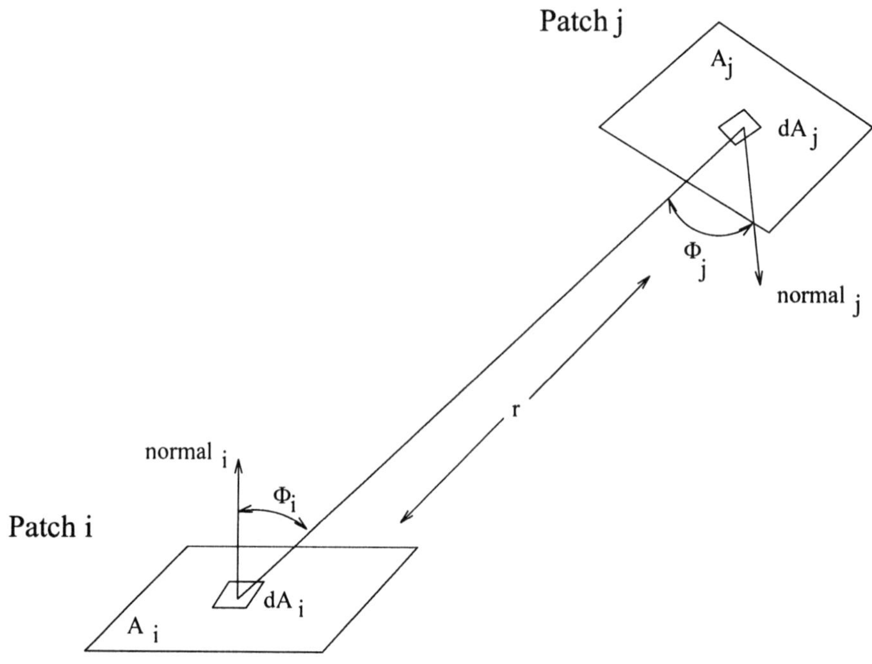

Figure 7.16   The geometry used for calculating form factors

$$
\begin{pmatrix}
1 - \rho_1 F_{11} & -\rho_1 F_{12} & \cdots & -\rho_1 F_{in} \\
-\rho_2 F_{21} & 1 - \rho_2 F_{22} & \cdots & -\rho_2 F_{2n} \\
\vdots & \vdots & \ddots & \vdots \\
-\rho_n F_{n1} & -\rho_n F_{n2} & \cdots & 1 - \rho_n F_{nn}
\end{pmatrix}
\begin{pmatrix}
b_1 \\ b_2 \\ \vdots \\ b_n
\end{pmatrix}
=
\begin{pmatrix}
e_1 \\ e_2 \\ \vdots \\ e_n
\end{pmatrix}.
\tag{7.5}
$$

7.7.2 Parallel requirements

From the description of the problem we can see that it has two distinct stages:

1. Set up the matrix of form factors

2. Solve for the unknown radiosities.

Stage 1: Examination of the problem description reveals that a task for the first stage of the problem could be the projection of one patch onto the hemi-cube positioned at the centre of another patch, that is, to calculate one element of the form factor matrix. However, the possibility of occluded surfaces requires the algorithm to check every time a projection is performed onto a hemi-cube positioned at a patch to ensure that no other patch has projected onto the same portion of the hemi-cube. Thus there are data dependencies present in the calculation of the individual elements of one row of the form factor matrix and

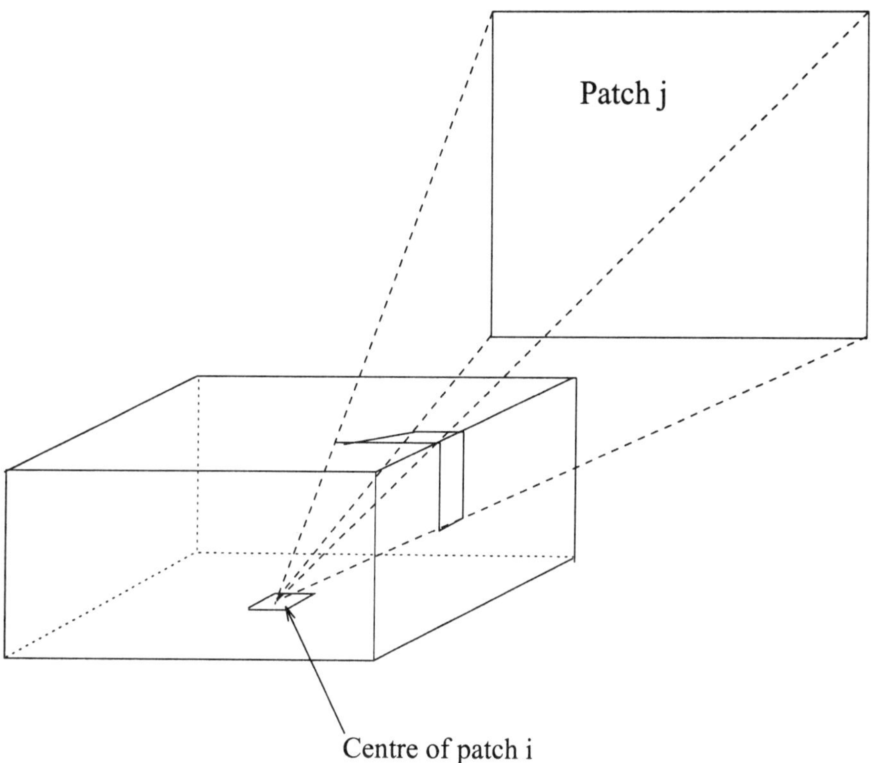

Figure 7.17   Projection of a single patch onto a hemi-cube

so it is preferable to treat this as a sequential operation. A task should therefore be the calculation of one row of the form factor matrix.

The choice of task now identifies the principal and additional data items. Each receiving patch is a principal data item. The algorithm positions a hemi-cube about the centre of this patch and then projects all other patches onto this hemi-cube. All the other patches are therefore the additional data items for this task. With the task and principal and additional data items established, we are now in a position to choose the correct computational model. Figure 7.18(a)(1) shows the choices we make. The number of patches in the environment are fixed and thus so is the number of tasks. Patches which face away from the receiving patch do not have to be projected, and having determined this from the corresponding normals, these patches do not need to be considered further. The computational complexities associated with a simple comparison of normals and a projection of a patch onto a hemi-cube are very different. Furthermore, these computational complexity variations are unknown for each task as this depends entirely on the nature of the environment. Thus, a demand driven approach must be chosen as the computational model.

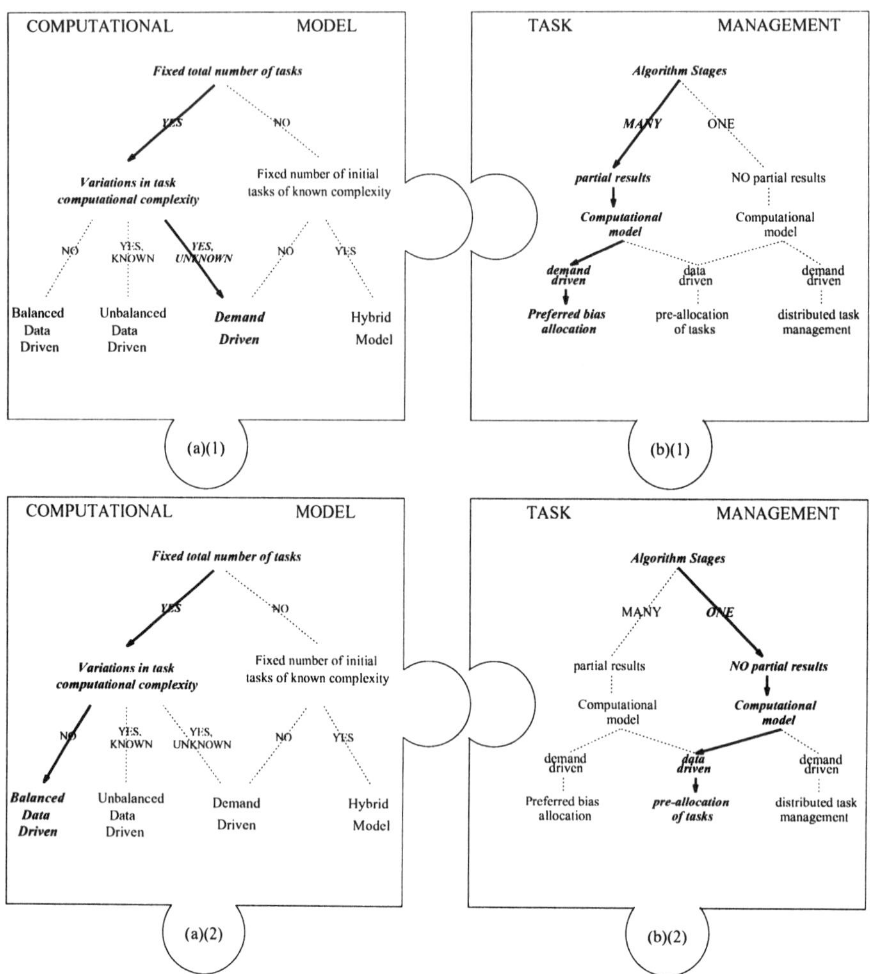

Figure 7.18   Choice of correct computational model and task management strategy for steps 1 and 2

Figure 7.18(b)(1) shows the choice we must make for the task management strategy now that we have chosen a demand driven model. There is another stage of the algorithm after the form factor matrix has been established, and that is the solution of this matrix. The resultant rows of the form factor matrix will be the principal data items of the second stage. A preferred bias allocation strategy will ensure these partial results are positioned correctly in anticipation of the second stage.

Stage 2: The second stage of the algorithm is the solution of the matrix of form factors to determine the unknown radiosities. The sequential solution of this problem typically uses a Gauss–Seidel iterative solver. We have already seen in section 7.2.2 that this method is inappropriate for parallel processing so we will use the 'Block Gauss–Seidel–Global Jacobi' method. The tasks for this second stage of the problem will be the solution of one row of the form factor matrix. There are a fixed number of tasks and the computational complexity to solve one row is the same for all rows and so, as shown in figure 7.18(a)(2) we should adopt a balanced data driven model. There is no subsequent stage once the matrix has been solved and so from figure 7.18(b)(2) we should select a pre-allocation of tasks as the task management strategy.

Having made the correct choice of the appropriate computational model and task management strategy for both stages of the problem we may now proceed with the parallel implementation.

7.7.3 Results

The thermal engineering problem was solved on different sizes of AMP configuration (which will be explained in Chapter 9) ranging from 1 to 63 processing elements. The thermal radiations were calculated for an environment of 448 patches. Table 7.1 shows the time in seconds for the setup and solution stages of the problem.

PEs	Setup	Solve	Total
1	1874.460	78.859	1953.527
2	938.570	42.819	981.597
4	473.570	23.749	497.533
8	238.452	22.924	261.595
13	147.626	20.918	168.771
16	121.294	18.946	140.453
23	85.561	24.151	109.935
32	63.487	28.096	91.807
42	49.911	35.525	85.664
53	40.830	43.732	84.782
63	35.053	49.956	85.229

Table 7.1 Times in seconds for 448 patches on different AMP configurations

The high computational effort required by the matrix setup stage allows good parallel performance to be achieved for this stage. Looking at the graphs of speed-up for this stage in figure 7.19 we see that a 63-processing element AMP shows a speed-up of 53.5. The speed-up graphs have yet to reach their peaks and we can, therefore, say that the optimum number of processing elements, n_{opt}, for this matrix setup stage is greater than 63 processing elements.

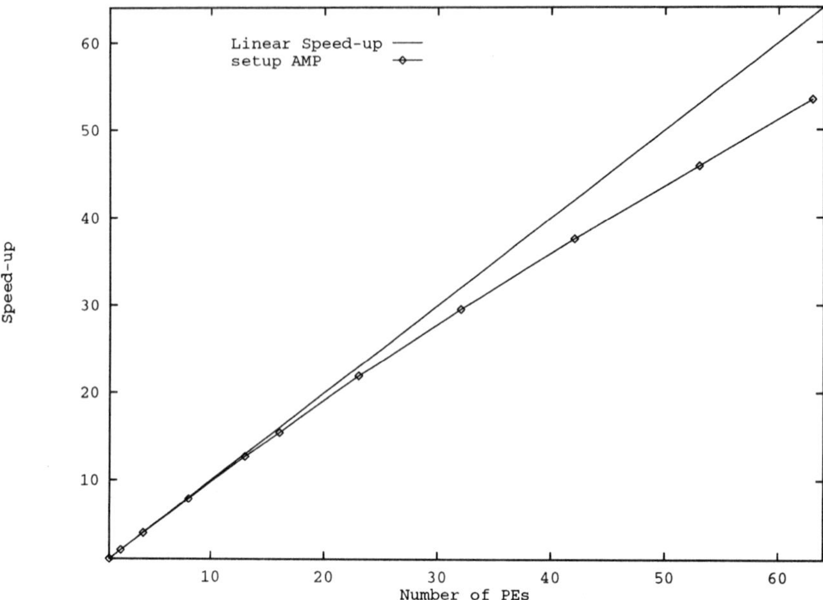

Figure 7.19   Speed-up for the matrix setup stage of the 448 patch problem

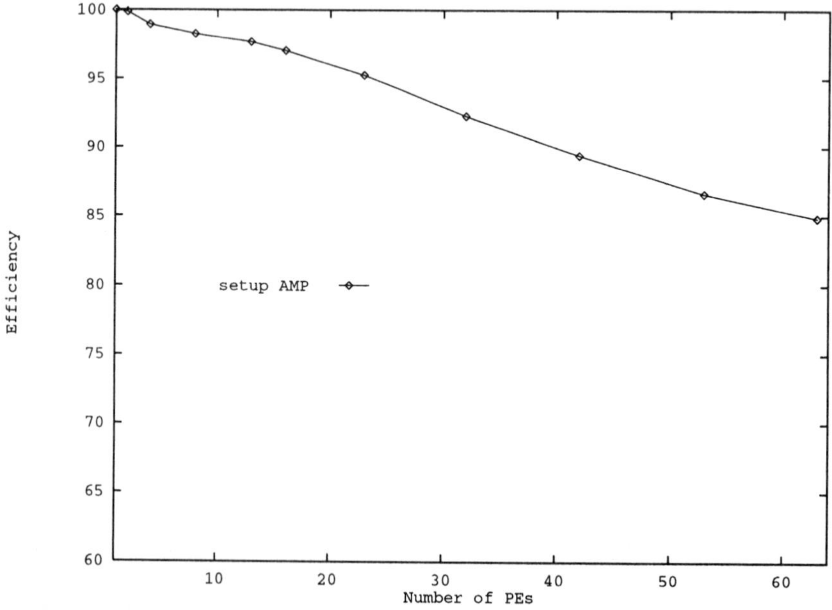

Figure 7.20   Efficiencies of the matrix setup stage of the 448 patch problem

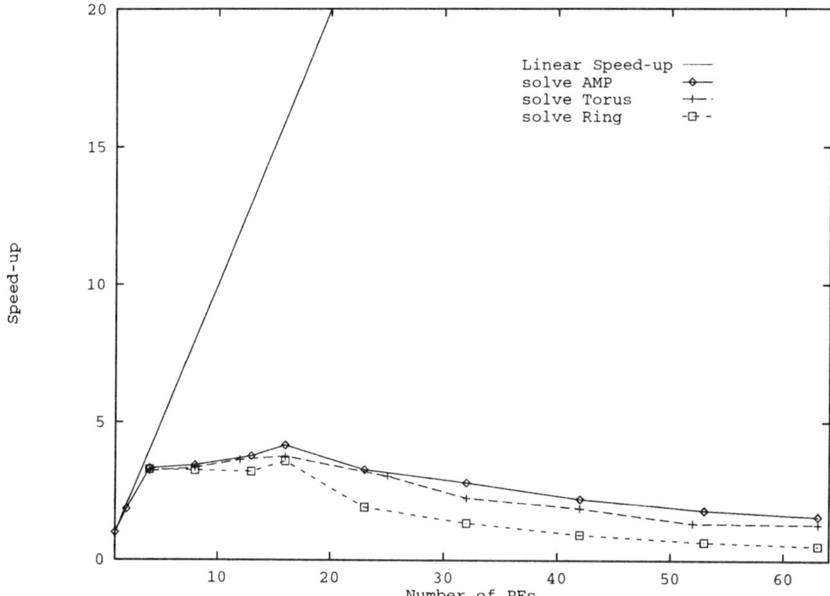

Figure 7.21   Speed-up for the matrix solution stage of the 448 patch problem

If we now examine the efficiency values for this stage of the computation in figure 7.20, we see that the setting up of the form factor matrix on a 63-processing element AMP is 85% efficient. This means that during this first stage, each processing element is able to devote 85% of its time to performing useful computation.

The communication overheads for the matrix solution stage of the gather method are considerably higher than the setup stage because every processing element has to exchange its partial results with all other processing elements at each iteration. As can be seen from table 7.1, the time taken to solve the matrix initially decreases as the number of processing elements is increased until a certain point and then this time increases as more processing elements are added. The maximum speed-up achieved for this stage of the gather method is just over 4. Figure 7.21 shows the speed-up achieved for this matrix solution stage on the AMP and other configurations, while figure 7.22 shows the corresponding efficiencies.

7.7.4 Conclusions

The correct choice of the computational model and task management strategy resulted in a speed-up of 53 and 85% efficiency in the parallel implementation on 63 processing elements of the first stage of the problem, but only a maximum speed-up of 4 for the second stage.

These discrepancies in the speed-ups and efficiencies between the matrix setup and matrix solution stages are important in so far as they affect the scalability of this application. From figure 7.19 we can see that the optimum number of processing

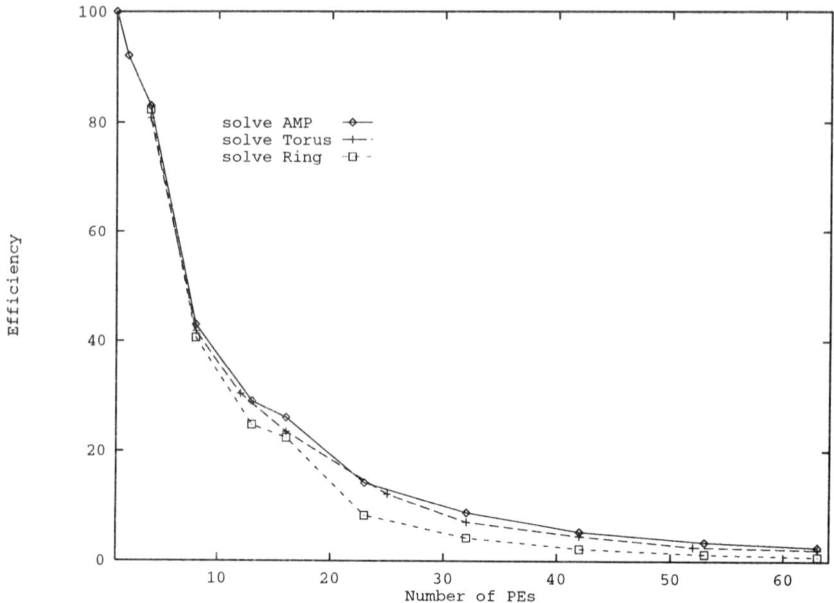

Figure 7.22 Efficiencies of the matrix solution stage of the 448 patch problem

elements for the setup stage is more than 63, whereas from figure 7.21 n_{opt} is somewhere in the region of 20 processing elements for the solution stage. Closer examination, as shown in figure 7.23, reveals that, for this 448 patch problem, on a single processing element the setup stage occupies 96% of the total solution time, and the solution stage just 4% of the total solution time, but for the 63-processing element AMP solution, this ratio has changed to 42% for the setup stage and 58% for the solution stage. We, therefore, need to re-examine the algorithm we have chosen to solve the matrix because the communication requirements for the current algorithm grow rapidly as more processing elements are added, while for the fixed size problem the computational requirements decrease. Only by selecting a matrix solution algorithm with lower communication requirements, such as a conjugate gradient method, can we hope to maintain some form of balance in the computation to communication ratio.

7.8 Exercises and Project Suggestions

1. In the case study presented in this chapter we have adopted the 'Block Gauss–Seidel–Global Jacobi' matrix solver. Would the traditional Jacobi solver have given better or worse speed-up and efficiency results for this problem? Justify your answer in terms of the implications to the computation to communication ratio.

2. Implement a processor farm on a chain of up to ten parallel processors. Your

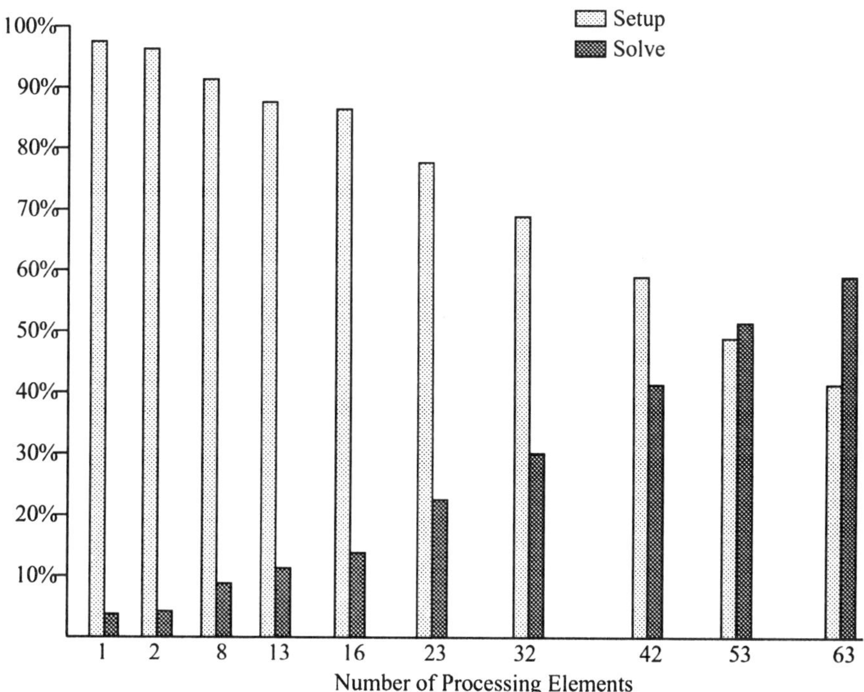

Figure 7.23   Percentages of time taken for a problem size of 448 patches on AMP configurations

system should perform 100 tasks each with the same fixed, pre-determined simulated computational times, say 0.001, 0.01, 0.1 and 1 second. Draw the speed-up graph as the number of processing elements is increased. Now implement the same problem on a single processor using concurrent processing elements. Under what circumstances would it still be possible to obtain meaningful speed-up results for this single processor implementation?

3. Implement a simple processor farm using PVM, described in section 3.7, on a network of autonomous computers. Now, compare and contrast the computation to communication ratio for a simulated computation on this and your parallel implementation of the previous question. How is it possible to reduce processor idle time in each system when the computation to communication ratio is low?

4. Write the pseudo-code to implement the three levels of local task pool described in section 7.4.1. You may assume that, on request, the router will provide an indication of the current level of message density within the system.

5. One possible way of attempting load balancing when using a demand driven computational model may be to allocate many tasks per task packet early on in the computation and then fewer per packet as the number of tasks in the task pool diminishes. Towards the end of computation only one task is contained in

each packet. Discuss the advantages and potential dangers of such an allocation scheme. Use pseudo-code to design this task allocation strategy for the global controller process of the system controller.

Chapter 8

Data Management

There is no problem so big that it cannot be run away from.

Richard Bach

The data requirements of many problems may be far larger than can be accommodated at any individual processing element. Rather than restricting ourselves to only solving those problems that fit completely within every processing element's local memory, we can make use of the combined memory of all processing elements. The large problem domain can now be distributed across the system and even secondary storage devices if necessary. For this class of application some form of data management will be necessary to ensure that data items are available at the processing elements when required by the computations.

Virtual shared memory regards the whole problem domain as a single unit in which the data items may be individually referenced. This is precisely how the domain could be treated if the problem was implemented on a shared memory multiprocessor system. However, on a distributed memory system, the problem domain is distributed across the system and hence the term **virtual***. Virtual shared memory systems may be implemented at different levels, such as in hardware or at the operating system level. In this chapter we will see how the introduction of a data manager process at each processing element can provide an elegant virtual shared memory at the system software level of our parallel implementation.*

The problem domains of many science and engineering applications are very large. The size of these domains are typically far more than can be accommodated within the local memory of any processing element (or indeed in the memory of many sequential computers). Yet it is precisely these complex problems that we wish to solve using parallel processing, and we do not want to 'run away from them'.

Consider a multiprocessor system consisting of 64 processing elements each with 4 Mbytes of local memory. If we were to insist that the entire problem domain were to reside at each processing element then we would be restricted to solving problems with a maximum domain of 4 Mbytes. The total memory within the system is $64 \times 4 = 256$ Mbytes. So, if we were to consider the memory of the multiprocessor system as a whole, then we could contemplate solving problems with domains of up to 256 Mbytes in size; a far more attractive proposition. (If the problem domain was even larger than this, then we could also consider the secondary storage devices attached to the system controller as part of the combined memory and that should be sufficient for most problems.)

There is a price to pay in treating the combined memory as a single unit. Data management strategies will be necessary to translate between the conceptual single memory unit and the physical distributed implementation. The aims of these strategies will be to keep track of the data items so that an item will always be available at a processing element when required by the task being performed. The distributed nature of the data items will thus be invisible to the application processes performing the computation. However, any delay between the application process requesting an item and this request being satisfied will result in idle time. As we will see, it is the responsibility of the data manager process to avoid this idle time. We will also see that the computational model adopted for the system software can influence the choice of data management strategy, as illustrated in figure 8.1.

8.1 World Model of the Data: No Data Management Required

Not all problems possess very large data domains. If the size of the domain is such that it may be accommodated at every processing element then we say that the processing elements have a *world model* of the data. A world model may also exist if all the tasks allocated to a processing element only ever require a *subset* of the problem domain and this subset can be accommodated completely. In the world model, all principal and additional data items required by an application process will always be available locally at each processing element and thus there is no need for any data item to be fetched from another remote location within the system. If there is no requirement to fetch data items from remote locations as the solution of the problem proceeds then there is no need for any form of data management.

The processor farm described in section 7.3.2 is an example of a parallel implementation which assumes a world model. In this approach, tasks are allocated to processing elements in an arbitrary fashion and thus there is no restriction on which tasks may be computed by which processing element. No provision is made for data management and thus to perform any task the entire domain must reside at each processing element.

Data items do not always have to be present at the processing element from the start of computation to avoid any form of data management. As discussed in section 7.1, both principal and additional data items may be included within a task packet. Provided no further data items are required to complete the tasks specified in the task packet then no data management is required and this situation may also be said to be demonstrating a world data model.

8.2 Virtual Shared Memory

Virtual shared memory provides all processors with the concept of a single memory space. Unlike a traditional shared memory model, this physical memory is dis-

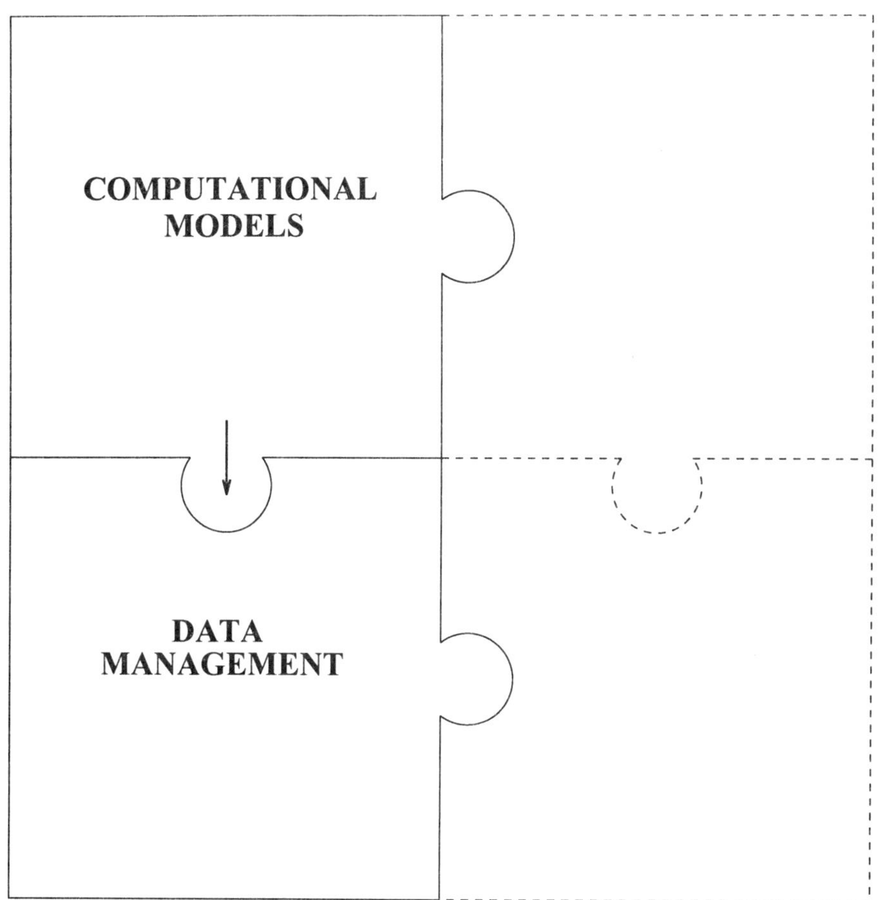

Figure 8.1   The choice of computational model influences the data management strategy

tributed amongst the processing elements. In the SAMD approach, a virtual shared memory environment can be thought of as providing each processing element with a *virtual world model* of the problem domain. So, as far as the application process is concerned, there is no difference between requesting a data item that happens to be local or remote; only the speed of access can be (very) different.

Virtual shared memory can be implemented at any level in the computer hierarchy. Implementations at the hardware level provide a transparent interface to software developers, but requires a specialised machine, such as the DASH system [128]. There have also been implementations at the operating system and compiler level. However, as we shall see, in the absence of dedicated hardware, virtual shared memory can also be easily provided at the system software level. At this level, a great deal of flexibility is available to provide specialised support to minimise any implementation penalties when undertaking the solution of problems with very

Higher level	System Software	Provided by the Data Manager process
	Compiler	High Performance Fortran[113], ORCA[18]
	Operating System	Coherent Paging[130]
Lower level	Hardware	DDM [182], DASH [128], KSR-1 [121]

Figure 8.2 The levels where virtual shared memory can be implemented

large data requirements on multiprocessor systems. Figure 8.2 gives four levels at which virtual shared memory (VSM) can be supported, and examples of systems that implement VSM at that particular level.

8.2.1 Implementing virtual shared memory

At the *hardware level* virtual shared memory intercepts all memory traffic from the processor, and decides which memory accesses are serviced locally, and which memory accesses need to go off-processor. This means that everything above the hardware level (machine code, operating system, etc.) sees a virtual shared memory with which it may interact in exactly the same manner as a physically shared memory. Providing this so-called transparency to the higher levels means that the size of data is not determined by the hardware level. However, in hardware, a data item becomes a fixed consecutive number of bytes, typically around 16–256. By choosing the size to be a power of 2, and by aligning data items in the memory, the physical memory address can become the concatenation of the 'item identifier' and the 'byte selection'. This strategy is easier to implement in hardware.

31	...	6	5	...	0
	item identifier			byte selection	

In this example, the most significant bits of a memory address locates the data item, and the lower bits address a byte within the item. The choice of using 6 bits as the byte selection in this example is arbitrary.

If a data structure of some higher level language containing two integers of four bytes each happened to be allocated from, say, address ...1100 111100 to ...1101 000100, then item ...1100 will contain the first integer, and item ...1101 will contain the other one. This means that two logically related integers of data are located in two physically separate items (although they could fit in a single data item).

Considered another way, if two unrelated variables, say x and y are allocated at addresses ...1100 110000 and ...1100 110100, then they reside in the same data item. If they are heavily used on separate processors, this can cause inefficiencies when the machine tries to maintain sequentially consistent copies of x and y on both processors. The machine cannot put x on one processor and y on the other, because it does not recognise x and y as different entities; the machine observes it as a single item that is shared between two processors. If sequential consistency has to be maintained the machine must update every write to x and y on both processors, even though the variables are not shared at all. This phenomenon is known as *false sharing*.

Virtual shared memory implemented at the *operating system level* also uses a fixed size for data items, but these are typically much larger than at the hardware level. By making an item as large as a page of the operating system (around 1–4 Kbyte), data can be managed at the page level. This is cheaper, but slower than a hardware implementation.

When the *compiler* supports virtual shared memory, a data item can be made exactly as large as any user data structure. In contrast with virtual shared memory implementations at the hardware or operating system level, compiler based implementations can keep logically connected variables together and distribute others. The detection of logically related variables is in the general case very hard, which means that applications written in existing languages such as C, Modula-2 or Fortran cannot be compiled in this way. However, compilers for specially designed languages can provide some assistance. For example, in High Performance Fortran the programmer indicates how arrays should be divided and then the compiler provides the appropriate commands to support data transport and data consistency.

Implementing virtual shared memory at the *system software* level provides the greatest flexibility to the programmer. However, this requires explicit development of system features to support the manipulation of the distributed data item. A *data manager* process is introduced at each processing element especially to undertake this job.

8.3 The Data Manager

Virtual shared memory is provided at the system software level by a data manager process at each processing element, as shown in figure 8.3. The aim of data management within the parallel system is to ensure the efficient supply of data items to the processing elements. The data manager process manages data items just as the task manager was responsible for maintaining a continuous supply of tasks. Note that the data items being referred to here are the principal and additional data items as specified by the problem domain and explained in section 4.3 and not every variable or constant the application process may invoke for the completion of a task.

The application process now no longer deals with the principal and additional data items directly, but rather indirectly using the facilities of the data manager. The application process achieves this by issuing a data request to the data manager process every time a data item is required. The data manager process assumes the responsibility for ensuring that every request for a data item from the application process will be satisfied. The data manager attempts to satisfy these requests by maintaining a local data cache.

The data management strategies implemented by the data manager and outlined in the following sections are *active*, dynamically requesting and acquiring data items during computation. This means that an application process should always have its request for a data item satisfied immediately by the data manager unless

- at the start of the problem the application processes make requests before any initial data items have been provided by the system controller, or

- the data manager's data fetch strategy has failed in some way.

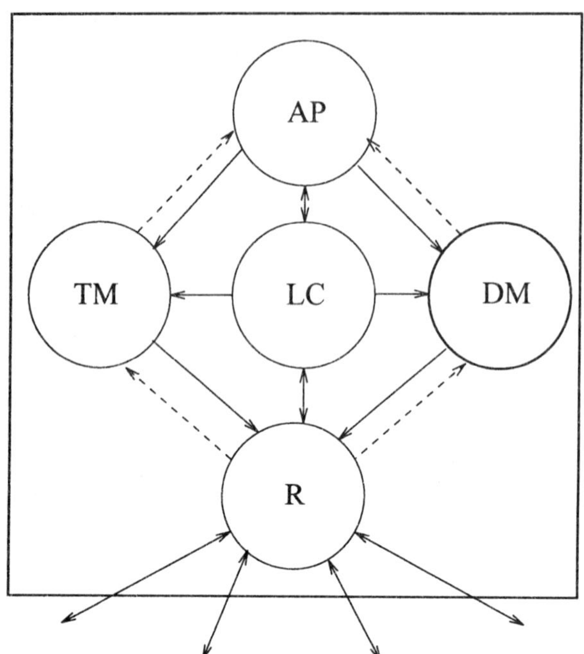

Figure 8.3 The Data Manager process at each processing element

8.3.1 The local data cache

The concept of *data sharing* may be used to cope with very large data requirements [44, 86]. Data sharing implements virtual shared memory by allocating every data item in the problem domain a unique identifier. This allows a required item to be 'located' from somewhere within the system, or from secondary storage if necessary. The size of problem that can now be tackled is, therefore, no longer dictated by the size of the local memory at each processing element, but rather only by the limitations of the combined memory plus the secondary storage.

The principal data item required by an application process is specified by the task it is currently performing. Any additional data item requirements are determined by the task and by the algorithm chosen to solve the problem. These additional data items may be known *a priori* by the nature of the problem, or they may only become apparent as the computation of the task proceeds.

To avoid any processing element idle time, it is essential that the data manager has the required data item available locally at the moment the application process issues a request for it. In an attempt to achieve this, the data manager maintains a local cache of data items as shown in figure 8.4. The size of this cache, and thus the number of data items it can contain, is determined by the size of a processing element's local memory.

Each data item in the system is a packet containing the unique identifier, shown

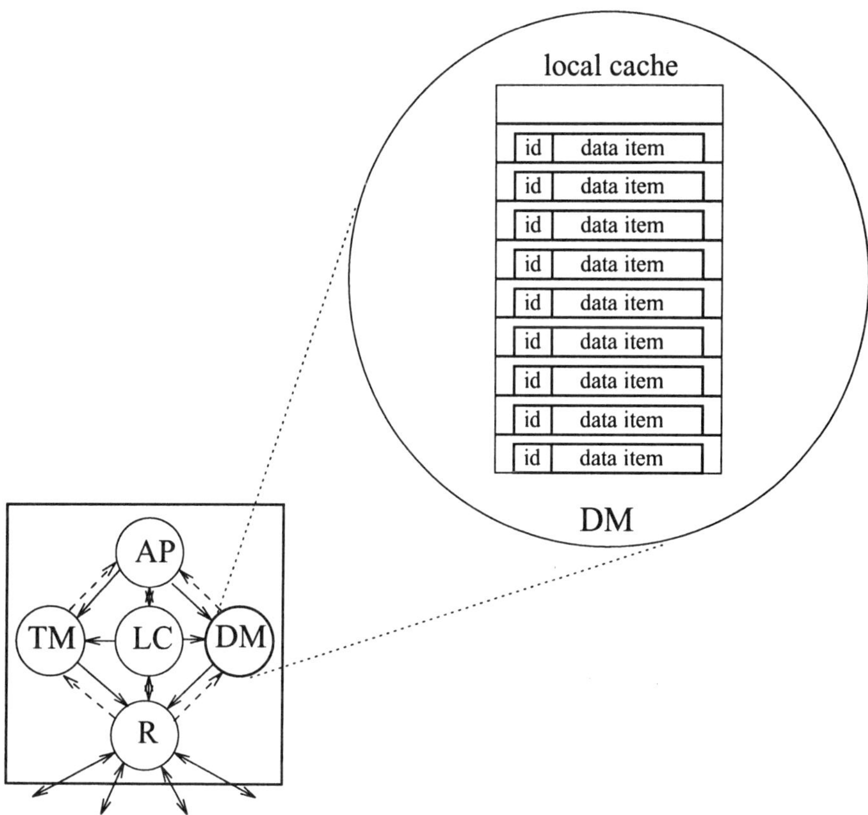

Figure 8.4   The local cache at the data manager

in figure 8.4 as id, together with the actual data which makes up the item. The data items may be permanently located at a specific processing element, or they may be free to migrate within the system to where they are required. When a data manager requires a particular data item which is not already available locally, this data item must be fetched from some remote location and placed into the local cache. This must occur before the application process can access the data item. The virtual shared memory of the system is thus the combination of the local caches at all the processing elements plus the secondary storage which is under the control of the file manager at the system controller. Figure 8.5 shows the composition of the virtual shared memory.

In certain circumstances, as will be seen in the following sections, rather than removing the data item from the local cache in which it was found, it may be sufficient simply to take a copy of the data item and return this to the local cache. This is certainly the case when the data items within the problem domain are *read-only*, that is the values of the data items are not altered during the course of the parallel solution of the problem (and indeed the same would be true of sequential implementation). This means that it is possible for copies of the same data item to

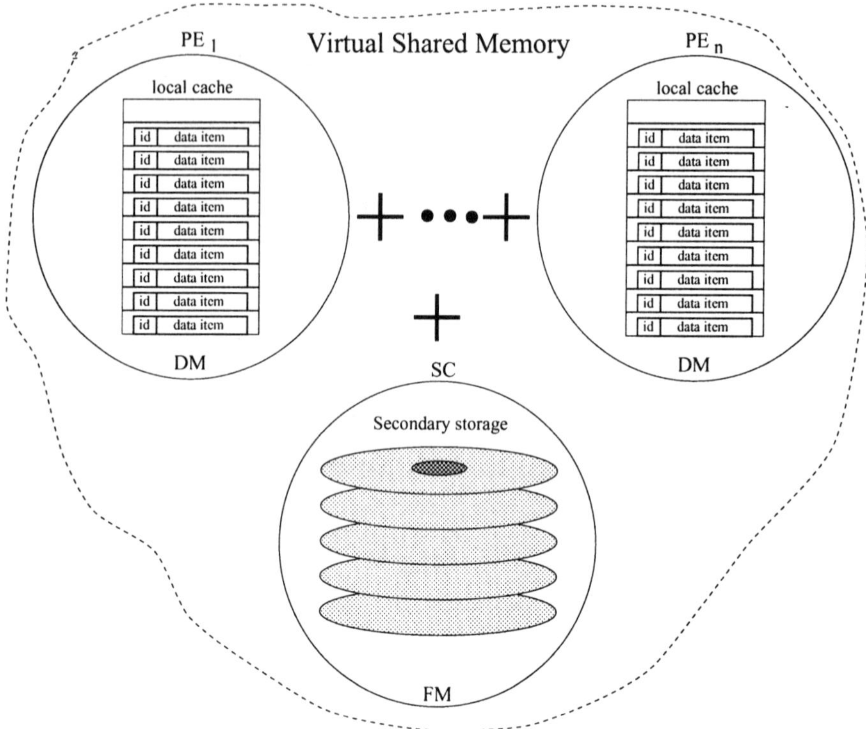

Figure 8.5   The composition of the virtual shared memory

be present in a number of local caches. Note that it is no advantage to have more than one copy of any data item in one local cache.

There is a limited amount of space in any local cache. When the cache is full and another data item is acquired from a remote location, then one of the existing data items in the local cache must be replaced by this new data item. Various strategies for implementing this replacement will be described in section 8.5.3. Care must be taken to ensure that no data item is inadvertently completely removed from the system by being replaced in all local caches. If this does happen then, assuming the data item is read-only, a copy of the entire problem domain will reside on secondary storage, from where the data items were initially loaded into the local caches of the parallel system. This means that should a data item be destroyed within the system, another copy can be retrieved from the file manager of the system controller.

If the data items are *read-write* then their values may be altered as the computation progresses. In this case, the data managers have to beware of consistency issues when procuring a data item. The implications of consistency will be discussed in section 8.4.

As we will now see, the strategies adopted in the parallel implementation for acquiring data items and storing them in the local caches can have a significant effect on minimising the implementation penalties and thus improving overall system

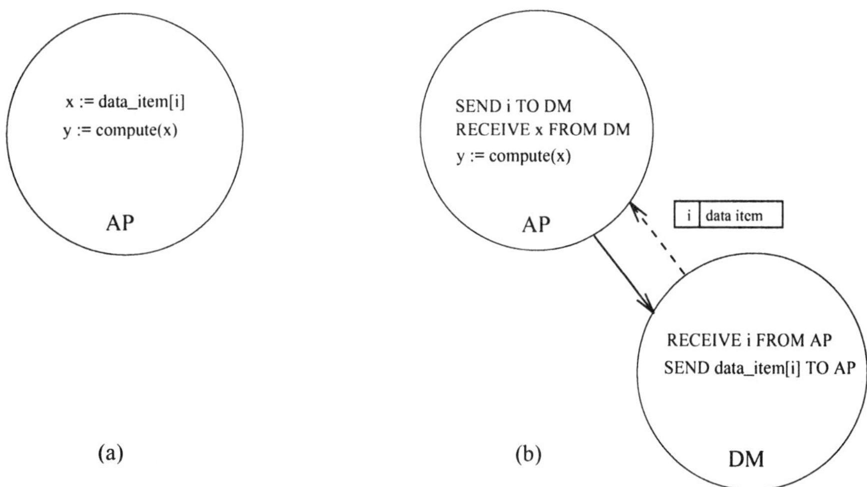

Figure 8.6   Accessing a data item (a) with and (b) without a data manager

performance. The onus is on the data manager process to ensure these strategies are carried out efficiently.

8.3.2 Requesting data items

The algorithm being executed at the application process will determine the next data item required. If the data items were all held by the application process, requesting the data item would be implemented within the application process as an *assignment statement*. For example a request for data item i would simply be written as x := data_item[i]. When all the data items are held instead by the data manager process, this assignment statement must be replaced by a request from the application process to the data manager for the data item followed by the sending of a copy of the data item from the local cache of the data manager to the waiting application process, as shown in figure 8.6.

The data item's unique identifier enables the data manager to extract the appropriate item from its local cache. If a data item requested by the application process is available, it is immediately transferred, as shown in figure 8.7(a). The only slight delay in the computation of the application process will occur by the need to schedule the concurrent data manager and for this process to send the data item from its local cache. However, if the data item is not available locally then the data manager must 'locate' this item from elsewhere in the system. This will entail sending a message via the router to find the data item in another processing element's local cache, or from the file manager of the system controller. Having been found, the appropriate item is returned to the requesting data manager's own local cache and then finally a copy of the item is transferred to the application process.

If the communicated request from the application process is asynchronous and this process is able to continue with its task while awaiting the data item then

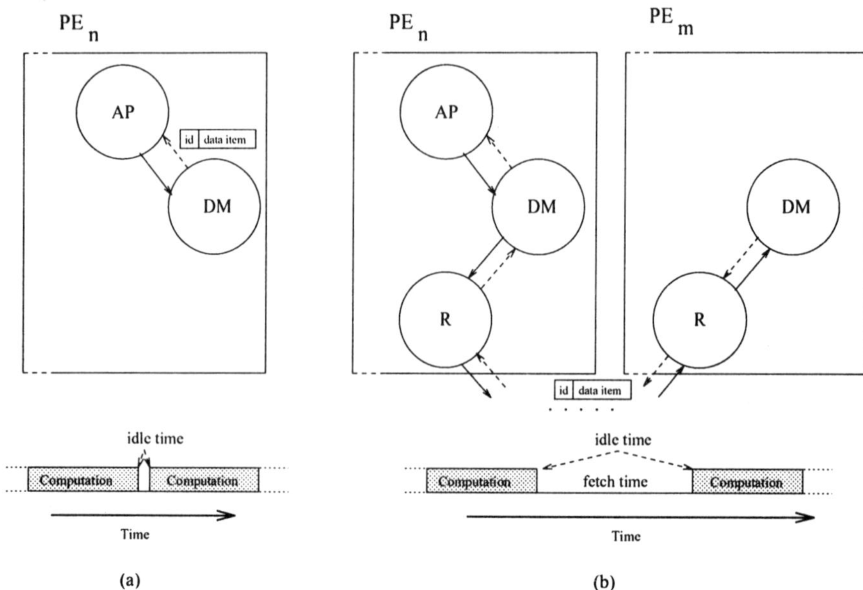

Figure 8.7 AP idle time due to (a) data item found locally (b) remote data item fetch

no idle time occurs. However, if the communication with the data manager is synchronous, or if the data item is essential for the continuation of the task then idle time will persist until the data item can be fetched from the remote location and a copy given to the application process, as shown in figure 8.7(b). Unless otherwise stated, we will assume for the rest of this chapter that an application process is unable to continue with its current task until its data item request has been satisfied by the data manager.

The control loop of a simple data manager to deal with requests from the application process, issue external request commands and handle external requests from other data managers is as follows:

```
PROCESS Data_Manager()
  Begin
    busy := TRUE
    WHILE busy DO
      PRIORITISED INPUT ALTERNATIVES
        1. RECEIVE id FROM AP   (* data request from AP *)
            IF (data_item[id] in local_cache) THEN
              SEND data_item[id] TO AP
            ELSE
              SEND external_request_for_id TO R
            ENDIF

        2. RECEIVE data_item[id] FROM R (* remote data item *)
            Begin
```

```
              Add_To_Local_Cache(data_item[id])
              (* data must have been requested previously  *)
              SEND data_item[id] TO AP
            End

     3. RECEIVE external_request_for_id FROM R (* external *)
          IF (data_item[id] in local_cache) THEN
            SEND data_item[id] TO requesting_PE via R
          ELSE
            SEND not_found_id TO R
          ENDIF
End (* Data_Manager *)
```

8.3.3 Locating data items

When confronted with having to acquire a remote data item, two possibilities exist for the data manager. Either it knows exactly the location of the data item within the system, or this location is unknown and some form of search will have to be instigated.

Resident sets

Knowing the precise location of the requested data item within the system enables the data manager to instruct the router to send the request for the data item, external_request_for_id, directly to the appropriate processing element. Just how this is done is explained in Chapter 9.

One of the simplest strategies for allocating data items to each processing element's local cache is to divide all the data items of the problem domain evenly amongst the processing elements before the computation commences. Providing there is sufficient local memory and assuming there are n processing elements, this means that each processing element would be allocated $\frac{1}{n}^{th}$ of the total number of data items. If there is not enough memory at each processing element for even this fraction of the total problem domain then as many as possible could be allocated to the local caches and the remainder of the data items would be held at the file manager of the system controller. Such a simplistic scheme has its advantages. Provided these data items remain at their predetermined local cache for the duration of the computation, then the processing element from which any data item may found can be computed directly from the identity of the data item.

For example, assume there are 12 data items, given the unique identification numbers $1, \ldots, 12$, and three processing elements, PE_1, PE_2, and PE_3. A predetermined allocation strategy may allocate data items $1, \ldots, 4$ to PE_1, data items $5, \ldots, 8$ to PE_2 and $9, \ldots, 12$ to PE_3. Should PE_2 wish to acquire a copy of data item 10, it may do so directly from the processing element known to have that data item, in this case PE_3.

It is essential for this simple predetermined allocation strategy that the data items are not overwritten or moved from the local cache to which they are assigned initially. However, it may be necessary for a processing element to also acquire

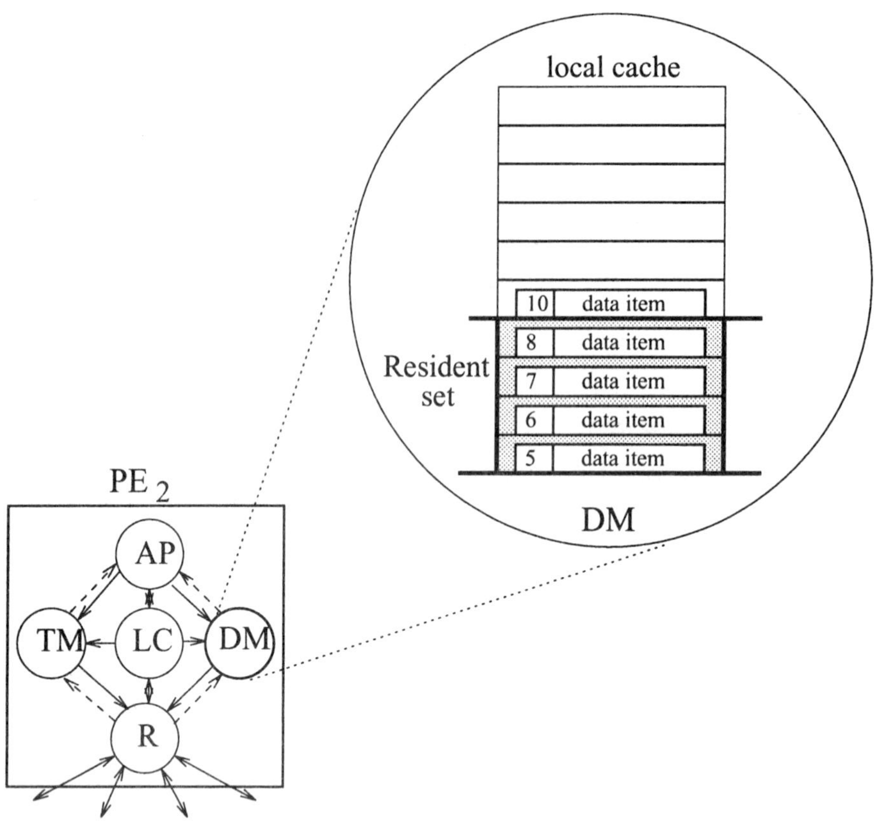

Figure 8.8 Resident set of the local cache

copies of other data items as the computation proceeds, as we saw with PE_2 above. This implies that the local cache should be partitioned into two distinct regions:

- a region containing data items which may never be replaced, known as the *resident set*, and

- a region for data items which may be replaced during the parallel computation.

The size of the resident set should be sufficient to accommodate all the pre-allocated data items, as shown for PE_2 from the above example in figure 8.8. The remaining portion of the local cache will be as large as allowed by the local memory of the processing element. Note that this portion needs to have sufficient space to hold a minimum of one data item as this is the maximum that the application process can require at any specific point during a task's computation. To complete a task an application process may require many data items. Each of these data items may in turn replace the previously acquired one in the single available space in the local cache.

The balanced data driven model of computation is well suited to a simple pre-determined even data item allocation scheme. In this model the system controller knows prior to the computation commencing precisely which tasks are to be assigned to which processing elements. The same number of tasks is assigned to each processing element and thus the principal data items for each of these tasks may be pre-allocated evenly amongst the local caches of the appropriate processing elements. Similar knowledge is available to the system controller for the unbalanced data driven model, but in this case the number of tasks allocated to each processing element is not the same and so different numbers of principal data items will be loaded into each resident set. Note that the algorithm used to solve the problem may be such that, even if a data driven model is used and thus the principal data items are known in advance, the additional data items may not be known *a priori*. In this case, these additional data items will have to be fetched into the local caches by the data managers as the computation proceeds and the data requirements become known.

More sophisticated pre-allocation strategies, for example some form of hashing function, are possible to provide resident sets at each processing element. It is also not necessary for each data item to be resident at only one processing element. Should space permit, the same data item may be resident at several local caches. This is particularly useful when a few data items are used frequently by most tasks, as discussed in sections 8.5.3 and 8.5.4 on caching and profiling.

The pre-allocation of resident sets allows the location of a data item to be determined from its unique identifier. A pre-allocated resident set may occupy a significant portion of a local cache and leave little space for other data items which have not been pre-allocated. The shortage of space would require these other data items to be replaced constantly as the computation proceeds. It is quite possible that one data item may be needed often by the same application process either for the same task or for several tasks. If this data item is not in the resident set for that processing element, then there is the danger that the data item will be replaced during the periods that it is not required and thus will have to be re-fetched when it is required once more. Furthermore, despite being pre-allocated, the data items of a resident set may in fact never be required by the processing element to which they were allocated. In the example given earlier, PE_2 has a resident set containing data items $5, \ldots, 8$. Unless there is *a priori* knowledge about the data requirements of the tasks, there is no guarantee that PE_2 will ever require any of these data items from its resident set. In this case, a portion of PE_2's valuable local cache is being used to store data items which are never required, thus reducing the available storage for data items which are needed. Those processing elements that do require data items $5, \ldots, 8$ are going to have to fetch them from PE_2. Not only will the fetches of these data items imply communication delays for the requesting data managers, but also the need for PE_2's data manager to service these requests will imply concurrent activity by its data manager which will detract from the computation of the application process.

The solution to this dilemma is not to pre-allocate resident sets, but to build up such a set as computation proceeds and information is gained by each data manager as to the data items most frequently used by its processing element. Profiling can also assist in establishing these resident sets, as explained in section 8.5.4. The price to pay for this flexibility is that it may no longer be possible for a data manager to determine precisely where a particular data item may be found within the system.

Searching for data at unknown locations

Acquiring a specific data item from an unknown location will necessitate the data manager requesting the router process to 'search' the system for this item. The naive approach would be for the router to send the request to the data manager process of each processing element in turn. If the requested data manager has the necessary data item it will return a copy and then there is no need for the router to request any further processing elements. If the requested data manager does not have the data item then it must send back a not_found message to the router, whereupon the next processing element may be tried. The advantages of this *one-to-one* scheme is that as soon as the required data item is found, no further requests need be issued and only one copy of the data item will ever be returned. However, the communication implications of such a scheme for a large parallel system are substantial. If by some quirk of fate (or Murphy's law), the last processing element to be asked is the one which has the necessary data item, then one request will have resulted in 2 × (*number of* PEs − 1) messages, a quite unacceptable number for large systems. Furthermore, the delay before the data item is finally found will be large, resulting in long application process idle time.

An alternative to this communication intensive one-to-one approach, is for the router process to issue a global broadcast of the request; a *one-to-many* method. A bus used to connect the processing elements is particularly suited to such a communication strategy, although, as discussed in section 2.1.4, a bus is not an appropriate interconnection method for large multiprocessor systems. The broadcast strategy may also be used efficiently on a more suitable interconnection method for large systems, such as interconnections between individual processors. In this case, the router issues the request to its directly-connected neighbouring processing elements. If the data managers at these processing elements have the required data item then it is returned, if not then these neighbouring processing elements in turn propagate the request to their neighbours (excluding the one from which they received the message). In this way, the request propagates through the system like ripples on a pond. The message density inherent in this approach is significantly less than the one-to-one approach, however one disadvantage is that if the requested data item is replicated at several local caches, then several copies of the same data item will be returned to the requesting data manager, when only one is required. How such a broadcast is implemented and techniques for reducing these redundant messages are described fully in sections 9.2.3 and 9.3.

For very large multiprocessor systems, even this one-to-many approach to discovering the unknown location of a data item may be too costly in terms of communication latency and its contribution to message density within the system. A compromise of the direct access capabilities of the pre-allocated resident set approach and the flexibility of the dynamic composition of the local caches is the notion of a *directory* of data item locations.

In this approach, it is not necessary to maintain a particular data item at a fixed processing element. We can introduce the notion of a *home*-processing element that knows where that data item is, while the data item is currently located at the *owner*-processing element. The home-processing element is fixed and its address may be determined from the identifier of the data item. The home-processing element

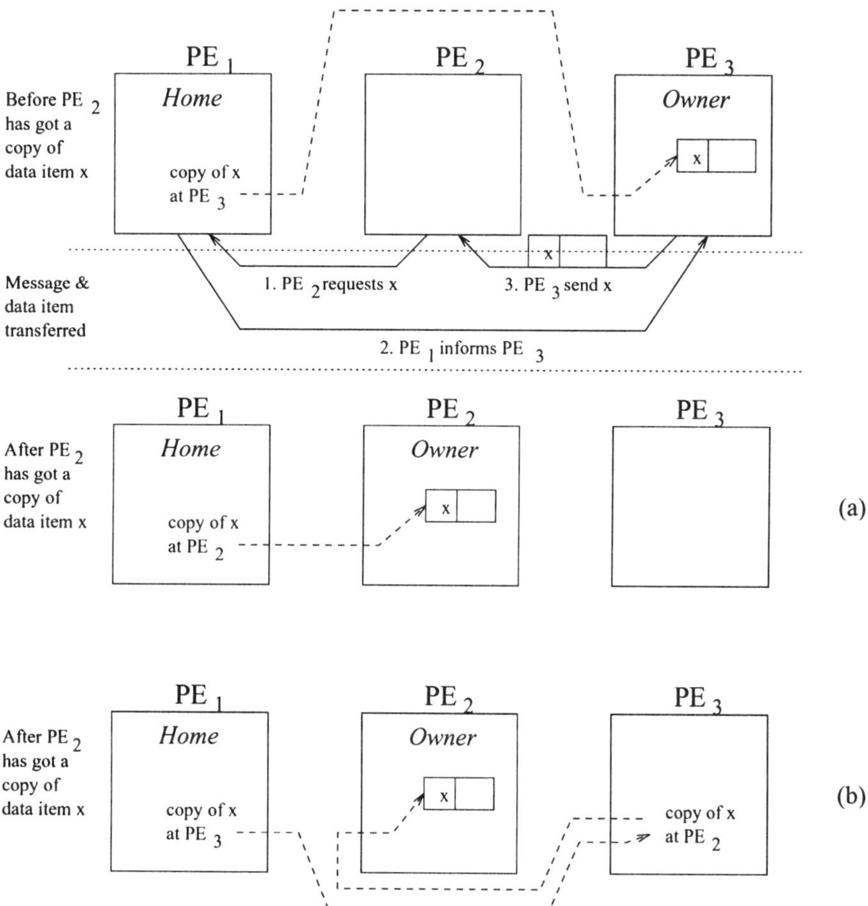

Figure 8.9   An example with a home-processing element PE_1, an owner PE_3, and a request by PE_2

knows which processing element is currently owning the data item. Should this data item be subsequently moved and the one at the owner-processing element removed, then either the home-processing element must be informed as to the new location of the data item, as shown in figure 8.9(a), or the previous owner-processing element must now maintain a pointer to this new location, as shown in figure 8.9(b). (For clarity no internal processes are shown at each processing element in these figures.) The first scheme has the advantage that a request message can be forwarded directly from the home-processing element to the current owner. The second strategy may be necessary, at least for a while after the data item has been moved from an owner, to cope with any requests forwarded by the home-processing element before it has received the latest location update.

Finally, it is also possible to do away with the notion of a home-processing element, by adding a hierarchy of directories. Each directory on a processing element 'knows' which data items are present on the processing element. If the required data item is not present, a directory higher up in the hierarchy might know if it is somewhere nearby. If that directory does not know, a higher level directory can be checked. This is much like the organisation of libraries; you first check the local library for a book, if they do not have it you ask the central library, and so on until you finally query the national library. With this organisation there is always a directory that knows the whereabout of the data item, but it is very likely that the location of the data item will be found long before asking the highest directory. (The Data Diffusion Machine [182] and KSR-1 [121] use a similar strategy implemented in hardware.)

8.4 Consistency

Copies of *read-only* data items may exist in numerous local caches within the system without any need to 'keep track' of where all the copies are. However, if copies of *read-write* data items exist then, in a virtual shared memory system, there is the danger that the data items may become inconsistent. The example in figure 8.10 illustrates this problem of inconsistency. Suppose that we have two processing elements PE_1 and PE_2, and a data item y with a value 0, that is located at processing element PE_1. Processing element PE_2 needs y, so it requests and gets a copy of y. The data manager on processing element PE_2 decides to keep this copy for possible future reference. When the application at processing element PE_1 updates the value of y, for example by overwriting it with the value 1, processing element PE_2 will have a *stale* copy of y. This situation is called *inconsistent*: if the application running at processing element PE_1 requests y it will get the new value (1), while the application at processing element PE_2 will still read the old value of y (0). This situation will exist until the data manager at processing element PE_2 decides to evict y from its local memory.

The programming model of a physical shared memory system maintains only one copy of any data item: the copy in the shared memory. There is only one copy so the data items cannot become inconsistent. Hence, naive virtual shared memory differs from physical shared memory in that virtual shared memory can become inconsistent.

To maintain consistency all copies of the data items will have to be 'tracked down' at certain times during the parallel computation. Once again one-to-one or one-to-many methods could be used to determine the unknown locations of copies of the data items. If the directory approach is used then it will be necessary to maintain a complete 'linked list' through all copies of any data item, where each copy knows where the next copy is, or it knows that there are no more copies. A consistency operation is performed on this list by sending a message to the first copy on the list, which then ripples through the list. These operations thus take a time proportional in the number of copies. This is expensive if there are many copies, so it can be more efficient to use a tree structure (where the operation needs logarithmic time). (A combination of a software and a hardware tree directory of this form is used in the LimitLESS directory [37].)

There are several ways to deal with this inconsistency problem. We will discuss three options: data items are kept consistent at all times (known as sequential

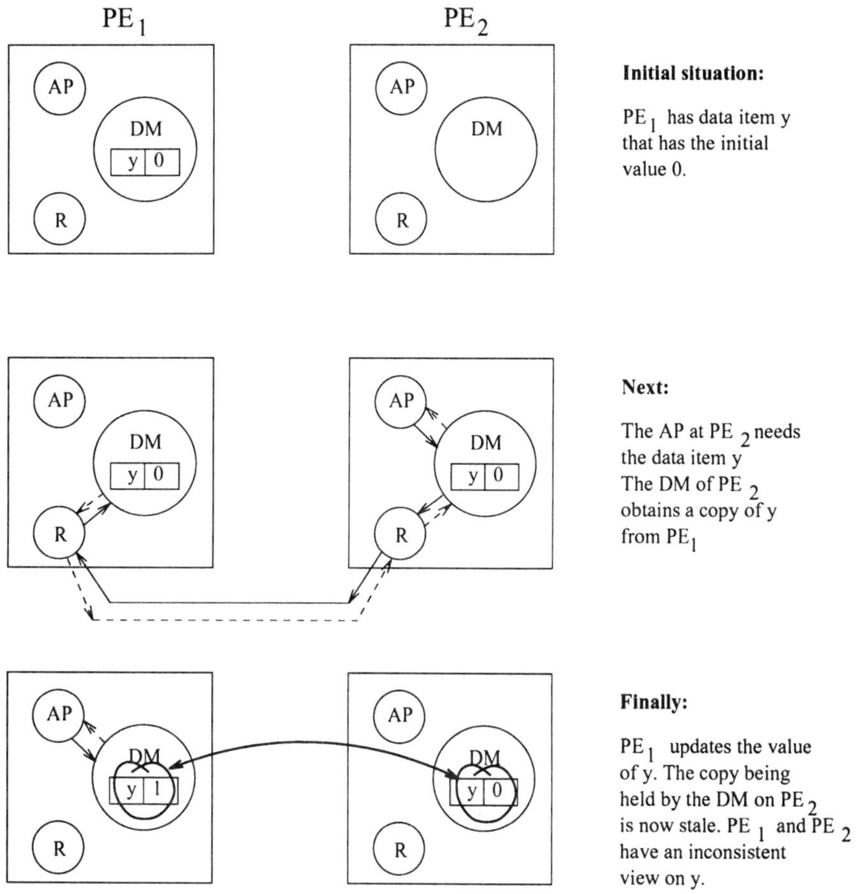

Figure 8.10   An example how an inconsistency arises. There are two processing elements, PE_1 and PE_2 and a data item y. PE_2 keeps a copy of y, while y is updated at PE_1.

consistency); the actual problem somehow copes with the inconsistencies (known as weak consistency); and finally, inconsistent data items are allowed to live for a well-defined period (the particular scheme discussed here is known as release consistency).

8.4.1 Keeping the data items consistent

The first option is that the data manager will keep the data items consistent at all times. To see how the data items can be kept consistent, observe first that there are two conditions that must be met before a data item can become inconsistent. Firstly, the data item must be duplicated; as long as there is only a single copy of the data item, it cannot be inconsistent. Secondly, some processing element must update one of the copies, without updating the other copies. This observation leads to two protocols that the data manager can observe to enforce consistency, while still allowing copies to be made:

1. Ensure that there is not more than a single copy of the data item when it is updated. This means that before a write all but one of the copies must be deleted. This solution is known as an *invalidating protocol*.

2. Ensure that all copies of the data item are replaced when it is updated. This solution is known as an *updating protocol*.

It is relatively straightforward to check that the invalidating option will always work; all copies are always identical, because a write only occurs when there is only a single copy. In the example, the copy of y at processing element PE_2 will be destroyed before y is updated on processing element PE_1.

For the updating protocol to be correct, the protocol must ensure that all copies are replaced 'at the same time'. Suppose that this is not the case: in the example the value on processing element PE_1 might be updated, while processing element PE_2 still has an old value for y. If the data managers running on processing elements PE_1 and PE_2 communicate, they can find out about this inconsistency. In order for the update protocol to work, the updating data manager must either ensure that no other data manager is accessing the data item while it is being updated, or that it is impossible for any communication (or other update) to overtake this update.

It is not easy to decide in general whether an invalidating or an updating protocol is better. Below are two examples that show that invalidating and updating protocols both have advantages and disadvantages. In both cases we assume that the problem is running on a large number of processing elements, and that there is a single shared data item that is initially replicated over all processing elements.

1. A task, or tasks, being performed by an application process at one processing element might require that the data item be updated at this data manager many times, without any of the other processing elements using it. An updating protocol will update all copies on all processing elements during every update, even though the copies are not being used on any of the other processing elements.

   An invalidating protocol is more efficient, because it will invalidate all outstanding copies once, whereupon the application process can continue updating the data item without extra communication.

2. Suppose that instead of ignoring the data item, all other processing elements do need the updated value. An invalidating protocol will invalidate all copies and update the data item, whereupon all other processing elements have to fetch the value again. This fetch is on demand, which means that they will have to wait on the data item.

   An updating protocol does a better job since it distributes the new value, avoiding the need for the other processing elements to wait for it.

There is a case for (and against) both protocols. It is for this reason that these two protocols are sometimes combined. This gives a protocol that, for example, invalidates all copies that have not been used since the last update, and updates the copies that were used since the last update. Although these hybrid protocols are potentially more efficient, they are unfortunately often more complex than a pure invalidating or updating protocol.

8.4.2 *Weak consistency: repair consistency on request*

The option to maintain sequential consistency is an expensive one. In general, an application process is allowed to proceed with its computation only after the invalidate or update has been completed. In the example of the invalidating protocol, all outstanding copies must have been erased and the local copy must have been updated before the application process can proceed. This idle time may be an unacceptable overhead. One of the ways to reduce this overhead is to forget about maintaining consistency automatically. Instead, the local cache will stay inconsistent until the application process orders the data manager to repair the inconsistency.

An example shows what the application processes must do in order to work on a weak consistent system. There are two application processes at PE_1 and PE_2, that share two data items with identifiers X and Y. Suppose that the tasks being performed at these application processes consists of the alternate phases shown in figure 8.11. First PE_1 will work on X and PE_2 will work on Y. During the second phase PE_1 will work on Y and PE_2 will work on X. Then PE_1 will work on X again and PE_2 on Y, and so on.

If we start with a situation where X and Y are at processing elements PE_1 and PE_2 respectively, then the local caches are consistent. Y will then be used (and updated) by PE_1 and X will be used by PE_2. At this moment, there are stale copies of X and Y around, as sketched in figure 8.12. This will not be a problem as long as no process ever uses these copies. When the third phase is entered, X and Y will be used on their old processing elements however. The stale copies must therefore be made consistent before this phase is entered. The same must be done before phase 4 is entered. Only the application process knows when the data items must be made consistent, and so it must issue an explicit command, SEND `make_consistent` X TO DM, or SEND `make_consistent` Y TO DM to instruct the data manager to make the appropriate data items consistent, as shown in figure 8.13.

There are two important advantages of weak consistency. Firstly, the local cache is made consistent at certain points in the task execution only, reducing the overhead. Secondly, local caches can be made consistent in parallel. Recall for example, the updating protocol of the previous section. In a weakly consistent system we can envisage that every write to a data item is asynchronously broadcasted to all remote copies. Asynchronously means that the processing element performing the write continues whether the update has been completed or not. Only when a consistency command is executed must the application process wait until all outstanding updates are completed. In the same way, a weakly consistent invalidating protocol can invalidate remote copies in parallel. These optimisations lead to further performance improvement. The disadvantage of weak consistency is the need for the explicit commands within the algorithm at each application process so that when a task is being executed, at the appropriate point, the data manager can be instructed to make the local cache consistent.

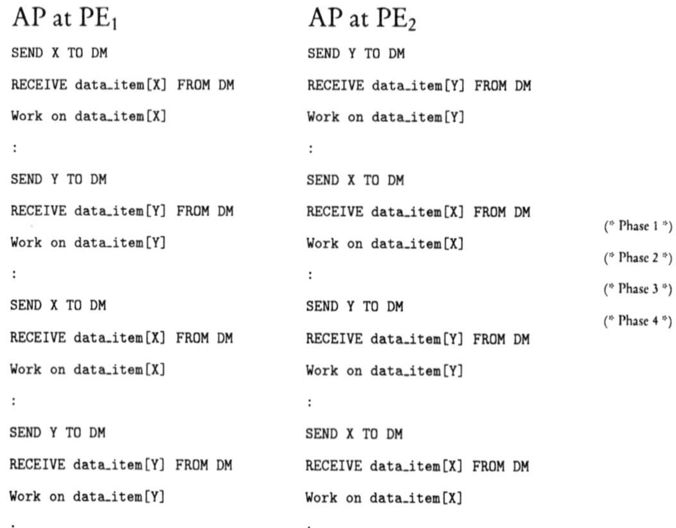

Figure 8.11   Example problem that requires consistency

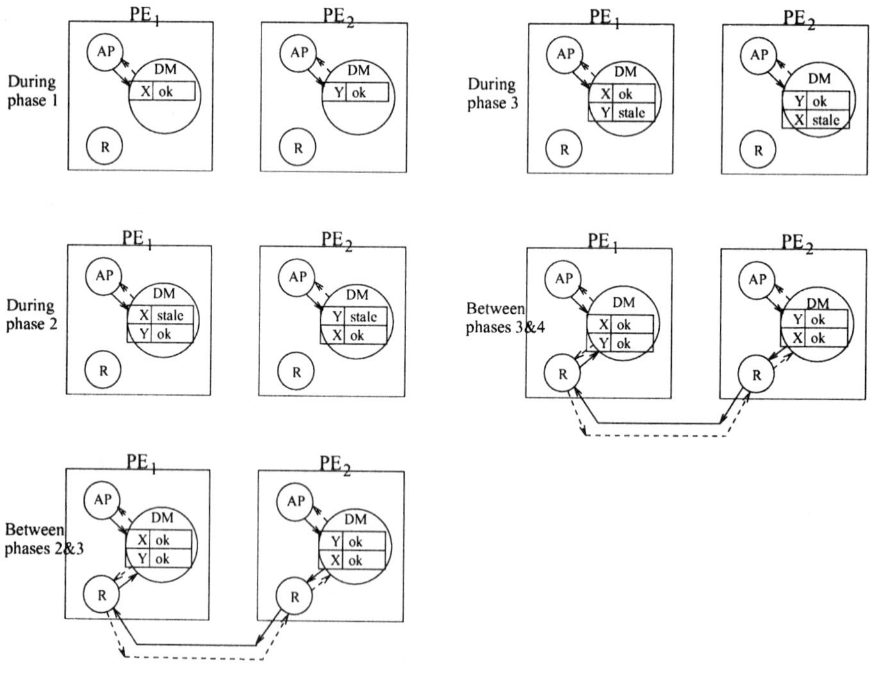

Figure 8.12   The communications required to get the program of figure 8.11 to work.

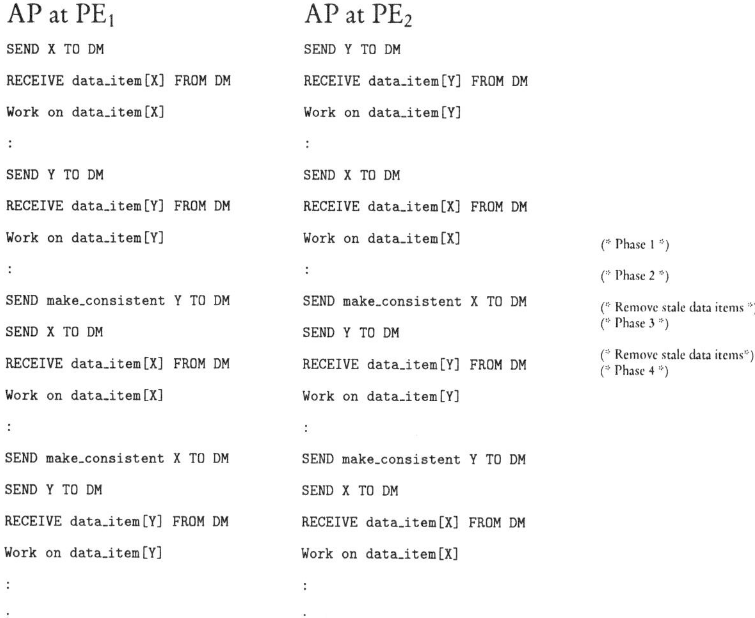

Figure 8.13   The program of figure 8.11 including explicit consistency operations.

8.4.3 *Repair consistency on synchronisation: Release consistency*

A weak consistency model as described above requires the programmer of the algorithm to ensure consistency at any moment in time. Observe the last example program in figure 8.13; the inconsistency need only be repaired when the algorithm goes from one phase to the next. Release consistency is based on the observation that algorithms do not go from one phase to the other without first synchronising. So it suffices to make the local caches consistent during the synchronisation operation. This means that immediately after each synchronisation the local caches are guaranteed to be consistent.

In the case of the example algorithm in figure 8.13 there will be some synchronisation operation between each phase. During each of these operations the local caches will be made consistent. This is in general slightly more often than strictly necessary, but it is far less often than would be the case when using sequential consistency. More importantly, the application process itself does not have to make the local caches consistent any more, it is done 'invisibly'.

Note that although invisible, consistency is only restored during an explicit synchronisation operation; release consistency still behaves very differently from sequential consistency. As an example, an application process at PE₁ can poll a data item in a loop, waiting for the data item to be changed by the application process at PE₂. Under sequential consistency any update to the data item will be propagated, and cause the application process at PE₁ to exit the loop. Under release consistency updates do not need to be propagated until a synchronisation point, and because it does not recognise that the polling loop is actually a synchronisation point the application process at PE_1 might be looping for ever.

8.4.4 Summary of consistency models

The above models, sequential-, release- and weak-consistency, are only three out of a spectrum of consistency models that have been created over the past years. The choice to opt for a strong model or for a less strong model is a choice between performance on the one hand, and ease of implementation on the other. Sequential consistency has a very simple and clear behaviour, the programmer can reason what will happen to the data items. Reasoning about weaker consistency is much harder.

This is not to say that weaker consistency models are useless. There are problems where weak or release consistency is perfectly sufficient, and so the debate about the best consistency model will continue.

8.5 Minimising the Impact of Remote Data Requests

Failure to find a required data item locally means that the data manager has to acquire this data item from elsewhere within the system. The time to fetch this data item and, therefore, the application process idle time, can be significant. This *latency* is difficult to predict and may not be repeatable due to other factors, such as current message densities within the system. The overall aim of data management is to maximise effective processing element computation by minimising the occurrence and effects of remote data fetches. A number of techniques may be used to reduce this latency by:

Hiding the Latency: – overlapping the communication with the computation, by:

> **Prefetching** – anticipating data items that will be required
>
> **Multi-threading** – keeping the processing element busy with other useful computation during the remote fetch

Minimising the Latency – reducing the time associated with a remote fetch by:

> **Caching & profiling** – exploiting any coherence that may exist in the problem domain

8.5.1 Prefetching

If it is known at the start of the computation which data items will be required by each task then these data items can be *prefetched* by the data manager so that they are available locally when required. The data manager thus issues the requests for the data items before they are actually required and in this way overlaps the communication required for the remote fetches with the ongoing computation of the application process. This is in contrast with the simple fetch-upon-demand strategy where the data manager only issues the external request for a data item at the moment it is requested by the application process and it is not found in the local cache.

By treating its local cache as a 'circular buffer' the data manager can be loading

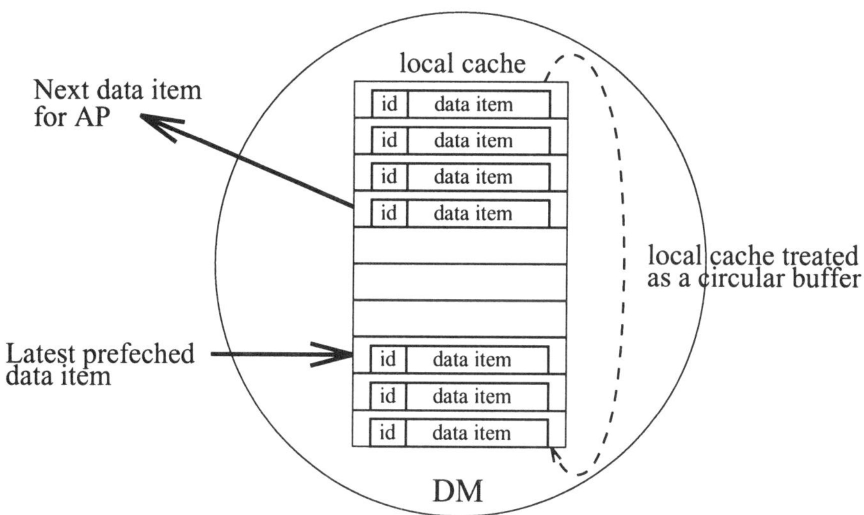

Figure 8.14 Storing the prefetched data items in the local cache

prefetched data items into one end of the buffer while the application process is requesting the data items from the other end, as shown in figure 8.14. The 'speed' at which the data manager can prefetch the data items will be determined by the size of the local cache and the rate at which the application process is 'using' the data items.

This knowledge about the required data items may be known *a priori* by the nature of the problem. For example, in the parallel solution of the thermal radiation simulation discussed as the case study in Chapter 7, the data manager knows that each task, that is the computation of a single row of the matrix of form factors, requires all the environment's patch data. The order in which these data items are considered is unimportant, as long as all data items are considered. The data manager can thus continually prefetch those data items which have yet to be considered by the current task. Note that in this problem, because all the data items are required by every task and the order is unimportant (we are assuming that the local cache is not sufficiently big to hold all these data items), those data items which remain in the local cache at the end of one task are also required by the subsequent task. Thus, at the start of the next task, the first data item in the local cache can be forwarded to the application process and prefetching can commence once more as soon as this has happened.

The choice of computation model adopted can also provide the information required by the data manager in order to prefetch. The principal data items for both the balanced and unbalanced data driven models will be known by the system controller before the computation commences. Giving this information to the data manager will enable it to prefetch these data items. A prefetch strategy can also be used for principal data items within the preferred bias task allocation strategy for the demand driven computation model, as described in section 7.5. Knowledge of its processing element's conceptual region can be exploited by the data manager to prefetch the principal data items within this region of the problem domain.

8.5.2 Multi-threading

Any failure by the data manager to have the requested data item available locally for the application process will result in idle time unless the processing element can be kept busy doing some other useful computation.

One possibility is for the application process to save the current state of a task and commence a new task whenever a requested data item is not available locally. When the requested data item is finally forthcoming either this new task could be suspended and the original task resumed, or processing of the new task could be continued until it is completed. This new task may be suspended awaiting a data fetch and so the original task may be resumed. Saving the state of a task may require a large amount of memory and indeed, several states may need to be saved before one requested data item finally arrives. Should the nature of the problem allow these stored tasks to in turn be considered as task packets, then this method has the additional advantage that these task packets could potentially be completed by another processing element in the course of load balancing, as explained in section 7.4.2 on distributed task management.

Another possible option is multi-threading. In this method there is not only one, but several application processes on each processing element controlled by an application process controller (APC), as shown in figure 8.15. Each application process is known as a separate *thread* of computation. Now, although one thread may be suspended awaiting a remote data item, the other threads may still be able to continue. It may not be feasible to determine just how many of these application processes will be necessary to avoid the case where all of them are suspended awaiting data. However, if there are sufficient threads (and of course sufficient tasks) then the processing element should always be performing useful computation. Note that multi-threading is similar to the Bulk Synchronous Parallel paradigm discussed in section 3.3.

One disadvantage of this approach is the overhead incurred by the additional context switching between all the application processes and the application process controller, as well as the other system software processes: the router, local controller, task manager and data manager, that are all resident on the same processor. A variation of multiple active threads is to have several application processes existing on each processing element, but to only have one of them active at any time and have the application process controller manage the scheduling of these processes explicitly from information provided by the data manager. When an application process' data item request cannot be satisfied locally, that process will remain descheduled until the data item is forthcoming. The data manager is thus in a position to inform the application process controller to activate another application process, and only reactivate the original application process once the required data has been obtained. This process is outlined in the code segment below. Note the application process controller schedules a new application process by sending it a task to perform. Having made its initial demand for a task to the application process controller (and not the task manager as discussed in section 7.3.2)

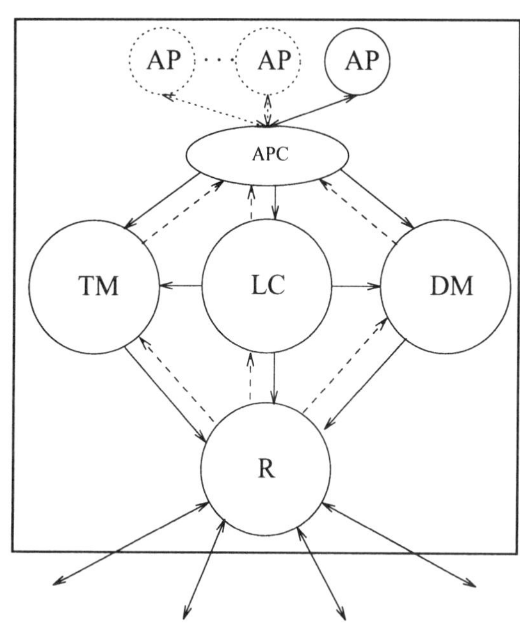

Figure 8.15 Several application processes per processing element

an application process will remain descheduled until explicitly rescheduled by the application process controller.

```
PROCESS Application_Process(AP_id)
  Begin
    busy := TRUE  (* continue whilst tasks remain *)
    WHILE busy DO
      Begin
        (* demand task *)
        SEND request_for_task TO APC (* assume DEMAND driven *)
        (* task only received when APC schedules this AP *)
        RECEIVE task FROM APC

        (* compute task *)
        WHILE more data items are needed DO
          Begin
            SEND id of required data item TO DM
            RECEIVE data_item[id] FROM Data Manager
            (* if this data item is not forthcoming then this *)
            (* process is descheduled until it is available  *)
            Compute_Further(data_item[id])
          End
      End
  End (* AP *)
```

```
PROCESS Application_Process_Controller()
  Begin
    busy := TRUE
    current_AP_id := 1  (* id of currently active AP *)
    SEND next_task TO AP[current_AP_id]
    WHILE busy DO
      PRIORITISED INPUT ALTERNATIVES
        1. RECEIVE id FROM AP[current_AP_id] (* data request *)
            Begin
              SEND id TO DM
              RECEIVE message FROM DM
              IF (message = data_item[id]) THEN
                SEND data_item[id] TO AP[current_AP_id]
              ELSEIF (message = not_found) THEN
                Begin
                  (* select next AP *)
                  current_AP_id := current_AP_id + 1
                  (* schedules this AP *)
                  SEND next_task TO AP[current_AP_id]
                End
              ENDIF
            End

        2. (* other alternatives *)
  End (* APC *)


PROCESS Data_Manager()
  Begin
    busy := TRUE
    WHILE busy DO
      PRIORITISED INPUT ALTERNATIVES
        1. RECEIVE id FROM APC
            IF (data_item is available locally) THEN
              SEND data_item[id] TO APC
            ELSE
              Begin
                SEND not_found TO APC
                SEND external_request_for_id TO R
              End
            ENDIF

        2. (* other alternatives *)
  End (* DM *)
```

Both forms of multi-threading have other limitations. The first of these is the extra memory requirements each thread places on the processing element's local memory. The more memory that each thread will require, for local constants and variables etc., the less memory there will be available for the local cache and thus fewer data items will be able to be kept locally by the data manager. A 'catch-22' situation now arises as fewer local data items implies more remote data fetches and thus the possible need for yet more threads to hide this increase in latency.

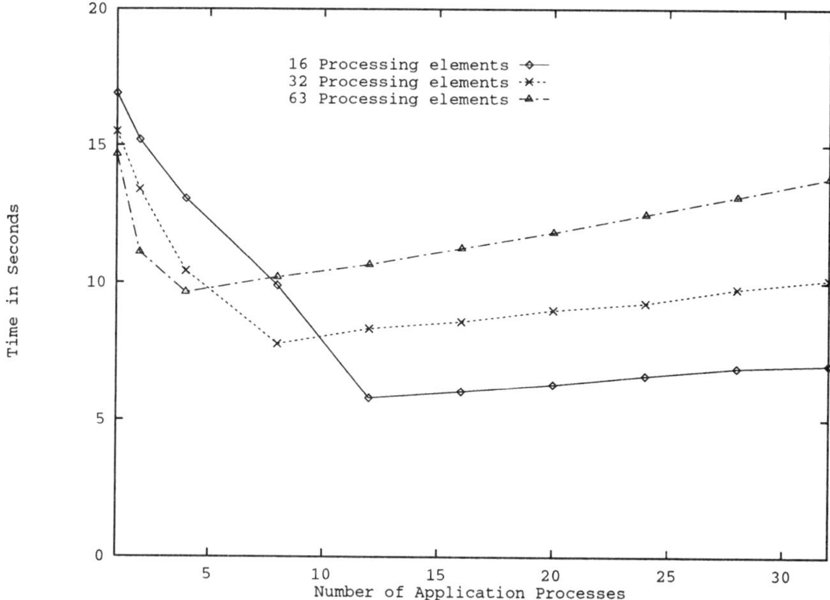

Figure 8.16 Problem solution times using multi-threading

The second difficulty of a large number of threads running on the same processing element is the unacceptably heavy overhead that may be placed on the data manager when maintaining the local cache. For example, a dilemma may exist as to whether a recently fetched data item for one thread should be overwritten before it has been used if its 'slot' in the local cache is required by the currently active thread.

Figure 8.16 shows results for a multi-threaded application. The graph shows the time in seconds to solve a complex parallel ray tracing problem with large data requirements using more than one application process per processing element. As can be seen, increasing the number of application processes per processing element produces a performance improvement until a certain number of threads have been added. Beyond this point, the overheads of having the additional threads are greater than the benefit gained, and thus the times to solve the problem once more increase. The number of threads at which the overheads outweigh the benefits gained is lower for larger numbers of processing elements. This is because the more application processes there are per processing element, the larger the message output from each processing element will be (assuming an average number of remote fetches per thread). As the average distances the remote data fetches have to travel in larger systems is greater, the impact of increasing numbers of messages on the overall system density is more significant and thus the request latency will be higher. Adding more threads now no longer helps overcome communication delays, but in fact the increasing number of messages actually exacerbates the communication difficulties. Ways must be found of dynamically scheduling the optimum number of application processes at each processing element depending on the current system message densities.

Despite these shortcomings, multi-threading does work well, especially for low numbers of threads and is a useful technique for avoiding idle time in the face of unpredictable data item requirements. Remember that multiple threads are only needed at a processing element if a prefetch strategy is not possible and the data item required by one thread was not available locally. If ways can be found to try and guess which data items are likely to be required next then, if the data manager is right at least some of the time, the number of remote fetches-on-demand will be reduced. Caching and profiling assist the data manager with these predictions.

8.5.3 Caching

Cache memories are used in conventional computers as high-speed buffers between the processor and main memory. The access time of the caches are typically ten times faster than a conventional memory access. Arranging that the data items frequently in use by the processor are kept in the cache, can thus significantly improve the average memory access time.

A cache normally consists of two parts: a *directory* of the items in the cache, and the *cache memory* itself. The cache memory is divided into a number of uniform sized *block frames*. Each of these correspond to one of the blocks which make up the main memory. The design of a cache memory is determined by its *placement policy*, which specifies the mapping from the blocks of main memory to those of the cache, and the *replacement policy* which determines which entries in the cache must be overwritten to make way for new arrivals.

In data management strategies, the local caches at each data manager assume the rôle of the cache memories of conventional processors (hence the choice of the name 'local cache'). The local caches of other processing elements and the secondary storage of the file manager are the equivalent of the 'main memory' of conventional processors. The access time for a data manager to fetch data item from these external 'memories' will be substantially higher than a fetch from its local cache. We may also use the terminology of traditional memory management and say that a *cache-hit* occurs if a data item is found in the local cache when required by an application process, and a *cache-miss* occurs when the data item is not found and a remote fetch must be initiated.

Coherence

In many problems the sequence in which references are made to data items is not random, but occurs in a somewhat predictable manner. This is due to a property which has been termed *coherence* (also known as *locality*); it is observed that the data item requests which are generated by a 'typical' program tend to be restricted to a small subset of the whole problem. Conventional virtual memory management systems depend on exploiting this feature for their success. Coherence refers to three concepts:

1. Temporal coherence. If a problem has good *temporal coherence* it means that if a task uses a data item at time T, it is likely that the task will use it again in the near future, at time $T + \delta t$.

2. Spatial coherence, in the problem domain. If a problem shows good *problem domain coherence* it means that if a data item at position A of the problem domain is accessed, it is likely that items in the neighbourhood of A $(A \pm \delta a)$ will be accessed soon.

3. Spatial coherence, in the network. If an application has good *network coherence* it means that data items that are available on processing element PE_1 are more likely to be used at processing element PE_1 and the processing elements in the neighbourhood of PE_1 than on processing elements further away.

All virtual shared memory systems benefit from this last form of coherence. If data is used that is already nearby, there will be less network traffic. As we will see in Chapter 9 the definition of 'neighbourhood' is highly configuration dependent; there are few neighbours in a ring network, but many neighbours in the hypercube or AMP configurations outlined in Chapter 9.

As an example of the significance of spatial coherence in the problem domain, in [85] a *normalised cumulative usage frequency* was defined and used to measure the frequencies of reference of the problem domain for a ray tracer application. The graphs produced illustrated immediately the coherence present in image space; that far from references being made uniformly to entries of the domain, a small subset of the entries account for a very large fraction of the domain. In some cases more than 70% of all references were made to as little as 10% of the domain. Although the temporal effects were excluded, these results are indicative that some uniformity amongst data references is evident. Techniques for exploiting coherence of reference in virtual memory systems can be applied to solutions when only limited memory resources are available.

A simple example of spatial coherence of the problem domain is shown in figure 8.17. This figure is derived from figure 4.9 which showed how the principal data item (PDI) and additional data items (ADIs) made up a task. In figure 8.17 we can see that task i and task j come from the same region of the problem domain and spatial coherence of the problem domain has meant that these two tasks have two additional data items in common. Task k, on the other hand, from a different region of the problem domain, requires only one additional data item which is not common to either task i or task j.

Temporal coherence is important for any system that relies on caching. A cache improves performance only if the data is reused, which is the case when the application has good temporal coherence. Almost all implementations of virtual shared memory rely on caching, so the more temporal coherence a problem exhibits, the better suited the problem is for implementing in parallel on a system utilising virtual shared memory.

Placement policies

Of the four basic placement policies which have been used in memory management systems, namely *direct*, *fully-associative*, *set-associative* and *sector* mappings, only

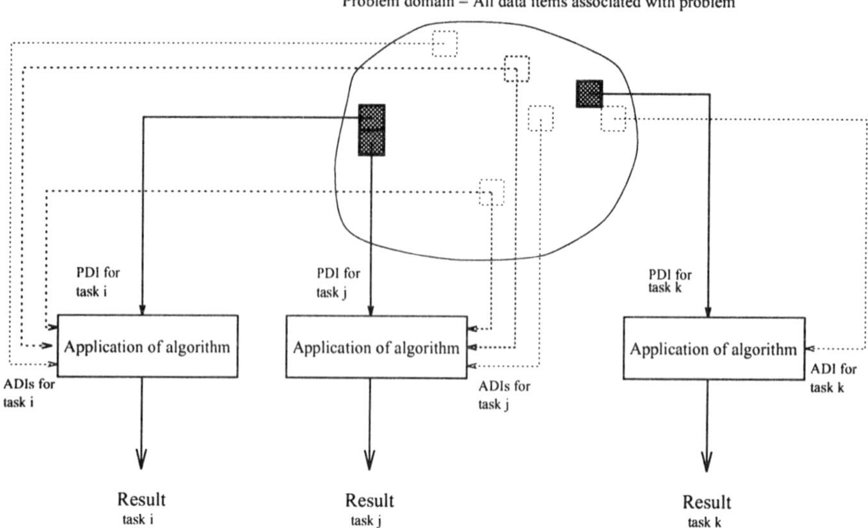

Figure 8.17   Common additional data items due to spatial coherence of the problem domain

the first three are suitable for data management in message passing systems, and the latter is not discussed further here [85]. In the following description of direct, fully-associative and set-associative mappings for the cache structure, we will assume a local cache with M 'slots' and a problem domain of N data items, with $N > M$.

Direct mapping: This placement policy can be described by the simple mapping:

$$\text{object } i \rightarrow \text{slot } (i \textbf{ MOD } M)$$

There is a disadvantage when using direct mapping. Because two or more memory locations can map to the same cache location, a cache replacement may occur even though the cache is not full. This is inefficient, especially when the data items concerned are used frequently.

Fully-associative mapping: With this mapping strategy, an entry in memory can map to any position in the cache:

$$\text{object } i \rightarrow \text{any slot}$$

Such a flexible placement strategy can be complex and expensive to implement. The whole cache may need to be examined in order to determine the appropriate cache location of any particular data item. The inefficiency of this extensive search can result in longer access times than those of the fully-associative mapping, despite the higher hit ratio of this approach.

Set-associative mapping This mapping represents a compromise between the simplicity of the direct mapping and the flexibility of the fully-associative mapping.

In this scheme, the cache is divided into K partitions, each partition consisting of $E = \frac{M}{K}$ slots.

The mapping is then described by:

$$\text{ojbect } i \rightarrow \text{ any slot in partition } i \textbf{ MOD } K$$

A straightforward mapping, comparable with direct mapping, determines the partition in which a data item may reside. This partition must then be searched to test if the data item is present.

Replacement policies

A replacement policy is necessary to determine which local cache positions, and thus which data items in the local cache, will be overwritten when the cache becomes full. If direct mapping is used, then the local cache position to be overwritten is known. If either of the other mapping strategies are used, then an appropriate chache position must be determined before the replacement (a, so-called, *cache-write*) can occur. A popular replacement policy is the *Least Recently Used*) (LRU) strategy. Each time a data item is referenced in the cache, it is marked as the most recently used, and all other data items are adjusted accordingly. When a replacement is necessary, the data item which was least recently used is chosen for overwriting.

The difficulty of deciding which data item to replace is greatly exacerbated when multi-threading is used. An important data item for one thread may not be used by another. When using the policy of only one active thread the least recently used replacement strategy is not appropriate for those data items not used by the active thread. As discussed in section 8.5.2, it is particularly important that the data item which has recently been fetched for a delayed application process is not overwritten before there has been a chance to forward it to the stalled process. One solution to this dilemma is to subdivide the local cache into separate portions for use by each thread, but of course this limits the size of the local cache 'available' to each thread. This is likely to increase the number of remote fetches per thread unless there is good temporal coherence within each task or good spatial coherence within the problem domain between tasks. The preferred bias task allocation strategy described in section 7.5 is one way of trying to ensure coherence between tasks on the same processing element, profiling is another.

8.5.4 Profiling

Although primarily a task management technique, profiling is used explicitly to assist with data management, and so is discussed here. At the start of the solution of many problems, no knowledge exists as to the data requirements of any of the tasks. (If this knowledge did exist then a prefetching strategy would be applicable.) Monitoring the solution of a single task provides a list of all the data items required by that task. If the same monitoring action is carried out for all tasks then at the completion of the problem, a complete 'picture' of the data requirements of all tasks would be known. Profiling attempts to predict the data requirements of future tasks from the list of data requirements of completed tasks.

Any spatial coherence in the problem domain will provide the profiling technique with a good estimate of the future data requirements of those tasks from a similar region of the problem domain. The data manager can now use this profiling information to prefetch those data items which are likely to be used by subsequent tasks being performed at that processing element. If the data manager is always correct with its prediction then profiling provides an equivalent situation to prefetching in which the application process is never delayed awaiting a remote fetch. Note in this case there is no need for multi-threading.

Thus, the more successful the predictions are from the profiling information, the higher will be the cache-hit ratios. From figure 8.17 we can see that if the completion of task i was used to profile the data item requirements for task j then, thanks to the spatial coherence of task i to task j in the problem domain, the data manager would have a 66% success rate for the additional data items for task j. However, a similar prediction for the additional data items for task k would have a 0% success rate and result in a 100% cache-miss, so the additional data items for task k would have to be fetched-on-demand.

8.6 Data Management for Multi-Stage Problems

In section 7.2.1 we discussed the algorithmic and data dependencies that can arise in problems which exhibit more than one distinct stage. In such problems, the results from one stage become the principal data items for the subsequent stage as was shown in figure 7.3. So, in addition to ensuring the application processes are kept supplied with data items during one stage, the data manager also needs to be aware as to how the partial results from one stage of the computation are stored at each processing element in anticipation of the following stage.

This balancing of partial result storage could be achieved statically by all the results of a stage being returned to the system controller. At the end of that current stage the system controller is in a position to distribute these data evenly as the principal and additional data items for the next stage of the problem. The communication of these potentially large data packets twice, once during the previous stage to the system controller and again from the system controller to specific processing elements, obviously may impose an enormous communication overhead. A better static distribution strategy might be to leave the results in place at the processing elements for the duration of the stage and then have them distributed from the processing elements in a manner prescribed by the system controller. Note that in such a scheme the local cache of each processing element must be able to hold not only the principal and additional data items for the current stage, but also have space in which to store these partial results in anticipation of the forthcoming stage. It is important that these partial results are kept separate so that they are not inadvertently overwritten by data items during the current stage.

In a demand driven model of computation the uneven computational complexity may result in a few processing elements completing many more tasks than others. This produces a flaw in the second static storage strategy. The individual processing elements may simply not have sufficient space in their local cache to store more than their fair share of the partial results until the end of the stage.

Two dynamic methods of balancing this partial result data may also be considered.

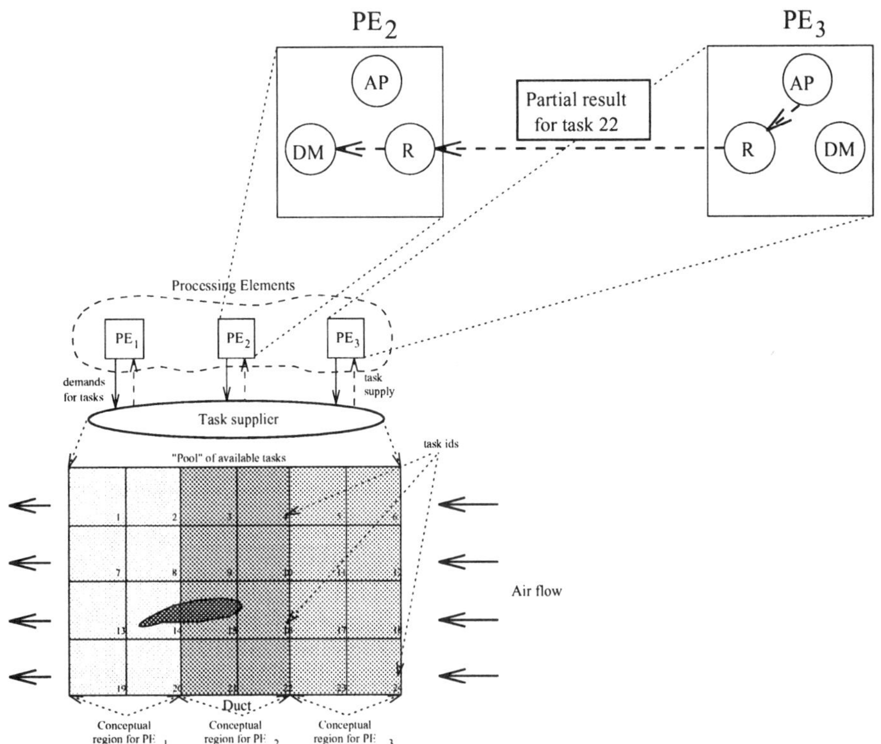

Figure 8.18 Storing a partial result at its conceptual processing element

Adoption of the preferred bias task management strategy, as discussed in section 7.5, can greatly facilitate the correct distribution of any partial results. Any results produced by one processing element from another's conceptual portion, due to task load balancing, may be sent directly to this other processing element. The initial conceptual allocation of tasks ensures that the destination processing element will have sufficient storage for the partial result. In figure 8.18, let us assume that, to achieve load balancing, PE_3 computes *task*$_{22}$ from the conceptual region of PE_2. When the application process at PE_3 has completed the task, the partial result is sent for storage to the data manager at PE_2.

If this conceptual allocation is not possible, or not desirable, then balancing the partial results dynamically requires each processing element to be kept informed of the progress of all other processing elements. This may be achieved by each processing element broadcasting a short message on completion of every task to all other processing elements. To ensure that this information is as up to date as possible, it is advisable that these messages have a special high priority so that they may be handled immediately by the router processes, by-passing the normal queue of messages. Once a data manager's local cache reaches its capacity the results from the next task are sent in the direction of the processing element that is known to have completed the least number of tasks and, therefore, the one which will have the most available space. To further reduce the possible time that this data packet may exist in the system, any processing element on its path which has storage capacity available may absorb the packet and thus not route it further.

8.7 Summary

Problems with small data requirements, or those which only require a subset of the problem domain, may be implemented with little need for a sophisticated data management strategy. In these cases the entire problem domain or the appropriate subset can be accommodated at every processing element. We say that the processing elements possess a world model of the data. Apart from the initial effort to distribute this data to the processing elements there is no further need to fetch data items as the computation proceeds.

The local memory available at each processing element should not restrict the problems we would like to solve in parallel. If the size of the problem domain is too large to be accommodated in its entirety at any processing element then it may be distributed across all the processing elements and, if necessary, across the secondary storage devices as well. This distribution of the problem domain means that processing elements may now have to fetch data items from elsewhere in the system as the computation proceeds. A data manager process is introduced at each processing element to minimise the time that an application process has to wait for a remotely fetched data item. No apparent delay in having a data request satisfied will provide an application process with the illusion that the entire problem domain is indeed available locally. In such a situation the application process has a virtual shared world model. All the distributed locations of the problem domain in this desirable state comprise the virtual shared memory.

In a parallel implementation, computational idle time should be avoided at all costs and so it may be necessary for the data manager to have the support of other techniques, such as multi-threading, to reduce this idle time should the delay for a remote fetch be unavoidable. Figure 8.19 shows how the correct data management strategy should be chosen.

As we have said, a small data requirement may be dealt with by the simple world data model. For large data requirements it is helpful to know whether these requirements are known or unknown. Known requirements can be prefetched by the data manager so they are available locally when required by an application process. The fetching of remote data items is thus overlapped with the current computation of the application process. Apart from the small overhead caused by the concurrent activity of the data manager, successful prefetching means that an application process should never have to wait for a data item.

A data item is termed unknown if it only becomes apparent that the data item is required once the task being executed by an application process is part-way through its algorithm. The data manager, therefore, has no prior warning as to which data item will be required next. If the necessary data item is not available locally when required then the application process will be delayed while it is fetched. Caching and profiling techniques can be used to exploit any coherence that may exist in the tasks' data requirements. These techniques allow the data manager to 'guess' what data items are likely to be required next, and they can be fetched in advance.

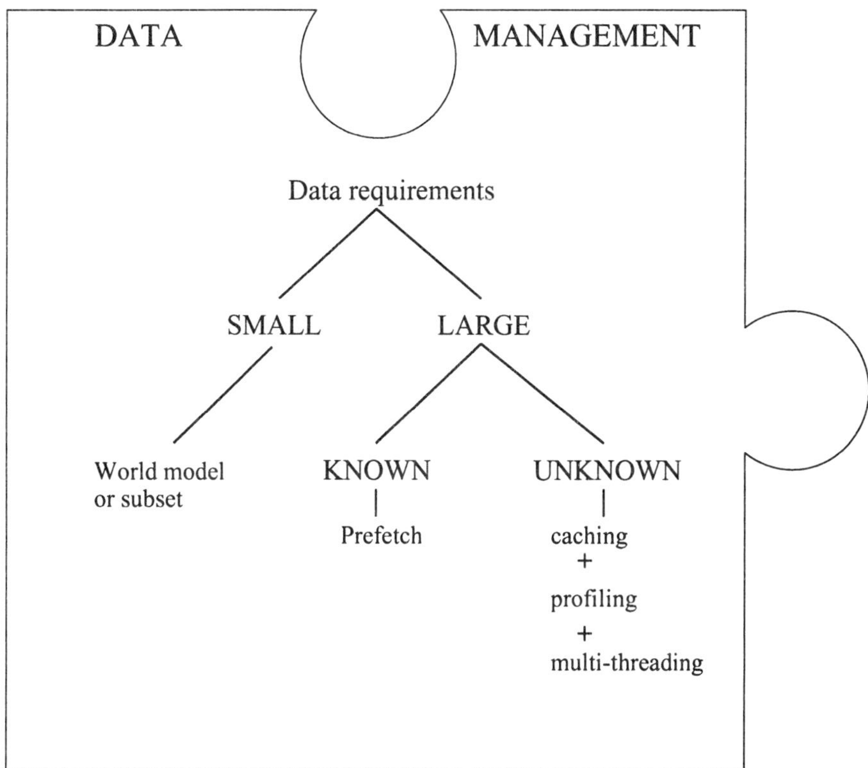

Figure 8.19   Selecting the appropriate data management strategy from the problem's data requirements

If the data manager's predictions are right then such a strategy will provide the same virtual world model that was possible with the prefetch strategy. If the guess was wrong then the application process has to wait. Multi-threading allows several application processes to execute concurrently on a single processor. If one of these application processes is delayed on a remote data fetch the others should still be busy performing tasks and thus the processing element will be still carrying out useful computation.

Some of the issues of data management will be considered in the following case study which involves the parallel implementation of the photo-realistic ray tracing technique from computer graphics.

8.8 Case Study: Rendering Complex Scenes using Ray Tracing

Photo-realistic results are achievable in geological time units!

François Sillion

Applications involving very large data requirements will necessitate data being fetched from remote processing elements during computation. Data management may significantly reduce the delay induced by this procedure. Ray tracing is a photo-realistic image synthesis technique for visualising a three-dimensional scene. Modelling complex scenes, possibly involving thousands of objects, may require far more data storage than can be accommodated at any individual processing element. This case study demonstrates how system performance of a parallel ray tracer for complex environments can be enhanced by exploiting coherence in the data requests and utilising multiple threads of execution.

8.8.1 Problem description

Visualisation is an important aspect of the engineering process. Often the more realistic the image, the better the evaluation of the results will be. The goal of photo-realistic computer graphics methods is to produce images which are indistinguishable from photographs of real three-dimensional scenes. Ray tracing is one such method.

In all image synthesis techniques, the fundamental step is computing the amount and nature of the light from the three-dimensional environment which reaches the eye from any given direction. This computation proceeds by simulating the physical behaviour of light and produces a two-dimensional representation on an image plane. Ray tracing computes the colour intensity of each pixel (picture element) of the image plane by calculating the path of a ray of light through the pixel and its interaction with objects in the scene. The computational effort required is dependent upon the number of pixels in an image plane and the complexity of the environment. High quality images of real scenes are extremely computationally intensive, prompting Sillion's above comment.

The algorithm

The ray tracing algorithm reverses the way in which light reaches the eye, by tracing a ray from the viewpoint backwards into the scene in order to calculate the colour and intensity of each pixel in the image plane. The illumination of objects intersected by the ray on its path through the environment contribute to the value of this pixel. The ray is traced through the pixel until its first intersection with an object. The ambient light and local illumination of this object combine to form this object's contribution. In addition, further contributions arise from subsidiary rays generated by the reflective and refractive properties of this object. The process is repeated to determine the colour parameters for each of these secondary rays. This recursive procedure is terminated either after a certain number of recursive steps, or when the contribution of any ray is below a given threshold.

A two-dimensional representation of the path of a single ray into a simple environment is shown in figure 8.20. Figure 8.21 illustrates how tracing a primary ray results in the generation of further reflected and refracted rays at each intersection point. In this example the algorithm was terminated at depth three.

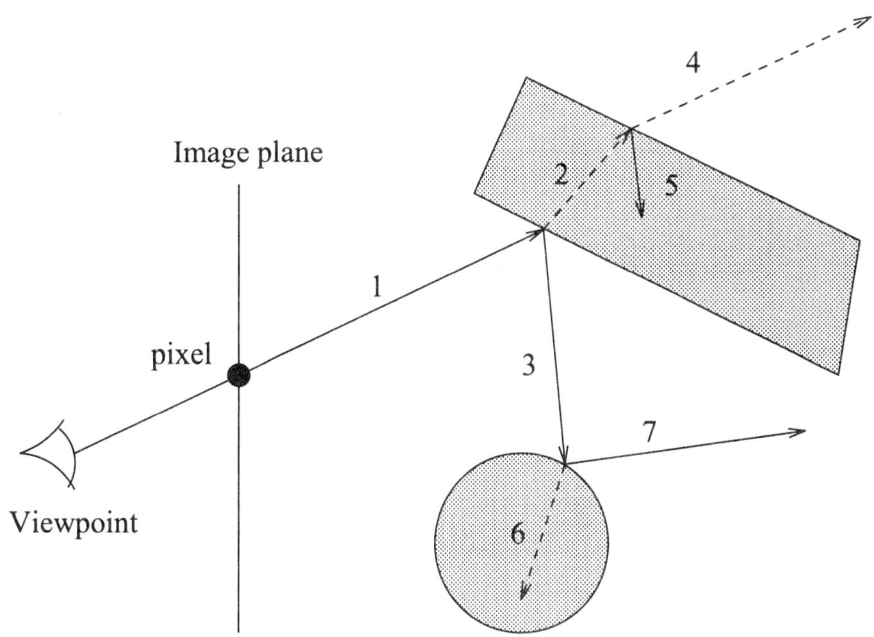

Figure 8.20   Two-dimensional representation of ray tracing algorithm

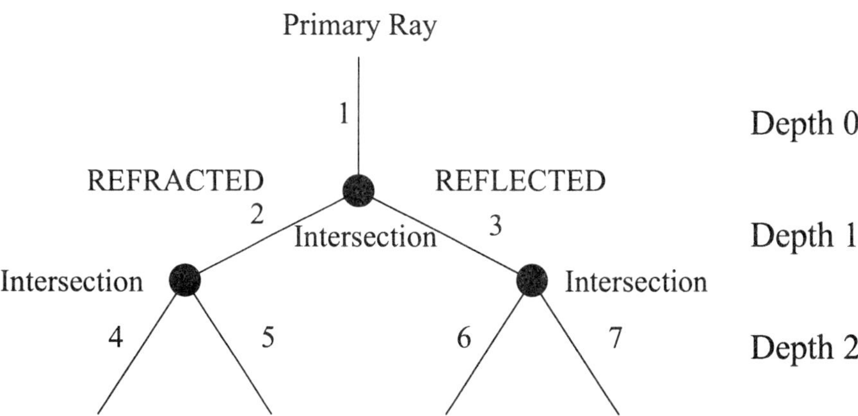

Figure 8.21   New rays generated at object intersection

The following code segment outlines the ray tracing algorithm.

```
PROCEDURE Raytrace(origin, direction, depth VAR colour)
  Begin
    IF depth > max_depth THEN
      colour := black
    ELSE
      Begin
        (* find the closest object intersecting the ray *)
        Intersect_Ray()
        IF no_intersection THEN
          colour := background_colour
        ELSE
          Begin
            (* Get local_colour contribution from OBJECT *)
            local_colour := Local_Contribution(object)

            (* Get colour contribution from REFLECTED ray *)
            reflected_direction :=_Reflection(direction)
            Raytrace(intersection_point,
                     reflected_direction,
                     depth+1,
                     reflected_colour)

            (* Get colour contribution from REFRACTED ray *)
            refracted_direction := Refraction(direction)
            Raytrace(intersection_point,
                     reflected_direction,
                     depth+1,
                     refracted_colour)

            (* Combine colours into returned value *)
            colour := Combine (local_colour,
                               reflected colour,
                               refracted_colour)


          End
        ENDIF
      End
    ENDIF
  End  (* Raytrace *)
```

Spatial subdivision

Numerous modifications have been suggested to improve the solution time of the standard ray tracing algorithm. Foremost of these are the spatial subdivision techniques. Spatial subdivision exploits the coherence that exists in the environment by subdividing it into a number of distinct regions. The octree method, put forward by Glassner [78], establishes a hierarchical data structure that specifies the occupancy of cubic regions, known as *voxels*, of object space. To determine the intersection point of a ray, it is now no longer necessary to check the ray against all the objects in the scene. The ray only has to be checked against the objects in the voxel through which it is currently passing. This voxel may contain a small subset of the total objects, or none at all. If the ray fails to intersect the objects in its current voxel it then passes into the next adjacent voxel and the check for intersection is performed again.

8.8.2 Parallel requirements

The computation associated with an individual ray is completely independent of all other rays. As such, ray tracing has often been described as an 'embarrassingly' parallel problem, and has been implemented on multiprocessor systems many times, for example [85, 119, 153]. However, the majority of these implementations utilise scene data sufficiently small to be accommodated at each processing element, that is, the world model approach. Each ray computation can then proceed more or less independently, with very little communication. This type of problem can usually be very easily adapted for parallel solution. The difficulty associated with parallel ray tracing arises when dealing with complex environments consisting of thousands of objects. In this situation, the world model is no longer possible, and data must be managed as the computation progresses. This introduces the need for communication as ray tasks request the appropriate data to enable the computation to be completed.

From the problem description we can see that it consists of only one stage. Each task is to trace a single ray from the viewpoint, through a particular pixel and into the scene. The result of this task will be the colour value for that pixel. The principal data items of this problem are the coordinates of the pixels and the additional data items will be the set of all objects in the scene.

A ray may pass right through the scene and not hit any objects, or it may interact with many surfaces. The computational complexity of each task varies and this complexity is unknown as it depends on the nature of the scene being considered and the chosen viewpoint. From figure 8.22(a) we see that a demand driven computational model is the correct choice.

Only one stage to the algorithm means we do not have to worry about partial results and so, as shown in figure 8.22(b), we should adopt a distributed task management strategy to ensure an efficient, load balanced system.

The path of a ray through the scene is dependent on the point from which it originated, its initial direction and the subsequent directions that result from its interaction with surfaces in the scene. The surfaces that a ray will intersect can thus only be determined as the ray traverses the scene. Subdividing the scene into voxels has the advantage that it is no longer necessary to check the ray against all objects in the scene to determine the point of intersection; only the objects in the current voxel need to be examined. However, the voxel that needs to be examined next is dependent on the path of the ray and thus will only become apparent as the computation of the task proceeds.

The data requirements for this problem are thus large and unknown. Thus, as we see from figure 8.22(c), a data management scheme which incorporates caching, profiling and multi-threading should be adopted.

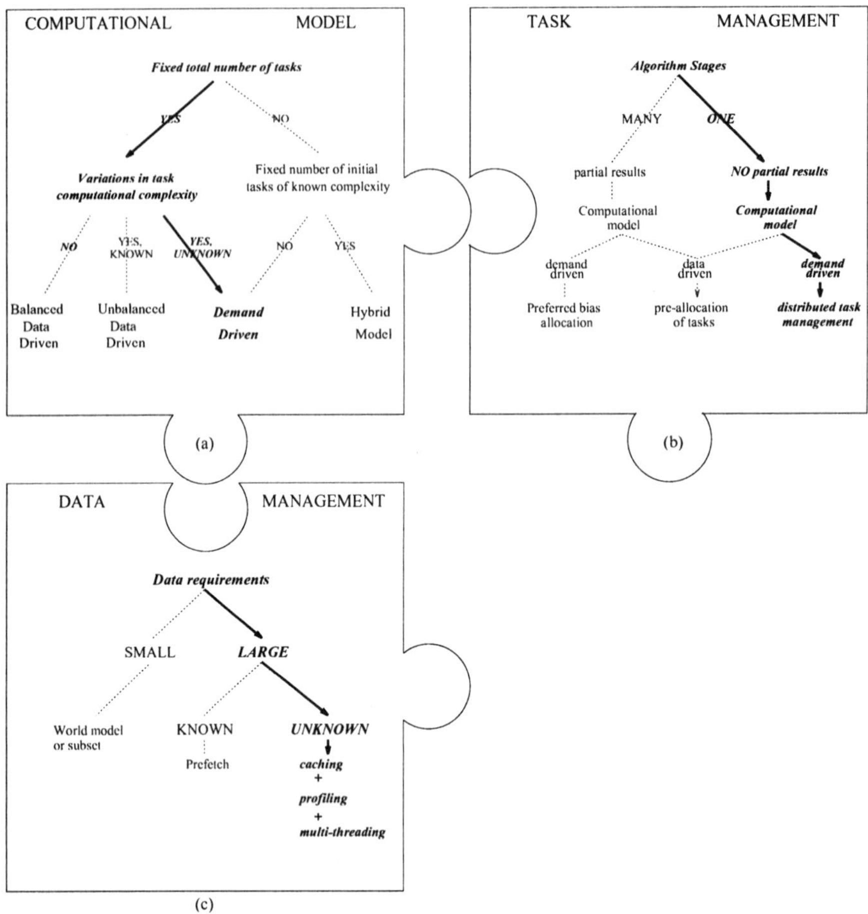

Figure 8.22   Choice of correct computational model, task management and data management strategy

8.8.3 Results

The ray tracing problem was solved on a 32-processing element AMP configuration (which is described in Chapter 9). The scene consisted of 2000 objects subdivided into an octree hierarchy. Figure 8.23 highlights the coherence that exists in the scene. The graph shows the percentage for which sample voxels were requested in this scene when considering different numbers of pixels. The 20 voxels illustrated were chosen as being representative of the large number of voxels within this complex scene. Each request occurs as a ray passes through the environmental volume defined by that voxel and results in data requests for objects contained within the voxel. The results illustrate that using a small profiling 'run' it is possible to determine those voxels that are likely to be required when considering a larger number of tasks.

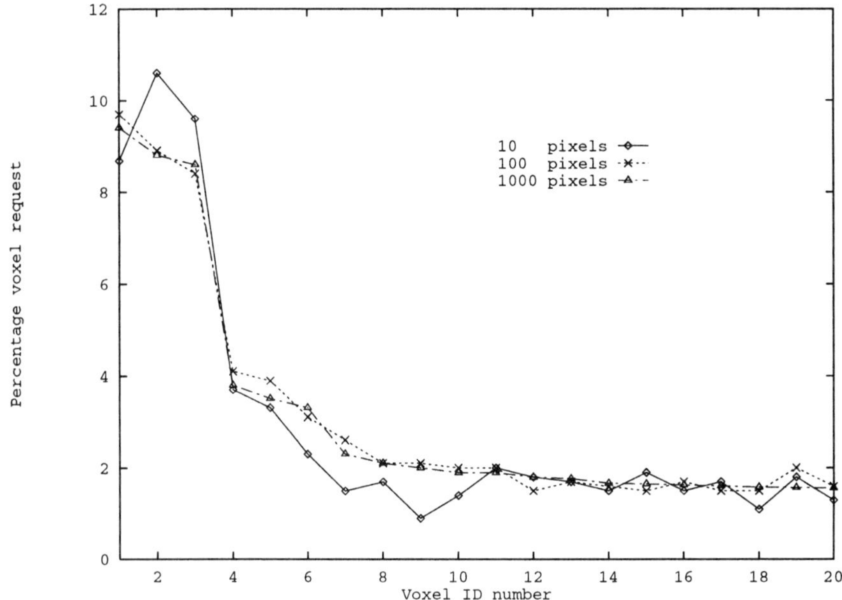

Figure 8.23 Distribution of a sample of voxel requests in a typical scene

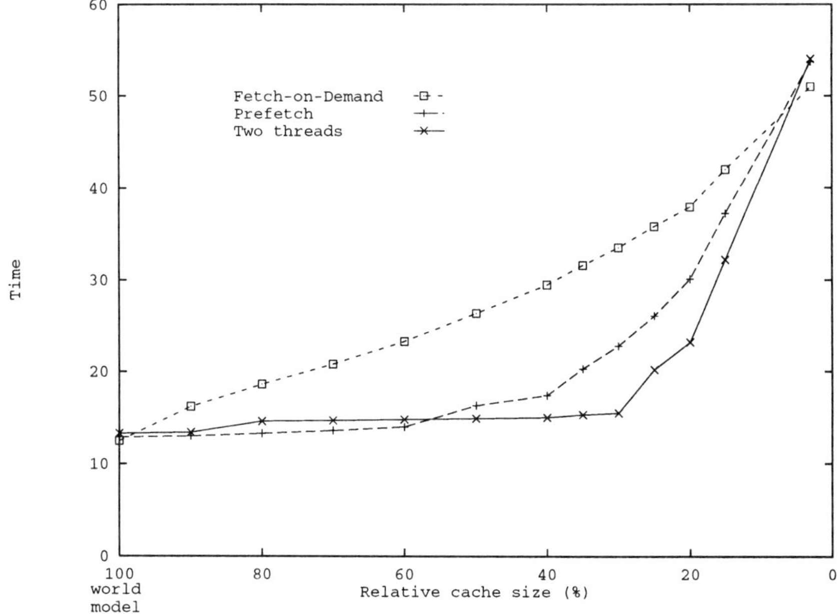

Figure 8.24 Problem solution for different data management strategies

Figure 8.24 shows the time required to solve the ray tracing problem using three different data management strategies: fetch-on-demand; prefetch based on profiling; and caching, profiling and multi-threading. A cache size of 100% is equivalent to a world model. As the cache size decreases so the likelihood of a cache-miss increases. A cache-miss with the fetch-on-demand approach causes application process idle time as the data is fetched from a remote location. Caching and profiling try to improve the cache-hit ratio by using the results, such as those shown in figure 8.23 to attempt to predict a task's data requirements. While these predictions may be successful some of the time, as the cache size decreases so the cache-misses and the resultant remote fetches increase. Multi-threading keeps the processing element doing useful computation when one application process is delayed. The communication overheads brought about by several threads can be seen in figure 8.24. It is only once profiling is no longer able to predict the correct data requirements and cache-misses start to occur (in this case with a relative cache size of about 58%) that the benefits of multi-threading become apparent.

8.8.4 Conclusions

The correct choice of data management strategy has been able to achieve solution times for the virtual shared memory implementation, approximating that achieved for the world data model. Overlapping the remote data fetches with the current computation and exploiting any coherence in the problem domain by predicting and fetching in advance likely data items has resulted in significant performance improvements compared with the naive fetch-on-demand approach. As we will see in the next chapter this difference in performance will be more noticeable as we increase the size of our multiprocessor system.

Multi-threading is essential to avoid processing element idle time when a cache-miss occurs. The smaller the cache size, the higher the number of cache-misses and the greater the need for more threads. However, the number of threads we can support at any processing element is limited by the associated increase in communication overheads and so eventually even the powerful combination of profiling, caching and multi-threading is unable to prevent a significant increase in the problem solution time. In our problem this situation only occurred when each processing element was reduced to holding less than 17% of the entire problem domain.

8.9 Exercises and Project Suggestions

1. What should the correct choice of data management strategy be if we had not adopted a spatial subdivision for our scene in the ray tracing case study?

   Hint: In this case all objects must be intersected with each ray.

2. Rewrite the global controller process shown in section 8.5.2 to implement the form of multi-threading that allows more than one active application process. How will the application process given have to be modified to deal with this alternative form of multi-threading?

3. An application process can be delayed awaiting either a task or a data item. In a multi-threading environment, the application process controller has to be aware as to why each thread is suspended. Assume we are using the form of multi-threading which allows only one active thread. Expand the pseudo-code given for the application process controller in section 8.5.2 to deal with a task request from an application process. What are the implications if no tasks are currently available at that processing element?

4. Failure to achieve linear speed-up of a parallel problem implementation means that the implementation has suffered a realisation penalty. Discuss how the data requirements for the problem affect this realisation penalty and describe how data management strategies can help improve the speed-up obtained.

5. Compare and contrast the data management strategy provided by the hierarchical directories of the Data Diffusion Machine given in appendix A with a strategy implemented on an AMP using a spanning tree (as discussed in Chapter 9) to locate a data item in an unknown location.

Chapter 9

System Communication

Good, the more communicated, more abundant grows.

John Milton

The performance of a distributed memory multiprocessor depends in large part on the efficiency of the message transfer system that provides the interface between the co-operating processors. Two of the important components of this message transfer system are the underlying processor interconnection network which provides the routes along which the messages may travel and the routing strategy which establishes the communication protocols. Although an overview will be given of both dynamic and static methods of configuration, this chapter will concentrate on static interconnection strategies. Greater care has to be taken with static configurations to ensure efficient system communication, than with dynamic configurations. Not all the techniques illustrated in this chapter will be necessary to achieve a high level of efficiency within a dynamic configuration, whereas they may be essential within a static configuration.

System communication is the foundation of a multiprocessor architecture. A parallel system simply could not exist without the communication facilities to transfer data, tasks and results to and from the system controller, thus enabling the processing elements to co-operate during the course of the computation. Communication overheads inhibit overall system performance. Thus the efficiency of system communication plays a crucial rôle in reducing implementation penalties and improving the scalability of the parallel solution of any problem.

System communication consists of two elements:

1. The configuration used to connect processing elements, and

2. The routing strategy that is employed to provide communication across this configuration.

As shown in figure 9.1, decisions taken concerning the best task and data management strategies for the problem being considered will affect the choice of the most efficient system configuration. Whilst a number of physical factors may be beyond our control, such as the architecture of the multiprocessor system, nev-

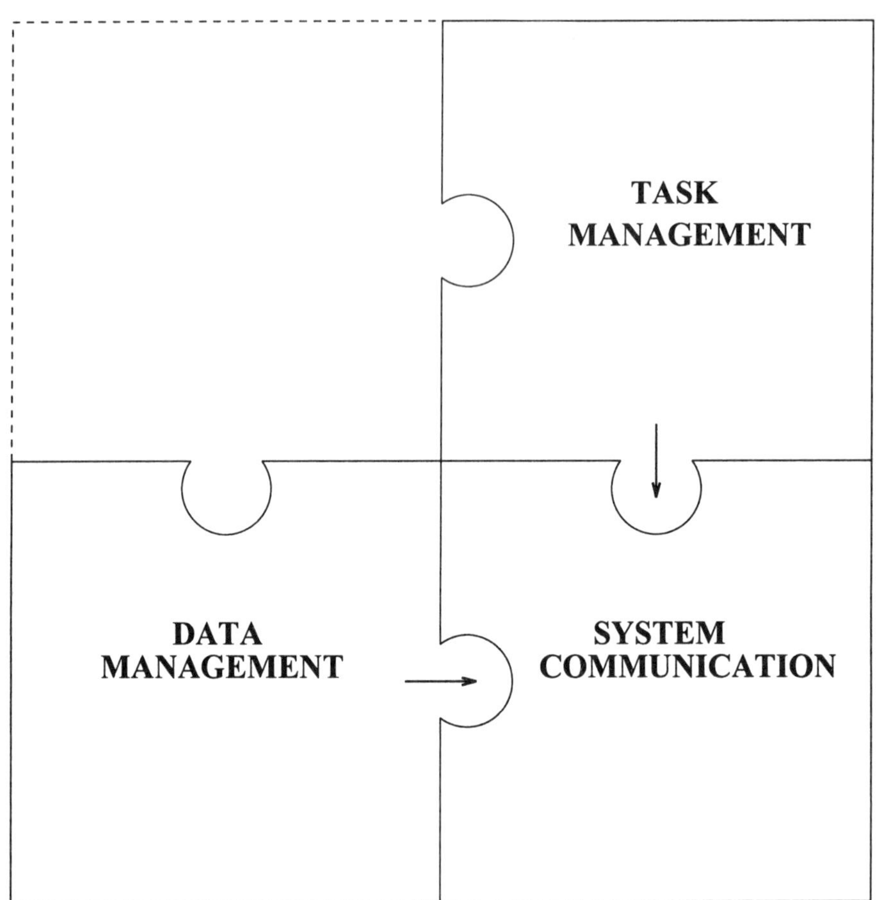

Figure 9.1 Task and data management strategies influence the system communication

ertheless, we must make the best possible choice of implementation within these constraints in this most crucial aspect of parallel processing.

In multiprocessor systems which have a dynamic routing capability, messages are passed between processors via specialised hardware routing components. The hardware thus assumes total responsibility for delivering messages efficiently. Dynamic systems possess the ability to *reconfigure* the interconnection network during the course of the computation by means of specialised switching devices, such as the dynamic crossbar switch discussed in section 2.1.4. Processors in such a system are effectively directly connected with no need to pass messages via any intermediate processors. Dynamic configurations are not without their problems including: messages still have to travel across a limited number of physical links; routing devices have a fixed number of inputs and outputs, and so to achieve a large system it may be necessary to connect several of these devices together; and congestion within these devices will still exist under heavy message loading conditions.

Static interconnection networks, on the other hand, are configured before commencing the parallel implementation and remain fixed throughout the course of the computation. As we will see, messages between processors may need to be routed through several intermediary processors. A router process will be introduced at each processing element to provide efficient transfer of messages within these static networks. Such a router is equally applicable within a dynamic network.

9.1 Configurations

The suitability of the underlying processor interconnection network, also known as the topology, plays a significant part in determining the overall system performance. In a fully connected configuration every processor is adjacent to every other processor, connected by a single link. The time required to send a message from a source processor to a destination processor is simply the time it takes to transfer the message physically across the link. However, for an n processor system, a fully connected configuration requires each processor to have $(n - 1)$ links available for interconnection. For large values of n this may not be feasible, in which case processors will have to communicate with each other not directly, but via intermediate processors. For a constant number of links per processor, the number of intermediate processors through which a message must be routed increases as the number of processors in the configuration increases. This increase in the number of intermediate processors between any two processors is a function of the interconnection network.

As we are discussing the connection of the actual processors, this term, rather than processing element, will be used in this section. Where appropriate, the processors within the figures depicting the configurations will be labelled from 0 to $(n - 1)$ for an n-processor configuration. So, for example, the processors in an 8-processor chain will be labelled from 0 to 7. The system controller will not be directly included in any of the traditional configurations discussed, but will be assumed to be present, for example, by the provision of additional links at some processors. In later sections when we discuss the routing strategies within these configurations which is part of the system software, the term processing element will be used once more.

9.1.1 A taxonomy for interconnection networks

In 1981 Feng produced a survey of interconnection networks [67], in which he attempted to identify four design decisions that could be used to classify networks. These include the mode of operation, control strategy, switching method and network topology. While covering a number of key differences between interconnection networks, his effort to cover all possible network types results in his classification of topologies, shown in figure 9.2, being too general to differentiate the particular class of static networks in which we are interested.

Six years before Feng's classification, in 1975, Anderson and Jensen introduced a taxonomy for identifying various systems of interconnected hardware units on

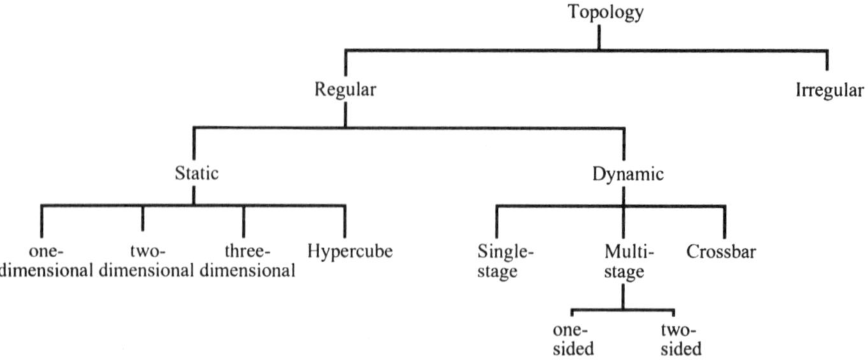

Figure 9.2   Feng's classification of topologies

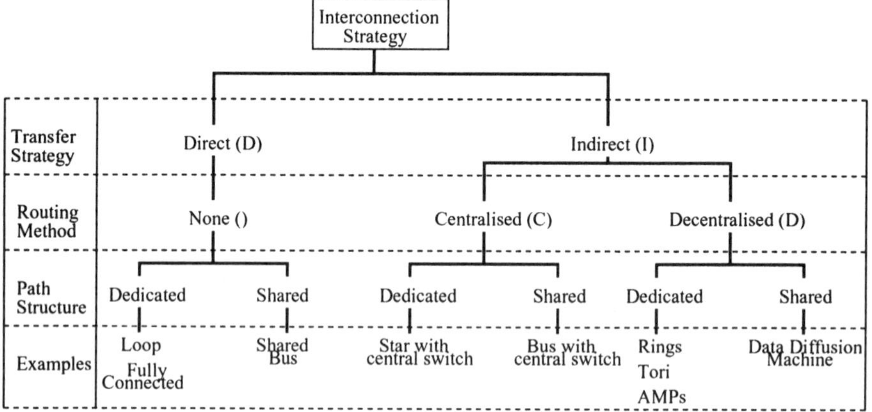

Figure 9.3   Taxonomy for interconnection strategies

which processes can run [9]. The taxonomy only deals with static networks and also excludes SIMD architectures. Anderson and Jensen's classification scheme uses a four letter code. The first letter of the code indicates whether messages may be transferred between processors directly (D) or indirectly (I). A direct transmission implies no intervention is required by either the source processor or an intermediary processor when routing a message. With indirect transmission a processor makes some decision regarding the link on which the message should be communicated. The second letter specifies the control of the routing within the system which can be none (), centralised (C) or decentralised (D). The third letter indicates whether the links are dedicated (D) or shared (S), while the fourth letter usually abbreviates the common name for the configuration. This taxonomy is shown diagrammatically in figure 9.3.

In the example configurations given in figure 9.3, the loop is a unidirectional ring configuration, and thus has a direct transfer strategy which will always be in the same direction. A ring configuration, on the other hand, requires a source processor to decide which direction will give the shortest path to the destination processor, and thus the ring may be classified as having an indirect transfer strategy. Anderson and Jensen conceded that often configurations are not clear and unambiguous and so there may be mixtures of their scheme. The Data Diffusion Machine [182] is one such hybrid. Originally envisaged as a hierarchical structure of busses connecting small numbers of processors (hence its IDS classification), the architecture now conceptually embraces a hierarchical structure of any interconnection strategy, for example, a hierarchical structure of rings as described in [157], and so could now be classified as either IDD or IDS.

In this chapter we shall primarily be examining interconnection strategies of distributed memory MIMD processors which fall into the IDD classification apart from the fully connected configuration which may be classified as DDD.

9.1.2 Criteria for evaluating interconnection strategies

Over the years a number of strategies have been proposed for interconnecting multiprocessor systems according to the IDD classification. Before examining these strategies it is necessary to establish some criteria by which we can compare them later. An evaluation of any multiprocessor configuration should take into account all factors that may effect system performance. Several different criteria have been used to study a wide range of configurations, for example [6, 180, 185]. In determining the most appropriate configuration on which to implement our problem, we will use the following criteria to evaluate the different configurations:

- the diameter of the configuration, D_{Diam},

- the average interprocessor distance and the normalised average interprocessor distance between any two processors, D_{Avg} and D_{Navg},

- the maximum number of routes on any link of the configuration, r_{max}, and

- the average link load, $load_{avg}$, and the resultant total number of messages, $message_{tot}$.

Two other criteria, expandability and fault tolerance, are also often used to compare configurations. Expandability is not such an important factor as the realisation penalties confronting the parallel implementation may determine the maximum number of processors we can effectively use for solving our problems. As the problems in which we are interested are not, in general, safety critical and thus if a link or processor is faulty we can tolerate the inconvenience of reloading the system, or even calling out an engineer if necessary, we shall also not rate *fault tolerance* as a high priority when selecting the desired configuration. For other applications, fault tolerance may be the overriding feature which determines the desired system, and to this end a number of special-purpose configurations have been proposed, for example [97, 151, 165, 166].

Configuration diameter

The diameter of a multiprocessor configuration, D_{Diam}, may be defined as the maximum direct distance between any two processors in the system, that is, the maximum number of links a message has to traverse from a source processor to a destination processor. The number of intermediate processors that have to forward the message is thus $(D_{Diam} - 1)$.

Average and normalised average interprocessor distance

The average interprocessor distance is the number of links on average that a message has to traverse between a source processor and a destination processor. This average interprocessor distance will depend on the source processor's position within a configuration and thus may not necessarily be the same for all processors in the configuration. Therefore, we shall use the *average* of the average interprocessor distances of all the processors in the configuration in this study.

Whenever possible, a closed formula will be derived for this average interprocessor distance of a configuration, otherwise the average of all the average interprocessor distances for the n processors will be expressed, for a configuration with a diameter of D_{Diam}, as:

$$D_{Avg} = \frac{\sum_{p=1}^{n} \frac{\sum_{d=1}^{D_{Diam}} d \times n_{pd}}{n}}{n}, \tag{9.1}$$

where n_{pd} is the number of processors distance d away from processor p.

In order to distinguish between systems with different number of links available per processor, Bhuyan and Agrawal [24] suggested the normalised average interprocessor distance D_{Navg}, which they defined as:

$$D_{Navg} = D_{Avg} \times (\text{number of links per processor}). \tag{9.2}$$

Maximum number of routes on any link

The routes messages follow within a configuration may be critical if bottlenecks and message congestion are to be avoided. If every processor needs to communicate with all other processors in the configuration then ideally every link should be on the same number of routes. If, however, the routes within a configuration must be chosen to meet certain criteria, for example, to be less than the diameter, then certain links within the configuration may be included in more routes than others. The maximum number of routes for any link in the configuration, r_{max}, indicates one or more links that may be carrying more than their 'fair' load and thus indicates possible places where message congestion can occur under heavy message loading.

Average link load and total resultant messages

The average link load, $load_{avg}$, may be measured as the average number of messages that are expected to pass over a link per unit time for a given number of source messages. The total number of messages that pass over a link at a distance d from a single source processor may be defined as:

$$load_d = \frac{load_{d-1} - abs_d}{outlinks_d}, \tag{9.3}$$

where abs_d is the number of messages destined for a processor at that distance d

from the source and therefore are absorbed at that processor and not routed further. If, on average, the number of messages destined for all processors is assumed to be the same, then for a system of n processors:

$$abs_d = \frac{\text{total messages}}{n-1}.$$

(9.4)

Furthermore, we may use $outlinks_d$ to represent the average number of links emanating from each processor at distance d that can be used to route messages further, so:

$$outlinks_d = \frac{n_d}{n_{d-1}},$$

(9.5)

where $n_0 = 1$. Also, defining $load_1$ as:

$$load_1 = \frac{(\text{total messages})}{outlinks_1},$$

(9.6)

we get $load_{d-1}$ as:

$$load_{d-1} = \frac{(\ldots[\frac{([\frac{(load_1 - abs_1)}{outlinks_1}] - abs_2)}{outlinks_2}]\ldots - abs_{d-1})}{outlinks_{d-1}}.$$

(9.7)

Then, assuming all processors are issuing the same number of messages in unit time, we may determine the average load on any link as:

$$load_{avg} = \sum_{d=1}^{D_{Diam}} n_d \times load_d,$$

(9.8)

where, once again, n_d is the number of processors that are distance d from the source processor.

The total number of messages that result within a configuration for a given number of source messages may now be derived, from the average link load, as:

$$message_{tot} = load_{avg} \times n.$$

(9.9)

9.1.3 Common configurations

Ways of connecting processors in some multiprocessor configuration have been investigated ever since parallel processing was first considered. A popular connection strategy has always been a *bus*. However, as discussed in section 2.1.4, because of contention difficulties a bus is only appropriate for low numbers of processors and so networks are constructed by connecting processors together by dedicated links.

We will now examine some of the more common interconnection networks and then introduce a new configuration, A Minimum Path (AMP) configuration, that minimises the interconnection distances between processors within the constraints of a fixed number of links per processor.

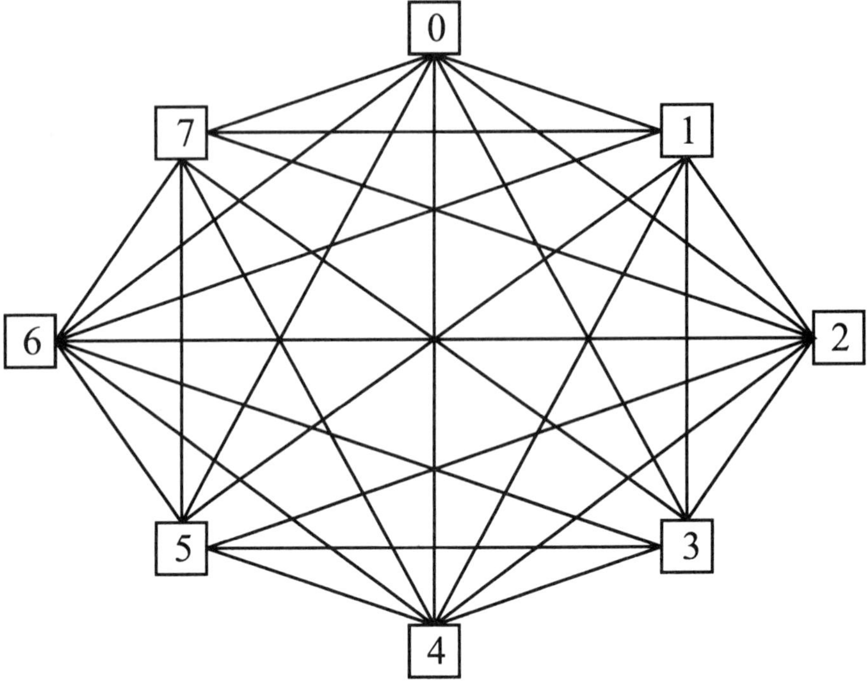

Figure 9.4   8-processor fully connected configuration

Fully connected configuration

As their name implies, fully connected configurations provide a link between a processor and all other processors within the configuration. Messages may, therefore, be routed directly from the source processor to the destination processor. Figure 9.4 shows an 8-processor fully connected configuration.

As every processor in the configuration is directly connected to every other processor, the maximum distance between any two processors is 1 ($D_{Diam} = 1$). All processors within a fully connected configuration will obviously have the same average interprocessor distance value, which for a configuration of n processors is:

$$D_{Avg} = \frac{n-1}{n}.$$

The direct connections between processors means that no processor is required to act as an intermediary for messages between distant processors. Messages generated locally are routed to the destination processor directly on the appropriate link, which is why this configuration may be classified as DDD. Every time a processor is added to a fully connected configuration an additional link must be provided at each processor in the configuration. The diameter of a fully connected configuration remains 1 regardless of how many additional processors are added. All links within a fully connected configuration will only be used for passing messages directly between the source and destination processors, and so $r_{max} = 2$.

Figure 9.5 8-processor chain

Chain

We have seen the chain configuration before as the interconnection strategy used in the processor farm in section 7.3.2. This configuration consists of processors arranged in a linear fashion as shown for an 8-processor chain in figure 9.5. All the processors are connected to two other processors, apart from the processors at the 'front' and 'back' of the chain which are only connected to one processor each.

The diameter of the chain configuration is one less than the number of processors in the chain which is the distance between the processor at the front of the chain and the processor at the back ($D_{Diam} = n - 1$). The average interprocessor distance will vary with position in the chain. The average interprocessor distance for the chain of n processors may be calculated as:

$$D_{Avg} = \frac{((n + 1) \ DIV \ 3) \times \frac{(n-1)(n)(n+1)}{n+(((n+1) \ MOD \ 3) \ DIV \ 2)-((n \ MOD \ 3) \ DIV \ 2)}}{n^2}.$$

Where DIV signifies integer division, and MOD is the remainder after the integer division.

The link (or links if the number of processors in the chain is odd) in the middle of the chain will obviously be on a larger number of routes than the other links of the chain. The maximum number of routes this middle link (or links) is on may be calculated as:

$$r_{max} = 2 \times ((n \ DIV \ 2)^2 + ((n \ MOD \ 2) \times (n \ DIV \ 2))).$$

Two-dimensional mesh

A two-dimensional mesh of processors, also known as an array, consists of processors arranged in a grid, as shown for a 20-processor mesh in figure 9.6. If more than four links are available at each processor then higher dimensional meshes may be constructed. We will restrict this discussion to two-dimensional meshes and for simplicity we shall refer to the two-dimensional mesh configuration simply as the *mesh* configuration.

Each processor in the mesh may be considered as part of a chain in the horizontal direction and a chain in the vertical direction. A mesh of n processors may be constructed by decomposing n into two factors cfp_1 and cfp_2 such that: ($cfp_1 \times cfp_2 = n$); cfp_1 is greater than or equal to cfp_2; and the difference between cfp_1 and cfp_2 is minimised. We shall term these factors the *closest factor pair (cfp)*. The mesh may now be constructed of cfp_1 processors in each of the horizontal chains which will give cfp_2 processors in each of the vertical chains. A mesh constructed from a prime number of processors will, therefore, be equivalent to a chain of the same number of processors.

The diameter of the mesh configuration is equal to the sum of the diameter of the

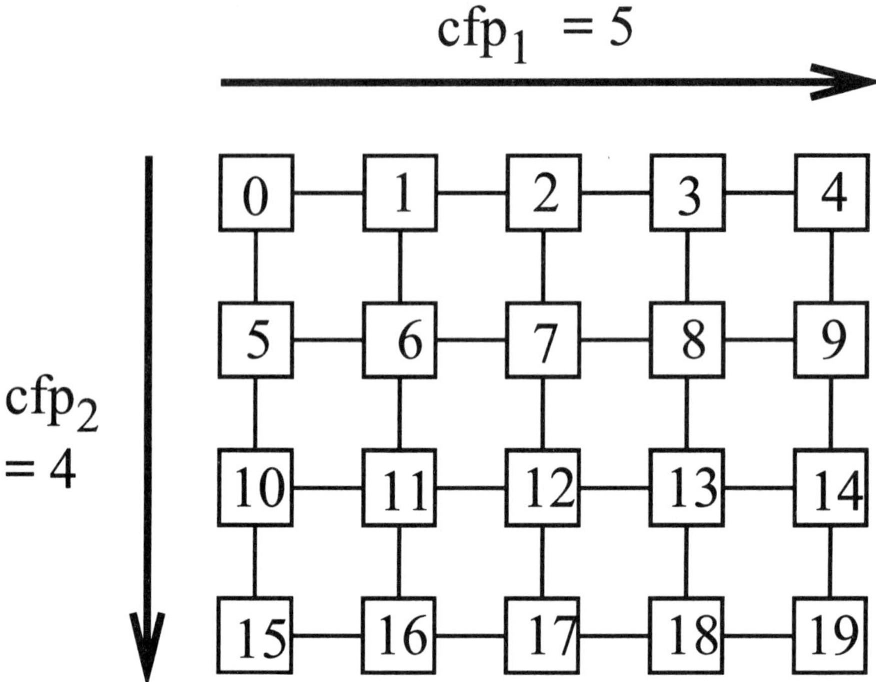

Figure 9.6 20-processor mesh

chain in the horizontal direction and the diameter of the chain in the vertical direction ($D_{Diam} = (cfp_1 - 1) + (cfp_2 - 1)$). The average interprocessor distance varies at different points within the mesh, and may be calculated as the average interprocessor distance of the chain of processors in the horizontal direction, $D_{Avg}(cfp_1)$, plus the average interprocessor distance of the vertical chain, $D_{Avg}(cfp_2)$. Thus, the average interprocessor distance $D_{Avg} = D_{Avg}(cfp_1) + D_{Avg}(cfp_2)$.

The number of corner processors in a mesh will remain at four, while the number of edge and interior processors will grow accordingly. No processor in a mesh requires more than four links. When constructing a mesh we may assume with no loss of generality that the number of processors in the horizontal chain, cfp_1, is always greater than or equal to the number of processors in the vertical chain, cfp_2, and so the links in the middle of any horizontal chain will be on more routes than any other links. The number of routes for these links may be computed as:

$$r_{max} = r_{max}(chain_{cfp_1}) \times cfp_2,$$

where $r_{max}(chain_{cfp_1})$ is the maximum number of routes on any link of a chain consisting of cfp_1 processors.

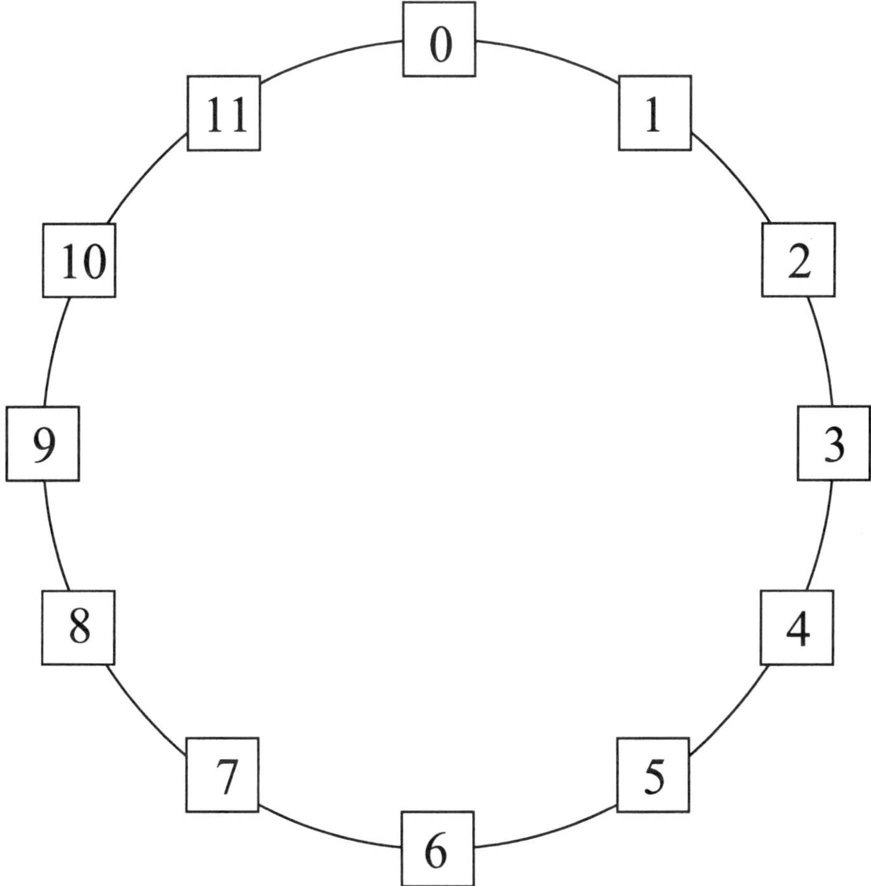

Figure 9.7   12-processor ring

Ring

Like the chain, the ring is one of the simplest and the most popular configurations. Rings have been used in such diverse area as: local area computer networks, for example, the token ring network; data flow architectures; and for solving a whole host of applications on multiprocessor systems, see for example [62]. A 12-processor ring is shown in figure 9.7. In a bidirectional ring, as opposed to a unidirectional loop, messages are able to be transmitted in both directions around the ring.

The diameter of the bidirectional ring configuration is equal to half the number of processors (ignoring fractions) in the ring for both even and odd numbers of processors ($D_{Diam} = n \; DIV \; 2$). All processors will have the same average interprocessor distance value due to the symmetric nature of the ring. The average interprocessor distance for processors in a ring with an odd number n of processors is:

$$D_{Avg} = \frac{D_{Diam} \times (D_{Diam} + 1)}{n},$$

while for an even number n of processors:

$$D_{Avg} = \frac{(D_{Diam})^2}{n}.$$

The symmetric nature of a ring ensures that all links will be on the same number of routes and so taking into account whether the number of processors in the ring is odd or even:

$$r_{max} = (n\ DIV\ 2)^2 + ((n\ MOD\ 2) \times (n\ DIV\ 2)).$$

Torus

In this section we will only examine torus configurations for processors with four links, although torus configurations for processors with more that four links have also been proposed, for example, the CLIP image processing system [63] and the three-dimensional torus configuration of the Cray T3D massively parallel system. Figure 9.8 shows how the torus configuration consists of rings of rings of processors. This is equivalent to an edge-connected mesh of processors.

As with the mesh, to minimise the diameter of the torus it is preferable that the number of processors within the horizontal rings is approximately the same as the number of processors in the vertical rings. This minimises the difference between the closest factor pairs cfp_1 and cfp_2, leading to a diameter of :

$$D_{Diam} = (cfp_1\ DIV\ 2) + (cfp_2\ DIV\ 2).$$

Tori are symmetric configurations so all processors will have the same average interprocessor distance value. This average interprocessor distance of a processor may be calculated as the sum of the average interprocessor distance of a horizontal ring plus the average interprocessor distance of a vertical ring, $D_{Avg} = D_{Avg}(cfp_1) + D_{Avg}(cfp_2)$.

The diameter of torus configurations increases depending on how close the closest factor pair are to the square root of the number of processors. So, if the number of processors, n, is a perfect square then the diameter of the torus is $2 \times (\sqrt{n}\ DIV\ 2)$. A torus configuration consisting of a prime number, n, of processors would have a cfp_2 value of 1 and would thus be equivalent to an n-processor ring and have a diameter of $n\ DIV\ 2$. The maximum number of routes on any link of a torus may be calculated as:

$$r_{max} = r_{max}(ring_{cfp_1}) \times cfp_2,$$

where $r_{max}(ring_{cfp_1})$ is the maximum number of routes on any link for cfp_1 processors arranged in a ring configuration and defined previously.

Hypercube

A hypercube configuration consists of 2^k processors with each processor connected to k other processors. This value k is referred to as the dimension of the hyper-

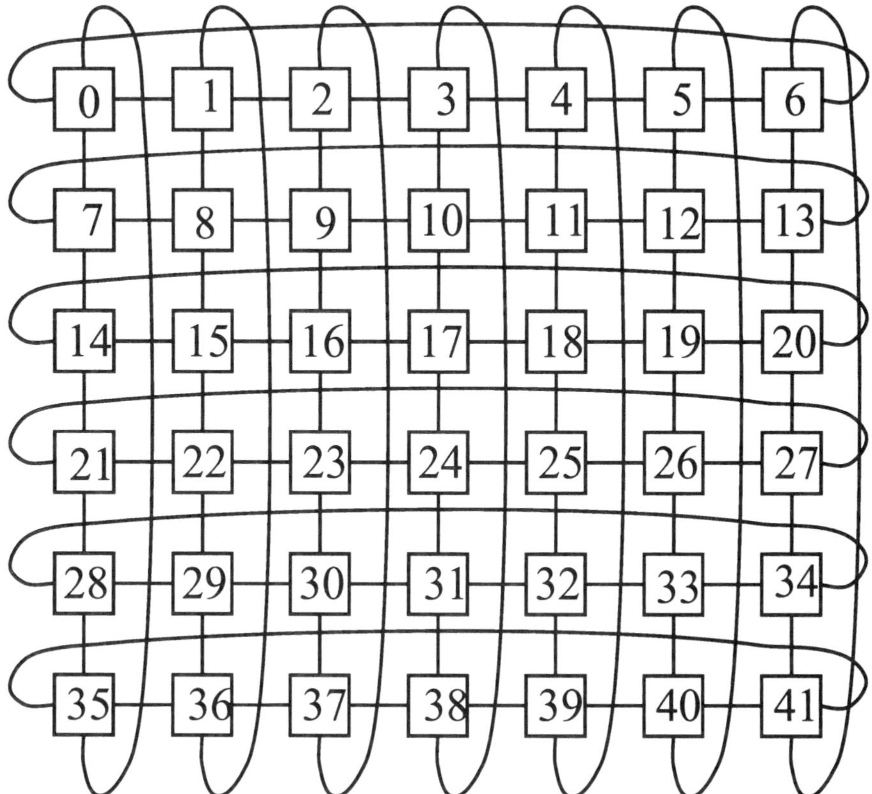

Figure 9.8   42-processor torus

cube. Hypercubes may, therefore, only be constructed from specific numbers of processors (powers of 2), and each processor requires a number of links equal to the dimension of the hypercube. A 4-dimensional hypercube is shown in figure 9.9. The 4-bit binary code shown is used for routing and is explained in section 9.2.

A hypercube of dimension k has a maximum distance between any two processors equal to this dimension, so $D_{Diam} = k$. The symmetric nature of the hypercube means that all processors will have the same average interprocessor distance value. The average interprocessor distance for a hypercube with $n = 2^k$ processors is:

$$D_{Avg} = \frac{k \times 2^{k-1}}{n}.$$

Hypercubes may be expanded only in powers of 2 processors, and an additional processor link is required each time this happens. As the dimension of a hypercube increases, the diameter increases as the logarithm of the number of nodes [140]. The symmetric structure and routing strategy of the hypercube ensures an equal number of routes on each link. For an n-processor hypercube $r_{max} = n$.

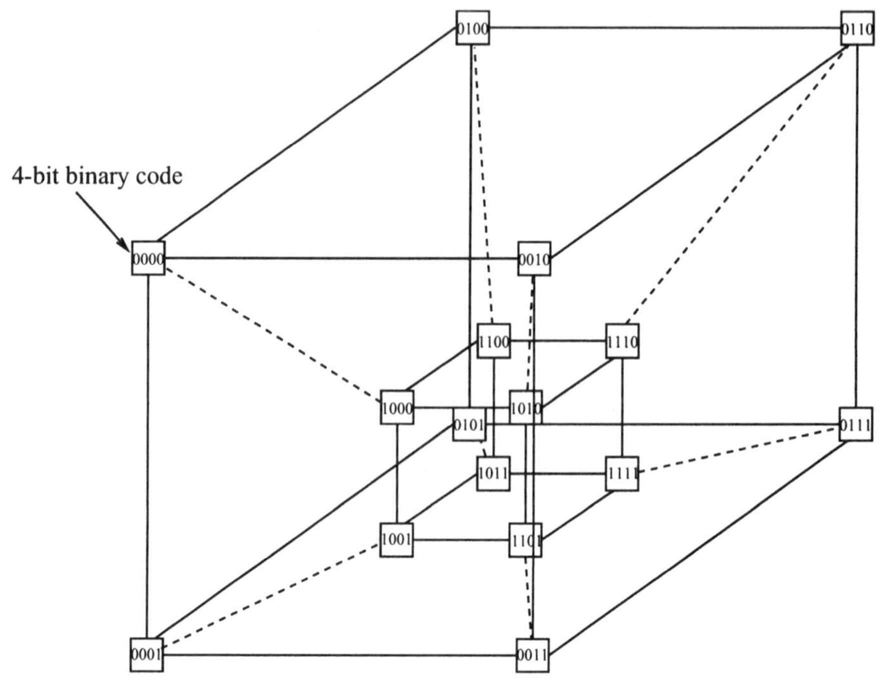

Figure 9.9 16-processor hypercube

Cube connected cycle

First proposed by Preparata and Vuillemin [152] this configuration interconnects 2^k processors such that groups of 2^r form a $(k - r)$-dimension hypercube, where r is the smallest integer such that $r + 2^r \geq k$. So in the $2^5 = 32$-processor cube connected cycle shown in figure 9.10, four processors are connected in a cycle (a ring) in each of the 'corners' of a 3-dimensional hypercube.

A slightly different cube connected cycle is discussed by Wittie [185]. This cube connected cycle of dimension D consists of $D \times 2^D$ processors, arranged as a ring of D processors around each of the 2^D 'corners' of the D-dimension hypercube. Only Preparata's cube connected cycle is considered here. The diameter may be calculated as the sum of the diameter of the source ring plus the diameter of the hypercube plus the diameter of the destination ring. So for a cube connected cycle of $n = 2^{r+k}$ processors the maximum distance between any two processors is:

$$D_{Diam} = 2^{r-1} + (k - r) + 2^{r-1}$$
$$= (2^r) + (k - r).$$

The average interprocessor distance cannot be defined for a generic cube connected cycle, and must be calculated for each specific example using:

$$D_{Avg} = \frac{\sum_{p=1}^{n} \frac{\sum_{d=1}^{D_{Diam}} d \times n_{pd}}{n}}{n},$$

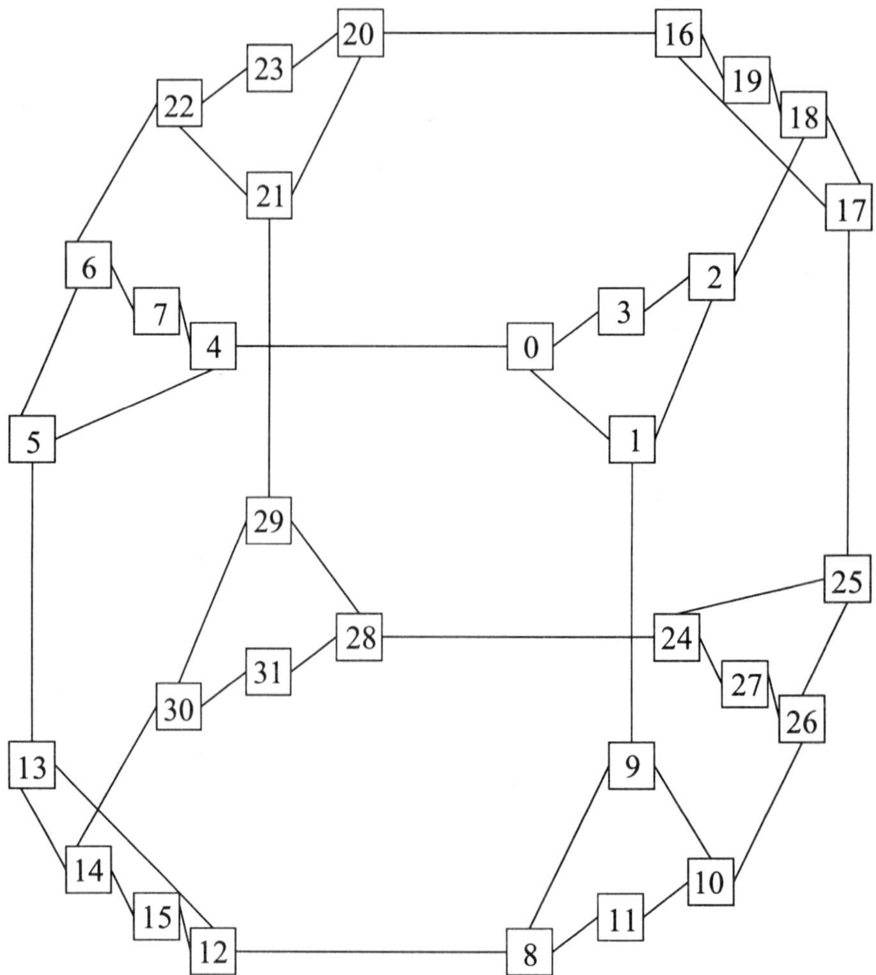

Figure 9.10   32-processor cube connected cycle

where n_{pd} is the number of processors distance d away from processor p.

As with hypercubes, cube connected cycles may only be expanded in powers of 2 processors, however, unlike hypercubes, there is no need to provide extra links as the configuration is increased. Routes on a cube connected cycle must traverse both the ring portion and the hypercube structure of this configuration. The links connecting the rings, and thus the dimensions in the hypercube structure, will be on the most number of routes and, due to the symmetric nature of the cube connected cycle, will each have the same maximum value. However, unlike the hypercube, the shortest path between two processors on different 'dimensions' of the hypercube may be unique and so $r_{max} = 2^{(k+r)}$.

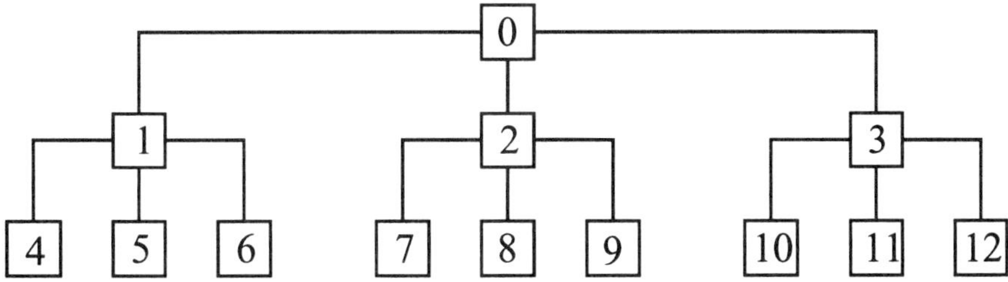

Figure 9.11 A full 13-processor tree of degree 3 and height 2"

Trees

The tree configuration has been widely used for solving a variety of applications in parallel. We have already seen it being used in the image processing case study described in Chapter 6. A tree of degree d and height h consists of a single processor at the top level, the *root processor*, connected to d other processors, each of which is a root processor of a subtree of degree d and height $(h-1)$. The processors at the lowest level of the tree, the *leaf processors*, are only connected to their 'parent' tree. The other processors in the tree, the so-called *branch* processors, have a maximum of $d+1$ links. One of these branch processor's links connects it to the processor directly 'above' it in the tree, and there are up to d links for connecting to processors 'below' it in the tree. A *full* tree is one in which every branch processor is connected to d processors below it in the tree. The total number of processors in a full tree of degree d and height h is $\frac{d^{h+1}-1}{d-1}$. Figure 9.11 shows a full tree configuration of degree 3 and height 2.

The maximum distance between two processors of a full tree is the distance from a leaf processor in one subtree of the root processor and a leaf processor in a different subtree, and so $D_{Diam} = 2 \times h$. Processors within a full tree configuration will have different average interprocessor distance values depending on their position within the tree. The root processor will obviously have the best average interprocessor distance value, while the values will be the worst for the leaf processors. The average interprocessor distance for the whole tree may be calculated as:

$$D_{Avg} = \frac{D_{Diam} \times (D_{Diam} + 1)}{n}.$$

To maintain a full tree as it is expanded to a new height $h+1$ requires an additional d^{h+1} processors, but no further links are required at each processor. It is possible to add any number of processors to a tree if a full tree is not required. The links connecting the root to the other processors in the tree configuration will be on the maximum number of routes. If a tree with degree d consisting of n processors is full, then all d links of the root processor will have this maximum number of routes which may be calculated as:

$$r_{max} = 2 \times (((((n-1)\ DIV\ d) \times (d-1)) + 1) \times ((n-1)\ DIV\ d))$$

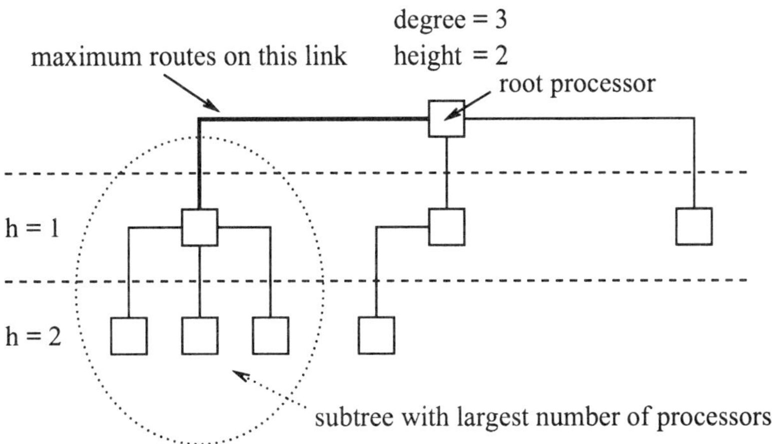

Figure 9.12 Calculating the maximum number of routes on a link of a non-full tree

where $((n - 1)\ DIV\ d)$ is the number of processors in each subtree of the root processor.

If the tree is not full and has height h, then the maximum number of routes will still traverse one of the root processor's links and this value may now be calculated as 2 multiplied by the number of processors in the subtree with the largest number of processors multiplied by the number of processors not in this subtree (including the root). This may best be illustrated by an example.

Given an 8-processor tree of degree 3 and height 2, as shown in figure 9.12, the number of processors not in the subtree connected to the root processor's left link including the root is 4, and the number of processors in the subtree is also 4, and so the number of routes on the root processor's left link and therefore, the maximum number of routes on any link of the tree, is:

$$r_{max} = 2 \times 4 \times 4$$
$$= 32$$

Other configurations

The chordal ring configuration may be constructed by adding 'chords' to processors arranged in a ring [13, 60]. A message now no longer has to circumvent at most half the processors in the ring, but may take a 'short cut' via the additional chords to its destination. Figure 9.13 shows a chordal ring of 18 processors. This configuration has a diameter of 5, which compares favourably with a ring of the same number of processors in which the diameter would be 9. Some of these chordal rings are simply another way of displaying cross connected meshes [116] and hypercubes [25]. Figure 9.14(a) shows a 16-processor chordal ring which is simply another representation of the 16-processor cross connected mesh in which the 'left' and 'right' edges are connected in a ring (as in the torus) and the 'top' and 'bottom' edges are connected in a cyclic manner, as shown in figure 9.15(b). Figure 9.15(a)

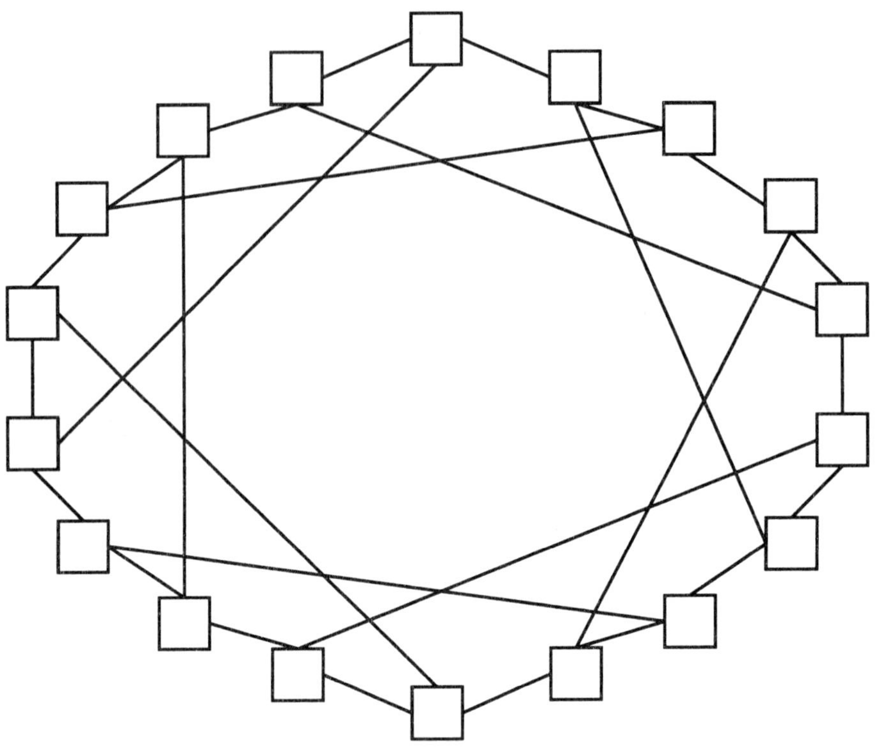

Figure 9.13   18-processor chordal ring

shows an 8-processor chordal ring which is simply another representation of the 3-dimensional hypercube shown in figure 9.14(b).

The X-tree [58] and the multitree structure [14] attempt to improve upon the tree configuration by connecting the leaf nodes in the X-tree and both the leaves and the roots in the case of the multitree structure. The 24-processor multitree structure shown in figure 9.16 has a diameter of 4.

Hypertrees [81] attempt to combine the expandability of a binary tree configuration with the compactness of a hypercube. Additional links in the hypertree are chosen to join processors in the same level of the tree such that these connections are the set of hypercube connections. Figure 9.17(a) shows a hypertree of 31 processors with a diameter of 6, whereas a binary tree of 31 processors has a diameter of 8. Other hierarchical structures include HINs [55] and pyramids [140].

The alpha network [24] is a generalised hypercube structure constructed from any nonprime number of processors. An alpha network is constructed for n processors by choosing integer values $m_1, m_2, \ldots, m_D$ such that:

$$\prod_{i=1}^{D} = n$$

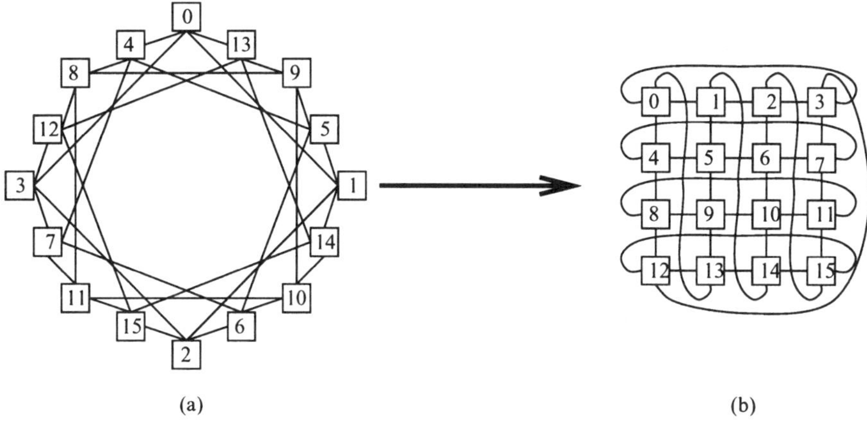

(a)

(b)

Figure 9.14 (a) 16-processor chordal ring (b) 16-processor cross connected mesh

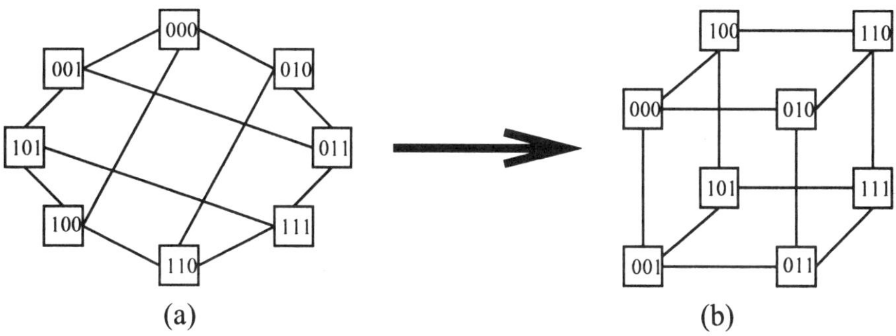

(a)

(b)

Figure 9.15 (a) 8-processor chordal ring (b) 8-processor hypercube

Figure 9.17(b) shows an alpha network of 24 processors. This alpha network has a diameter of 3, but requires six links per processor.

De Bruijn networks have been proposed as fault tolerant interconnection strategies for large numbers of processors [23, 61, 65]. A de Bruijn network of dimension k consists of processors labelled with a k-digit code and links connecting any pair of processors x and y if the last $(k-1)$ digits of the code for processor x are the same as the first $(k-1)$ digits of processor y [23, 140]. Figure 9.18 shows a de Bruijn network of dimension 3.

9.1.4 Minimum path configurations

The philosophy underlying the construction of the A Minimum Path (AMP) configuration is to minimise the diameter, D_{Diam}, of the interconnection network; that is, to minimise the number of links a message has to travel between any source processor and any other destination processor within the configuration. This principle is maintained even at the expense of the loss of regularity in a system. Another

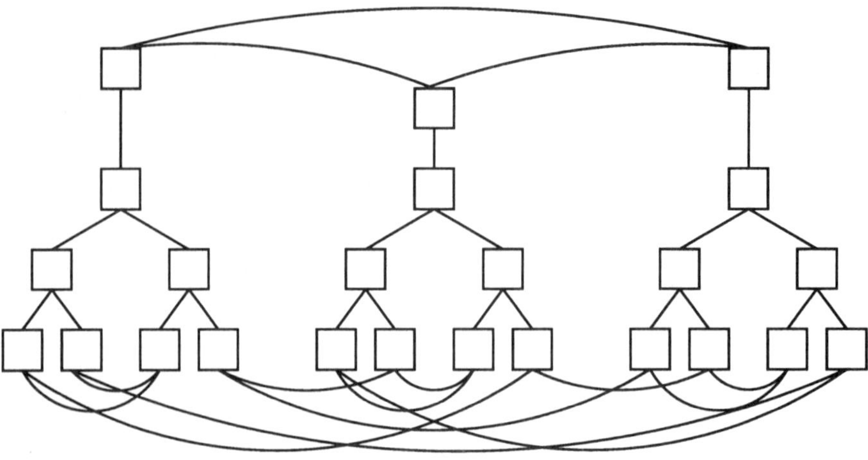

Figure 9.16   24-processor multitree structure

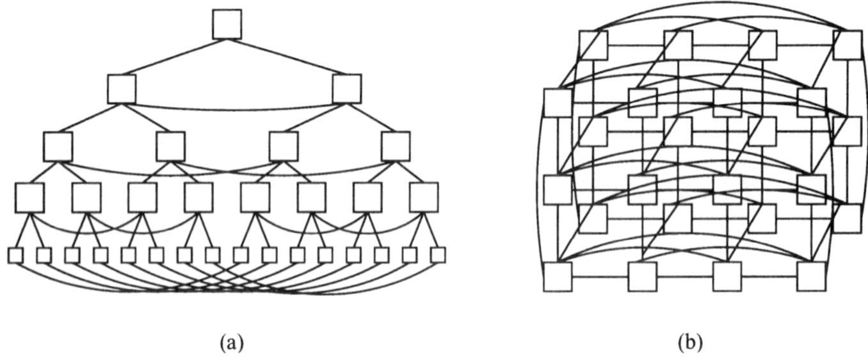

(a)   (b)

Figure 9.17   (a) 31-processor hypertree (b) 24-processor alpha network

feature of the AMP configuration is that every link of a processor within the configuration is connected to a different processor; that is, no two links of any processor are connected to the same processor. In the following description we will assume each processor has four links available for interconnection with other processors. The principles described here are, obviously, equally applicable to processors with any number of links.

As figure 9.19(a) shows, it is easy to construct a configuration of five processors with a diameter of 1. However, as discussed in section 4.4.2, to provide a useful parallel processing platform, a multiprocessor system must have access to input/output facilities. We achieved this by designating one processor as the *system controller* (SC) with the responsibilities of providing this input/output interface. The other processors, the *processing elements*, perform the actual processing of the problem. The inclusion of a system controller within a configuration may be

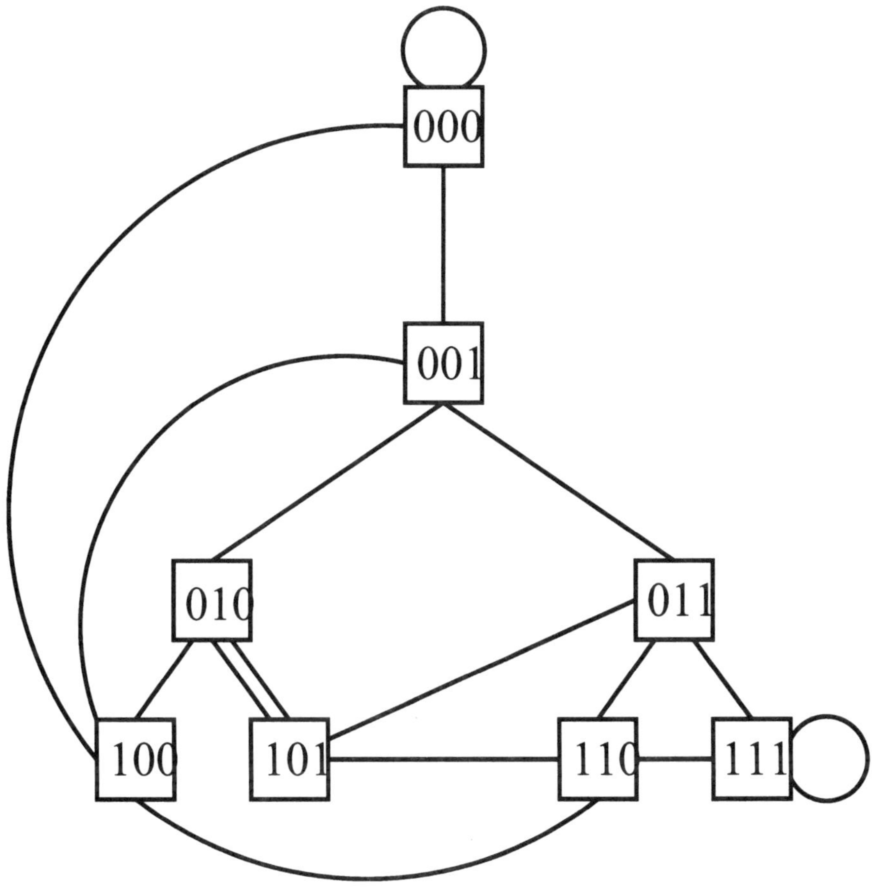

Figure 9.18   A de Bruijn network of dimension 3

achieved either by the provision of an additional link to one or more processors as shown in figure 9.19(b), or by using some of the existing links as shown in figure 9.19(c). In this last case the number of processors within the configuration must be reduced to four if the diameter of 1 is to be maintained.

If additional links are to be provided at some particular processors for connecting a configuration of n processors to the system controller then all n processors will have four links available for processor to processor interconnection. If no additional links are present for this purpose then two existing links must be used for connecting the system to the system controller (as the number of links is even, using only one link would leave another link unconnected). In such a configuration of n processors, two processors will have three links available and $(n-2)$ processors will have four links available for interconnection with other processors.

If the system controller is included in a system without the need to use any of the existing links of the processors, then the maximum number of processors

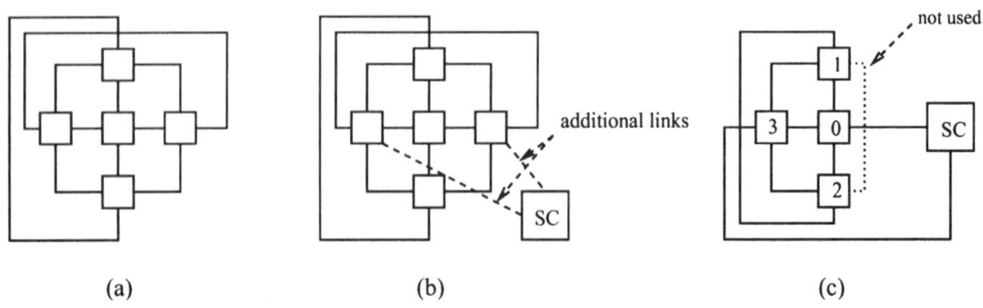

Figure 9.19 Processor systems with diameter of 1 (a) 5-processor system without SC (b) additional links for SC (c) no additional links used for SC

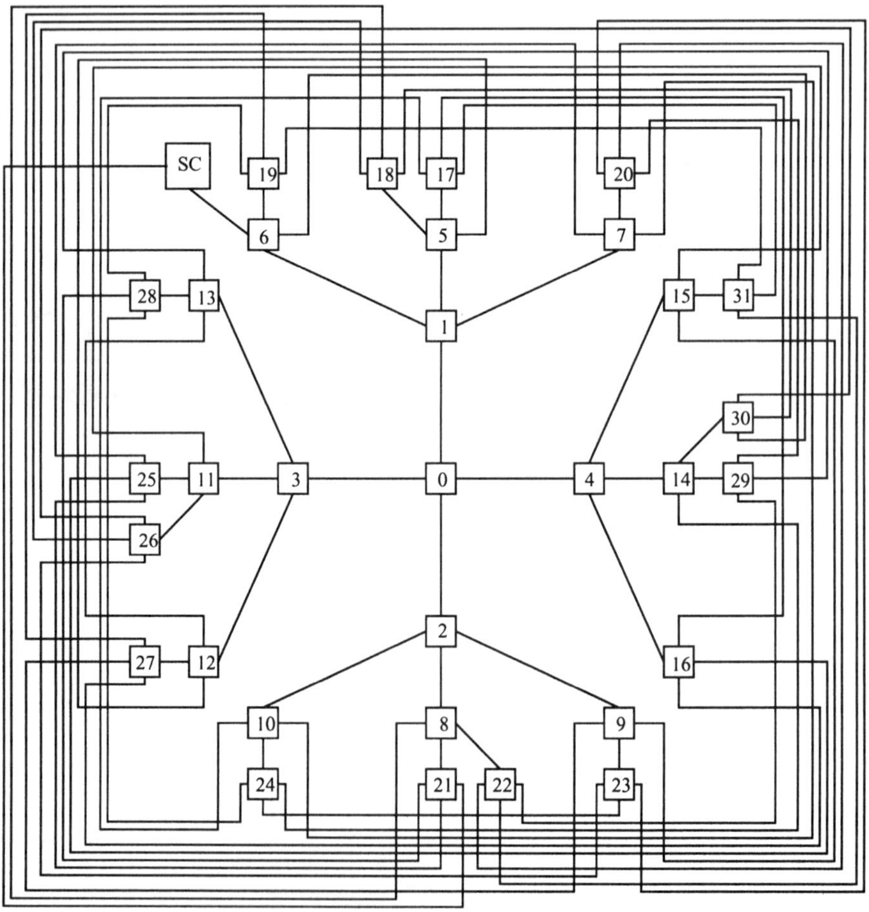

Figure 9.20 The 32-processor AMP configuration with system controller

that can be interconnected within a configuration of a certain diameter may be obtained from extremal graph theory [27]. If extra links are not available then, as demonstrated in figure 9.19(c), fewer processors may be interconnected in a system of a given diameter. In this situation an indication of the *upper bound* to the number of processors that can be connected in a system can be provided by extremal graph theory, as demonstrated in the following section. Figure 9.20 shows the 32-processor AMP which has a diameter of 3 with only four links per processor and including a system controller. AMP configurations have been generated using genetic algorithms and heuristic depth first search algorithms [33, 43].

Theoretical limits on optimal configurations

Each processor in a static distributed memory multiprocessor system has a number of links available for interconnection with other processors within the system. We are assuming that each processor has four links. (The T800 and T9000 transputers described in section 2.1.4 are examples of such a processor.)

Assuming that every processor in the configuration has the same number of links (or valency), Δ, the upper bound on the maximum number of processors in the configuration, usually called the *Moore bound*, can be found by counting the number of processors which are at distances of $0, 1, 2, \ldots, D_{Diam}$ links from a given processor. This gives at most

$$1 + \Delta + \Delta(\Delta - 1) + \Delta(\Delta - 1)^2 + \ldots + \Delta(\Delta - 1)^{D_{Diam}-1} \qquad (9.10)$$

processors for a diameter D_{Diam}. Graphs achieving this bound are called Moore graphs. Biggs [26] shows that (except for $D_{Diam}=1$ or $\Delta=2$), Moore graphs can exist only for the cases $D_{Diam}=2$ and $\Delta=3, 7,$ or 57; but in all other cases, graphs can be found that approach these bounds.

For practical configurations, we have assumed that two existing links from the configuration are used for connection to the system controller, since as the number of links per processor is even, using one or three links would leave another link unconnected. We have also assumed that at least one of the system controller's links is used to interface with the input/output facilities. In such a configuration of n processors, two processors will have three links available and $(n - 2)$ processors will have four links available for interconnection with the other processors. This results in a smaller upper bound on the maximum number of processors that can be obtained by considering the number of processors at different distances from a processor connected to the system controller. Since such a processor has $(\Delta - 1)$ links available for interconnection with other processors, this gives

$$1 + (\Delta - 1) + (\Delta - 1)^2 + \ldots + (\Delta - 1)^{D_{Diam}} \qquad (9.11)$$

processors.

It is possible to consider an optimal configuration of n processors as a combination of two nodes containing the system controller connections and $(n - 2)$ other nodes. The two nodes can then be considered to be connected to all the other nodes by a spanning tree (explained below) with a root node of valency 3, as represented by formula 9.11, and the other $(n - 2)$ nodes by a spanning tree with root node of valency 4, as represented by formula 9.10. It is then possible to calculate the average interprocessor distance, D_{Avg}, of this configuration, and the number of shortest paths which are equal to the diameter, which we shall term P_{diam} [33]. Table 9.1 shows some results for actual AMP configurations of valency 4 compared with the theoretical optimum configurations, which we know are unobtainable.

Processors	Actual AMP configurations			Theoretical Limit		
	D_{Diam}	P_{Diam}	D_{Avg}	D_{Diam}	P_{Diam}	D_{Avg}
12	2	43	1.514	2	43	1.514
13	2	53	1.550	2	53	1.550
14	3	2	1.602	3	1	1.592
32	3	247	2.297	3	244	2.291
36	3	349	2.374	3	346	2.368
40	4	15	2.456	3	464	2.431
53	4	171	2.694	4	13	2.578
64	4	492	2.885	4	365	2.821
128	5	899	3.523	5	7	3.409
256	6	1505	4.192	5	12200	4.154

Table 9.1   Comparison of results with theoretical limits

Spanning trees

Within a non-disjoint interconnection network, routes exist from every processor to all other processors. These routes initially traverse one of the source processor's links and from there travel across other processor's links until reaching their destination. More than one route may exist between any processor pair and these routes may differ in length. We shall term the set of routes which give the shortest distance between a processor and all other processors, the *spanning tree* for that processor. Figure 9.21 shows the 53-processor AMP and figure 9.22 shows the spanning tree for the processor labelled 0 in the 53-processor AMP.

Figure 9.23 shows the spanning tree for the processor labelled 9 in the 53-processor AMP. The irregular nature of the AMP configurations means that processor 9's spanning tree has a slightly different structure to that of processor 0, but both processors have a diameter less than or equal to that of the 52-processor AMP, that is 4. Figure 9.24 shows a spanning tree for processor 7 in the 20-processor mesh shown in figure 9.6. Spanning trees will play a significant rôle when considering the routing strategies for static configurations in section 9.2.3.

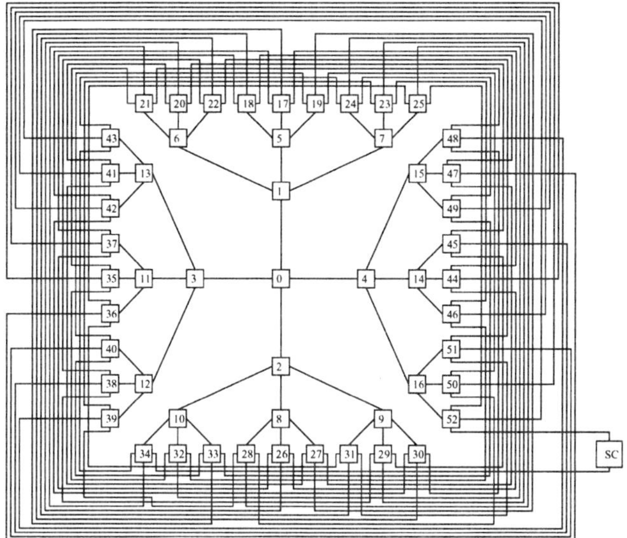

Figure 9.21   The 53-processor AMP configuration

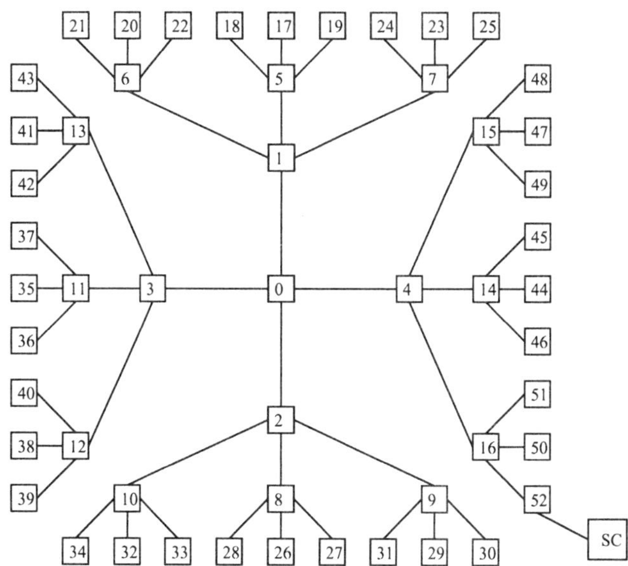

Figure 9.22   The spanning tree for processor labelled 0 in the 53-processor AMP configuration

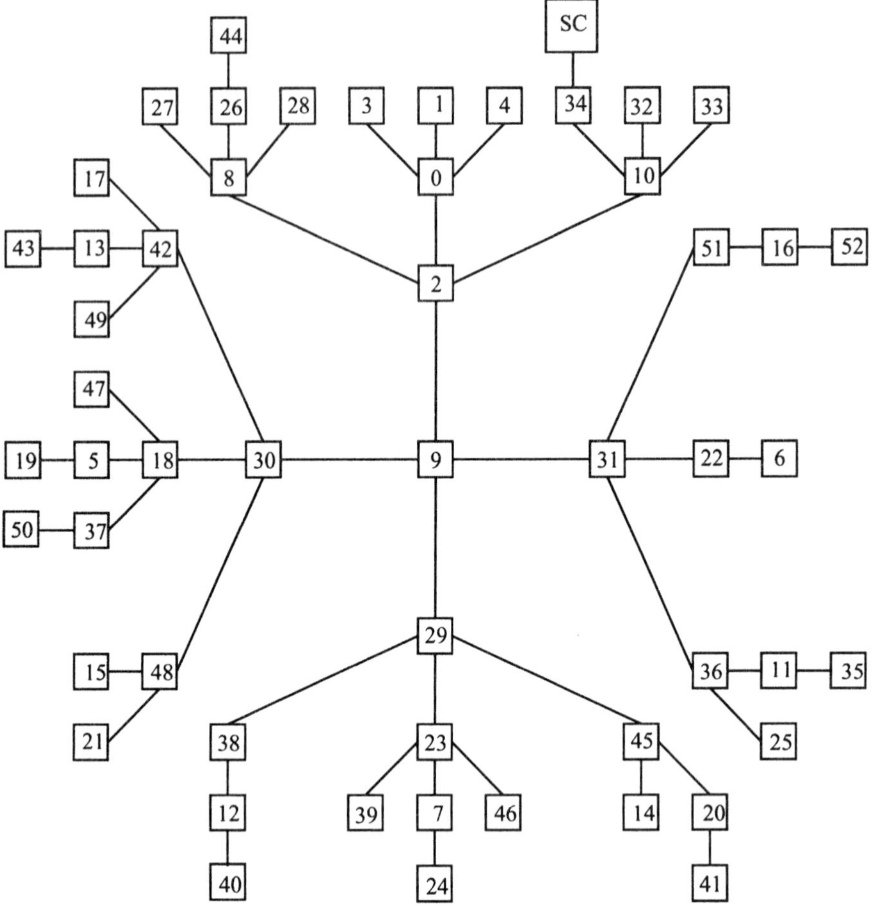

Figure 9.23   The spanning tree for processor labelled 9 in the 53-processor AMP configuration

9.1.5 Comparison of configurations

The physical distances messages have to travel within a multiprocessor system have important implications for the efficiency of the message transfer system. Our choice of configuration should reflect this. Comparing some of the configurations we have described, using the criteria put forward in section 9.1.2, will assist us when we come to choose the most appropriate configuration for the parallel implementation of the problem, later on in this chapter. Tables of results are given for only a small number of processors. You are encouraged to extend the tables to include the number of processors in your multiprocessor system.

Table 9.2 gives the diameters of a number of processors arranged in some of the configurations. As can be seen from the table, for a given number of processors, the diameter of AMP configurations are less than any of the other configurations,

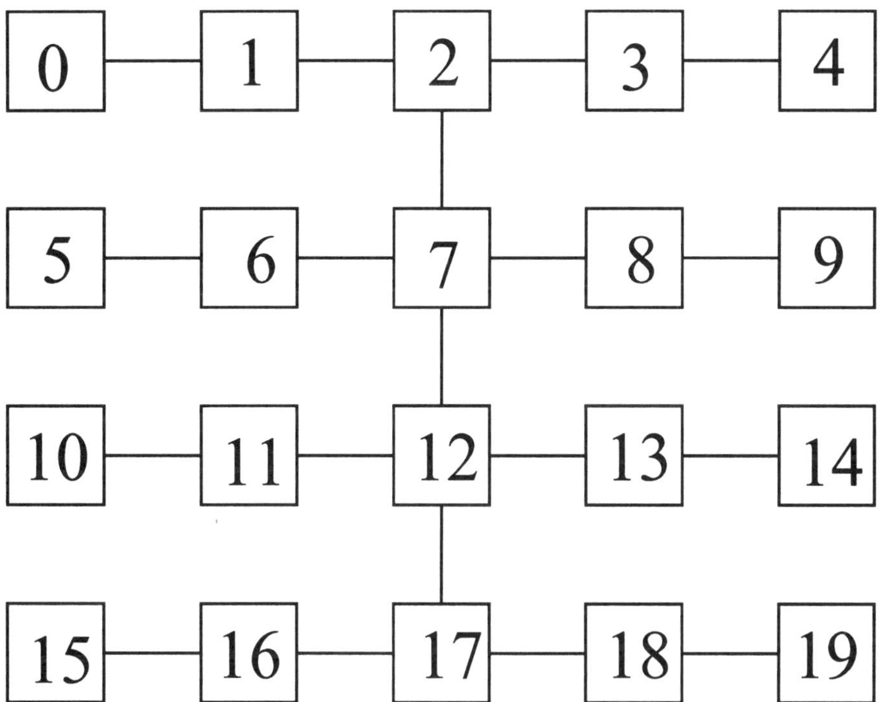

Figure 9.24   The spanning tree for processor labelled 7 in the 20-processor mesh configuration

and indeed the 64-processor AMP configuration has the same diameter as an 8-processor ring.

Table 9.3 gives the average interprocessor distance values, D_{Avg}, for different configurations. This average interprocessor distance is equivalent to the average number of links a message has to cross from any source processor to its desired destination processor. So, for example, a message from a source processor in a 64-processor AMP would have to cross 2.92 links on average while, for a processor on a 64-processor ring, the same message would have to traverse on average 16 links.

Table 9.4 gives the average number of links per processor in each of the configurations for the different numbers of processors. These averages are then used to calculate the normalised average interprocessor distances shown in table 9.5. Note that the links connecting the AMP configurations to the system controller are not included in this discussion and hence the values for the average number of links per processor in the AMP configurations are less than 4.

The normalised average interprocessor distances of ternary trees are low compared to AMP configurations due to their lower average number of links per processor. The hypercube of 3 processors has a normalised average interprocessor distance of 12.5 due to the requirement of 5 links per processor, whereas the 32-processor

	Processors								
	8	13	16	23	32	40	53	64	128
AMP	2	2	3	3	3	4	4	4	5
Hypercube	3	-	4	-	5	-	-	6	7
Torus	3	-	4	-	6	7	-	7	12
Ternary Tree	4	4	5	6	6	6	8	8	10
Mesh	4	-	6	-	10	11	-	14	22
Ring	4	6	8	11	16	20	26	32	64
Chain	7	12	15	22	31	39	52	63	127

Table 9.2   Comparison of configuration diameters

	Processors								
	8	13	16	23	32	40	53	64	128
AMP	1.28	1.55	1.73	2.05	2.31	2.53	2.76	2.92	3.58
Hypercube	1.50	-	2.00	-	2.50	-	-	3.00	3.50
Torus	1.50	-	2.00	-	3.00	3.50	-	4.00	5.64
Ternary Tree	1.97	2.56	2.91	3.39	3.93	4.25	4.77	5.01	6.25
Mesh	1.75	-	2.5	-	3.88	4.23	-	5.26	7.94
Ring	2.00	3.23	4.00	5.74	8.00	10.00	13.25	16.00	32.00
Chain	2.63	4.31	5.31	7.65	10.67	13.99	17.66	21.33	42.66

Table 9.3   Comparison of average interprocessor distances

AMP has a normalised average distance of 9.1 and only requires on average 3.94 links per processor.

Communication patterns

While the normalised average interprocessor distances give an interesting means of comparing configurations, the maximum number of routes on any link, r_{max}, and the average message load and total resultant number of messages, $load_{avg}$ and $message_{tot}$, may provide a better insight into the communication patterns within the configurations and, therefore, the possible communication overheads that may occur when *global* communication patterns exist in the system. Global communication will put the biggest strain on the communication facilities as, in this situation, every processor is required to communicate with all other processors.

| | \multicolumn{8}{c}{Processors} | | | | | | | |
	8	13	16	23	32	42	53	63
AMP	3.75	3.85	3.88	3.91	3.94	3.95	3.96	3.97
Hypercube	3.00	-	4.00	-	5.00	-	-	6.00[a]
Torus	4.00	-	4.00	-	4.00	4.00	-	4.00
Ternary Tree	3.45	1.84	1.87	1.91	1.94	1.95	1.96	1.97
C. C. Cycle	3.00	-	2.50	-	2.75	-	-	-
Mesh	2.50	-	3.00	-	3.25	3.38	-	3.49
Binary Tree	1.75	1.84	1.88	1.91	1.94	1.95	1.96	1.97
Ring	2.00	2.00	2.00	2.00	2.00	2.00	2.00	2.00
Chain	1.75	1.85	1.88	1.91	1.94	1.95	1.96	1.97

[a] 64-processor hypercube

Table 9.4 Average number of links per processor

| | \multicolumn{8}{c}{Processors} | | | | | | | |
	8	13	16	23	32	42	53	63
AMP	4.80	5.96	6.74	8.06	9.10	10.07	10.98	11.59
Hypercube	4.50	-	8.00	-	12.50	-	-	18.00[a]
Torus	6.00	-	8.00	-	12.00	12.84	-	15.76
Ternary Tree	3.45	4.72	5.45	6.48	7.61	8.54	9.36	9.83
C. C. Cycle	6.00	-	7.65	-	10.56	-	-	-
Mesh	4.38	-	2.50	-	3.88	4.23	-	4.91
Binary Tree	3.88	5.59	6.45	7.81	9.48	10.74	11.93	12.76
Ring	4.00	6.46	8.00	11.48	16.00	21.00	26.50	31.50
Chain	4.60	7.97	9.98	14.61	20.70	27.28	34.61	41.35

[a] 64-processor hypercube

Table 9.5 Comparison of normalised average interprocessor distances

Table 9.6 shows the maximum number of routes on any link of each of the configurations. The values given in this table for the AMP configurations exclude the routes to the system controller. The shorter distances between processors in the AMP configurations result in an r_{max} substantially lower than the tree configurations. In fact, the binary tree is almost equivalent to the chain due to the need for messages from processors of one subtree of the root to traverse the links at the root of the tree in order to get to the processing elements of the other subtree. This bottleneck is only slightly alleviated by increasing the degree of the tree from two to three, and even this still results in an r_{max} value for 23 processors being higher for the ternary tree than the binary tree. The 'hypercube structure' of the hypercubes and cube connected cycles with alternative paths between the 'dimensions' is responsible for the low maximum number of routes on the links of these configurations.

	Processors							
	8	13	16	23	32	42	53	63
AMP	7	12	18	28	43	61	83	101
Hypercube	8	-	16	-	32	-	-	64[a]
Torus	8	-	16	-	64	72	-	140
Mesh	16	-	32	-	128	144	-	280
C. C. Cycle	16	-	64	-	128	-	-	-
Ring	16	42	64	132	256	441	702	992
Ternary Tree	32	72	126	260	494	810	1404	1944
Binary Tree	32	84	128	240	512	832	1240	1984
Chain	32	84	128	264	512	882	1404	1984

[a] 64-processor hypercube

Table 9.6   Maximum number of routes on any link

Finally we come to the average number of messages handled by each link, $load_{avg}$, and the resultant message total, $message_{tot}$, for the configurations. These values are functions of the number of messages transmitted and the distances these messages have to travel and so, to illustrate these average message values, we will examine the case where each processor within the configurations issues 200 messages within a considered time interval. The method of communication used is point-to-point with each source processor sending messages to specific destination processors. Also, because within some of the configurations examined different processors have different numbers of links, average values for the number of processors distance d away, n_d, will be used to calculate the $load_{avg}$ values and then the total number of resultant message, $message_{tot}$. Table 9.7 shows the values for n_d for some of the 32-processor configurations. Rings and chains are not shown in this table as

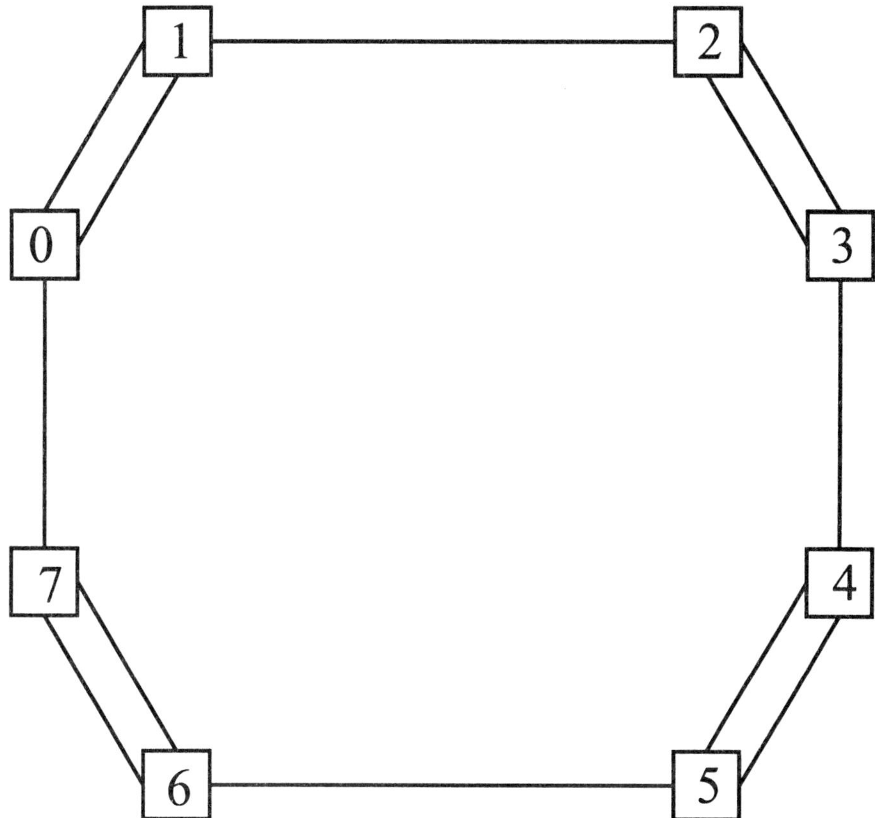

Figure 9.25   8-processor cube connected cycle

their diameters are too large to be easily accommodated. The 8-processor cube connected cycle, shown in figure 9.25, is unique amongst the configurations being examined as it has on occasion two links between the same pair of processors. These additional links may be used to reduce the link loads (but obviously not the number of messages that pass through a processor) and so the *load*$_{avg}$ value for the 8-processor cube connected cycle, given in table 9.8, reflects this, and thus is lower than the average message value for the 8-processor ring. The total resultant messages is the same for the 8-processor ring and the 8-processor cube connected cycle.

To illustrate the calculation of the average message values, we shall work through the example of a 32-processor AMP, with each processor issuing 200 messages. The number of messages destined for each processor and, therefore, absorbed is:

$$abs_d = \frac{200}{31} \simeq 6.45$$

	n_1	n_2	n_3	n_4	n_5	n_6	n_7	n_8	n_9	n_{10}
AMP	3.94	11.06	16.00							
Hypercube	5.00	10.00	10.00	5.00	1.00					
Torus	4.00	7.00	8.00	7.00	4.00	1.00				
Ternary Tree	1.94	3.63	4.69	7.44	7.13	6.19				
C. C. Cycle	2.75	3.75	5.00	6.75	7.00	4.50	1.25			
Mesh	3.25	5.13	5.75	5.25	4.25	3.25	2.25	1.25	0.50	0.13
Binary Tree	1.94	2.75	3.38	4.38	4.25	5.19	4.38	4.25	0.50	

Table 9.7 Average number of processors distance d away, n_d, in 32-processor configurations

Now, from equation (9.8) and table 9.7:

$$load_1 = \frac{200}{3.94}$$
$$load_2 = \frac{50.76 - 6.45}{2.81}$$
$$load_3 = \frac{15.77 - 6.45}{1.45}$$

If the results are not rounded to two decimal places, as we have shown, then the value of the average message loads, $load_3$ in this example, should be equal to the number of messages absorbed, abs_d. The $load_{avg}$ for the 32-processor AMP rounding to two decimal places each time is:

$$load_{avg} = (3.94 \times 50.76) + (11.06 \times 15.77) + (16.00 \times 6.43)$$
$$= 477.29$$

Table 9.8 shows the $load_{avg}$ values for the each of the configurations.

For a given number of source messages, the total number of messages, $message_{tot}$, that will result within the configuration may be obtained from equation (9.9) (except for the 8-processor cube connected cycle) as:

$$message_{tot} = load_{avg} \times n$$

Figure 9.26 shows a bar graph of some of these total numbers of resultant messages calculated for each of the configurations when each processor issues 200 messages. As can easily be seen, in configurations in which an increase in the number of processors leads to a marked increase in the average interprocessor distance between any two of these processors, the number of extra messages generated increases alarmingly. So, for a ring of 32 processors, 6400 source messages results in 52852 messages within the system, and even worse, although not shown in figure 9.26, for a 32-processor chain, 6400 source messages results in 70400 mes-

				Processors				
	8	13	16	23	32	42	53	63
AMP	292.86	335.90	371.67	430.83	477.23	523.13	563.86	593.45
Hypercube	342.86	-		-	516.10	-	-	609.52[a]
Torus	342.86	-	426.67	-	619.36	658.54	-	800.00
Ternary Tree	450.00	553.83	620.00	708.30	811.29	895.70	972.42	1014.85
C. C. Cycle	342.90	-	683.33	-	793.55	-	-	-
Mesh	400.00	-	533.33	-	800.00	866.67	-	1066.67
Binary Tree	507.14	654.41	733.33	853.76	1010.08	1127.29	1239.48	1317.36
Ring	457.14	683.33	853.33	1190.91	1651.61	2151.22	2696.15	3196.77
Chain	600.00	933.33	1133.33	1600.00	2200.00	2866.66	3600.00	4266.66

[a] 64-processor hypercube

Table 9.8 Comparison of $load_{avg}$ values

sages, an 11-fold increase. As the number of processors is increased to 63 in the chain, then 200 messages per processor results in more than a quarter of a million messages, an increase over the number of source messages of over 21-fold.

The average number of messages handled by each link and, therefore, the total resultant messages are lower for the AMP configurations than any of the other configurations considered. For an 8-processor AMP, 1600 source messages results in a modest 2343 total messages, only a 46% increase, while for a 63-processor AMP, 12600 source messages causes 37387 messages, an increase of 198%. Percentage increases for all of the configurations are shown in figure 9.27, while the same percentages in more detail, excluding the rings and chains are shown in figure 9.28.

If the same message needs to be sent to all processors, then a broadcast method of communication, as described in section 9.2.3, could be used. In this case each processor only sends one message on each of its links. This message is received and propagated further by the other processors. In this case the total number of messages that will result for each of the n processors issuing m broadcasts is thus

$$message_{tot} = m \times n(n - 1)$$

This total number of messages is configuration independent and will give significantly lower message totals than the point-to-point method discussed previously.

If the same number of messages, $\frac{200}{n-1}$, is used for the broadcast method as was used to construct table 9.8, then the total number of messages resulting from the broadcast is $(200 \times n)$, which produces the same number of resultant messages as there are source messages in the point-to-point method of communication.

9.2 Communication Strategies

Co-operation may be the key if complex problems are to be solved on distributed memory MIMD processors in desirable times. This co-operation is achieved in such

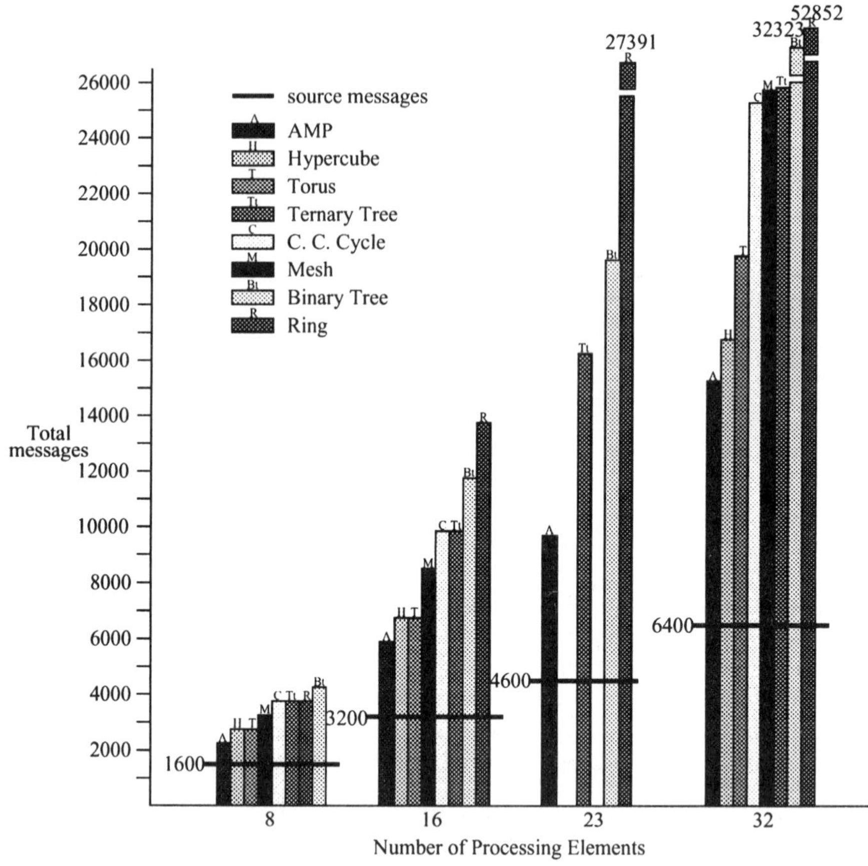

Figure 9.26 Bar graph of $message_{tot}$ values

a message passing environment by the processes sending and receiving messages. Communication is accomplished because a process, upon receiving a message, obtains the values sent from the source process and synchronisation is achieved because a message can only be dealt with after it has been sent [10]. If a link (either internal or external) exists between a source process A and a destination process B, then a message may be sent by process A executing the output command:

SEND *message* **TO** B

and received by process B performing the corresponding input command:

RECEIVE *message* **FROM** A

On the other hand, as the link specifies the connection of two processes, the message may also be sent by the source process A performing:

SEND *message* **ON** *link*

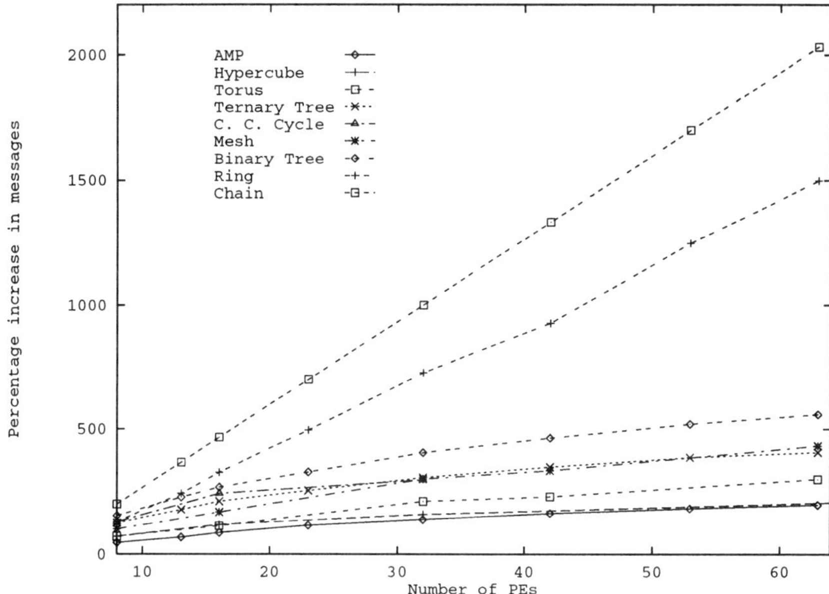

Figure 9.27 Percentage increase in messages for all configurations

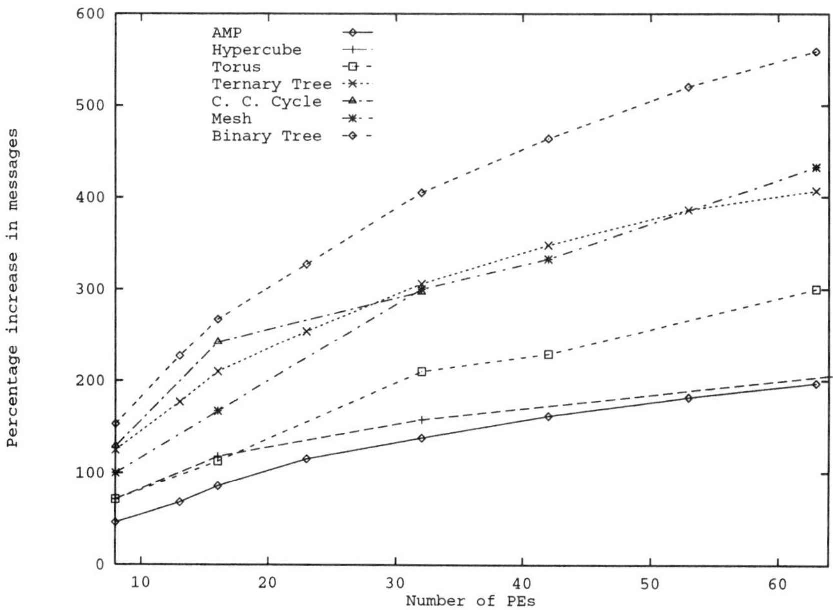

Figure 9.28 Percentage increase in messages for configurations excluding rings and chains

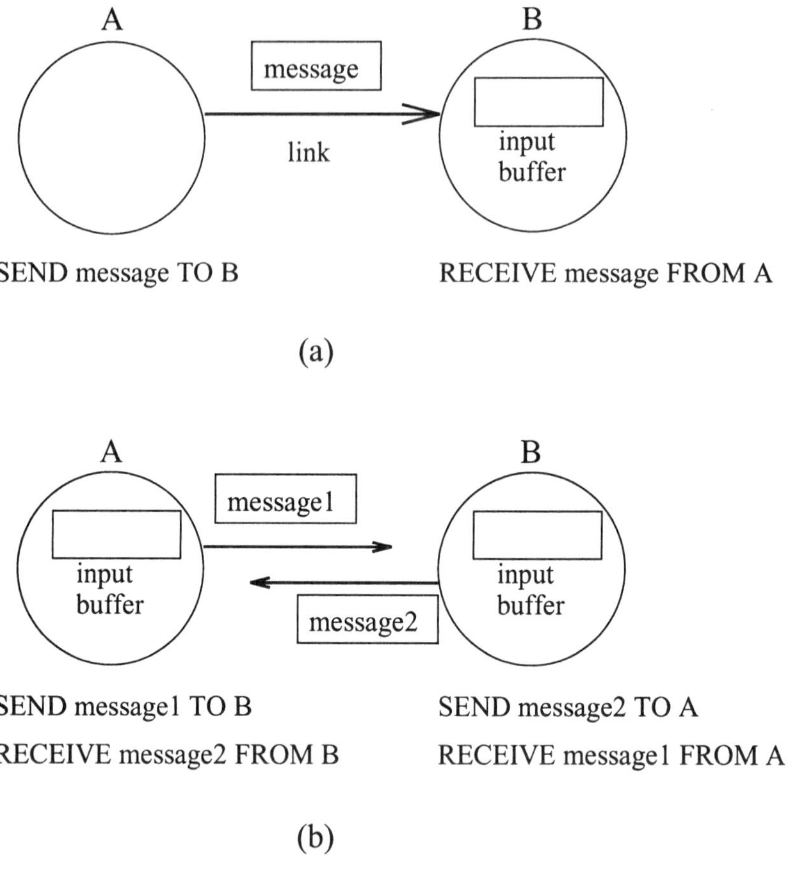

Figure 9.29   (a) Communication from process A to process B (b) deadlock

and received by the destination process *B* executing:

RECEIVE *message* **OFF** *link*

These two methods are equivalent. Both methods will be used in this description of communication strategy. Whichever method is used, the message is transferred from the source process *A* via the link to the destination process *B*, as shown diagrammatically in figure 9.29(a). An input buffer will be necessary to store the incoming message temporarily at process *B* for future interpretation. For the purposes of this discussion we will assume that a link connects two processes and is bidirectional.

In static topologies each processing element is connected to a fixed number of other processing elements, and may thus communicate directly with these processing elements. This communication may be handled by a router process at each processing element which is shown in the structure for the processing element in figure 4.13. To facilitate communication between processing elements that are not directly connected, each router should also provide the ability for passing on messages destined for processing elements other than itself. A router should thus monitor all external links coupling a processing element with other directly connected processing elements as well as those links connecting any other internal processes (such as the local controller, data manager, etc.) to the router. The router can now respond to inputs received off any of the links. During the course of this response, in accordance with the deadlock avoidance scheme described shortly, any additional incoming messages will be buffered. Having dealt with the original message the router is then free to tackle those messages that may have been buffered. The router continues these activities until the desired computation is complete and the system is closed down by the system controller. An outline of a router with four external links, with `external_link[0]` used for receiving the initialisation parameters, is:

```
PROCESS Router()
  Begin
    RECEIVE initialisation_parameters OFF external_link[0]
    busy := TRUE  (* until the problem is solved *)
    WHILE busy DO
      Begin
        INPUT ALTERNATIVES
          RECEIVE message OFF internal_link  (*all internals*)
            Handle(message)
          RECEIVE message OFF external_link  (*all externals*)
            Handle(message)

        Handle_Any_Buffered_Inputs()
      End
  End (* Router *)
```

The communication harness provided by the routers enables messages to be passed between the processing elements of the system. Thus, if the processing elements can be imagined as the bricks used for building a multiprocessor system, then the communication harness is the cement which holds the processing elements together.

As mentioned previously, the type of communication we are primarily concerned with is point-to-point. In such a communication paradigm, one process may communicate on one link to one other process. If this communication is synchronous then, whichever process performs the appropriate input or output command first is suspended until the other process reaches its corresponding command. The values are then transferred and both processes are free to continue. The order in which the inputs and outputs occur between processes is critical if a deadlock situation is to be avoided. Deadlock occurs if processes are waiting for communications that never materialise. For example, deadlock occurs in the segments of code shown in figure 9.29(b), because process A is waiting to output to process B which will never occur because at the same time process B is waiting to output to process A. The onus is on the programmer to ensure that this situation does not arise. Ensuring inputs and outputs are in the correct sequence is not a guarantee, however, that the spectre of subtle deadlock will never arise between processes executing on different processors. In figure 9.30 deadlock also occurs as once again no process is able to

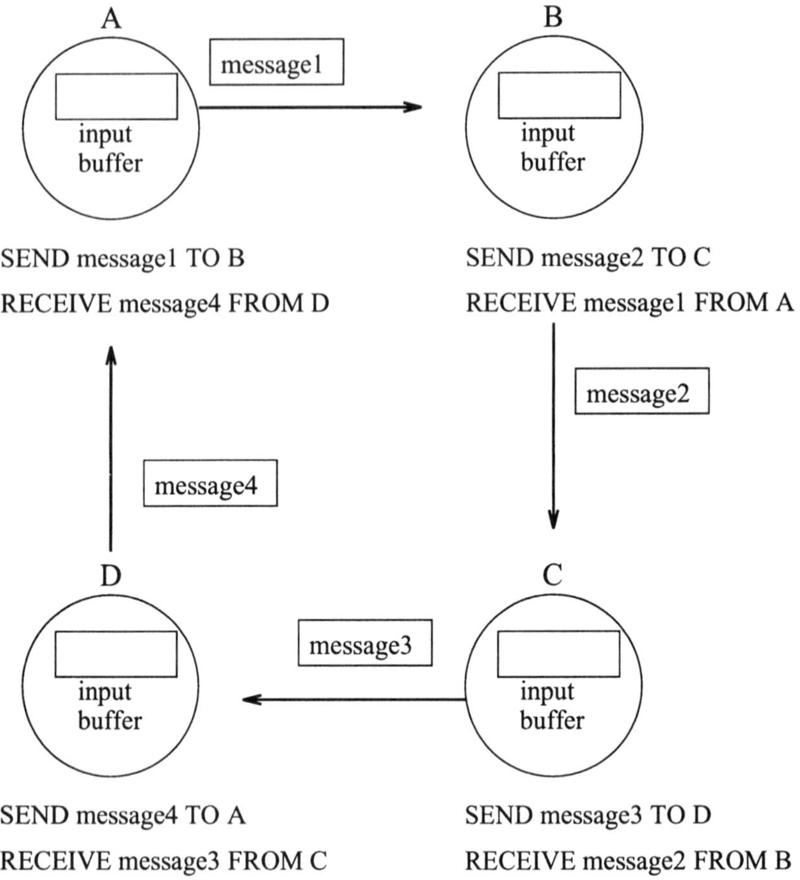

Figure 9.30   A deadlock situation

complete its output command. Additional measures have to be taken within the router to avoid deadlock.

9.2.1 Avoiding deadlock

Multiple processes executing on a single processor execute concurrently. Concurrent execution implies the processes share the processor time and so only one process will be executing at any point in time. A process can, therefore, be in one of three states: *executing*; *active*, that is waiting to be executed; or, *descheduled* waiting for an event, such as a communication, to occur. Assuming more than one level of scheduling priority exists, a high priority process will always be executed in preference to a low priority process if both are active. A low priority process is thus run until it is unable to proceed because it is waiting to output or input, or it is interrupted by a high level process. In addition, a low priority process will be descheduled and placed at the end of the schedule list after a certain timeslice period to allow other low priority processes to be executed. A high priority process will never be timesliced in this way to accommodate low priority processes.

This favoured scheduling of high priority processes can be used to form the basis for a deadlock avoidance scheme within the router. Communication by the router on any link is performed by two subprocesses shown in the following code segment. A high priority process Do_Output, performs the actual output on a specified link while a low priority process, Handle_Input receives and buffers any inputs from that link and any other links until the output has been completed. On completion of the output, the high priority process informs the low priority process of this fact and the communication is over. The router is then free to deal with any inputs that may have been buffered.

```
PROCESS Router()

  SUBPROCESS Do_Output(output_link)
    Begin
      SEND message ON output_link (* perform desired output *)
      SEND FALSE TO Handle_Input
    End (* Do_Output *)


  SUBPROCESS Handle_Input(input_links)
    Begin
      carry_on := TRUE
      WHILE carry_on DO
        PRIORITISED INPUT ALTERNATIVES
          1. RECEIVE carry_on FROM Do_Output
              (* sets carry_on to FALSE*)

          2. RECEIVE message OFF internal_link (* all internals *)
              Store_In_Buffer(message)
          3. RECEIVE message OFF external_link (* all externals *)
              Store_In_Buffer(message)
    End (* Handle_Input *)


  SUBPROCEDURE Handle(message)
    Begin
      Interpret(message)
      IF (message requires output) THEN
        PRIORITISED PARALLEL
          1. Do_Output(output_link)   (* high priority *)
          2. Handle_Input(input_link) (* low  priority *)
      ELSE
        Deal_With(message)
      ENDIF
    End (* Handle *)

  (* start of main body of Router *)
  Begin
```

```
RECEIVE initialisation_parameters OFF external_link[0]
busy := TRUE  (* until the problem is solved *)
WHILE busy DO
  Begin
    INPUT ALTERNATIVES
      RECEIVE message OFF internal_link (* all internals *)
        Handle(message)
      RECEIVE message OFF external_link (* all externals *)
        Handle(message)

    WHILE NOT buffer_empty DO
      Begin
        Remove_From_Buffer(buffered_message)
        Handle(buffered_message)
      End
  End
End (* Router *)
```

The output process, being a high priority process, immediately interrupts any low priority process and attempts to perform its output. If the destination process is ready for the communication, the transfer occurs and the `Handle_Input` process is notified. This notification terminates the `Handle_Input` process, and the router can thus return to its task of monitoring links. If, however, the destination process is currently not ready to receive the output, for example, if it is trying to perform an output itself, then the high priority `Do_Output` process is descheduled and the low priority process `Handle_Input` is run. This low priority process receives inputs from the multitude of sources and buffers these to be dealt with once the communication is complete. As soon as the `Do_Output` process is able to continue it will be rescheduled, interrupting the low priority process, and the desired transfer can occur. The communication is completed by the `Do_Output` process sending the value `FALSE` to the `Handle_Input` process which terminates the `WHILE carry_on DO` loop. The router must now deal with any messages that may have been buffered. These messages are handled in the order in which they were received, thus preserving the message sequence.

Although not shown in the code segment, the router is also able to take advantage should a processor be able to communicate on its external links simultaneously. If simultaneous output is being performed, then a high priority `Do_Output` process will be launched for each output, and the single low priority `Handle_Input` process will continue to receive and buffer incoming messages until all the `Do_Output` processes have completed.

Implementing the output as a high priority process avoids the subtle deadlock described in [40]. Buffering of the inputs not only helps prevent deadlock, but also allows other routers to terminate their communications and thus introduces a degree of asynchronous communication. The size of the input buffers and the time delay in dealing with the received messages can have implications for system performance. As mentioned above, the input process, `Handle_Input`, will only receive and buffer inputs as long as the output process (or processes) are delayed in their communication. As all outputs will in turn be received and buffered by

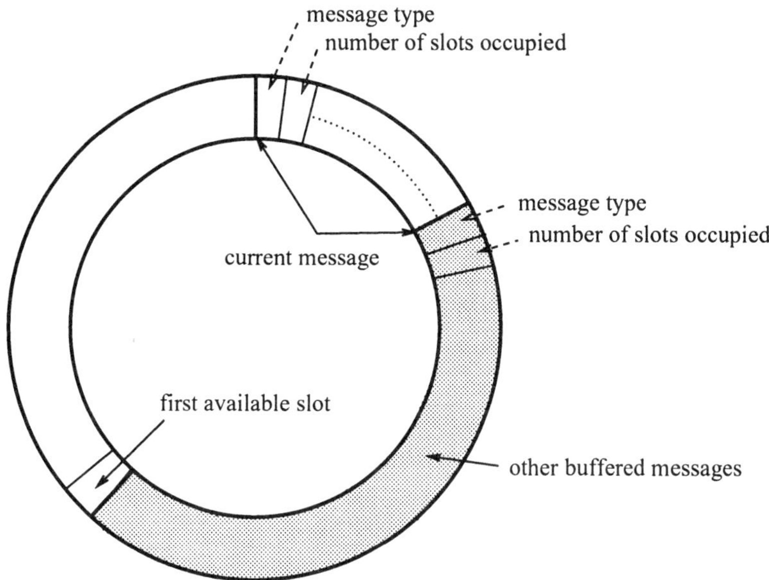

Figure 9.31 Circular buffer for storing input message

corresponding Handle_Input processes on other processing elements this delay should not be significant.

The incoming messages are stored in a circular buffer as shown in figure 9.31. A variety of message types and sizes may exist in a complex message passing system and so it is necessary to store the message type and the number of buffer slots that the message will occupy as the first two slots of a buffered message. When handling the buffered messages, the router process is able to reconstruct each message using these two slots and deal with this current message accordingly. It may happen that while dealing with a buffered message additional messages may arrive, for example, if the current buffered message involves an output. The additional messages will be added to the back of the circular buffer. Only after all buffered messages have been handled will the router return to its passive state of monitoring the links. In this way a form of asynchronous communication may proceed through a router while still preserving the order of the messages received.

As input message traffic is forthcoming from not only external links, but also from internal links (from the task manager, data manager and local controller), it is possible that the input process could be swamped by messages and the buffer overflow. To reduce the possibility of this swamping, a *saturation prevention* mechanism can be built into the communication scheme to restrict inputs on the internal links should the level of the buffer exceed a certain critical level. These restrictions will reduce the asynchronous nature of the communications, but this is obviously preferable to a saturation situation.

There are, of course, many other methods that can be used to avoid deadlock. Several of these impose a strict synchronous control on the communication. Pro-

Message Type:

specific_request_external_data	*tag* source_PE destination_PE data_id		

global_request_external_data	*tag* source_PE data_id	

return_data	*tag* destination_PE source_PE data_length data_item			

external_request_task	*tag* source_PE destination_PE task_id		

return_task	*tag* destination_PE source_PE task_length task_packet			

change_state	*tag* which_state

closedown_command	*tag*

Figure 9.32   The format of some example messages

cesses are only allowed to communicate on a link if they are in possession of the control token for that link. Having only one control token per link helps reduce the likelihood of deadlock. Other deadlock free routing schemes, such as the 'virtual channel' method are more flexible [54, 146]. In this approach, each link is substituted by a pair of virtual channels. Each process now passes messages on the virtual channel determined by its own process identity and the identity of the destination process. The choice of channels at each process is arranged to ensure the communication is deadlock free. This method of virtual channels has been shown in [54] to provide a deadlock free routing strategy for hypercubes of any dimension.

9.2.2 Message protocols

A variety of message types and sizes exist in a complex message passing system. To distinguish between them, each message is accompanied by a *tag* which specifies what type of message is currently being communicated and thus the format of the message. Certain messages will have a fixed size, while others will be of a variable length depending on the problem and the stage of the computation. To assist with the interpretation, these variable length messages must contain information about the size of the variable portions at known locations within the message packet. Figure 9.32 gives the format of some typical messages that will be required. Note that the source_PE of the data or task request will become the destination_PE of the returning data or task message.

9.2.3 Routing

In order to proceed from its source processing element to the desired destination processing element, a message must follow an existing path within the multiprocessor system. If the source and destination processing elements are adjacent then

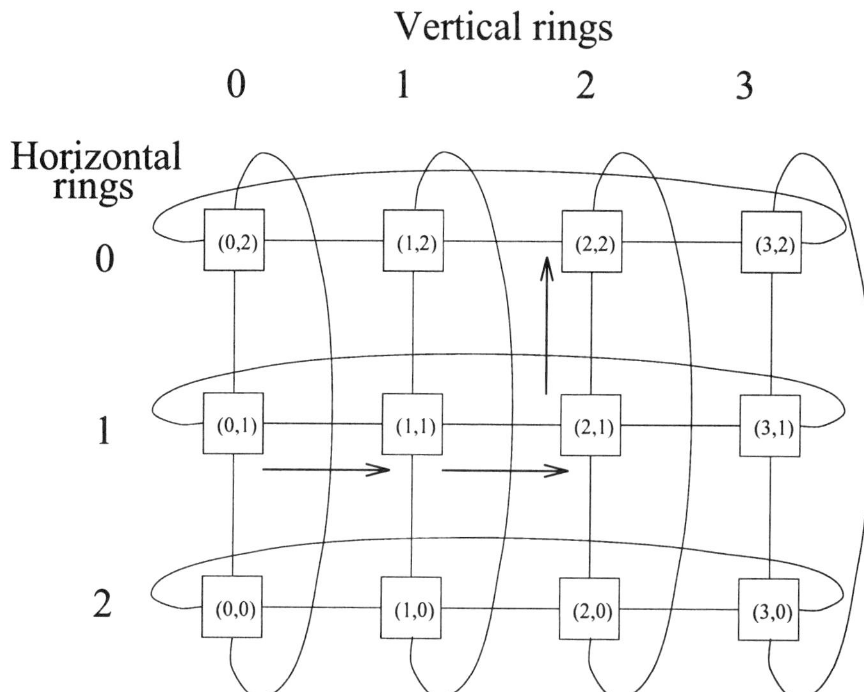

Figure 9.33 An example of routing in a 12-processing element torus

a direct path exists between these two processing elements. However, if source and destination processing elements are not directly connected then the path taken by the message will include other processing elements.

Regular configurations, such as tori and hypercubes are able to use a routing function to determine the route of any message between two processing elements within the system. The routing function works by computing the next link on which to send the message from the destination address contained in the message. This process is repeated at each processor visited on the path from source to destination. For example, in a torus several paths of minimum distance between processing elements exist. The following code segment uses the Cartesian coordinate labelling system illustrated in figure 9.33 to implement one possible routing strategy.

```
PROCESS Torus_Router()
  Begin
    busy := TRUE
    WHILE busy DO
      INPUT ALTERNATIVES
        RECEIVE message FROM internal_process (* INTERNAL *)
          Begin
            offset := (destination_coord[horiz] + cfp1 -
```

```
                    processor_coord[horiz]) MOD cfp1
        IF offset > (cfp1 DIV 2) THEN
          SEND message TO link_left
        ELSE
          SEND message TO link_right
        ENDIF
      End

    RECEIVE message FROM link_up      (* UP direction *)
      IF destination_coord = processor_coord THEN
        SEND message TO internal_process
      ELSE
        SEND message TO link_down
      ENDIF

  (* DOWN similar to UP *)

    RECEIVE message FROM link_left   (* LEFT direction *)
      IF destination_coord = processor_coord THEN
        SEND message TO internal_process
      ELSEIF destination_coord[horiz] =
                  processor_coord[horiz] THEN
        Begin
          offset := (destination_coord[vert] + cfp2 -
                  processor_coord[vert]) MOD cfp2
          IF offset > (cfp2 DIV 2) THEN
            SEND message TO link_down
          ELSE
            SEND message TO link_up
          ENDIF
        End
      ELSE
        SEND message TO link_right
      ENDIF
    (* RIGHT similar to LEFT *)
  End (* Torus_Router *)
```

Another example of an elegant routing function is routing messages within a hypercube. The processing elements in a k-dimensional hypercube may be labelled using a k-bit binary code in such a way that a processing element's links connect to those processing elements whose binary code differs in exactly one position [140]. Each link can thus be thought of as corresponding to a bit position shown in figure 9.9 for a 4-dimensional hypercube. Routing within the hypercube may now be achieved by comparison of the destination bit pattern with the processing element label [54]. This routing strategy is detailed in the following code segment.

```
PROCESS Hypercube_Router()
  Begin
    busy := TRUE
    WHILE busy DO
      INPUT ALTERNATIVES
      RECEIVE message FROM link[in]
```

```
        IF destination_label = PE_label THEN
          SEND message TO internal_process
        ELSE
          Begin
            bit := Find_Differing_Bit(destination_label,
                                      PE_label)
            SEND message TO link[bit]
          End
        ENDIF
      RECEIVE message FROM internal_process
        Begin
          bit := Find_Differing_Bit(destination_label,
                                    PE_label)
          SEND message TO link[bit]
        End
  End (* Hypercube_Router *)
```

The routing strategy for the hypercube may become clearer if illustrated by means of an example. Consider a 4-dimensional hypercube in which the processing element labelled 0100 received a message destined for the processing element labelled 0111. In this case the message should be sent further on the link connecting the receiving processing element and the processing element labelled 0110, as this processing element's label differs from the receiving processing element's label in the third bit (from the left) which is the same bit in which the receiving processing element's label differs from the label of the destination processing element. The route for a message from the processing element labelled 0000 to the processing element labelled 0111 in the 4-dimensional hypercube is shown graphically in figure 9.34.

The irregular nature of some configurations, such as the AMPs, precludes such a routing function. However, as the configurations are static we are able to determine *a priori* all possible paths from one processing element to any other processing element within the system. From this potentially large set of all the possible paths we are now in a position to select those paths that we may deem as desirable for the message to follow.

Two criteria are used for selecting the desired paths for messages. Firstly, the path should be chosen such that the distance between the source processing element and the destination processing element is as short as possible. This shortest path implies that the number of links the message has to traverse, and thus the number of intermediate processing elements the message has to negotiate, is minimised. The distance of all these chosen paths will fall within the diameter of the system. Secondly, where a choice of possible paths which satisfy the first criterion exist, then the path selected will be such that the number of paths traversing any link in the system will be approximately the same. Ideally all links should be included in the same number of paths, but due to the requirements of the first criterion and the irregular nature of the configurations this may not be possible. We shall term this path as the *primary path*. When certain links of the system are heavily loaded with messages, then it may be appropriate to choose an alternative path for a message. Methods for selecting these *secondary paths* are discussed later in this section. The set of primary paths from a processing element to all other processing elements is the spanning tree for that processing element, as discussed in section 9.1.4.

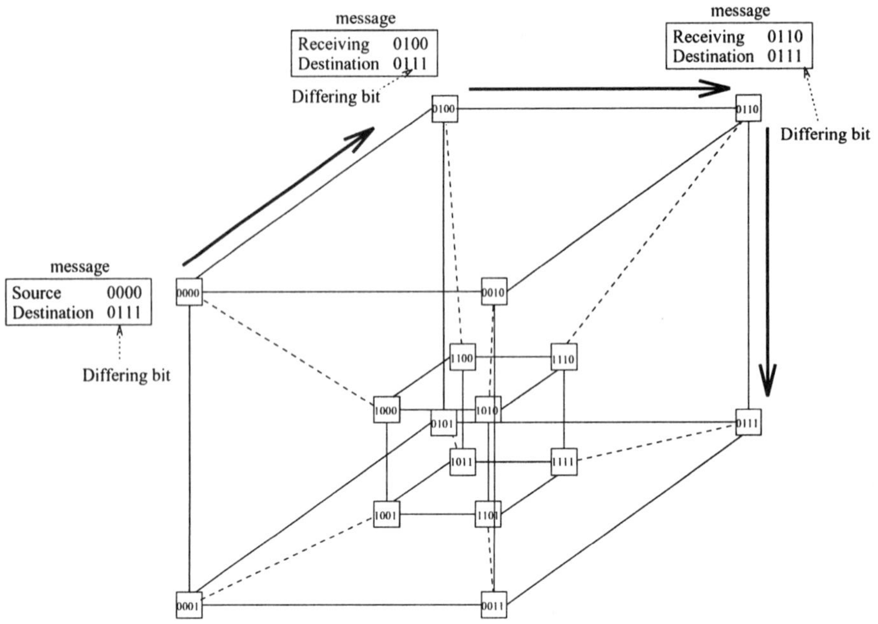

Figure 9.34   An example of routing within a 16-processing element hypercube

Given the selection strategy of always choosing the shortest path between any two processing elements as the primary path, we are able to avoid storing every spanning tree at each processing element. Instead it is sufficient to store the link which gives the shortest path. If we imagine the four links of each processing element as being in the *Up*, *Down*, *Left* or *Right* direction, then the choice of link may simply be the choice of one of these four directions. The storage of this information, therefore, only requires a 2-bit entry in a lookup, or *path table* for every processing element. A configuration of n processing elements would thus require a path table of $2 \times (n - 1)$ bits to be stored at each processing element. The path table for the 8-processing element AMP configuration, given in figure 9.35, is shown in table 9.9.

On receipt of a message from an external link, the router determines from the destination address in the heading of the message, `destination_PE`, whether this processing element is the destination of the message. If this is not the case, then the message is routed out on the link obtained from its path table. A description of this is shown in the following code segment. Messages from internal processes require no check and may be routed immediately on the external link obtained from the path table.

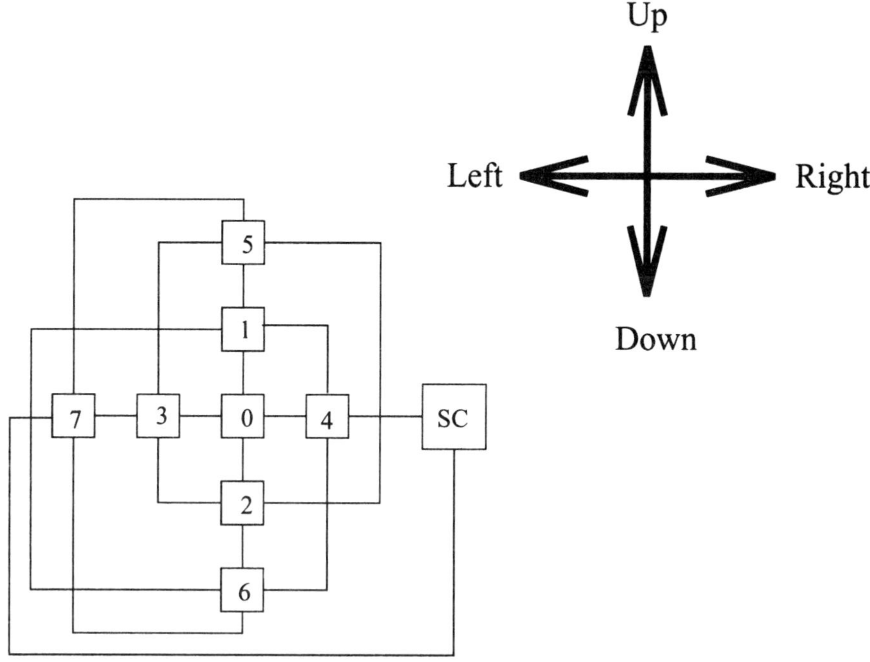

Figure 9.35 The 8-processing element AMP configuration

					Destination					
	PEs	0	1	2	3	4	5	6	7	SC
	0	.	Up	Down	Left	Right	Up	Down	Left	Right
S	1	Down	.	Left	Up	Right	Up	Left	Left	Right
o	2	Up	Right	.	Left	Down	Right	Down	Left	Down
u	3	Right	Up	Down	.	Right	Up	Down	Left	Left
r	4	Left	Up	Down	Left	.	Up	Down	Down	Right
c	5	Left	Down	Right	Left	Down	.	Up	Up	Up
e	6	Up	Left	Up	Down	Right	Down	.	Down	Right
	7	Right	Up	Right	Right	Down	Up	Down	.	Left
	SC	Left	Left	Left	Down	Left	Down	Down	Down	.

Table 9.9 The path table for the 8-processing element AMP configuration

```
PROCESS Router()

  (* Other Procedures & Subprocesses *)

  SUBPROCEDURE Handle(message)
    Begin
      Interpret(message)
      IF (message requires output) THEN
        Begin
          IF (destination_PE = PE_id) THEN
            (* send message to appropriate local process *)
            Communicate(internal_link[appropriate])
          ELSE
            Communicate(external_link[path_table[destination_PE]])
          ENDIF
        End
      ELSE
        Deal_With(message)
      ENDIF
    End (* Handle *)

  (*** start of main body of Router ***)
  Begin
    RECEIVE initialisation_parameters OFF external_link[0]
    busy := TRUE  (* until the problem is solved *)
    WHILE busy DO
      Begin
        INPUT ALTERNATIVES
          RECEIVE message OFF internal_link (* all internals *)
            Handle(message)
          RECEIVE message OFF external_link (* all externals *)
            Handle(message)

        Handle_Any_Buffered_Inputs()
      End
  End (* Router *)
```

The path tables for the configuration need only ever be computed once and then the appropriate row distributed to each processing element when the system is initialised. Provided the physical links are set correctly, this strategy allows the routing for any configuration to be carried out by simply acquiring the necessary path table. In this way, the complexity of the routing function for the torus shown in the appropriate code segment can be replaced for the 8-processing element torus by the path table shown in table 9.10. Note that the system controller can easily be included using a path table, but the use of existing links for the inclusion and the consequent loss of symmetry would require a modification to the routing function.

For the overhead of some additional storage requirements, the path tables are able to provide a simple routing strategy to enable the routers at each processing element to exchange messages with other processing elements. Indeed, determining the appropriate path using a path table is computationally quicker than the calculations

	PEs	0	1	2	3	4	5	6	7	SC
						Destination				
	0	.	Right	Right	Left	Down	Down	Down	Down	Up
S	1	Left	.	Right	Right	Down	Down	Down	Down	Left
o	2	Left	Left	.	Right	Down	Down	Down	Down	Right
u	3	Right	Left	Left	.	Down	Down	Down	Down	Down
r	4	Up	Up	Up	Up	.	Right	Right	Left	Up
c	5	Up	Up	Up	Up	Left	.	Right	Right	Left
e	6	Up	Up	Up	Up	Left	Left	.	Right	Right
	7	Up	Up	Up	Up	Right	Left	Left	.	Down
	SC	Up	Up	Down	Down	Up	Up	Down	Down	.

Table 9.10 The path table for the 8-processing element torus

required by the complex routing functions. Path tables provide the mechanism for point-to-point communication. Additional techniques are needed to implement global broadcasts.

The global broadcast mechanism

Point-to-point communication implies a *one-to-one* mapping of a message from one source processing element to one destination processing element, even though intermediate processing elements may be involved in the routing of the message. Often it may be desirable to communicate one message from one source processing element to all other processing elements. For example, we may require such a strategy for searching for data items in unknown locations, as discussed in section 8.3.3.

A global broadcast facility allows a *one-to-many* mapping of communication to processing elements. When performing a global broadcast, a message from the source processing element is communicated on all the top level links of the spanning tree. This message is then absorbed and routed further by every other processing element until all processing elements have received the message. Within a system containing four links per processor, each processing element will receive at most one message and route the message further at most three times.

Having received a message which has been globally broadcast, a processing element must know on which links, if any, this message should be routed onward so that all processing elements will receive the same message and no processing element will receive the message more than once. Every processing element must, therefore, have some knowledge of every other processing element's spanning tree. As the spanning trees are predetermined and thus fixed, it is sufficient that each processing element has a 4-bit code for every other processing element. In this code, each bit corresponds to a link, in the Up, Down, Left and Right directions respectively. If, within the code for a particular processing element the bit is set to 1, then on receipt of a broadcast message from that processing element the message must be routed further on that link. Alternatively, if the bit is set to 0 then the message must not be propagated on that link. The messages that are propagated may, of course, be routed further on the appropriate links simultaneously if the hardware allows it. The *broadcast table* for the processing element labelled 0 in the 8-processing element AMP system is shown in table 9.11. So, from this table, if processing element 0 gets a broadcast message from processing element 1, it knows this message has to be propagated further on its Down link (to processing element 2). Similarly if processing element 0 receives a broadcast message from processing element 4, it propagates the message on its Down and Left links, while if it receives a broadcast message from processing element 6, processing element 0 will not propagate the message further.

Source	Up	Down	Left	Right
1	0	1	0	0
2	1	0	0	0
3	1	0	0	1
4	0	1	1	0
5	0	0	0	0
6	0	0	0	0
7	0	0	0	0
SC	0	1	0	0

Table 9.11   The broadcast table for the processing element 0 in the 8-processing element AMP

The modification to the router process to allow it to sequentially route a globally broadcast message is given in the following code segment. Note that due to the nature of spanning trees, when a globally broadcast message is received on an external link, the appropriate bit in the broadcast table for the receiving processing element that corresponds to the source processing element and the link on which the message arrived will be set to 0.

```
PROCEDURE Handle(message)
  Begin
    Interpret(message)
    IF (message requires output) THEN
      Begin
        IF (message = global_broadcast) THEN
          Begin
            Communicate(internal_link[appropriate]) (* absorb *)
            FOR i = 1 TO number_of_external_links DO
              IF (broadcast_table[source_PE][i] = 1) THEN
                (* propagate the message further *)
                Communicate(external_link[i])
              ENDIF
      End
```

```
    ELSEIF (destination_PE = PE_id) THEN
       (* send message to appropriate local process *)
       Communicate(internal_link[appropriate])
    ELSE
       Communicate(external_link[path_table[destination_PE]])
  End
ELSE
  Deal_With(message)
ENDIF
End (* Handle *)
```

Other strategies

Routing strategies have been the subject of detailed research by the communications and networking communities. While the environments of a dedicated multiprocessor interconnection network and a global information super-highway are obviously different, a number of techniques may be adopted into the routing strategies of the system software from the communications industry as circumstances dictate. Some of these techniques are:

Dynamic monitoring: By monitoring its own communication, each router will be aware of its local message density and the delays in communicating messages with its neighbours. It may also be aware of delays elsewhere in the system, but this information should be treated with caution, due to the delay in actually acquiring this information. Armed with an indication of prevalent message densities, the router can make informed decisions about which path to select for a particular message. This would imply the router having access to several alternative path tables. Figure 9.36 shows an alternative path for a message from processing element 7 to processing element 14 in a mesh when a link on its primary spanning tree, shown in figure 9.24, is known to be heavily loaded.

Random: Random routing, also known as universal routing, has been proposed as a means to prevent certain links becoming more heavily loaded than others. The technique suggests that a message is sent out by the source processing element on a random link rather than the link specified by the path table. After this initial random direction, the message will then follow its primary spanning tree to the required destination.

Flooding: The technique of 'flooding' takes the 'brute-force' approach to broadcasting. Rather than following predetermined broadcast tables, the receiving processing element simply propagates the message on all its links except the link on which the message was received. This has the consequence that the message will appear on all links of the system and may thus reach a processing element quicker via an alternate path should a link on its established broadcast path be currently heavily loaded. However, the potential number of redundant messages that such a technique may generate has serious implications for the overall message densities within the system as well as the wasted effort of each processing element receiving the same message more than once.

There are many other techniques, for example 'hot-potato' routing. Detailed books on networking will provide further information on these strategies. Our

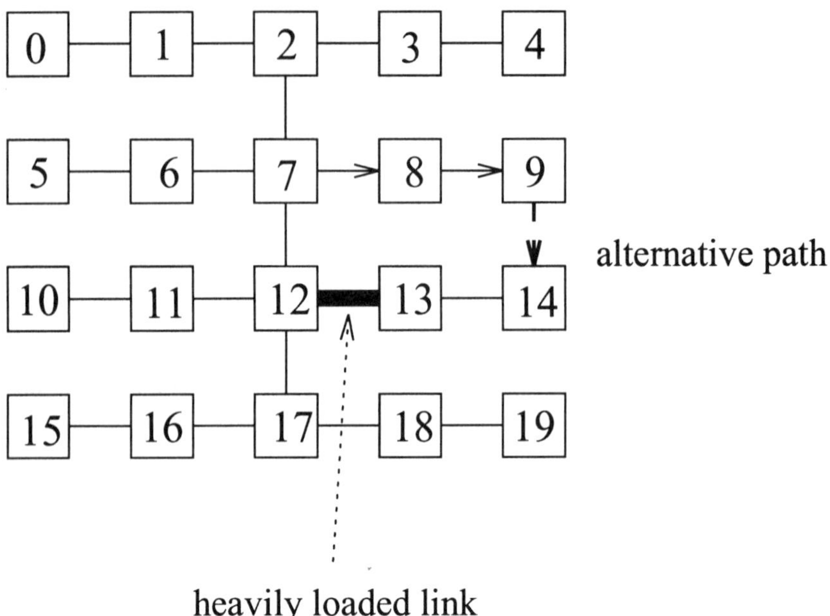

Figure 9.36   Alternative path from PE_7 to PE_{14}

advice is always, 'If a routing strategy can make a performance improvement for a particular implementation, then use it.'

9.3 Minimising Redundant Messages

Routing strategies such as flooding may serve a purpose, but they do introduce a number of redundant messages into the system, increasing the overall message densities and thus exacerbating message latencies. They should be avoided for this reason.   A point-to-point implementation of a desired broadcast also results in a significant number of redundant messages as we saw in table 9.8. A broadcast facility, such as that provided by the broadcast tables, will avoid redundant messages from the source processing element, but the source message may in turn generate redundant reply messages.

Requesting data items held in unknown locations, as we discussed in section 8.3.2, is one example where these redundant messages may occur. We will use this example to illustrate a number of methods that can be used to minimise the number of redundant messages that may otherwise be generated.

Just to recap, if a particular data item is required by an application process and that item is not currently held locally, then the data manager is responsible for fetching the item. If the location of this data is unknown, then the item may be found by simultaneously searching for that item on all branches of the spanning tree. As several copies of the item may exist in the system this simultaneous search may result in several messages containing the same requested data being returned.

All but one of these messages are redundant, and if message densities are to be reduced then ways must be found to 'destroy' these redundant messages as soon as possible, while at the same time ensuring that the one desired copy of the data item does indeed reach the data manager.

9.3.1 Non-propagation of data requests

An obvious way to prevent some redundant messages is for a processing element to recognise that it should not propagate a request further along the spanning tree if the data was found locally. This method prevents redundant request messages and in doing so obviously reduces the number of possible returning copies of the data item sought. The higher up the source processing element's spanning tree this non-propagating processing element is, the more effective this non-propagation of data requests will be.

In the example shown in figure 9.37, if the data item requested by the processing element labelled 9 is found at processing elements labelled 22 and 30, then the dotted lines and processing elements indicate which processing elements will not receive the request for that item. For processing element labelled 22, only one processing element, the processing element labelled 6, will not receive the request, while if the data is found at processing element labelled 30, fourteen request messages and therefore, fourteen possible return messages, are avoided.

9.3.2 Snooping

By maintaining knowledge of the progress of other processing elements, a processing element is able to destroy messages bound for these processing elements that are deemed to be 'out of date'. To achieve this, all appropriate messages from a processing element contain a message number. Each processing element has a *snoop table* which contains the `greatest_message_number_so_far` received from all other processing elements. These messages include not only those destined for this processing element, but also those that the router may have passed on in its rôle as intermediate node.

This snoop table is updated in one of two circumstances:

1. If a request is received with a message number greater than the value currently held then the snoop table is altered to reflect this new message number. (Note: the unique path of the spanning tree prevents requests arriving at a node that have message numbers less than or equal to that currently held in the snoop table.)

2. If a returning data item is received with a `message_number` greater than or equal to that currently held then the snoop table entry for the destination of this return is set to the value of `message_number` + 1.

Any return messages now received with a message number less than or equal to the value in the snoop table will not be routed further and therefore, effectively 'destroyed'.

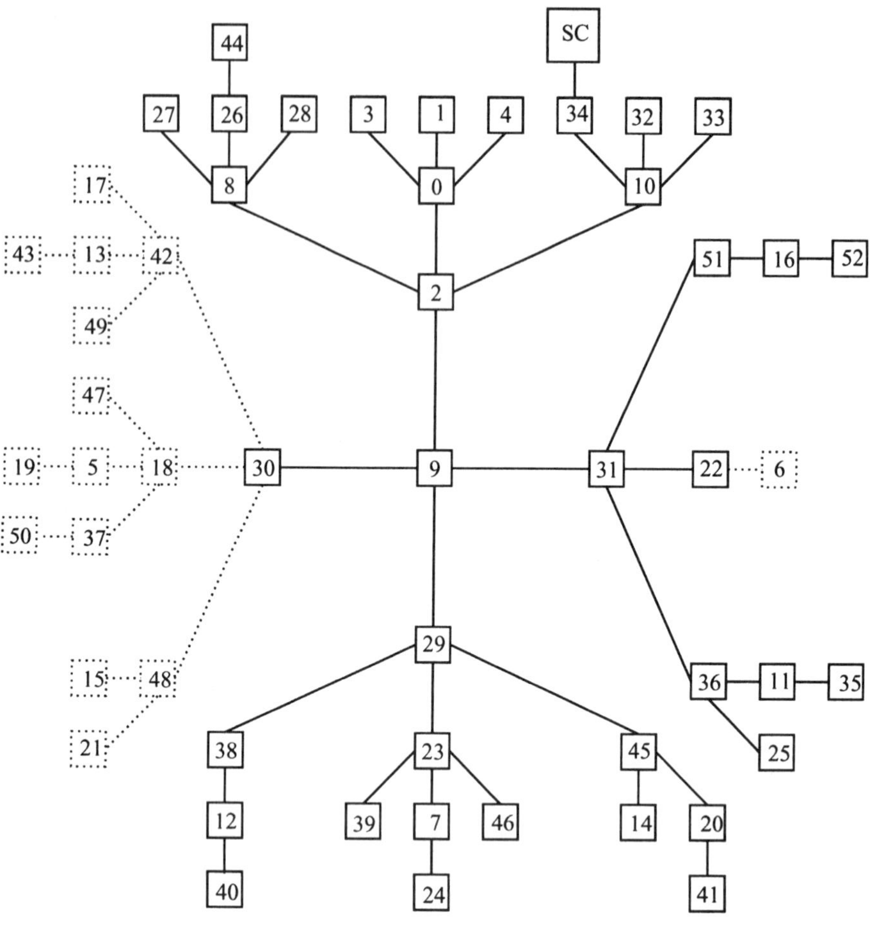

Figure 9.37   Reducing redundant messages by non-propagation

9.3.3 Poaching

Poaching is a technique that allows a processing element to take advantage of a required data item currently being routed through itself bound for another destination. This is easily achieved by the routing process noting the identifier of the data item that its own data manager is currently requesting, and then performing a simple check against the identifiers of all data items passing through it, for example, to satisfy requests from other processing elements. Should a match be found, then, as well as routing the data item further towards its destination (provided it passes the snoop table test), a copy of the item is also forwarded to the local data manager. While not immediately reducing message densities, poaching can have a significant impact as the satisfied application process is now in a position to request further data items, which may cause remote requests and so reduce the message density by snooping at distant nodes. The router is now also aware that the data item has been found and any subsequent return of requests for this processing element need not be forwarded to the data manager. If an item is poached, any requests stacked for that item (see below) will be fulfilled without further delay.

9.3.4 Stacking data requests

When a request for a particular data item arrives at a processing element one of three conditions will hold:

1. The data item is available locally and may be returned forthwith.
2. The data item is not available and the request is propagated further.
3. The data item is not available, but this processing element has already requested the same item.

Propagating the request onward in this third case would be redundant and so the request is *stacked* until such time as the requested data item is returned to this processing element (or is poached). Once this happens the stacked request is fulfilled, provided it still passes the snoop table test, and the appropriate data item is returned towards the requesting processing element.

9.3.5 Delayed broadcast of data requests

A further way to reduce redundant messages is for a processing element not to broadcast a request on all its links simultaneously, but rather on each link in turn with a suitable delay in between. This delay could be a specified time which is known to be long enough for the item to be returned if it is found on that branch of the spanning tree, or it could be until not_found messages have been returned from all nodes on that branch of the spanning tree. If, of course, the data item is returned before the end of the delay, then no further requests for that item need be broadcast.

While this method will reduce redundant messages, the choice of the initial spanning tree branch may be critical in ensuring that the data is returned within a suitable time. Good choices of initial branch might be: that branch of the spanning tree where a copy of the data item was previously found; the direction of the distant resident set location of the data item (note a point-to-point communication was not chosen here even with a known resident set location, as this may be 'far away' in the network, while a copy actually existed closer to the requested processing element); in the direction of the system controller which is known to have all data items; etc. Obviously, the higher the level of replication of data items in the system, the more successful this method is likely to be.

9.4 Wormhole Routing

Static networks typically use *packet-switching* techniques to physically pass a message from one processor to another. In this approach, a complete message is passed across the link connecting two router processes. The receiving router inputs this complete package before interpreting the message and passing it on to its destination, as in figure 9.38(a). In dynamic networks, the selection of a path between two

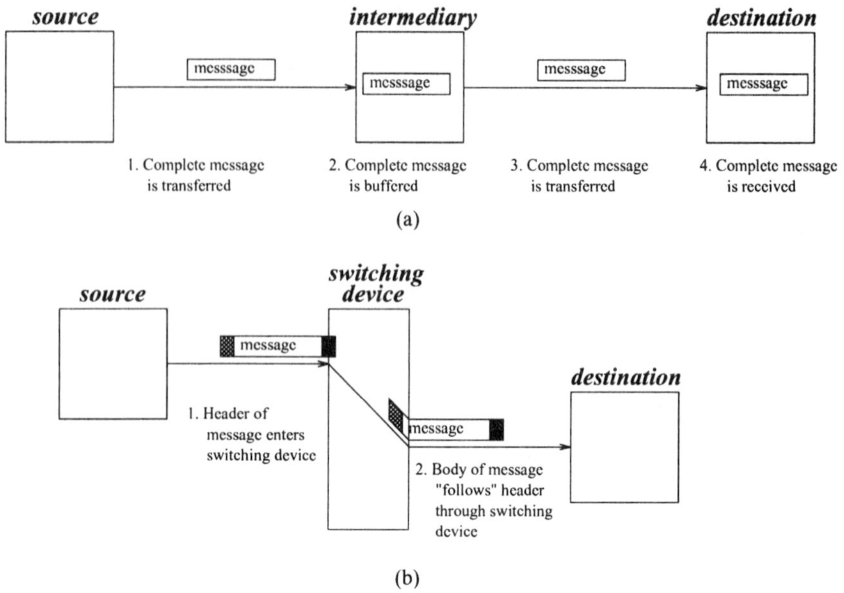

Figure 9.38   Passing messages between processing elements: (a) packet-switching (b) wormhole routing

processors is carried out by hardware through the dynamically configurable switching devices. Packet switching for dynamic networks would require the switching devices to have sufficient memory to store a complete message and only once this complete message had been received could the device select the appropriate output path.

Wormhole routing helps reduce communication delays in dynamic networks by allowing the 'head' of a message to be sent onward by the switching device before the 'tail' has been received, as shown in figure 9.38(b). This means that the header can be entering the destination processor, or another switching device while the body of the message is still passing through the previous switching device. A tail at the end of the message informs the switching device that the complete message has passed through and the input and output switches may be made available for use by other messages.

9.5 Summary

Communication is essential for any parallel implementation. In static interconnection networks, the choice of configuration can play a significant rôle in reducing communication overheads. To achieve the most efficient performance, the configuration chosen should be well suited to the communication patterns inherent in the parallel implementation.

Communication patterns manifest themselves in the parallel solution of a problem by:

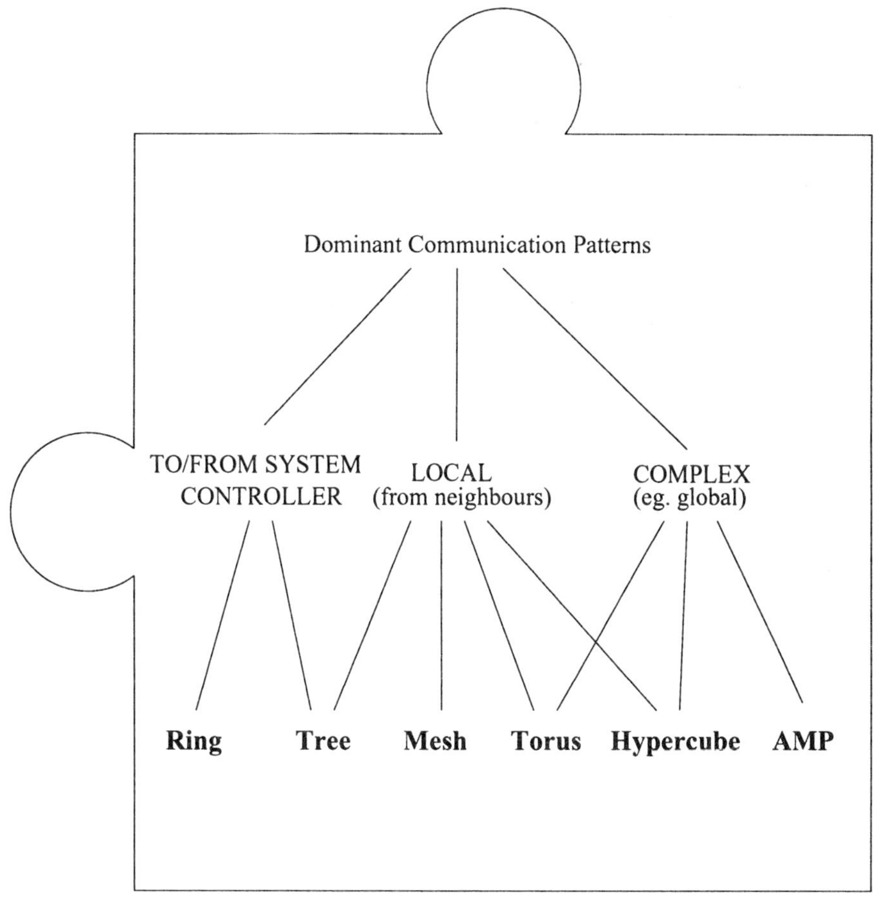

Figure 9.39   The dominant communication patterns help determine configuration

1. The nature of the algorithm adopted. Any inherent multiple stages or data dependencies will necessitate a certain required level of communication between processing elements within the system.

2. The data management or task management strategy required. For example, a world model of data requires no data management. However, the distribution of large problem domains across the multiprocessor system and the provision of a virtual shared memory environment introduces significant communication as processing elements fetch data items from remote locations. Similarly, distributed task management strategies have associated communication requirements.

The choice of the best configuration for these two conditions must be made from the 'worst case' communication pattern that exists. This 'worst case' pattern will dominate the communication requirements for the parallel implementation and thus must be tackled effectively.

Figure 9.39 shows how the appropriate configuration should be chosen depending on the dominant communication pattern. If no communication is required between parallel tasks and a world model of data is possible then the only communication required within the system will be: to distribute the data initially from the system controller, to supply tasks to the processing elements from the system controller; and to send the results back to the system controller for collating. A chain was used for this communication pattern in the processor farm that we examined in Chapter 7, however, as we have seen in this chapter, a better choice of configuration would be a ring, or even better still, a tree.

The parallel implementation of many algorithms, for example finite volume or finite difference methods, requires near-neighbour communication to update their portion of the problem domain at each new timestep [170]. Such a communication pattern may be termed *local*. Although there will still be the need to get data, tasks and results to and from the system controller, this local communication is not suitable for either a ring or tree configuration, and so a mesh or torus should be used.

Implementing a virtual shared memory environment across all processors of a multiprocessor system introduces a complex *global* communication pattern as processing elements may need to fetch data items from anywhere within the system. Global communication places the heaviest strain on any communication system. Section 9.1.5 shows that any implementation with such a communication pattern should be implemented on a torus, a hypercube, or the most appropriate, an AMP configuration.

The system software router is responsible for transferring messages between processing elements within the multiprocessor system. The messages handled by a router may originate from other processes within its own processing element, the task manager, data manager or local controller, or the router may have to act as an intermediate for messages from other processing elements.

Different levels of priority within the scheduler of a processing element can be used to develop a deadlock free routing strategy. The output command is executed at a high priority in parallel with a low priority input strategy which buffers any incoming messages. After the output is completed the buffered messages are dealt with. Provided there is sufficient buffer space the order of the messages can be preserved and deadlock avoided.

Regular configurations allow routing functions to be defined in order to determine the path between any two processing elements. Although often elegant, these functions may be computationally complex. Path and broadcast tables can be used for both regular and irregular configurations to provide an efficient means of ensuring messages transmitted within the system reach their destination in the quickest possible fashion.

The effect of the correct choice of configuration will now be demonstrated using a problem that requires frequent, global communication: simulating the flocking motion of birds.

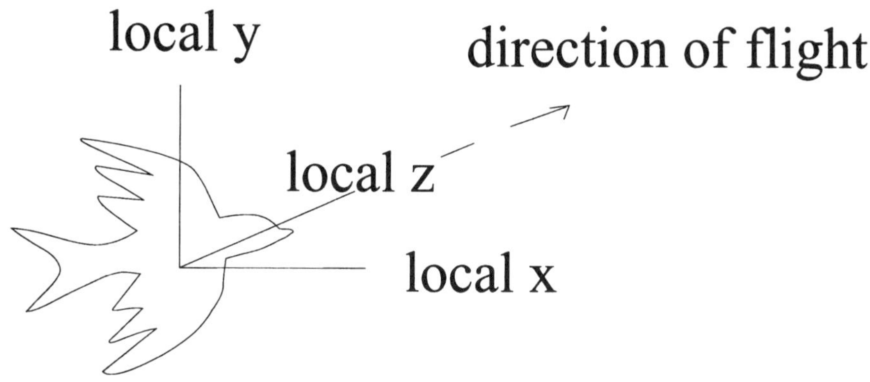

Figure 9.40 Flight path of a bird

9.6 Case Study: Bird Flocking Simulation

The dictionary definition of a flock is 'a number of animals or birds together'. To an external observer, the flying motion of a flock of birds appears fluid and synchronised, yet the flock is made up of a large number of individual birds acting without any form of central control. Computer simulations of this behaviour aim to model the interaction between the birds based on each bird's local perception of the environment [161]. A straightforward decomposition of this problem for parallel processing is to define a task as the computation of a single bird's motion. As we will see, deriving the motion of the flock in this case requires constant co-operation between the tasks with a resultant heavy communication requirement. As such, this problem is well suited to illustrate the system communication strategies we have studied in this chapter.

9.6.1 Problem description

For this case study, we will describe a simple flock model based on work by Reynolds [161]. In this model, the motion of the birds is based on calculations relating to their current velocity and position within the flock. As such, the model does not consider many of the forces normally associated with flying, such as lifts or drags. These can always be incorporated at a later stage. Each bird has its own local coordinate system providing orientation information which can be used with the determined velocity. The actual flight of the bird is based on incremental piecewise translations along its forward direction, as shown in figure 9.40. This flight path is not planned far in advance, but is dynamic, constantly being altered at discrete intervals to react to the overall behaviour of the flock.

The important constraints governing the flight of the birds in the flock are the needs to:

- avoid a collision with any other bird,
- maintain a similar velocity to nearby birds, and
- stay close to other members of the flock.

Each of these constraints independently suggests the best direction for the bird to travel in the next time step. The actual path must be computed by combining these, sometime opposing, desires.

As we will see, the calculation of the directions for each of the constraints produces a weighted vector sum based on the distance between pairs of birds and their relative position within the flock. Reynolds pointed out that birds were particularly sensitive to activities in the forward direction and related to speed and thus a 'zone of sensitivity' can be defined as an inverse exponential of distance from the bird, $\frac{1}{c^d}$, where c is a constant and d is distance [161]. This sensitivity zone helps simulate the birds limited perception range.

Collision avoidance

Birds may be treated as pointed charges repelling each other. The metric of repulsion and (attraction) that is used is the inverse of the square of distances, $\frac{1}{d^2}$. The collision avoidance vector for each bird is a weighted sum of the repelling forces asserted by each flockmate:

$$\text{avoidance} = \sum_{i=0}^{\text{no. of birds}} force_{ni} \times s_i$$

where $force_{ni}$ is a force of magnitude $\frac{1}{d_i}$ asserted by this bird on $bird_i$, and s_i is the value computed from the sensitivity function.

Maintaining similar velocity

If we take the simple case with only two birds with velocities v_1 and v_2 then at each discrete update we want to bring v_1 closer to v_2. We can achieve this by assigning to v_1 a new vector calculated as $(v_2 - v_1) \times s$, where s is a small positive constant related to the sensitivity constant. So for a large number n of birds, the velocity vector v_1 becomes:

$$v_1 = (v_2 - v_1) \times s_2 + \ldots + (v_n - v_1) \times s_n$$

Staying close to the flock

To achieve this we want to steer the birds towards the centre of the flock. This implies that birds at the outskirts of the flock should have a higher desire to head towards the centre than those birds already in the middle of the flock. Once again a weighted sum is computed, which for $bird_i$ would be:

$$\text{centring} = u_{i1} \times w_1 + \ldots + u_{in} \times w_n$$

where u_{i1} is a unit vector from $bird_i$ to the position of $bird_1$, $w_1 = s_1 \times force_1$ where s_1 is the sensitivity value and $force_1$ is the magnitude for the attraction for $bird_1$.

Combining these three vectors provides the new direction for the bird at the next update step. The position of the bird for that update can be computed for this direction and the velocity of the bird. Displaying each bird at every update provides an animated sequence which is the simulation of the flock's behaviour. The algorithm for this simulation is detailed below:

```
PROCEDURE Flock_Simulation()
  Begin
    Initialise_Birds()
    finished := FALSE
    REPEAT
      FOR i = 1 TO number_of_birds DO
        Begin
          FOR j = 1 TO number_of_birds DO
            IF j <> i THEN
              Begin
                Calculate_Collision(bird[i].old_status,
                                    bird[j].old_status)
                Calculate_Matching(bird[i].old_status,
                                   bird[j].old_status)
                Calculate_Centring(bird[i].old_status,
                                   bird[j].old_status)
              End
            ENDIF
          Combine_Contributions(bird[i])
          bird[i].new_status := Update(bird[i].old_status)
        End
    UNTIL finished
  End (* Flock Simulation *)
```

9.6.2 Parallel requirements

Simply stated, the problem the we are required to solve is to calculate the new position of every bird in a flock at a series of discrete time intervals. Calculation of the position of one bird is independent of similar calculations for all other birds for one particular time step. Furthermore, the computational complexity to compute a bird's new position is the same for all birds. To compute the position for a bird at time step t_i requires the positional and velocity information for all other birds at time step t_{i-1}. (Note this problem is very similar in structure to the Jacobi method of matrix solution described in section 7.2.)

An obvious choice of task for the parallel implementation of this problem is the calculation of a single bird's new position in one time step. The total number of tasks in the problem is thus equal to the number of birds in the flock we are simulating. Each task requires the same computational effort and the total number of tasks is known and so, from figure 9.41(a), we see that we should adopt a balanced data driven computational model. The parallel implementation thus involves each processing element computing position update calculations for a similar number of birds. If the number of birds that we wish to simulate in the flock is an exact multiple of the number of processing elements then each processing element will carry out the computations for the same number of birds.

This algorithm is multi-stage as the computation at each time step is distinct and is dependent on partial results (the birds' previous positions and velocities) from the previous time step. This information and the choice of computational model implies a pre-allocated task management strategy, as shown in figure 9.41(b). The

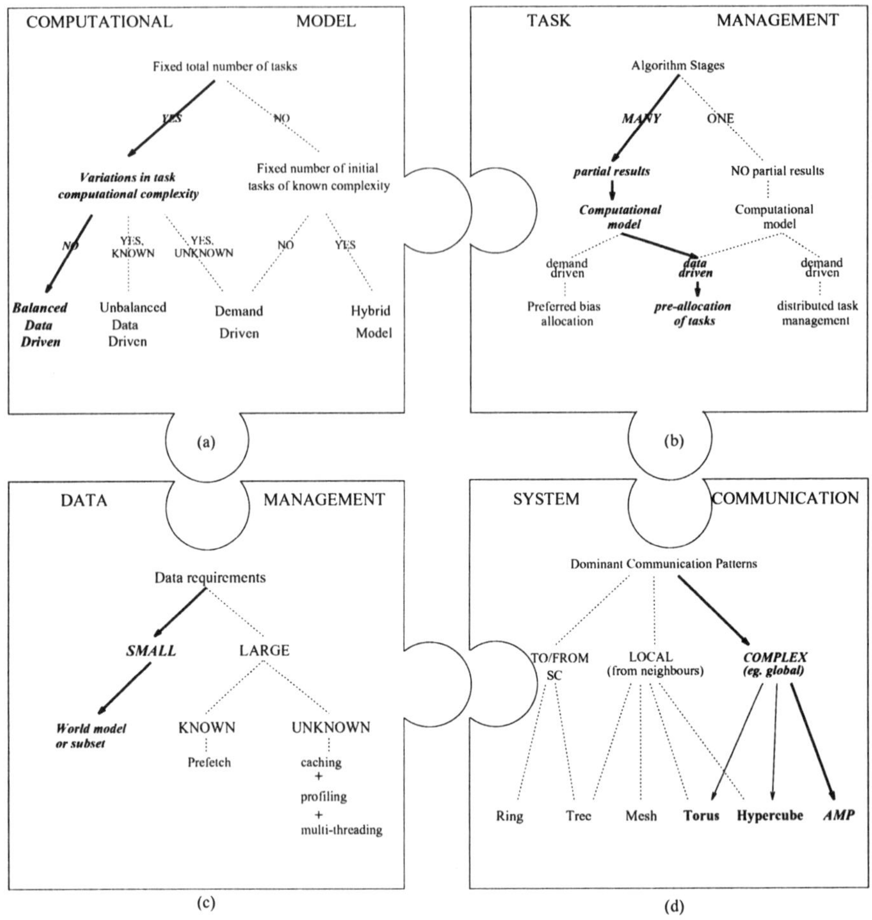

Figure 9.41 Choice of correct parallel implementation

computation for each stage is the same and so the choice for computational model is *balanced data driven* for every stage.

Fortunately for the parallel implementation of this problem, the data requirements are small and should have no difficulty in fitting completely in the local memory of each processing element. As shown in figure 9.41(c) a world model is thus sufficient with no need for any additional data management.

We have to ascertain what is the dominant communication pattern. Remember, this pattern is the 'worst case' of the communication patterns inherent in the algorithm and the data management strategy we have chosen. Taking the second part, first: our analysis of the data requirements of the problem identified that a world model was the correct choice of data management strategy. The only communication required for this strategy is to send initially all the data items from the system controller to each processing elements. A ring, or better, a tree configuration would

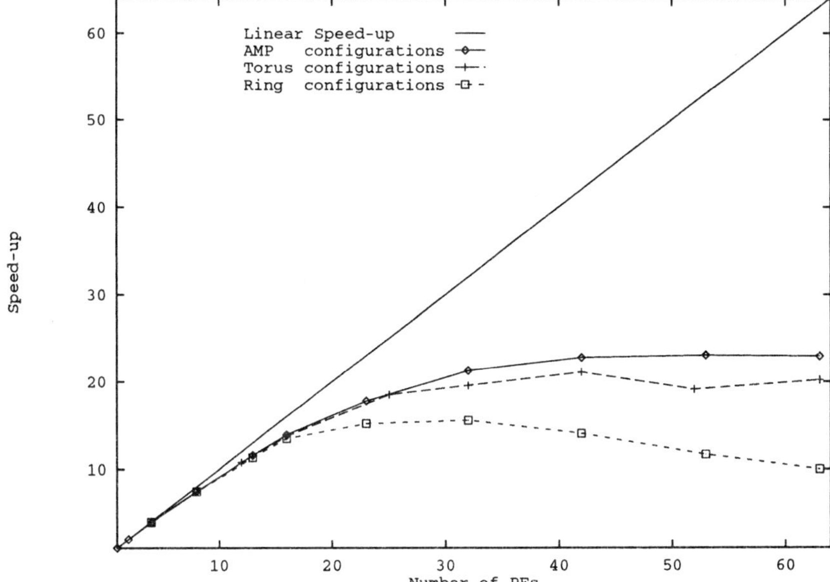

Figure 9.42 Speed-up for a flock size of 450 birds

be the appropriate configuration for this communication pattern. As discussed in
the problem description, at the conclusion of one time step, information concerning the current position of each bird must be supplied to every processing element
so that the next time step's calculations can be performed by a processing element
on the birds for which it is responsible. This is clearly a complex global communication pattern. The dominant communication pattern for this problem is thus
complex and either a torus, hypercube or AMP may be the chosen configuration.
Of these, the AMP will be shown to be the best choice.

9.6.3 Results

The bird flocking simulation was run on systems constructed from different numbers of processors, arranged in rings, tori and AMP configurations. The speed-up
achieved for the parallel implementation on a flock size of 450 birds with each of
the configurations is shown in figure 9.42. From the graphs it can be seen that in all
three cases a maximum speed-up has already been achieved before the 63-processing
element systems. The ring configurations have a value for n_{opt} of approximately
32 processing elements and achieve a maximum speed-up of less than 16, while the
torus configurations have a n_{opt} of close to 42 processing elements and a maximum
speed-up of around 21 is possible. The AMP configurations, on the other hand,
have a n_{opt} in the region of 53 processing elements and achieve a maximum speed-up
of just over 23.

Figure 9.43 plots the solution times for an increasing problem size for each of the

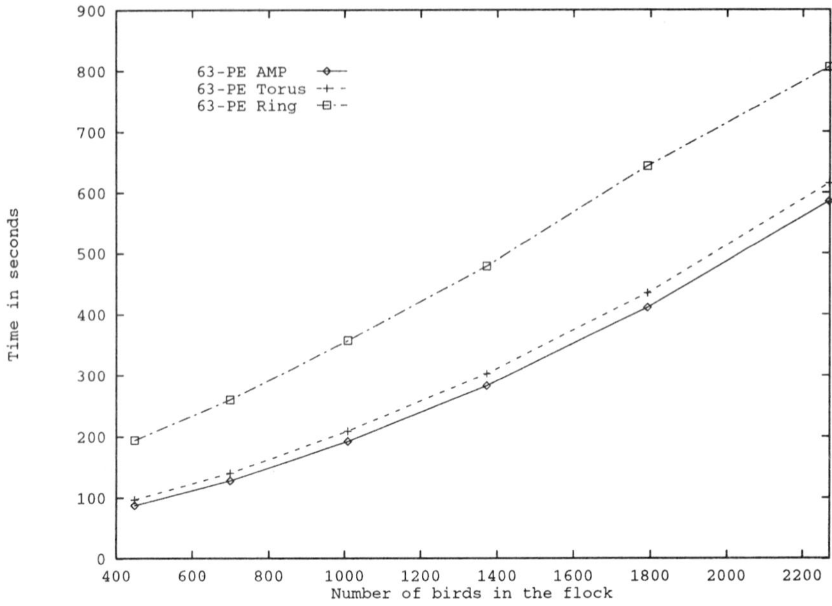

Figure 9.43   Time in seconds for increasing problem size on 63-processing element configurations

three configurations of 63 processing elements. While the size of flocks considered may not be too realistic, they do serve to highlight the difference in performance of the configurations as the problem size increases. Examining the percentage differences between the time required to solve the different sizes of problem, we see that the AMP is 11.2% faster than the torus and 122.7% faster than the ring for the 450-bird flock and 5.0% quicker than the torus and 37.7% quicker than the ring for the 2250-bird flock problem. The difference in the times taken between the AMP and the ring and torus configurations are 9.7 seconds and 107.0 seconds for the 450-bird problem and 29.5 seconds and 220.7 seconds when there are 2250 birds to be simulated.

9.6.4 Conclusions

Simulations of the motion of varying sizes of flocks of birds were carried out on processing elements arranged in ring, torus and AMP configurations. The problem sizes considered ranged from a flock size of 450 to 2250 birds. Figures 9.42 and 9.43 show that ring configurations consistently gave the worst performance for the parallel implementation of this problem, while AMP configurations consistently gave the best performance.

These results emphasize how the correct choice of configuration to match the dominant communication patterns within a problem can significantly improve overall system performance.

9.7 Exercises and Project Suggestions

1. A subtle deadlock situation can occur between the following two processes P1 and P2, especially when they are implemented on separate processors. The deadlock may occur when an input is received by process P1 from the keyboard in order to terminate the computation. Discuss why this subtle deadlock occurs and show how this may be avoided by:

   (a) a synchronous acknowledgement scheme (known as a handshake) between process P1 and P2, and

   (b) the use of the `PRIORITISED PARALLEL` construct.

```
PROCESS P1()
  Begin
    busy := TRUE
    WHILE busy DO
      PRIORITISED INPUT ALTERNATIVES
        1. RECEIVE key FROM keyboard
             Begin
               RECEIVE x FROM P2
               SEND FALSE TO P2
               busy := FALSE
             End
        2. RECEIVE x FROM P2
             Display(x)
  End (* P1 *)

PROCESS P2()
  Begin
    busy := TRUE
    WHILE busy DO
      PRIORITISED INPUT ALTERNATIVES
        1. RECEIVE busy FROM P1
             (* terminates P2 *)
        2. ELSE
             Begin
               Compute (x)
               SEND x TO P1
             End
  End (* P2 *)
```

2. Design a routing function for a full tree of degree 3 and height 4. The total number of processors in this tree is 121. How would your routing function be affected if there were only 100 processors available for this configuration?

3. Design the path and broadcast tables for a 48-processor torus configuration in which each processor has six links for interconnection. Now implement and compare the efficiency of this routing strategy with a routing function for the same configuration.

4. Using table 9.7, calculate the total number of messages that would result in each

of the configurations if the flooding method of broadcast (described in section 9.2.3) was used. You may once again assume that each of the 32 processors is issuing 200 messages.

5. Table 9.9 gives the broadcast table for the 8-processing element AMP. How many paths cross each link? Assume some data management requirement leads to a sudden upsurge of message traffic between processing elements 6 and 0 so that the communication between these two processors is now four times heavier than traffic between any other two processing elements. How could the path table be altered temporarily to ensure as even a link loading as possible during this upsurge?

Chapter 10

A Problem Solving Methodology

It is impossible to produce a useful system from a base in which no components are trusted.

attributed to Seneca (BC55–AD44)

This chapter brings together material from the previous chapters, integrating it into a methodology for approaching problem implementation. This involves extracting from a problem the criteria which are important for the parallel implementation. These criteria then determine the correct techniques that must be adopted to ensure efficient implementation. The aspects of the problem important for parallel processing are interdependent and must be considered together. The analysis examines:

- *the presence of any data dependencies ⇒ task definition and granularity,*
- *computational complexity variations ⇒ computational model,*
- *the distinct stages of the problem ⇒ task management strategy,*
- *data requirements ⇒ data management strategy, and*
- *dominant communication requirements ⇒ system communication.*

The software structure of a processing element capable of coping with the diverse nature of real problems is described. Finally, the application of the analysis is illustrated by considering a parallel implementation of the panel method from computational fluid dynamics.

The Sequential-Algorithm Multiple-Data model of parallelism requires each processing element of the multiprocessor system to apply the same sequential algorithm to different principal data items in parallel. The optimum implementation of the SAMD approach involves analysing the problem to determine the criteria which determine the nature of the system software.

The constituent parts of the methodology are interdependent, as shown in figure 10.1. Analysis of the problem must therefore first consider the correct computational model and then, using this in conjunction with the data and task requirements of the problem, ascertain the requisite data management and task management strategies. The dominant communication pattern inherent in the algorithm

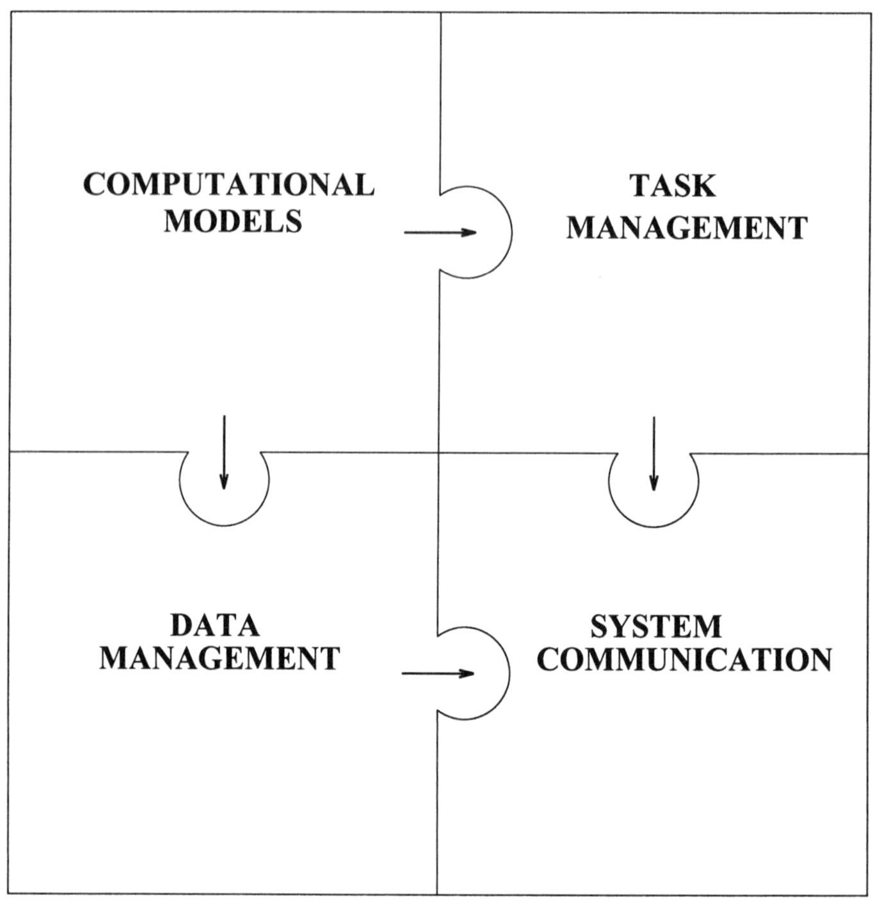

Figure 10.1 The interaction of components of the methodology

or introduced by the data or task management will now suggest the most efficient choice of system communication.

10.1 Problem Analysis

To analyse a problem correctly, a detailed knowledge of the problem formulation is not necessary. However, the eventual implementation of the problem will require expert knowledge. This suggests the parallel programmer can work in conjunction with scientists and engineers to implement their problems efficiently on multiprocessor systems.

The first order of business when confronted with a problem is to establish what constitutes a task. A task is the fundamental unit of computation adopted for the parallel implementation. The nature of a task is determined from the subdivision of the problem domain, that is how the complete problem can be divided into sub-problems. This is something we do regularly in our lives when confronted with a difficult dilemma, 'How can I solve this problem with the help of some friends?'

A problem's lowest computational element within the sequential algorithm is known as the atomic element for that problem. If data dependencies exist between atomic elements then these elements should be combined until a unit of computation is established which is independent of similar other units of computation – this is the task. In some problems it may not be possible to achieve these independent units of computation. In these cases, a task should be defined which minimises the associated data dependencies.

The choice of task for the problem also determines the principal and additional data items. Distribution of these tasks to the processing elements falls into the scope of task management which will be discussed shortly. Having established the task composition the analysis of the problem can begin. Figure 10.2 illustrates the decisions that have to be made.

10.1.1 Computational model

The computational model determines the manner in which the problem will be solved on the parallel system. Overall system performance is fundamentally linked to the model that is chosen. An incorrect choice of model could see some processing elements standing idle while others struggle to complete their computationally complex work, or could result in excessive communication overheads which could detrimentally affect the computational effectiveness of the processing elements.

The data driven computational models have low communication overheads, but are unable to cope with unknown complexity variations within the problem domain. The demand driven model has a higher communication requirement, but is able to adapt to the unknown variations and ensure that the processing elements are kept busy while there is still work to be done. The hybrid model is able to benefit from the low communication overheads of the data driven models and the dynamic load balancing properties of the demand driven approach. However, the hybrid model is only appropriate for problems which have an unknown total number of tasks, but a fixed number of initial tasks of known complexity. Figure 10.2(a) shows the information that is required to enable the correct choice of computational model to be made.

10.1.2 Task management

Task management controls the manner in which work is supplied to the processing element. Only by maintaining a continuous supply of tasks can the processing elements be kept busy performing useful computation and thus contributing to the solution of the problem. If all but one of the processing elements are idle then we are no better off than the sequential implementation of the problem. In fact, we are probably worse off as any parallel implementation has an associated communication overhead, so in this case the parallel implementation could take longer to solve the problem than the sequential version!

The distinct stages inherent in the algorithm chosen for the problem influence the task management strategy that should be adopted. The task management for multi-

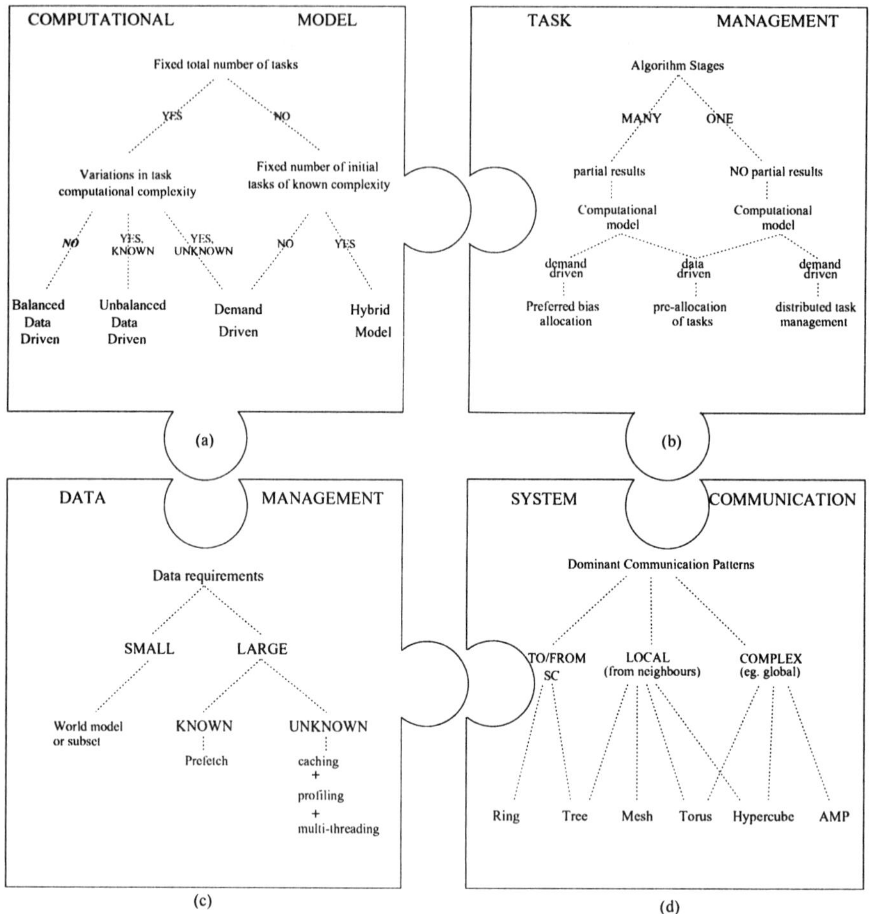

Figure 10.2 Design decisions in the SAMD model

stage problems cannot ignore the effect partial results from one stage must have on subsequent stages. Coupled with this is the influence of the chosen computational model. Data driven models can be supported by a simple pre-allocation of tasks to each processing element, whereas a demand driven computational model will need some form of distributed task management or a preferred bias allocation. The decisions that influence the choice of task management strategy are shown in figure 10.2(b).

10.1.3 Data management

The size of each processing element's local memory and the number of principal and additional data items required by a problem dominate the choice of data management strategy. If the local memory is sufficiently large to accommodate the entire data requirements then no significant data management is necessary. Remember, however, that partial results produced in multi-stage algorithms may also have to be accommodated locally during the current stage.

Large data requirements can be handled by a virtual shared memory approach. In virtual shared memory the local memories of the individual processing elements of the multiprocessor system are considered to form a single logical memory unit. In order to locate them, each data item is allocated a unique identifier. The application processes access these data items in a uniform manner and it is the responsibility of the data manager to ensure that an application process request for a data item is always satisfied. This request may be satisfied from amongst the data items available in the data manager's local cache, or it may require the data manager to fetch the item from the local cache of some other processing element. Obviously, the data manager's response time to a request will depend on the data item's location.

As can be seen in figure 10.2(c), if the data requirements for a problem are known *a priori* then the data manager can ensure the necessary data items are always available locally when they are required. Often the nature of the algorithm provides an indication as to future data requests. This is achieved by prefetching them from their remote locations in advance of the application process requests. If the data requirements are unknown then a combination of caching and profiling must be used to try to reduce the number of remote fetches by exploiting any coherence in the problem domain. Multi-threading minimises idle time by allowing the processing element to continue with executing other tasks even if one is currently delayed due to the need to fetch a data item from a remote location.

10.1.4 System communication

Communication is an integral part of any parallel implementation. However, communication overheads play a fundamental part in preventing a problem being solved on a large multiprocessor system. One of the major factors affecting the efficiency of communication within a multiprocessor system is the choice of configuration. Unfortunately, because of the fixed nature of many modern multiprocessor architectures, this is one option over which the user may have no control.

Figure 10.2(d) shows how the dominant communication patterns within the problem should suggest the correct choice of configuration. It is not only the communication requirements inherent in the choice of algorithm, that is the prevalent data dependencies, that must be considered, but also the communication patterns that may result from the choice of task and data management strategies.

Tree configurations are appropriate for the limited communication requirements to and from the system controller while minimum path (AMP) configurations, with their low diameters and average interprocessor distances, are most suitable for supporting global communication requirements.

10.2 Structure of the System Architecture

A parallel system consists of hardware processors connected in some manner by an interconnection network, plus the software infrastructure to enable the solution of problems on this multiprocessor machine. In this book we have examined the requirements for the efficient parallel implementation of complex problems and

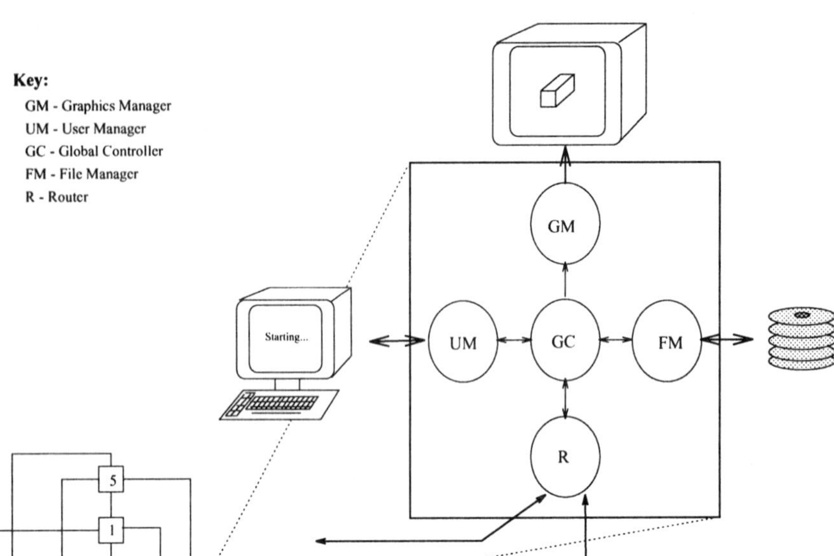

Figure 10.3   Structure of a system controller

developed the system software necessary to achieve this goal. This section sum-
marises the structure of the system architecture that forms this system software.

The system architecture consists of a system controller which supervises the
parallel solution, and two or more processing elements which perform the actual
computation of the tasks. The system controller and each processing element has
its own hardware processor and thus their activities take place truly in parallel. The
same structures for the system controller and the processing elements are used
regardless of the underlying hardware configuration.

The system controller provides the input/output interface for the multiprocessor system. In section 4.4.2 we identified the functions required from the system
controller. These functions are supported within the system controller by individual concurrent processes. Figure 10.3 shows the structure of a system controller.
Any input from the user is handled through the User Manager (UM) which is also
responsible for displaying pertinent progress information. For problems which
involve some form of high resolution visualisation, such as the ray tracing example
of Chapter 8, a Graphics Manager (GM) may be useful to manipulate any results
to the correct format before sending them to be displayed on a specialised device.

The integration of secondary storage devices, such as hard disks, into the virtual
shared memory may be necessary for problems with very large data requirements.
In addition, all problems will require certain information, such as path tables, data

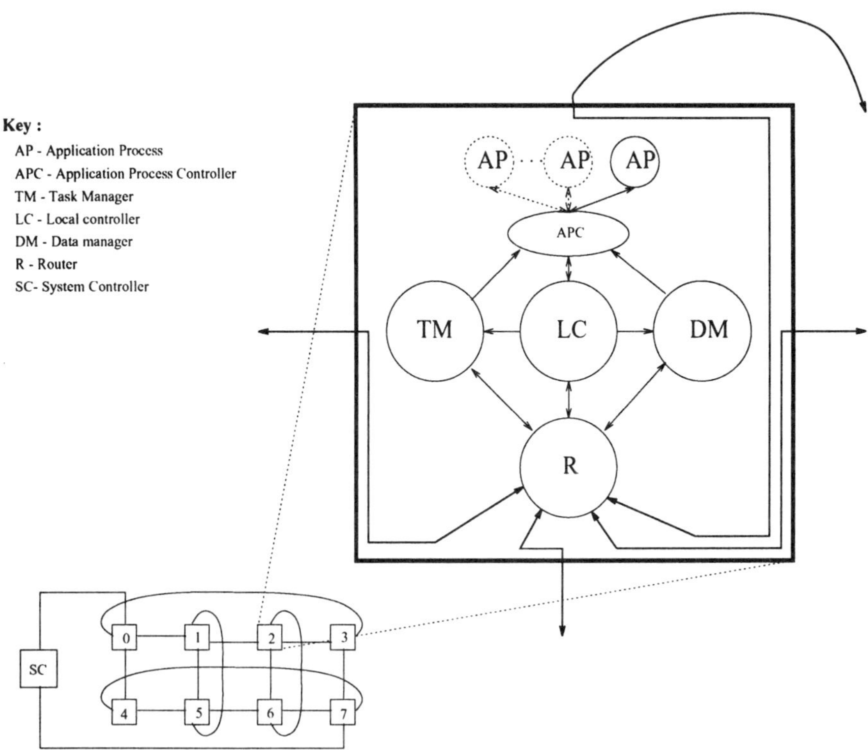

Figure 10.4   Structure of each processing element

items, etc., to be retrieved from the secondary storage devices prior to the parallel processing commencing, and may require results to be stored on these devices for later retrieval. The File Manager (FM) process provides these necessary services.

The Router (R) process provides the means of communicating with the processing elements of the parallel system. The activities of these processes are co-ordinated by the Global Controller (GC) process. This vital process ensures the processing elements are initially provided with the correct configuration information and problem parameters. The choice of computational model will determine whether the global controller has to play the additional rôle of task supplier in the case of a demand driven system, or task allocator for the data driven models. The global controller collates results and is also responsible for terminating the processing elements either when the computation is complete, or should the user wish to abort the system.

The structure of each processing element is shown in figure 10.4. Each Application Process (AP) has a copy of the sequential algorithm that has been chosen to solve the problem. On receipt of a task from the Task Manager (TM), the application process carries out the algorithm on the principal data item specified by the task. Additional data items may be required during the course of the computation and these are requested from the Data Manager (DM). More than one application process may be supported at each processing element to provide a multi-threading capability. In this case, an Application Process Controller (APC) is necessary to co-ordinate the task and data requests from these application processes. Results produced by an application process are passed to the Local Controller (LC). In a single stage problem these results may be returned to the system controller for collation, while when a multi-stage algorithm is being used these results may be stored as partial results at the data manager or the data manager of another processing element if necessary.

The task manager supplies the application process with tasks. For a data driven model, the pre-allocated tasks will be known to the task manager and supplied as an initial parameter to the application process. In a demand driven situation, on completion of its current task, the application process will demand the next task from the local task pool of the task manager. It is the responsibility of the task manager to ensure that while there is still a portion of the problem that has yet to be completed, there will be tasks available for the application process when required.

The data manager provides the virtual shared memory environment when problems with large data requirements are implemented. Requests for data items from the application processes are fulfilled by the data manager from its local cache. This data item may have been already available or may have had to be fetched by the data manager from elsewhere in the system.

The Router (R) at each processing element provides the communication mechanisms that allow the processing elements to exchange messages and thus co-operate in the parallel solution of the problem. The router is aware of the underlying hardware configuration and is able to exploit this to ensure that messages are transferred as efficiently as possible.

The local controller oversees the activities of the processing element and provides the control necessary to ensure such activities as the smooth changeover of the processing element from one stage of an algorithm to the next and the correct placement of partial results.

10.3 Summary

The choices that come out of the problem analysis must be fed into the system architecture to enable each process to perform its rôle in the appropriate manner. There is thus no such thing as general purpose parallel processing. The system architecture must be engineered so information from the analysis will cause, on initialisation, the system controller and every processing element to select the appropriate strategy from the list of possibilities. So, for example, informing the system that a choice of a demand driven model has been made, results in the global controller establishing a task pool of available tasks, the task managers setting up their own local task pools and endeavouring to keep these full, and the application processes actively demanding the next tasks for computation.

Each of the system processes has a vital rôle to play in the parallel implementation of any problem. Trusting each process to perform its function correctly will enable the system software to provide the environment in which the efficient parallel implementation of any problem may be contemplated. As Seneca would have agreed, this will be a useful system. *This is practical parallel processing.*

10.4 Case Study: Panel Methods for Computational Fluid Dynamics

Panel methods are used in computational fluid dynamics to calculate the flow about a three-dimensional body. The inherent computational complexity and frequent use of the panel method as a design tool means there is a strong incentive to implement it on a multiprocessor system. This case study gives the mathematical formulation of the panel method. The problem is then analysed for the parallel criteria, and the effects of the decisions on the solution of the panel method on a multiprocessor system are highlighted.

10.4.1 Problem description

The calculation of flow about a three-dimensional body is an important aspect of computational fluid dynamics. For example, according to Hess [99], a company such as Douglas Aircraft performs flow calculations about a complete aircraft approximately ten times per day. Calculation of an inviscid, incompressible potential flow about an arbitrary shape may be achieved by solving the linear equations that result from a discretisation of the boundary integral equation [53, 88, 100]. Panel methods have found a wide range of applications in aerospace and other industries, for example, the design of Formula-1 racing cars, sailing vessels, locomotives etc., where a need arises to predict the low speed flow past complex configurations.

Panel methods are applicable to any problem that is governed by Laplace's equation. Although, these methods were originally known as surface singularity methods, the technique of covering the domain of the problem with small quadrilaterals led to the name 'panel method'. The more general solution of linear partial differential equations by this method has become known as the boundary element method. In this case study we restrict our attention to non-lifting potential flow over three-dimensional bodies.

10.4.2 Problem formulation

The problem may be formulated as follows[1]: fluid velocity at a point may be expressed as the gradient of a potential function, Φ, which satisfies Laplace's equation in the region R' exterior to the body surface S, has a zero normal derivative on S, and approaches the proper uniform stream potential at infinity (figure 10.5).

$$\bigtriangledown \Phi = 0 \text{ in } R'$$

$$\frac{\partial \Phi}{\partial n} \Big|_S = \vec{n}.\mathrm{grad}\Phi \Big|_S = 0$$

$$\Phi \to (V_{\infty x}x + V_{\infty y}y + V_{\infty z}z) \text{ for } x^2 + y^2 + z^2 \to \infty$$

where $\vec{n}$ is the unit outward normal vector at a point on the surface S and the

---

[1] The methodology we have developed does not require a full understanding of the often complex mathematics of the problem to enable the identification of the correct choices for an efficient implementation. This level of detail in this case study has been deliberately included to show that real problems can be solved using these methods.

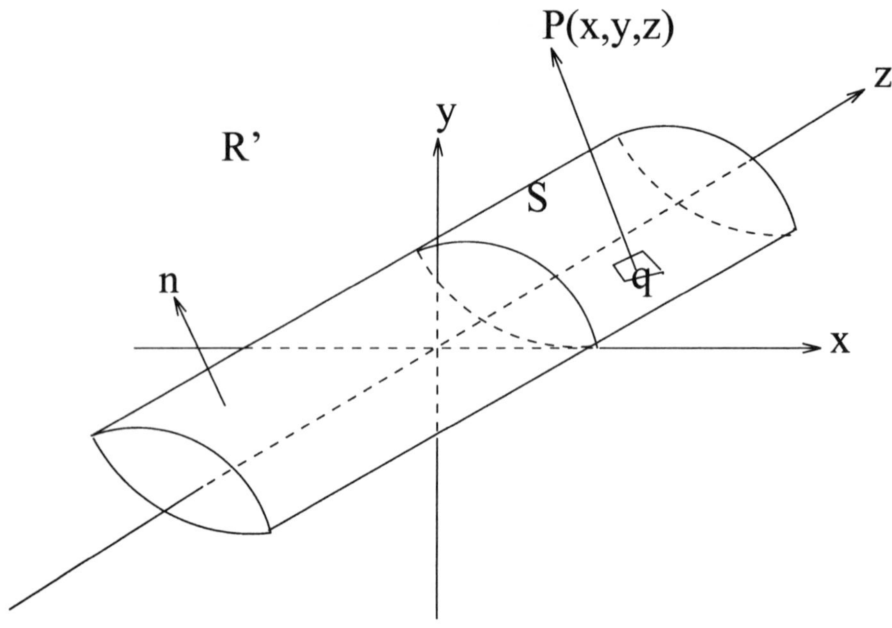

Figure 10.5   Notation used

undisturbed flow is represented by the constant vector $\vec{V}_\infty$ with components $V_{\infty x}, V_{\infty y}, V_{\infty z}$.

If Φ is written as the sum of the uniform stream potential ϕ_∞ and the disturbance potential due to the body ϕ:

$$\Phi = \phi_\infty + \phi$$

then ϕ satisfies:

$$\nabla \phi = 0 \text{ in } R' \tag{10.1}$$

$$\frac{\partial \phi}{\partial n}\,|_s = \vec{n}.\mathrm{grad}\phi\,|_s = -\vec{n}.\vec{V}_\infty\,|_s \tag{10.2}$$

$$\phi \to 0 \text{ for } x^2 + y^2 + z^2 \to \infty \tag{10.3}$$

The body surface is imagined to be covered with a surface source density distribution σ such that:

$$\phi(x,y,z) = \int\!\!\int_S \frac{\sigma(q)}{r(p,q)}\,dS \tag{10.4}$$

where $r(p,q)$ is the distance from the integration point q on the surface to the point in the flow p, with coordinates (x,y,z), where the potential is being evaluated. The function σ must be determined so that ϕ satisfies equation 10.2.

As the surface S is approached the derivative of equation 10.4 becomes singular

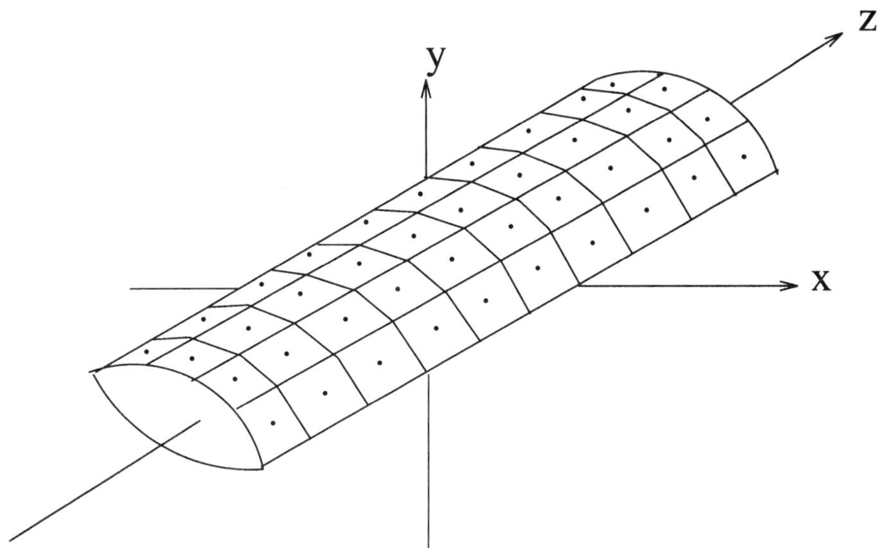

Figure 10.6 The approximate representation of the body surface

and its principal part, $2\pi\sigma(p)$, must be extracted. So, taking the normal derivative of ϕ on the body surface:

$$\frac{\partial\phi}{\partial n}\Big|_S = 2\pi\sigma(p) + \int\int \frac{\partial}{\partial n}\left(\frac{1}{r(p,q)}\right)\sigma(q)dS$$

and substituting it into equation 10.2 gives the integral equation for σ as:

$$2\pi\sigma(p) + \int\int_S \frac{\partial}{\partial n}\left(\frac{1}{r(p,q)}\right)\sigma(q)dS = -\vec{n}(p).\vec{V}_\infty \tag{10.5}$$

where $\vec{n}(p)$ indicates dependence on location.

Once this equation is solved for σ, the disturbance potential ϕ may be evaluated from equation 10.4 and the disturbance flow velocities in the coordinate directions from the derivatives of equation 10.4.

Numerical approximation

The body surface is approximated by a large number of small quadrilateral panels, as shown in figure 10.6, labelled with index j. An initially unknown source density σ_j is assumed to be constant over each panel, but may vary from panel to panel. By approximating the problem thus, it is reduced to finding the values of a finite number of values of σ_j. To find these values, the boundary condition given in equation 10.5 is applied at a finite number of collocation points, labelled with index i. These collocation points are usually at panel centres.

The discrete form of equation 10.5 is then:

$$2\pi\sigma_i + \sum_j \sigma_j \int\!\!\int_{S_j} \frac{\partial}{\partial n}\left(\frac{1}{r(i,j)}\right)dS = -\vec{n}_i.\vec{V}_\infty \tag{10.6}$$

This equation is applied to each collocation point. Note σ_i in equation 10.6 is the source strength of the panel containing collocation point i. The influence function:

$$a_{ij} = \int\!\!\int_{S_j} \frac{\partial}{\partial n}\left(\frac{1}{r(i,j)}\right)dS$$

may be evaluated analytically [100]. Thus the solution of σ_i is obtained from:

$$\sum_j a_{ij}\sigma_j = b_i$$

where b_i is $-\vec{n}_i.\vec{V}_\infty$, for each i, or in matrix form:

$$A\vec{\sigma} = \vec{b} \tag{10.7}$$

The exact expression for the influence calculation involves time consuming logarithm and arctangent calculations. If the collocation point is some distance from the panel then an asymptotic expansion of the exact expression may be used to produce much simpler expressions that are faster to evaluate with no substantial loss in accuracy. Indeed, these asymptotic expansions may produce a more accurate solution for panels that are 'far apart' [147]. This is because if the panels are far apart then the exact expression involves the difference of nearly equal quantities which are then subject to 'round-off' errors on computers.

Because each panel influences every collocation point, A is a dense, and usually non-symmetric, influence matrix. Iterative methods are usually employed for the solution of equation 10.7. Once the source vector $\vec{\sigma}$ has been found then velocities may be calculated anywhere in the flow field, and in particular on the body surface (see [100] for details).

10.4.3 Parallel requirements

From the description of the problem we can see that it has two distinct stages:

1. Set up the matrix of influences

2. Solve for the unknown source singularities

Examination of the problem description reveals that an atomic element for the first stage of the problem could be the calculation of the influence of one panel on another. This calculation produces one element of the influence matrix. There are no data dependencies between the influence calculations for a single panel and so we could choose this as our task. However, the second stage of the algorithm involves the solution of the influence matrix and this will require each processing element to be aware of complete rows of the influence matrix. In a realistic engineering application there are likely to be several hundreds, if not thousands, of panels to consider, it is therefore preferable to make a task the calculation of an entire row

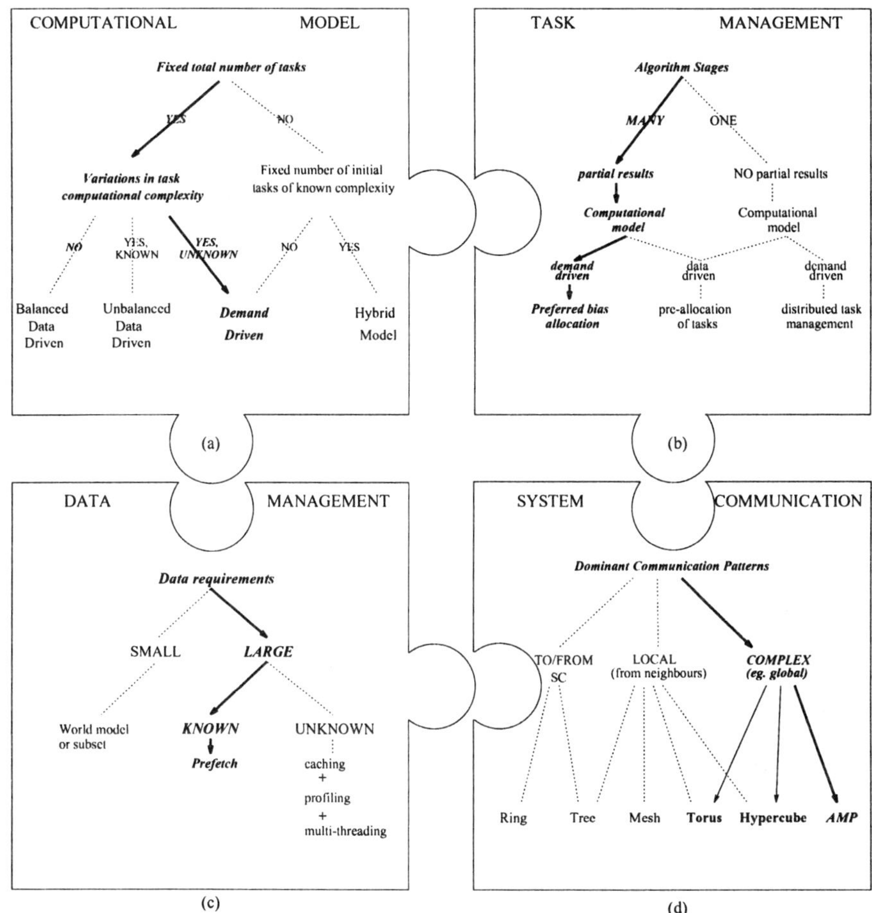

Figure 10.7   Choice of correct computational model and task management strategy for steps 1 and 2

of the influence matrix, that is the calculations of the influence on one panel from all other panels.

This choice of task identifies the principal data item as the panel being considered and the additional data items as all other panels in the problem domain. With this established we can choose the correct computational model as shown in figure 10.7(a). The computational complexity associated with each influence calculation is related to the panel's position relative to all other panels in the problem domain. If the other panels are 'close' then the full expression must be used, however, if they are further away then an asymptotic expansion of this expression may be used. These expansions are much simpler expressions and thus may be computed in a fraction of the time of the exact solution, as shown in table 10.1. The different computational effort required for these calculations and the fact that a panel's position on the body will determine its relative position to the other panels, means we must adopt a demand driven computational model to cope with these unknown variations in computational complexity associated with each of the tasks.

	near	mid	far
Influence calculation	1.000	0.221	0.151

Table 10.1 Normalised times required for near-, mid- and far-field calculations

Figure 10.7(b) shows the choice we must make for the task management strategy for stage 1 of this problem now that we have chosen a demand driven model. There is another stage of the algorithm after the influence matrix has been established, and that is the solution of this matrix. The resultant rows of the influence matrix will be the principal data items of this second stage. A preferred bias allocation strategy will ensure these partial results are positioned correctly in anticipation of the second stage.

A Jacobi iterative solver was selected for the second stage of this problem. As we discussed in section 7.2.2, this method is suitable for a balanced data driven approach and thus a pre-allocation of tasks can be adopted for this stage.

The data requirements for the panel method problem are large, typically far larger than can be accommodated within the local cache of every processing element. We know that to complete one task we have to compute the influence of all other panels on the panel specified by the task. Furthermore, the order in which we carry out these calculations is not important as long as all the panels are considered. The data requirements are thus known and we may adopt a prefetch data management strategy, as illustrated in figure 10.7(c).

In the first stage of the algorithm, each task may be computed independently of all other tasks and thus the communication pattern for this stage is to/from the system controller. However, the Jacobi algorithm adopted to solve the second stage requires information to be exchanged at each iteration – a global data requirement. Furthermore, the data management required for the first stage also implies a global communication pattern and thus, as shown in figure 10.7(d), a torus, hypercube, or better an AMP configuration should be chosen.

10.4.4 Results

To evaluate the suitability of the choices we have made, the panel method was implemented on AMP, torus and ring systems of 63 processing elements. Results were obtained for a test case of a 10% thick ellipsoid at incidence above the ground plane. The body was represented by an increasing number of panels from 196 (corresponding to a 15×15 mesh) to 2916 panels (corresponding to a 55×55 mesh).

Figure 10.8 shows the time taken in seconds for both the stages of the panel method for problem sizes increasing from 576 to 2916 panels, on the AMP, torus and ring configurations. Results were not possible for problem sizes greater than 1936 panels on 63-processing element rings because the resultant message densities

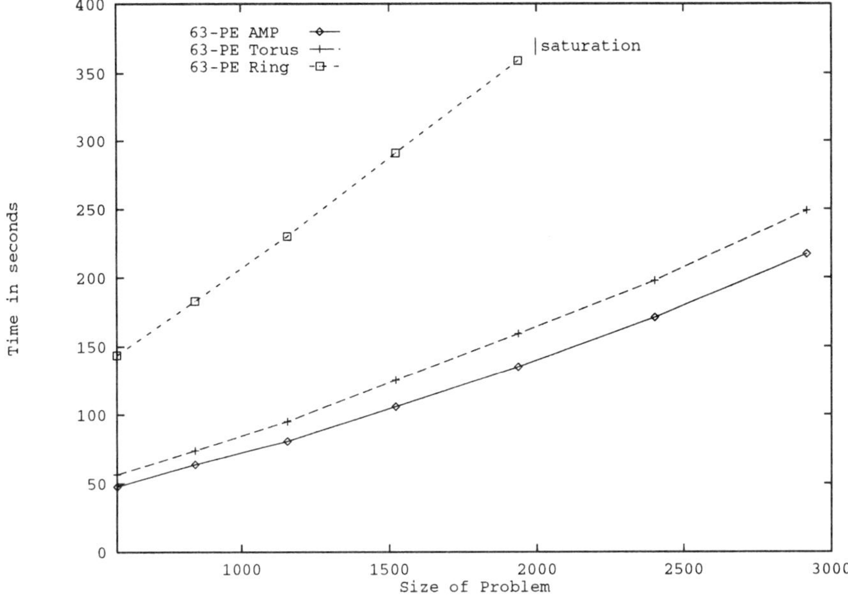

Figure 10.8 Total time taken in seconds for increasing problem size on 63-processing element configurations

were too high, overflowing the communication system. The solution of the 576 panel problem on the AMP configuration is 18% faster than the same problem on the torus and 200% faster than the same problem on the ring. For a problem size of 1936 panels, the AMP is still approximately 18% faster than the torus and 165% faster than the ring. When the problem size is increased to 2916 panels, the AMP configuration is still 15% faster than the torus.

10.4.5 Conclusions

The results clearly show how important the choice of configuration strategy is for any parallel implementation. AMP configurations are better suited to global communication and so they consistently perform better than both the torus and ring configurations.

The panel method is a particular example of a boundary element method and so the same techniques applied to the parallel implementation of the panel method can easily be applied to any other boundary element method. We can also see that the panel method exhibits many of the characteristics of the thermal radiation case study investigated in Chapter 7. Furthermore, the need to exchange information at each iteration for the second stage of the panel method is very similar to communication patterns that exists in the bird flock simulation of Chapter 9, for which an AMP configuration was also the most suitable.

It is these inherent characteristics that must be extracted from a problem to enable the most efficient parallel implementation to be chosen. A deep understanding of the intricacies of the problem formulation are not necessary to distill the appropriate characteristics, as long as the necessary questions can be answered. The answers to these questions will provide the correct choice of parallel implementation. The work presented in this case study was the result of a very successful collaboration between aerospace engineers, who understood the problem they wanted to solve, and parallel programmers who knew the right questions that needed to be asked in order to solve the problem most efficiently on a large multiprocessor system.

10.5 Exercises and Project Suggestions

1. Imagine your task is to implement a complex engineering problem, the simulation of nuclear particle movement, on a 64-processor distributed memory MIMD system. The nuclear particle simulation (the exact details of which you do not need to know) requires the paths of thousands of particles to be tracked as they move about an environment. The direction of these paths is determined by the surfaces with which the nuclear particles interact as they move through the environment. At certain surfaces the nuclear particle may be absorbed and thus the particle is not traced any further. Thus the path of one particle may be significantly shorter than another particle. In the simulation, it is assumed that the particles only interact with the surfaces and do not interact with each other. Therefore, each particle may be traced independently of all other particles. To achieve a reasonable solution many thousands of particles are traced in very complex environments. The data required to model the surfaces of any environment is large, far more than can be accommodated at any processor of your parallel system. However, there is sufficient memory for all the data to be distributed across the system.

   Given this information, discuss the most efficient way of implementing this problem on your parallel system. Your answer must justify your choice of method of domain decomposition, data and task management strategy, and configuration.

2. Imagine your task is to implement a complex engineering problem, the boundary element method, on a 64 processor distributed memory MIMD system. The boundary element method (the exact details of which you do not need to know) requires the influence of every quadrilateral surface to be calculated at every other quadrilateral surface, with the influence calculations varying in complexity from surface to surface. The order in which these computations are performed for each quadrilateral surface is not important as long as every other quadrilateral surfaces is considered. The problem being implemented involves many thousands of quadrilateral surface, far more than can be accommodated at any processor of your parallel system. However, there is sufficient memory for all the data to be distributed across the system.

   Given this information, discuss the most efficient way of implementing this problem on your parallel system. Your answer must justify your choice of method of domain decomposition, data and task management strategy, and configuration.

3. Implement your favourite complex problem using the SAMD approach on your parallel system!

Appendix A

The Data Diffusion Machine

The inability of physically shared memory multiprocessors to perform efficiently with more than tens of processors led, in the 1980's, to the development of the Virtual Shared Memory, or VSM, concept. VSM machines aimed at providing the functionality of a shared memory machine while offering the scalability of a distributed memory architecture. The Data Diffusion Machine [182], or DDM, is a good example of a VSM architecture developed in that period. This appendix provides a detailed description of the DDM, highlighting the manner in which this novel architecture addresses the consistency issues associated with distributed data management, which were discussed in chapter 8.

A.1 Background

The DDM design was motivated by the need to implement parallel Prolog systems, for which shared data is a fundamental component. Until then, such parallel Prolog systems had been developed on shared memory architectures. The DDM was therefore designed to mimic precisely a shared memory architecture in which all data should be accessible with equal costs to any processor.

Simple VSM models do not offer this uniform data access as they bind memory locations to specific processors. This means that certain memory locations are physically "closer" to some processors than others. This type of architecture may be classified as Non Uniform Memory Access, or NUMA, as described in Chapter 3. From the programmer's viewpoint, a UMA model, in which all memory is conceptually at the same distance, is preferable as this allows the program to access memory without regard to where the data will be allocated physically. The DDM implements the UMA model using associative memories.

Scalability was an important design issue of the DDM. Not only was it desirable that the performance of the DDM increased as more processors were added, but also there could not be any dramatic increase in cost, maintaining the system's overall cost effectiveness. The DDM attempts to bound all overheads by the logarithm of the number of processors. Data items can be located in a time bounded by $O(\log p)$ (where p is the number of processors). Broadcast operations (either to distribute data or to invalidate data) are performed in a time bounded by $O(\log p)$. The costs of the machine are $O(p \log p)$. This is accomplished by using hierarchical directories.

A.2 The Associative Memories

One of the main goals of the DDM design is to provide a memory supporting the UMA model. This means that the programmer need not be aware that certain areas of the memory require more time to access than others. This goal can be achieved by organising the hardware and system software in such a way that the data migrates to the processors where it is required. The DDM facilitates data migration by changing the hardware organisation of the memory, so that data addresses are not bound to the physical location of the data.

In traditional memories the address of a data item has a one-to-one mapping with a physical location. Given the address, it is known where the data may be found, and given this location, the address of the data item is fixed. The DDM uses a type of memory that does not suffer from this restriction: an *associative memory*. An associative memory decouples the notion of the address of a data item and the physical location of the data, by storing the data together with a tag containing the address of the data item. Given an address to read from or to write to, an associative memory compares this address with the tags, and performs the operation on the matching memory location.

When all processors in the parallel system have an associative memory, each data item can be stored at any processor. This enables the data to be moved to where it is required. Data can also be shared between various processors as copies may be kept at several processors. This effectively implements a UMA once the initial penalty has been paid to fetch a data item to the requesting processor, as this local copy can reused without any further overhead.

Although there is a great deal of freedom as to where data may be placed, there are some limits. Firstly, each processor has a limited memory, and so there is an upper-bound on the amount of data that can be stored locally. Secondly, the total machine has a finite amount of memory, which restricts the total number of data items that can be present within the system at any time. Should additional data items be required, then virtual memory techniques must be used to implement paging or segmentation to and from disk. Thirdly, data transportation is still necessary. Thus for a program to obtain maximal performance, data should be accessed infrequently by other processors, that is, the program should have good temporal locality, as discussed in section 8.5.3.

Fully associative memories are expensive to build, as for each memory location there is a need to store the tag and include a piece of hardware to compare the address with the tag. (All memory locations should also be processed in parallel in order to achieve a desirable performance). A set-associative memory, although limiting the associativity, may be used to reduce the complexity and price of a fully associative memory. Figure A.1 shows how a set-associative memory works. A hash function is used on the address to index a data item in each of the memory banks. A fully associative look-up is then performed to select the appropriate data item. Although a tag is still stored with each data item, there are significantly fewer comparators (one for each bank, typically 2-16), which reduces the cost considerably.

The DDM is not the only machine that uses associative memories. At the same time that the DDM was developed, Kendall Square Research independently de-

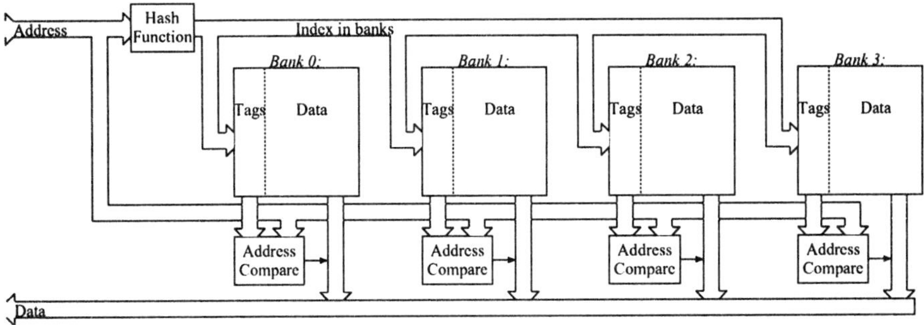

Figure A.1   The structure of a set-associative memory, this example shows a 4-way set-associative memory

signed the ALLCACHE^{TM} architecture, used in the KSR-1 [121] and KSR-2 machines. The ALLCACHE and the DDM are very similar architectures, both using associative memories and a hierarchical directory structure. Subsequently other architectures using associative memories have been designed, including the IACOMA, the DICE [126] and the COMA-F. The VSM architectures that depend on associative main memory are often referred to as Cache Only Memory Architectures, or COMAs.

A.3 Directory Structure and Interconnection Network

The associative memories allow the data to be relocated to where it is required. This flexibility creates a problem: because data can be stored at any place, a mechanism must be provided to locate a data item given its address. This mechanism is provided in the form of a *directory*, which is organised hierarchically.

A.3.1 The directory hierarchy

At the lowest level of the hierarchy, each processor has a local directory. This directory knows which data items reside on that particular processor. In fact, the associative memory implements this level of the directory, as the tags of the associative memory store which data items are present. At the next level of the hierarchy the machine is divided into groups containing a number of processors. Figure A.2 shows this structure with three processors per group. For each group, a directory maintains which of the data items are present in the group of processors below. At the next level, there is again a grouping, with level-3 directories knowing which data items are present in the groups of level-2 directories below.

As with the memories at the leaf-processors, the directories are implemented using associative memories, so that bookkeeping about any data item can be stored in any directory. Note that the higher level directories lack *precise* information on the whereabouts of the data. The only information maintained is whether the data item is present in the tree below it, and whether the data item is copied outside this tree. Going up in the tree, the information becomes less precise, but more global.

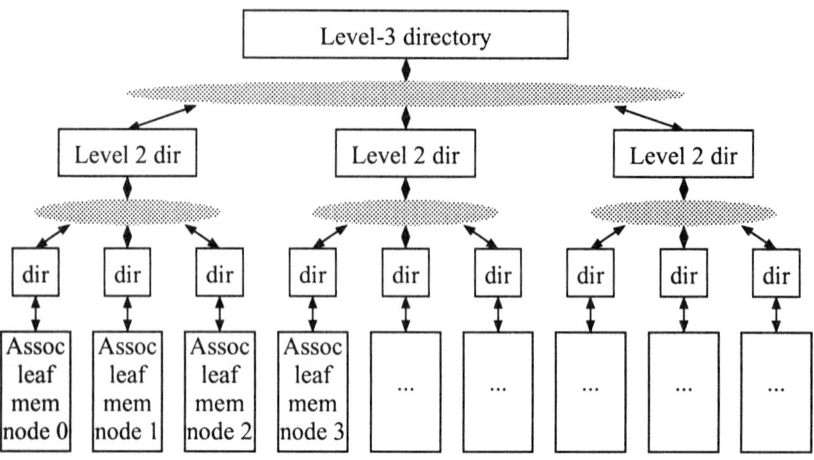

Figure A.2   The directory structure. The boxes marked "dir" are the local, or level-1 directories.

A directory higher up has information about the data items on a larger group of processors, but does not know where the copies reside.

The algorithm to locate a data item follows straightforwardly from the description of the tree. If a processor requires a data item, it posts a request to its local directory. If the data is not present locally, the local directory posts the request to the directory one level up; this directory knows if the data item is in one of the neighbouring processors. If the data item is unknown again, the request is posted to the next higher level until a directory in the tree is reached which is aware of the data item. The request now travels downwards until it reaches the processor at the bottom of the tree at which the data item resides. The data item is then forwarded to the original requester by retracing the steps made by the request. A more elaborate description of read and write operations is presented in section A.4.

Any request for a non-local data item proceeds up the tree until the data item is located in a branch below that current directory, and then down the tree to the appropriate processor. The maximum number of steps that need to be made for a request to be satisfied is thus $4 \log_f p$, where p is the number of processors, and f is the "fanout" of the tree (there are at most $\log_f p$ steps up, $\log_f p$ down, and then again $\log_f p$ up and down to bring the data back). This means that with an exponential increase in the number of processors the access time for a data item increases only linearly.

A.3.2 The directory interconnect

The precise way of interconnecting the directories is not specified in figure A.2. Before discussing the directory in more detail, we need to specify how the directories are connected with each other. Three basic schemes have been considered for the DDM: a bus, ring, and direct interconnect, as shown in figure A.3.

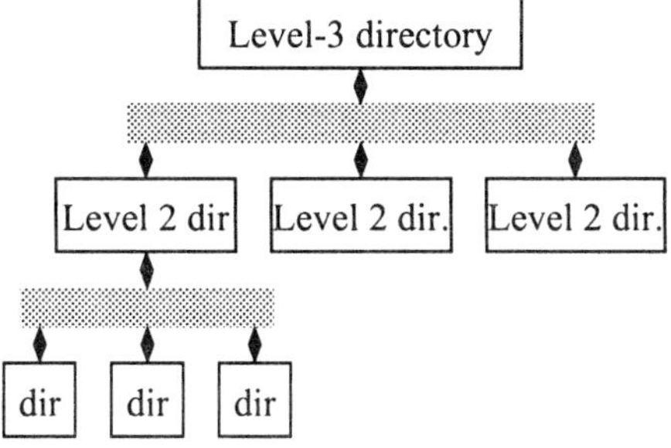

a) Bus based interconnection

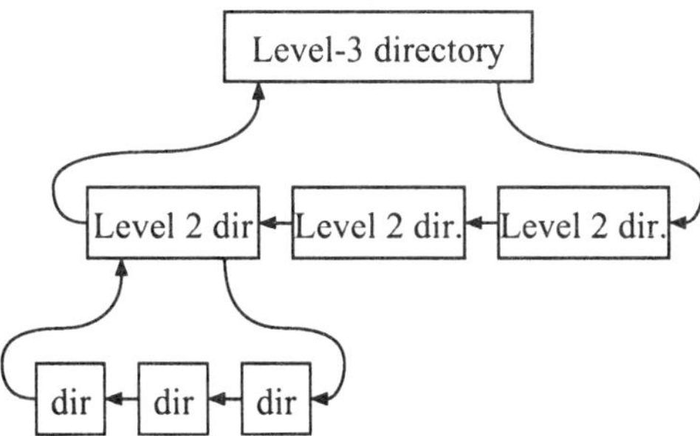

b) Ring based interconnection

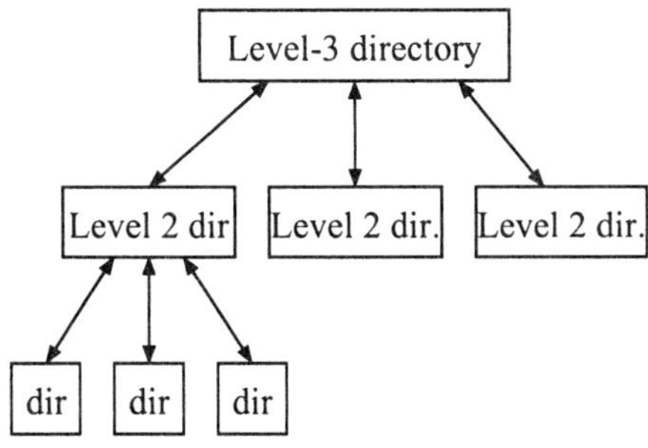

c) Link based interconnection

Figure A.3   Three interconnection structures, bus, ring and direct interconnection.

Bus interconnect

In the bus-based implementation the "children" and "parent" in a cluster are all connected to one central bus. Any message send by any of the processors connected to the bus will be seen all other processors. This means that when one of the children posts a request for a data item, all the children will see the request (as will the parent). The first child that can respond to the request may do so. A bus based DDM is presented in [94].

Using a bus has two disadvantages. Firstly, if the parent wants to send a message to one specific child, communication between any other pair of processors on the bus is blocked. Secondly, buses are not easy to construct physically and require an arbiter to ensure only one processor at a time posts a request.

Ring interconnect

An alternative is to use a ring interconnect, which connects all the children and the parent processor in a unidirectional ring network. A message is posted by sending it to a neighbouring processor. When a processor receives a message, it will be passed on to the next processor on the ring, unless it has to be delivered to that particular processor. Broadcasting is supported naturally, as all processors can read a message that is passed around the ring. The KSR-1 uses a ring interconnect.

The advantage of a ring network over a bus network is twofold. Firstly, the ring is easier to construct. The communication channels between the processors are point-to-point unidirectional channels and thus there is no need for an arbiter. Secondly, because there are many ring segments, many messages can travel through the ring at the same time. The ring is thus similar to a pipeline: while a message is underway from the parent to a child, messages from other processors can be initiated in the ring and travel at the same time. However, as discussed in Chapter 9, the diameter of a ring increases linearly as more processors are added, significantly increasing the delay in message response times.

Direct interconnect

The third possibility considered for the DDM is to provide direct bidirectional communication channels, or *links*, between the parent and each of its children. These links can be, for example, similar to the links provided by a transputer [4]. Direct links reduce the latency that exists in a ring, and are easier to implement than a bus because there is no need for an arbiter or multicasting hardware [141, 156].

The disadvantage of using bidirectional communication channels between the parent and each of the children is that the broadcast is no longer a simple operation. On a bus or a ring, the broadcast is inherent, but using direct connection, a broadcast must be implemented explicitly by sending a message to all the children that need to receive a copy. This requires the parent to maintain additional administration information for each data item. Not only does the parent need to know whether a copy is present in any of the branches below, but also it must know which branches have a copy, so that the broadcast can be directed to the appropriate branches. This administration can be maintained efficiently in a bitmask. In the example shown in figure A.2, a 4-bit bitmask is sufficient; one bit for each of the branches below,

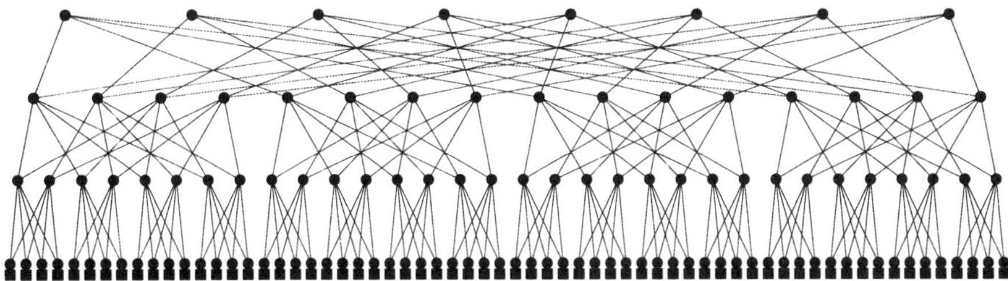

Figure A.4   An example of a split tree

and one bit to signal whether there is a copy outside this tree (the "branch" going up to the parent). In this appendix we focus on the version of the DDM that uses such a link interconnect. However, all principles presented have a direct equivalent in DDMs implemented with buses or rings.

A.3.3 Scalable split directories

The tree shown in figure A.2 is the conceptual structure of the directory. The actual implementation of the directory structure has to be different for two reasons:

1. The amount of traffic in the higher levels of the tree increases as there are fewer directories servicing the requests. There are p directories at the lowest level (one for each p processors), but there is only one top-level directory which potentially handles the same amount of traffic as the p directories below.

2. Although the top directory structure does not have to store precisely where data items are located, it must store some information for *all* items below it. This means that the size of the top directory is linear in the number of items stored in the machine. Even if many items are shared, so a only a fraction of the items on each processor are unique, this would still mean that the top-level directory must increase as more processors are added. The implementation of such a huge top-level directory might be prohibitively expensive.

The solution adopted in the DDM is to subdivide directories higher up in the tree. At each level of the tree, directories are split so that instead of big monolithic directories handling many transactions, many smaller directories exist that handle only a fraction of the traffic.

The directories are divided so that each directory receives the administration of a fraction of the data items. The last few bits of the item address determine the distribution of the data item over the directories. This can be implemented simply in hardware, and generally results in an equal amount of traffic in all branches. An additional advantage is that the addresses become shorter higher up in the tree. Since the directory will only store items with an address ending in a certain bit pattern, these bits do not have to be stored in the associative memories of the directories.

Figure A.4 shows the interconnection of 64 processors with a splitting of 2 at each level. The circles represent directories and the squares are the leaf-processors.

The topology that results is still a hierarchical structure, but no longer a tree, and is termed a Banyan graph [116], or a fat-tree [127].

A.4 The Coherency Protocol

The associative memories in the leaf-processors store the actual data items, and the directories in between maintain pointers to data items so that data can be located efficiently. When data is transferred from one processor to another, the pointers in the directories must be adjusted so that the new copies are recorded. Also, when a data item is deleted from a processor, the associated pointers in the directory must be removed. The coherency protocol of the DDM transports the data and updates the pointers. It ensures that the directories and memories are always in a consistent state.

The coherency protocol works on an item basis. *Transactions* (asynchronous messages) are exchanged between processors, signalling a request to perform some operation or an answer to a previous request. A transaction always operates on the data item specified in the transaction header. There are six important transactions: **Read** and **Copy** transactions are needed to read data; and, **Erase, Exclusive, Fetch** and **Data** transactions implement write operations. There are no special transactions to handle synchronisation operations. Instead these operations are supported on top of the ordinary protocol support for reads and writes.

A.4.1 Reading data

A memory that receives a request from the processor for a data item that is not available locally initiates a **Read** transaction to the directory immediately above it. A directory that receives a **Read** transaction propagates it to the nearest copy. If the directory knows that a copy of the data is present below it, the request is sent in the direction of that copy, otherwise the request is sent further up the hierarchy. When the transaction reaches a processor with the data, a copy of the data item is taken and sent back in a **Copy** transaction to the processor from where the request originated.

To be able to retrace the route from where the original transaction came, the state of the data item is changed in a directory when a **Read** transaction is handled. The branch via which the request was received is stored. When the **Copy** transaction comes back, it can be sent back to the appropriate branch of the tree, and the administration is updated to record the presence of a new copy of the data item. The four actions in the read part of the protocol are shown schematically in figure A.5.

A.4.2 Writing data

The DDM supports a sequential consistency model implemented with an invalidating protocol (see section 8.4 for a discussion on invalidating protocols). When the processor wants to overwrite data, the local directory knows whether other copies exist. If there are other copies present, the processor issues an **Erase** transaction before the write can be performed. This transaction is a command to the directory that all copies that the directory knows of must be destroyed, leaving

The processor wants to read data ⇒
    Is the data present ?
        Yes: perform the read
        No: Issue a **Read** transaction

On receipt of a **Read** transaction by a directory ⇒
    Store the identification of the originating branch
    Is there a copy below ?
        Yes: propagate the transaction in the direction of the copy
        No: propagate the transaction upwards

On receipt of a **Read** transaction by a leaf-processor ⇒
    Fetch the data, and send a **Copy** transaction upwards
    Update the administration to reflect that there is another copy

On receipt of a **Copy** transaction by a directory ⇒
    Propagate to the originating branch
    Update the administration to reflect that that branch has got a copy

On receipt of a **Copy** transaction by a leaf-processor ⇒
    Store the data, and notify the processor that the data has arrived

Figure A.5   The part of the protocol that processes read operations.

only the copy at the originating processor to remain. A directory will therefore propagate an **Erase** transaction along all branches of the tree that are known to have a copy. Because this propagation goes over multiple branches, multiple copies may be invalidated in parallel. In fact, all copies are reached in a time bounded by $O(\log p)$.

When a leaf-processor receives the **Erase** transaction, it destroys its copy of the data item (by marking the entry in the associative memory as "Invalid"), and an **Exclusive** transaction is sent back. This transaction is the acknowledgement that the destruction of the data has been completed. A directory will wait for the acknowledgements that all outstanding copies known to that directory have been destroyed, before sending an **Exclusive** transaction to the originating processor. The return path to the originating processor is stored in the same way as for the Read transaction: when the **Erase** transaction is handled, the branch along which the **Erase** was received is stored. Each **Exclusive** that comes in is used to remove that branch from the list of branches that had a copy. When the last **Exclusive** comes in, an **Exclusive** transaction is sent to the originator.

Eventually, the processor requesting the **Erase** will receive an **Exclusive**. This means that the processor is guaranteed to have the sole copy of the data item. This copy can, therefore, be updated safely. After the update, copies can be made again if other processors request the freshly updated data item.

The processor wants to write data $\Rightarrow$
    Is the data present ?
      No: Issue a **Fetch** transaction
      Yes, one copy: perform the write
      Yes, but other copies exist: issue an **Erase** transaction

An **Erase** transaction is received by a directory $\Rightarrow$
    Store the identification of the originating branch
    Propagate the transaction to all branches with a copy

An **Erase** transaction is received by a leaf-processor $\Rightarrow$
    Destroy the data, and send an **Exclusive** transaction upwards

An **Exclusive** transaction is received by a directory $\Rightarrow$
    Update the administration to reflect that the copy is invalidated
    If the destruction is complete:
        Send an **Exclusive** transaction to the originating branch

An **Exclusive** transaction is received by a leaf-processor $\Rightarrow$
    Notify the processor that the write can be performed

On receipt of a **Fetch** transaction by a directory $\Rightarrow$
    Store the identification of the originating branch
    Is there a copy below ?
      Yes: propagate the transaction in the direction of the copy
      No: propagate the transaction upwards
    Send an **Erase** transaction to all other branches with a copy

On receipt of a **Fetch** transaction by a leaf-processor $\Rightarrow$
    Fetch the data, and send a **Data** transaction upwards
    Destroy the data, and send an **Exclusive** transaction upwards

On receipt of a **Data** transaction by a directory $\Rightarrow$
    Propagate to the originating branch
    Update the administration to reflect that that branch has got a copy

On receipt of a **Data** transaction by a leaf-processor $\Rightarrow$
    Store the data.

Figure A.6   The part of the protocol that processes write operations.

The **Erase** transaction is only issued if the processor has a copy of the data already. If the processor does not have a copy of the data item, a copy must be obtained in the process of erasing all copies. In this case, the requesting processor issues a **Fetch** transaction. This transaction is a command to obtain one copy, and to destroy all other copies. When a directory receives a **Fetch** transaction, it will propagate the **Fetch** to the nearest copy that is available (following the same algorithm as the **Read**). If there are any other copies present, an **Erase** transaction is propagated to these.

The **Fetch** transaction is in the first instance answered with a **Data** transaction. This transaction carries the requested data, which can be propagated to the originating processor. Later on an **Exclusive** transaction will be received signalling that the invalidation of the other copies has been completed. The protocol for dealing with the four transactions needed to write data is shown in figure A.6.

A.4.3 *Multiple read and/or write operations*

The two cases above show how a single read or write operation is dealt with. During the normal operation of a DDM, multiple read and write operations will execute simultaneously. Most of these operations will be performed on different memory locations and will therefore not interfere with each other (each data item has its own private administration information). However, it does happen that multiple operations need to be performed on the same item simultaneously.

The most common case is multiple reads. If, for example, two adjacent processors both want to read the same data, then the directory above these two processors will receive two **Read** transactions. When the second **Read** is received, the directory will note that a transaction is in progress. The directory then simply stores the branch from which the second **Read** was received, so that when the **Copy** transaction carrying the data returns it can be propagated to both sources simultaneously. An arbitrary number of **Read** transactions can be combined in this way. Note that transaction combining can dramatically reduce the number of messages, as only one **Read** actually progressed up the tree. In the extreme case where all processors simultaneously wish to obtain a copy of the same data item present on one processor, all reads will combine in the various directories in the tree, resulting in a spanning tree through which the **Copy** transaction will be returned.

Fetch and **Erase** transactions cannot be executed in parallel, as the protocol requires that there is only a copy at one processor in the machine. The requests are still combined, suspended, and eventually dealt with in a round robin manner, thereby guaranteeing that each request will be serviced. It is also possible to handle multiple **Read**, **Erase** and **Fetch** transactions; the interested reader is referred to an article discussing this protocol in [141].

A.4.4 *Synchronisation operations*

The protocol of the DDM does not have explicit support for synchronisation operations. Because efficient synchronisation operations are crucial for parallel programming, the protocol has been designed so that the shared memory primitives for a *lock* and a *barrier* can be implemented easily and efficiently on top of the existing protocol either in software or hardware. The basic support for the synchronisation operations is an atomic operation on the DDM memory at the leaf-processor (no special support is needed for this in the protocol). This atomic operation is the Fetch-and-add operation [83]: a value is taken from the memory, one is added to it, and the value is written back again.

A lock can be implemented in a variety of ways using this Fetch-and-add. The simplest implementation polls on a memory location to wait for it to become zero. When the value is zero, a Fetch-and-add is performed so that the location is non zero, which sets the lock. The protocol can deal with this efficiently, because multiple read and write operations can be combined. Therefore, only a very limited number of transactions is needed, even for locks that are temporarily highly congested. Slightly more complex implementations allow fair locks to be implemented.

The barrier primitive is implemented in a similar manner. A counter counts how many of the processors are waiting for the barrier. This counter is incremented (atomically) when a processor enters a barrier, and will start waiting for a second variable to change value. The last processor entering the barrier will note that the counter reaches the desired value, whereupon the processor increments the second variable to release all waiting processors. The protocol will distribute the value that is updated in the second variable efficiently because multiple reads are combined.

A.5 Summary

Since the original paper on the DDM, several versions have been developed. SICS in Sweden has built a hardware prototype of the DDM, based on bus interconnects, and with 88000 processors [94]. Although this small prototype does not demonstrate that the architecture is scalable, it showed that the DDM could be implemented in hardware. Kendall Square Research has industrially developed COMAs that are very similar to the DDM, the KSR-1 [121] and KSR-2. These machines use a ring network and custom-built processors. At the University of Bristol, two versions of the DDM have been developed that use a link interconnect [156, 141]. Although no hardware prototype exists, an emulator has been developed which implements every detail of the machine. Shared memory programs can be executed on an emulated large-scale DDM (72 processors) running on a Inmos transputer-based system.

The measured performance for a set of benchmark programs showed that the design of the DDM appeared to be scalable, and managed to exploit most of the parallelism inherent in the programs. However, as with other virtual shared memory architectures, the DDM struggles to exploit the parallelism that exists in programs with poor locality, as a significant amount of time is lost waiting on the data to be transported. Nevertheless, the baseline cost and performance are competitive and, for a machine of p processors, the costs increases with only $O(\log p)$, and the performance loss is at most $O(\log p)$. The DDM thus met its design requirements of a scalable shared memory with a UMA model. The interested reader is referred to the following papers for more detailed information on the DDM: [141, 142, 143, 144, 145].

Appendix B

Understanding the Pseudo-code

Throughout this book we have made extensive use of a pseudo-code to illustrate how a number of the ideas presented may be implemented. Whilst not designed to be any standard programming language, the pseudo-code has been chosen to minimise the effort required to translate it into an actual parallel implementation language such as C, Fortran, Ada and occam.

This appendix provides additional explanations for each of the constructs used within the pseudo-code. Note that indentation has been used in all cases to highlight the level of scope of the constructs.

B.1 Sequential Constructs

B.1.1 Variables

All variables in the code are shown as underscored lowercase names, such as `variable_name`. Wherever possible the names of variables have been chosen to show clearly their intended purpose. Reserved words are usually shown in uppercase.

Array variables are indexed within square brackets as `array_variable[index]`. Record-like structures use a dot to separate the field from the record name, `record.field`. For example, the four questions of one of the exam scripts, i, being marked by the teachers in section 4.2 are referred to as `Script[i].Question[1]`, ..., `Script[i].Question[4]`.

The symbol `:=` is used to denote an assignment operation,

```
variable_name := value
```

while tests for equality and inequality use =, < and > respectively.

```
variable_name = value
variable_name < value
variable_name > value
```

Comments are enclosed within starred brackets and are used to provide additional information where required.

```
(* Everything within these brackets is a comment *)
```

B.1.2 Statements

Statements are single instructions, procedure calls or sequences of statements within a Begin-End construct. Indentation also assists in identifying those statements which are within the same scope.

```
Begin
  statement_1
  statement_2
End
```

B.1.3 Procedures

Procedures and subprocedures are sequential code segments used to improve overall code readability.

```
PROCEDURE Procedure_Name(parameter_list)
  statement

SUBPROCEDURE Sub_Procedure_Name(parameter_list)
  statement
```

Here `parameter_list` declares one or more variables passed into the procedure. These may be of two forms: value parameters, or variable parameters prefixed by keyword `VAR`. A value parameter's content is not altered during execution of the procedure, while those of a variable parameters contents may be changed.

A procedure may return a value, that is play the role of a function, by including the reserved word RETURN.

```
PROCEDURE Function_Name(parameter list)
  Begin
    statement
    RETURN value
  End
```

B.1.4 Logical & mathematical expressions

Logical and mathematical operations are equivalent to most other languages and are shown in upper case.

```
TRUE, FALSE      - boolean values
AND, NOT         - logical and, logical not
DIV, MOD         - Integer division, integer remainder
```

B.1.5 Loop constructs

Three loop constructs are used: FOR, WHILE and REPEAT.

```
FOR loop_counter = start_value TO finish_value DO
  statement
```

This loop repeatedly executes `statement` whilst incrementing `loop_counter` from `start_value` to `finish_value`.

```
WHILE condition DO
  statement
```

The while loop will execute `statement` whilst `condition` is TRUE, whereas the repeat loop executes `statement` (at least once) until `condition` is TRUE.

```
REPEAT
  statement
UNTIL condition
```

B.1.6 Selection constructs

Selection constructs allow one of a number of possible statements to be executed depending on the value of some condition.

```
IF condition THEN
  statement
ENDIF


IF condition THEN
  statement_1
ELSE
  statement_2
ENDIF


IF condition_1 THEN
  statement_1           (* condition_1 TRUE *)
ELSEIF condition_2 THEN
  statement_2           (* condition_1 FALSE, condition_2 TRUE *)
ELSE
  statement_3           (* condition_1 & condition_2 FALSE *)
ENDIF
```

B.2 Parallel Constructs

B.2.1 Initiating parallelism

The sequential constructs chosen for this pseudo-code are very similar to those used in most sequential languages such as Pascal or Modula-2. Additional constructs need to be introduced to indicate the parallel (or concurrent) execution of some statements. In the following code segment:

```
PARALLEL
  statement_1
  statement_2
```

`statement_1` and `statement_2` will execute concurrently if this code segment is implemented on one processor and in parallel if it is implemented on two processors, as explained in section 1.2 and figure 1.7.

A PARALLEL construct thus causes the execution of the code to *fork* at that point into the specified number of parallel (or concurrent) processes. Once all of these processes have terminated, the code "rejoins" and continues executing sequentially. Figure B.1 shows the flow of execution for a simple code segment.

```
Begin
  statement_a
  PARALLEL
    statement_b
    statement_c
    statement_d
  statement_e
  statement_f
End
```

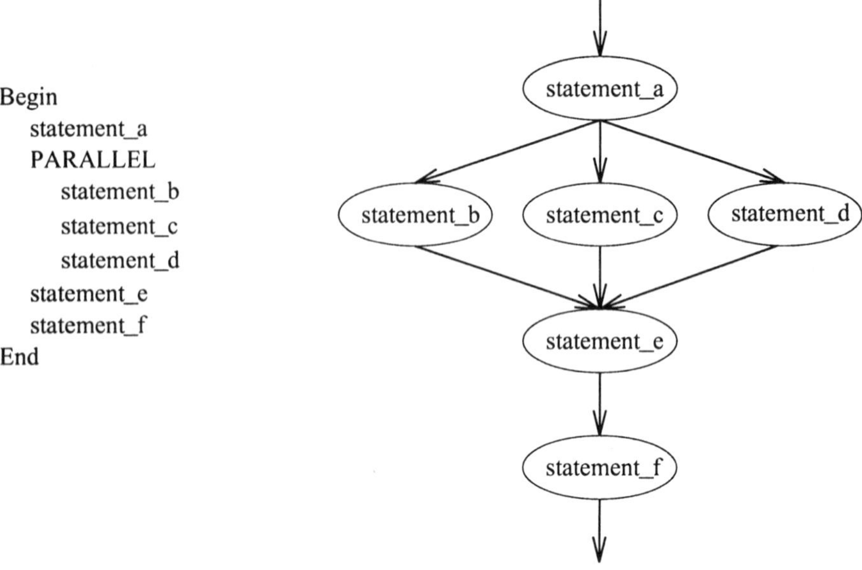

Figure B.1   Flow of execution using the PARALLEL construct

B.2.2 Processes

As explained in section 4.4.2, a process is a segment of code that runs concurrently with other processes on a single processor, or in parallel with other processes on different processors. The reserved word PROCESS is used distinguish these processes from sequential procedures. The processor farm described in section 7.3.2 consists of a number of parallel processes, Processing_Element, each containing three concurrent processes: Task_Router; Application_Process; and, Result_Router.

```
PROCESS Processing_Element(id_number)

  PROCESS Task_Router()
    Begin
      (* Body of the Task_Router *)
    End

  PROCESS Application_Process()
    Begin
      (* Body of the Application_Process *)
    End

  PROCESS Result_Router()
    Begin
      (* Body of the Result_Router *)
    End

  Begin
```

```
    PARALLEL
      Application_Process()
      Task_Router()
      Results_Router()
  End (* Processing_Element *)
```

A number of similar processes or statements may be executed in parallel (or concurrently) by means of the replicated `PARALLEL` construct.

```
PARALLEL FOR counter = 1 TO number_of_times
    statement
```

So, for the processor farm, the parallel execution of a system controller and ten processing elements would be initiated as:

```
Begin
  PARALLEL
    System_Controller()
    PARALLEL FOR id_number = 1 TO 10
        Processing_Element(id_number)
End (* Processor_Farm *)
```

On the few occasions where it has been necessary to "launch" any additional concurrent processes from within a top level process we have used the term `SUBPROCESS` to distinguish these lower level processes.

B.2.3 *Prioritised parallelism*

Within a `PARALLEL` construct we will assume that all the processes are executed with the same *priority*. On separate processors this is certainly the case as the processes are running in parallel, but on a single processor this implies that each process is given an equal allotment of the processor's time. The processes are therefore *timesliced* with each concurrent process being allocated the processor for a portion of time before transferring control of the processor to another concurrent process. The sharing of the processor continues until all concurrent processes have terminated.

The `PRIORITISED PARALLEL` construct may be used to impose levels of priority on concurrent processes. In this construct, the process with the highest priority will be allocated control of the processor first. This highest priority process will keep control of the processor until either it has terminated or it is suspended. The process may be suspended waiting for a communication to occur. Once the highest priority process has terminated or is suspended, control of the processor passes to the process with the next highest priority. As soon as the condition for suspending the higher priority process is satisfied, this higher priority process will interrupt the execution of the lower priority process and once more assume control of the processor.

```
  PROCESS Process_A()
    Begin
      (* Body of Process_A *)
    End
```

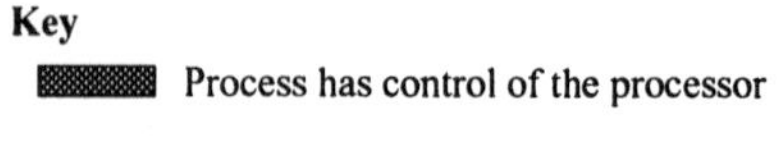

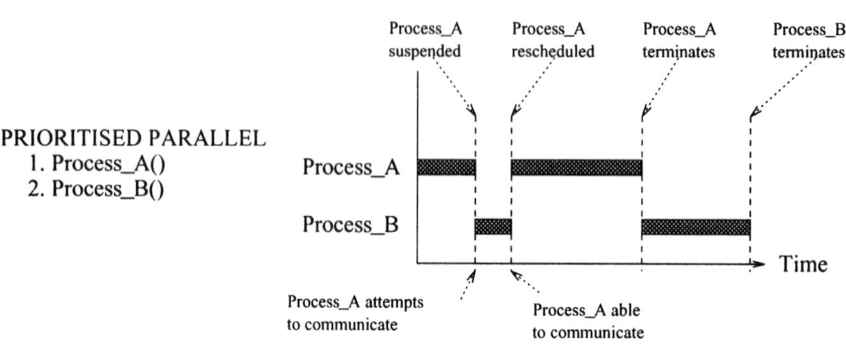

Figure B.2   Processor utilisation for the `PRIORITISED PARALLEL` construct

```
PROCESS Process_B()
  Begin
    (* Body of Process_B *)
  End

Begin
  PRIORITISED PARALLEL
    1. Process_A()
    2. Process_B()
End
```

In this example, `Process_A` has a higher priority than `Process_B` and so, provided its execution is not somehow suspended, `Process_A` will continue to execute until it has terminated and only then will `Process_B` gain control of the processor. Figure B.2 shows processor utilisation for this example. We used this `PRIORITISED PARALLEL` construct to form the basis of our deadlock avoidance scheme discussed in section 9.2.1.

```
PROCESS Router()

  SUBPROCESS Do_Output(output_link)
    Begin
      (* Body of Do_Output *)
    End


  SUBPROCESS Handle_Input(input_links)
    Begin
      (* Body of Handle_Input *)
    End
```

```
SUBPROCEDURE Handle(message)
  Begin
    Interpret(message)
    IF (message requires output) THEN
      PRIORITISED PARALLEL
        1. Do_Output(output_link)   (* high priority *)
        2. Handle_Input(input_link) (* low priority  *)
    ELSE
      Deal_With(message)
    ENDIF
  End (* Handle *)

Begin (* Router *)
  (* Main body of Router *)
End    (* Router *)
```

B.2.4 *Communication constructs*

In a message passing environment, co-operation between processes is achieved by sending and receiving messages. Two different forms of communication constructs are used in this book, as described in section 9.2. In the first type of construct, message are sent to and received from named processes:

```
SEND message TO Process_A
RECEIVE message FROM Process_B
```

In the second type, messages are sent on and received off a named link:

```
SEND message ON link_1
RECEIVE message OFF link_2
```

These two constructs are equivalent. So, in both SEND cases the message is transferred from a source process via a link to the destination process. The two methods of describing communication are used interchangeably; the choice of structure being selected to aid clarity.

B.2.5 *Communication selection constructs*

Communication selection constructs allow one of a number of possible statements to be executed depending on the availability of some incoming message. If several incoming messages are waiting to be handled then the INPUT ALTERNATIVES construct will select one of these inputs non-deterministically; receive the message and then execute the associated statements. So, in the following code segment example:

```
INPUT ALTERNATIVES
  RECEIVE message_1 FROM process_1
    statement_1
  RECEIVE message_2 FROM process_2
    statement_2
```

```
RECEIVE message_3 FROM process_3
  statement_3
```

If `message_1` and `message_3` are both waiting to be dealt with, the INPUT
ALTERNATIVES construct will select one of these, say `message_3`. This message
will now be received from `process_3` and `statement_3` will be executed. This
communication selection structure only deals with one of the possibly many waiting messages. In order to deal with any outstanding messages, or more messages
from the same process as the one selected, this construct should be placed in some
loop construct, as we saw for the Router process in section 9.2:

```
PROCEDURE Router()
  Begin
    RECEIVE initialisation_parameters OFF external_link[0]
    busy := TRUE  (* until the problem is solved *)
    WHILE busy DO
      Begin
        INPUT ALTERNATIVES
          RECEIVE message OFF internal_link
            Handle(message)
          RECEIVE message OFF external_link
            Handle(message)

        Handle_Any_Buffered_Inputs()
      End
End (* Router *)
```

If no message is waiting to be received then the process executing the INPUT
ALTERNATIVES is suspended until a message is forthcoming. If suspension is un-
desirable then an ELSE clause may be used within this construct. If no messages
are waiting to be received then the ELSE clause will always be selected.

```
INPUT ALTERNATIVES
  RECEIVE message_1 FROM process_1
    statement_1
  ELSE
    statement_2
```

A priority ordering for selecting the waiting messages may be achieved using the
PRIORITISED INPUT ALTERNATIVES construct.

```
PRIORITISED INPUT ALTERNATIVES
  1. RECEIVE message_1 FROM process_1
       statement_1
  2. RECEIVE message_2 FROM process_2
       statement_2
  3. RECEIVE message_3 FROM process_3
       statement_3
```

In this example, if `message_1` and `message_3` are both waiting to be dealt with,
the PRIORITISED INPUT ALTERNATIVES construct will always select `message_1`
as it has the highest priority. This message will now be received from `process_1`
and `statement_1` will be executed.

B.3 Pseudo-code Example: The Structure of the SAMD System

This book describes the SAMD method for solving complex problems using parallel processing. Implementation of this methodology has required the development of a system architecture consisting of a system controller and one or more processing elements, as discussed in section 4.4.2. The structure of these two components of our system are shown in figures 4.12 and 4.13 respectively. The pseudo-code for the overall system is:

```
SYSTEM SAMD

  PROCESS System_Controller()
    PROCESS User_Manager()
      Begin
        (* Body of User_Manager *)
      End
    PROCESS File_Manager()
      Begin
        (* Body of File_Manager *)
      End
    PROCESS Graphics_Manager()
      Begin
        (* Body of Graphics_Manager *)
      End
    PROCESS Global_Controller()
      Begin
        (* Body of Global_Controller *)
      End
    PROCESS Router()
      Begin
        (* Body of Router *)
      End
    Begin   (* System_Controller *)
      PARALLEL
        User_Manager()
        File_Manager()
        Graphics_Manager()
        Global_Controller()
        Router()
    End      (* System_Controller *)

  PROCESS Processing_Element(id_number)
    PROCESS Application_Process_Controller()
      Begin
        (* Body of Application_Process_Controller *)
      End
    PROCESS Application_Process(thread_number)
      Begin
        (* Body of Application_Process *)
      End
    PROCESS Data_Manager()
```

```
      Begin
        (* Body of Data_Manager *)
      End
  PROCESS Task_Manager()
      Begin
        (* Body of Task_Manager *)
      End
  PROCESS Local_Controller()
      Begin
        (* Body of Local_Controller *)
      End
  PROCESS Router()
      Begin
        (* Body of Router *)
      End
  Begin  (* Processing_Element *)
      PARALLEL
        Application_Process_Controller()
        PARALLEL FOR i = 1 FOR number_of_threads
          Application_Process(i)
        Data_Manager()
        Task_Manager()
        Local_Controller()
        Router()
  End     (* Processing_Element *)

Begin    (*** SAMD ***)
  PARALLEL
    System_Controller()
    PARALLEL id_number = 1 FOR number_of_processing_elements
      Processing_Element(id_number)
End      (*** SAMD ***)
```

Glossary

ADI: See Data item, Additional data item.

AMP: A Minimum Path system configuration constructed so that the diameter and average interprocessor distance is minimised.

AP: See Application Process.

APC: See Application Process Controller.

Application Process: The concurrent process of a processing element which performs the computation specified by the algorithm.

Application Process Controller: The concurrent process of a processing element which controls the execution of one or more application processes.

Atomic element (of computation): The lowest form of computation in the sequential algorithm.

Broadcast: Communicating a message from one processing element to all other processing elements.

Computational model: The work allocation scheme dividing computation between processing elements.

Conceptual allocation: See Preferred bias allocation.

Data coherence: The phenomenon that data requests are not arbitrary, but related to previous requests.

Data driven: Allocation of work to the processing elements in a predetermined fashion.

Data item: An element of the problem domain.

> **Principal data item:** The data item on which the algorithm is to be applied.
>
> **Additional data item:** Any other data that may be needed to complete the computation on the principal data item.

Data dependency: Data dependencies exist in the problem domain when work (tasks) have to be completed in a specified order.

Data Manager: The concurrent process of the processing element responsible for providing the data required by the application process.

Deadlock: A system state in which computation is unable to proceed as processes are waiting for a condition which will never occur.

Demand driven: The processing elements "drive" the parallel implementation by demanding, on completion of their current task, the next task to be performed.

Distributed memory: Each processing element has its own associated memory component.

DM: See Data Manager.

FM: See File Manager.

File Manager: The concurrent process of a system controller which is responsible for accessing secondary storage devices such as hard disk units.

GC: See Global Controller.

Global Controller: The concurrent process of a system controller which supervises problem computation.

GM: See Graphics Manager.

Graphics Manager: The concurrent process of a system controller which is responsible for driving specialist graphics display devices.

LC: see Local Controller.

Load balancing: The practice of endeavouring to distribute the workload of the problem evenly amongst the processing elements.

Local Controller: The concurrent process of a processing element which co-ordinates the local activities of a processing element.

Multi-threading: The practice of having more than one application executing concurrently at each processing element.

Overhead: A factor which detrimentally affects overall system performance.

Packet: See Task-packet.

Parallel processing: The solution of a problem on more than one processor.

PDI: See Data item, Principal data item.

PE: See Processing Element.

Preferred bias allocation: Allocation of tasks to processing elements in a predetermined manner to ensure the correct distribution of any partial results.

Prefetch data management: Known data items are fetched by the data manager process in advance, so that they are available locally when required.

Process: Software component of the multiprocessor system.

Processor: The hardware component from which the multiprocessor system is constructed.

Processor farm: Realisation of a demand driven computational model by May and Shepherd.

Processing Element: A combination of hardware and system software which performs the parallel computation. A multiprocessor system is constructed from a number of processing elements.

Profiling: Predicting the data requirements of the problem from the pattern of data requests generated by a few selected tasks.

Router: The concurrent process of the processing element responsible for passing messages and data within the multiprocessor system.

SC: See System Controller.

Scalability: The suitability of the adopted parallel approach for implementation on larger multiprocessor systems.

Shared memory: A single memory component which is utilised by more than one processing element.

Speed-up: A measure of the merit of a parallel implementation on a specified number of processing elements. Speed-up is calculated as a ratio of the time to solve the problem on a single processing element versus the time required for the multiprocessor solution.

System Controller: A dedicated processing element which provides input and output facilities, and controls the operation of the processing elements performing the computations.

TM: See Task Manager.

Task: The application of an algorithm to a specific principal data item. As such, a task is the smallest element of problem computation within the parallel system.

Task granularity: The number of atomic elements which constitute a task.

Task Manager: The concurrent process of the processing element which supplies the application process with the next task to be performed.

Task-packet: The grouping of one or more tasks into one message to be supplied to a processing element.

UM: See User Manager.

User Manager: The concurrent process of a system controller which is responsible for interaction with the system user (for example, via keyboard and screen).

References

[1] *Alliant Product Summary*. Alliant Computer Systems, Littleton, MA, 1987.

[2] *CRAY-1 system hardware reference manual*. Cray Research Institute, 1977.

[3] *The T9000 transputer*. SGS-Thomson Microelectronics, Bristol, 1st edition, 1991.

[4] *Transputer Reference Manual*. INMOS Ltd, 1988.

[5] W. B. Ackerman. Data flow languages. In N. Gehani and A. D. McGettrick, editors, *Concurrent Programming*, chapter 3, pages 163–181, Addison-Wesley, 1988.

[6] D. P. Agrawal and G. C. Pathak. Evaluating the performance of microcomputer configurations. *IEEE Computer*, 19:23–37, 1986.

[7] G. S. Almasi and A. Gottleib. *Highly Parallel Computing*. Benjamin/Cummings, Redwood City, California, 2nd edition, 1994.

[8] G. M. Amdahl. Validity of the single-processor approach to achieving large scale computing capabilities. In *AFIPS*, AFIPS Press, Reston, Va, Apr. 1967.

[9] G. A. Anderson and E. D. Jensen. Computer interconnection structures: Taxonomy, characteristics, and examples. *Computing Surveys*, 7(4):197–213, Dec. 1975.

[10] G. R. Andrews and F. B. Schneider. Concepts and notations for concurrent programming. *Computing Surveys*, 15(1):3–43, 1983.

[11] M. Annaratone et al. Warp architecture and implementation. In 13th *Annual International Symposium on Computer Architecture*, pages 346–356, Tokyo, June 1986.

[12] M. Annaratone, C. Pommerell, and R. Rühl. Interprocessor communication speed and performance in distributed-memory parallel processors. In 16th *Annual Symposium on Computer Architectures*, pages 315–324, June 1989.

[13] B. W. Arden and H. Lee. Analysis of chordal ring networks. *IEEE Transactions on Computers*, 30(4):291–295, Apr. 1981.

[14] B. W. Arden and H. Lee. A regular network for multicomputer systems. *IEEE Transactions on Computers*, 31(1):60–69, Jan. 1982.

[15] Arvind, L. Bic, and T. Ungerer. Evolution of dataflow computing. In Gaudiot and Bics, editors, *Advanced topics in dataflow computing*, pages 3–34, Prentice-Hall, Englewood Cliffs, NJ, 1991.

[16] Arvind et al. *The tagged token dataflow architecture*. Technical Report MA 02139, MIT Laboratory for Computer Science, Cambridge, MA, 1984.

[17] J. Backus. Can programming be liberated from the von Neumann style functional style and its algebra of programs. *Communications of the ACM*, 21(8):613–641, 1978.

[18] H. Bal. *Programming Distributed Systems*. Silicon Press, Summit, New Jersey, 1990.

[19] A. Basu. A classification of parallel processing systems. In *ICCD*, 1984.

[20] K. Batcher. Design of a massively parallel processor. *IEEE Transactions on Computers*, 29(9):836–840, Sep. 1980.

[21] G. Bell. Ultracomputer: A TeraFLOP before its time. *Communications of the ACM*, 35(8):26–47, 1992.

[22] M. Ben-Ari. *Principles of Concurrent and Distributed Programming*. Addison-Wesley, Wokingham, England, 1990.

[23] J. C. Bermond, N. Homobono, and C. Peyrat. Large fault tolerant interconnection networks. *Graphs and Combinatorics*, 5:107–123, 1989.

[24] L. N. Bhuyan and D. P. Agrawal. A general class of processor interconnection strategies. In *9th Annual Symposium of Computer Architecture*, pages 90–98, Austin, Texas, Apr. 1982.

[25] L. N. Bhuyan and D. P. Agrawal. Generalised hypercube and hyperbus structures for a computer network. *IEEE Transactions on Computers*, 33(4):323–333, Apr. 1984.

[26] N. Biggs. *Algebraic Graph Theory*. *Cambridge Tracts in Math. No. 67*, Cambridge University Press, London, 1974.

[27] B. Bollobás. *Extremal Graph Theory*. Academic Press, London, 1978.

[28] S. Borkar, R. Cohn, G. Cox, et al. Supporting systolic and memory communication in iWarp. In *17th Annual International Symposium on Computer Architecture*, pages 70–81, May 1990.

[29] P. Brinch Hansen. Structured multiprogramming. *Journal of the ACM*, 15(7):574–578, July 1972.

[30] P. Brinch Hansen. A comparison of two synchronising concepts. *Acta Informatica, Springer Verlag*, 1:190–199, 1972.

[31] P. Brinch Hansen. *Operating systems principles*. Prentice-Hall Inc, Englewood Cliffs, New Jersey, 1973.

[32] P. Brinch Hansen. Distribute processes: a concurrent programming concept. *Communications of the ACM*, 21(11):934–941, Nov. 1978.

[33] C. J. Burgess and A. G. Chalmers. Optimum transputer configurations for real applications requiring global communications. In *18th World Occam and Transputer Users Group Conference*, IOS Press, Manchester, Apr. 1995.

[34] A. W. Burks. Programming and structural changes in parallel computers. In W. Händler, editor, *Conpar*, pages 1–24, Springer, Berlin, 1981.

[35] A. Burns and G. Davies. *Concurrent Programming*. Addison-Wesley, 1993.

[36] N. Carriero and D. Gelernter. *How to Write Parallel Programs*. MIT Press, Cambridge, Massachusetts, 1990.

[37] D. Chaiken, J. Kubiatowicz, and A. Agarwal. LimitLESS directories: a scalable cache coherence scheme. In *Proceedings of the 4th International Conference on Architectural Support for Programming Languages and Operating Systems, ASPLOS-IV*, pages 224–234, Apr. 1991.

[38] A. G. Chalmers. Concurrent features in CLANG. In *Symposium and Workshop on Computer Science Theory and Practice*, Grahamstown, South Africa, Nov. 1983.

[39] A. G. Chalmers. Occam - the language for educating future parallel programmers? *Microprocessing and Microprogramming*, 24:757–760, 1988.

[40] A. G. Chalmers. Useful titbits. *Occam User Group Newsletter*, 5, 1988.

[41] A. G. Chalmers. *A Minimum Path system for parallel processing*. PhD thesis, University of Bristol, Department of Computer Science, Aug. 1991.

[42] A. G. Chalmers, N. W. Campbell, and B. T. Thomas. Computational models for real-time tracking of aircraft engine components. In A. Wagner, editor, *6th North American Transputer Users Group conference*, IOS Press, Vancouver, May 1993.

[43] A. G. Chalmers and S. Gregory. Constructing minimum path configurations for multiprocessor systems. *Parallel Computing*, 19:343–355, Apr. 1993.

[44] A. G. Chalmers and D. J. Paddon. Communication efficient MIMD configurations. In *4th SIAM Conference on Parallel Processing for Scientific Computing*, Chicago, 1989.

[45] A. G. Chalmers and D. J. Paddon. Parallel radiosity methods. In D. L. Fielding, editor, *4th North American Transputer Users Group*, pages 183–193, IOS Press, Ithaca, NY, Oct. 1990.

[46] K. M. Chandy and J. Misra. *Parallel Program Design*. Addison-Wesley, 1988.

[47] P. Chaudhuri. *Parallel Algorithms: Design and analysis*. Prentice-Hall, Australia, 1992.

[48] D. Chen, M. Su, and P. Yew. The impact of synchronisation and granularity on parallel systems. In *17th Annual Symposium on Computer Architecture*, pages 239–248, June 1990.

[49] H. Cheng. Vector pipelining, chaining and speed on the IBM 3090 and Cray X/MP. *IEEE Computer*, 22(9):31–44, 1989.

[50] B. Codenotti and M. Leonici. *Introduction to parallel processing*. Addison-Wesley, Wokingham, England, 1993.

[51] M. F. Cohen and D. P. Greenberg. The hemi-cube: A radiosity solution for complex environments. *ACM Computer Graphics*, 19(3):31–40, July 1985.

[52] M. Cosnard and D. Trystram. *Parallel Algorithms and Architectures*. International Thomson Computer Press, Boston, 1995.

[53] R. Courant and D. Hilbert. *Methods of Mathematical Physics*. Interscience, New York, 1953.

[54] W. J. Dally and C. L. Seitz. Deadlock-free message routing in multiprocessor interconnection netwroks. *IEEE Transactions on Computers*, C-36(5):547–553, May 1987.

[55] S. P. Dandamudi and D. L. Eager. Hierarchical interconnection networks for multicomputer systems. *IEEE Transactions on Computers*, 39(6):786–797, June 1990.

[56] L. Davis, editor. *Handbook of Genetic Algorithms*. Van Nostrand Reinhold, 1991.

[57] A. L. DeCegama. *The Technology of Parallel Processing: Parallel Processing Architectures and VLSI Design*. Prentice-Hall International Inc., 1989.

[58] A. M. Despain and D. A. Patterson. X-tree: A tree structured multiprocessor computer architecture. In 5th *Symposium on Computer Architecture*, pages 144–151, Apr. 1978.

[59] E. W. Dijkstra. Co-operating sequential processes. In F. Genuys, editor, *Programming Languages*, Academic Press, New York, 1968.

[60] K. W. Doty. New designs for dense processor interconnection networks. *IEEE Transactions on Computers*, 33(5):447–450, 1984.

[61] D. Z. Du and F. K. Hwang. Generalised de Bruijn digraphs. *Networks*, 18:27–38, 1988.

[62] I. S. Duff. The influence of vector and parallel processors on numerical analysis. In A. Iserles and M. J. D. Powell, editors, *The State of the Art in Numerical Analysis*, Clarendon Press, Oxford, 1987.

[63] M. J. B. Duff. Review of the CLIP image processing system. In *AFIPS National Computer Conference*, pages 1055–1060, 1978.

[64] D. L. Eager, J. Zahorjan, and E. D. Lazowska. Speedup versus efficiency in parallel systems. *IEEE Transactions on Computers*, 38(3):408–423, March 1989.

[65] A. B. Esfahanian and S. L. Hakimi. Fault-tolerant routing in de Bruijn communication networks. *IEEE Transactions on Computers*, 34(9):777–788, Sep. 1985.

[66] V. Faber, O. M. Lubeck, and A. B. White Jr. Super-linear speedup of an efficient sequential algorithm is not possible. *Parallel Computing*, 3:259–260, 1986.

[67] T. Feng. A survey of interconnection networks. *IEEE Computer*, 12–27, Dec. 1981.

[68] J. A. Fisher. Microprogramming, microprocessing and supercomputing. In *Microprocessing and Microprogramming*, pages 17–20, Aug. 1988.

[69] H. P. Flatt and K. Kennedy. Performance of parallel processors. *Parallel Computing*, 12:1–20, 1989.

[70] M. J. Flynn. Some computer organisations and their effectiveness. *IEEE Transactions on Computers*, 21(9):948–960, 1972.

[71] S. Fortune and J. Wyllie. Parallelism in Random Access Machines. In *Proceedings of ACM Symposium on the Theory of Computing*, pages 114–118, 1978.

[72] I. T. Foster. *Designing and Building Parallel Programs*. Addison-Wesley, Reading, Massachusetts, 1995.

[73] G. Fox et al. *Solving problems on concurrent processors*. Volume 1, Prentice-Hall, 1988.

[74] B. Gebhart. *Heat Transfer*. McGraw Hill Book Company, New York, second edition, 1971.

[75] N. Gehani and A. D. McGettrick, editors. *Concurrent Programming*. Addison-Wesley, Wokingham, 1988.

[76] D. Gelernter. Generative communication in Linda. *ACM Transactions on Programming Languages and Systems*, 7(1):81–112, Jan. 1985.

[77] C. F. Gerald and P. O. Wheatley. *Applied numerical analysis*. *World Student Series*, Addison-Wesley, Reading, MA, 5th edition, 1994.

[78] A. S. Glassner. Space Subdivision for Fast Ray Tracing. *IEEE Computer Graphics and Applications*, 4(10):15–22, Oct. 1984.

[79] A. S. Glassner, editor. *An introduction to ray tracing*. Academic Press, London, 1989.

[80] D. E. Goldberg. *Genetic Algorithm in search, optimisation and machine learning*. Addison-Wesley, 1989.

[81] J. R. Goodman and C. H. Seéquin. Hypertree: A multiprocessor interconnection topology. *IEEE Transactions on Computers*, C-30(12):923–933, Dec. 1981.

[82] C. M. Goral, K. E. Torrance, D. P. Greenberg, and B. Battaile. Modelling the interaction of light between diffuse surfaces. *ACM Computer Graphics*, 18(3):213–222, July 1984.

[83] A. Gottlieb, R. Grishman, C. P. Kruskal, K. P. McAuliffe, L. Rudolph, and M. Snir. The NYU Ultracomputer designing a MIMD, shared-memory parallel machine. *IEEE Transactions on Computers*, C-32(2):175–189, Feb. 1983.

[84] A. Gottlieb, B. D. Lubachevsky, and L. Rudolph. Basic techniques for the efficient coordination of very large numbers of cooperating sequential processors. *ACM Transactions on Programming Languages and Systems*, 5(2):164–189, 1983.

[85] S. A. Green. *Parallel Processing for Computer Graphics*. *Research Monographs in Parallel and Distributed Computing*, Pitman Publishing, London, 1991.

[86] S. A. Green and D. J. Paddon. A non-shared memory multiprocessor architecture for large database problems. In M. Cosnard, M. H. Barton, and M. Vanneschi, editors, *Proceedings of the IFIP WG 10.3 Working Conference on Parallel Processing*, Pisa, 1988.

[87] D. P. Greenberg, M. F. Cohen, and K. E. Torrance. Radiosity: A method for computing global illumination. *The Visual Computer*, 2(5):291–297, Sep. 1986.

[88] P. H. L. Groenenboom and B. V. Neratoom. The application of boundary elements to steady and unsteady potential fluid flow problems in two and three dimensions. In C. A. Brebbia, editor, *Proceedings of the 3rd International Seminar on Boundary Element Methods*, pages 37–52, Soringer-Verlag, Irvine, California, July 1981.

[89] H. A. Grosch. High speed arithmetic: The digital computer as a research tool. *Journal of the Optical Society of America*, 43(4):306–310, Apr. 1953.

[90] H. A. Grosch. Grosch's law revisited. *Computerworld*, 8(16):24, Apr. 1975.

[91] J. R. Gurd, C. Kirkham, and J. Watson. The Manchester prototype dataflow computer. *Communications of the ACM*, 28(1):36–45, 1985.

[92] J. L. Gustafson. Re-evaluating Amdahl's law. *Communications of the ACM*, 31(5):532–533, May 1988.

[93] B. K. Haddon. Nested monitor calls. *ACM Operating systems review*, 11(4):18–23, Oct. 1977.

[94] E. Hagersten. *Toward Scalable Cache Only Memory Architectures*. PhD thesis, Swedish Institute of Computer Science, 1992.

[95] W. Händler. The impact of classification schemes on computer architecture. In *IEEE International Conference on Parallel Processing*, pages 7–15, IEEE, New York, Aug. 1977.

[96] D. R. Hartree. The ENIAC, an electronic computing machine. *Nature*, 158:500–506, 1946.

[97] L. W. Hawkes. A regular fault-tolerant architecture for interconnection networks. *IEEE Transaction on Computers*, 34:677–680, July 1985.

[98] J. L. Hennessy and D. A. Patterson. *Computer Architecture: A quantitative approach*. Morgan Kaufmann, San Mateo, CA, 1990.

[99] J. L. Hess. Panel methods in computational fluid dynamics. *Annual Review of Fluid Mechanics*, 22, 1990.

[100] J. L. Hess and A. M. O. Smith. *Calculation of Non-Lifting Potential Flow about Arbitrary Three-Dimensional Bodies*. Technical Report ES 40622, Douglas Aircraft Company Inc., March 1962.

[101] J. L. Hess and A. M. O. Smith. 'Calculation of Potential Flow about Arbitrary Bodies'. *Progress in Aeronautical Sciences*, 8, 1966.

[102] T. Hey. Scientific applications. In G. Harp, editor, *Transputer Applications*, chapter 8, pages 170–203, Pitman Publishing, 1989.

[103] D. W. Hillis. *The Connection Machine*. The MIT Press, 1985.

[104] C. A. R. Hoare. Monitors: An operating system structuring concept. *Communications of the ACM*, 17(10):549–557, Oct. 1974.

[105] C. A. R. Hoare. Communicating sequential processes. *Communications of the ACM*, 21(8):666–677, Aug. 1978.

[106] C. A. R. Hoare. *Communicating Sequential Processes. International Series in Computer Science*, Prentice-Hall International, London, 1985.

[107] R. W. Hockney and C. R. Jesshope. *Parallel Computers 2: Architecture, Programming and Algorithms*. Adam Hilger, Bristol, 1988.

[108] R. W. Hockney and C. R. Jesshope. *Parallel Computers 2: Architecture, Programming and Algorithms*, chapter 1, pages 60–81. Adam Hilger, 1988.

[109] J. H. Holland. *Adaptions in natural and artificial systems*. University of Michigan Press, Ann Arbor, 1975.

[110] M. Homewood, M. D. May, D. Shepherd, and R. Shepherd. The IMS T800 transputer. *IEEE Micro*, 10–26, 1987.

[111] R. M. Hord. *Parallel Supercomputing in MIMD Architectures*. CRC Press, Boca Raton, 1993.

[112] R. J. Hosking, D. C. Joyce, and J. C. Turner. *First steps in numerical analysis*. Hodder and Stoughton, Lonfon, 1978.

[113] HPF Forum. High Performance Fortran language specification. *Scientific Programming*, 2(1), June 1993.

[114] M. E. C. Hull, D. Crookes, and P. J. Sweeney. *Parallel processing: The transputer and its applications. International Computer Science Series*, Addison-Wesley, Wokingham, 1994.

[115] K. Hwang. *Advanced Computer Architecture. McGraw-Hill Series in Computer Science*, McGraw-Hill, New York, 1993.

[116] K. Hwang and F. A. Briggs. *Computer Architecture and Parallel Processing*. McGraw-Hill, New York, 1985.

[117] J. L. Keed. On structuring operating systems with monitors. *The Australian Computer Journal*, 10(1):5–9, Feb. 1978.

[118] D. E. Knuth. *Sorting and Searching*. Volume 3 of *The Art of Computer Programming*, Addison-Wesley, 1973.

[119] H. Kobayashi, T. Nakamura, and Y. Shigei. 'Parallel Processing of an Object Space for Image Synthesis Using Ray Tracing'. *The Visual Computer*, 3(1):13–22, Feb. 1987.

[120] E. V. Krishnamurthy. *Parallel processing: principles and practice. International Computer Science Series*, Addison-Wesley, 1989.

[121] KSR. *KSR Technical Summary*. Kendall Square Research, Waltham, MA, 1992.

[122] V. Kumar, A. Grama, A. Gupta, and G. Karyps. *Introduction to Parallel Computing*. Benjamin/Cummings, Redwood City, California, 1994.

[123] H. T. Kung. *VLSI array processors*. Prentice-Hall, Englewood Cliffs, NJ, 1988.

[124] H. T. Kung and C. E. Leiserson. Systolic arrays (for VLSI). In Duff and Stewart, editors, *Sparse Matrix proceedings*, SIAM, Philadelphia, 1978.

[125] C. Lazou. *Supercomputers and Their Use*. Claredon Press, Oxford, revised edition, 1988.

[126] G. Lee, B. W. Quattlebaum, S. Jamil, M. Agarwal, L. Kinney, , and D. J. Lilja. *DICE Prototype Specification*. Technical Report #06, Dept. of EE, Univ. of Minnesota, Aug. 1993.

[127] C. E. Leiserson. Fat-Trees: universal networks for hardware-efficient supercomputing. *IEEE Transactions on Computers*, C-34(10):892–901, Oct. 1985.

[128] D. Lenoski, J. Laudon, T. Joe, D. Nakahira, L. Stevens, A. Gupta, and J. Hennessy. The DASH prototype: logic overhead and performance. *IEEE Transactions on Parallel and Distributed Systems*, 4(1):41–61, Jan. 1993.

[129] T. Lewis and H. El-Rewini. *Introduction to parallel computing*. Prentice-Hall, 1992.

[130] K. Li. Ivy: a shared virtual memory system for parallel computing. *Proceedings of the 1988 International Conference on Parallel Processing*, 2:94–101, Aug. 1988.

[131] G. J. Lipovski and M. Malek. *Parallel Computing: Theory and comparisons*. John Wiley, New York, 1987.

[132] A. Lister. The problems of nested monitor calls. *ACM operating systems review*, 11(3):5–7, July 1977.

[133] K. O. May. Historiography: A perspective for computer scientists. In N. Metropolis, J. Howlett, and G. Rota, editors, *A History of Computing in the Twentieth Century*, pages 11–18, Academic Press, 1980.

[134] M. D. May and R. Shepherd. *Communicating Process Computers*. Inmos Technical Note 22, Inmos Ltd., Bristol, 1987.

[135] M. D. May, P. W. Thompson, and P. H. Welch, editors. *Network, routers & transputers*. IOS Press, Amsterdam, 1993.

[136] C. L. McCreary, M. E. McArdle, and J. D. McCreary. *Broadcast Communication Delay Metrics for the iPSC/2 and iPSC/860 Hypercubes*. Technical Report, Dept of Computer Science and Engineering, Auburn University, Alabama, USA 36849, 1991.

[137] L. F. Menabrea and A. Augusta(translator). Sketch of the Analytical Engine invented by Charles Babbage. In P. Morrison and E. Morrison, editors, *Charles Babbage and his Calculating Engines*, Dover Publications, New York, 1961.

[138] Message Passing Interface Forum. *Document for a standard message-passing interface*. Technical Report, University of Tennessee, Knoxville, 1993.

[139] J. Mohan. *Performance of Parallel Programs: Model and Analyses*. PhD thesis, Carnegie Mellon University, Pittsburgh, Philadelphia, USA 15213, July 1984.

[140] B. Monien and H. Sudborough. Comparing interconnection networks. In *13th Symposium on Mathematical Foundations of Computer Science*, pages 138–153, 1988.

[141] H. L. Muller, P. W. A. Stallard, and D. H. D. Warren. *The Data Diffusion Machine with a Scalable Point-to-Point Network*. Technical Report CSTR-93-17, Department of Computer Science, University of Bristol, Oct. 1993.

[142] H. L. Muller, P. W. A. Stallard, and D. H. D. Warren. An evaluation study of a link-based data diffusion machine. In *Proceedings of the International Workshop on Support for Large Scale Shared Memory Architectures*, pages 115–128, Cancun, Mexico, Apr. 1994.

[143] H. L. Muller, P. W. A. Stallard, and D. H. D. Warren. Hiding miss latencies with multi-threading on the data diffusion machine. In *Proceedings of the 1995 International Conference on Parallel Processing, volume I*, pages 178–185, Oconomowoc, Wisconsin, Aug. 1995.

[144] H. L. Muller, P. W. A. Stallard, and D. H. D. Warren. The role of associative memory in vsm architectures: a price-performance comparison. In *Proceedings of 4th EUROMICRO Workshop on Parallel and Distributed Processing*, IEEE Computer Society Press. To Appear, Braga, Portugal, Jan. 1996.

[145] H. L. Muller, P. W. A. Stallard, D. H. D. Warren, and S. Raina. Parallel evaluation of a parallel architecture by means of calibrated emulation. In *Proceedings of the 8th International Parallel Processing Symposium*, pages 260–267, IEEE Computer Society Press, Cancun, Mexico, Apr. 1994.

[146] C. Nevison et al. *Laboratories for Parallel Computing*. Jones & Bartlett, 1990.

[147] J. N. Newman. Distribution of sources and normal dipoles over a quadrilateral panel. *Journal of Engineering Mathematics*, 20:113–126, 1986.

[148] M. G. Norman. Bulk synchronous parallelism. *WoTUG Newsletter*, 17:32–35, July 1992.

[149] D. Nussbaum and A. Argarwal. Scalability of parallel machines. *Communications of the ACM*, 34(3):56–61, March 1991.

[150] D. L. Parnas. The non-problem of nested monitor calls. *ACM Operating System Review*, 12(1):12–14, Jan. 1978.

[151] D. K. Pradhan and S. M. Reddy. A fault tolerant communication architecture for distributed systems. *IEEE Transaction on Computers*, 31, Sep. 1982.

[152] F. P. Preparata and J. Vuillemin. The Cube-connected cycles: A versatile network for parallel computation. *Communications of the ACM*, 24(5):300–309, May 1981.

[153] T. Priol and K. Bouatouch. Static load balancing for a parallel ray tracing on a MIMD hypercube. *The Visual Computer*, 5(1):109–119, March 1989.

[154] B. Purvis. Programming the Intel i860. *Parallelogram International*, 6–9, Oct. 1990.

[155] M. J. Quinn. *Parallel Computing: Theory and practice*. McGraw-Hill, New York, 1994.

[156] S. Raina and D. H. D. Warren. Traffic patterns in a scalable multiprocessor through transputer emulation. In *Proceedings of the 25th Hawaii International Conference on System Sciences*, pages 267–276, 1992.

[157] S. Raina, D. H. D. Warren, and J. Cownie. Shared virtual memory on transputers via the Data Diffusion Machine. In H. Zedan, editor, *13th Occam User Group Technical Meeting*, pages 322–330, IOS Press, York, Sep. 1990.

[158] V. Rajaraman. *Elements of parallel computing*. Prentice-Hall of India, New Dehli, 1990.

[159] S. F. Reddaway. DAP - a Distributed Array Processor. In *1st Annual Symposium on Computer Architecture*, 1973.

[160] R. Rettberg and R. Thomas. Contention is no obstacle to shared memory multiprocessing. *Communications of the ACM*, 29(12):1202–1212, 1986.

[161] C. W. Reynolds. Flocks, herds and schools: a distributed behavioural model. *ACM Computer Graphics*, 21(4):25–34, July 1987.

[162] R. M. Russel. The CRAY-1 computer system. *Communications of the ACM*, 21:63–72, 1978.

[163] I. D. Scherson and P. F. Corbett. Communications overhead and the expected speed-up of multidimensional mesh-connected parallel processors. *Journal of Parallel and Distributed Computing*, 11:86–96, 1991.

[164] J. P. Secilla, N. Garcia, and J. Carrascosa. Template location in noisy pictures. *Signal Processing*, 14:347–361, 1988.

[165] A. Sengupta, P. D. Joshi, and S. Bandyopadhyay. A synthesis approach to design optimally fault tolerant network architecture. *IEEE Transaction on Computers*, 40(1), Jan. 1991.

[166] A. Sengupta, A. San, and S. Bandyopadhyay. On optimally fault-tolerant multiprocessor network architecture. *IEEE Transaction on Computers*, 36:619–623, May 1987.

[167] J. C. Sheperdson and H. E. Sturgis. Computability of recursive functions. *Journal of the ACM*, 10:217–255, 1963.

[168] J. E. Shore. Second thoughts on parallel processing. *Comput. Elect. Eng.*, 1:95–109, 1973.

[169] R. Siegel and J. R. Howell. *Thermal Radiation Heat Transfer*. Hemisphere Publishing Corporation, Washington D.C., 1981.

[170] D. M. Smith and S. P. Fiddes. Efficient parallelisation for implicit and explicit solvers on a MIMD computer. In R. B. Pelz, A. Ecer, and J. Haüser, editors, *Parallel Computational Fluid Dynamics '92*, pages 383–395, Elsevier Science Publisher B.V., Amsterdam, 1992.

[171] E. M. Sparrow and R. D. Cess. *Radiation Heat Transfer*. Books/Cole Publishing Company, Belmont, California, 1966.

[172] R. J. Swam, S. H. Fuller, and D. P. Siewiorek. 'Cm*—A Modular, Multi-Microprocessor'. In *Proc. AFIPS 1977 Fall Joint Computer Conference 46*, pages 637–644, 1977.

[173] S. Thakkar, P. Gifford, and G. Fiellamd. The Balance multiprocessor system. *IEEE Micro*, 8(1):57–69, Feb. 1988.

[174] L. C. Thomas. *Fundamentals of Heat Transfer*. Prentice-Hall INC, Englewood Cliffs NJ, 1980.

[175] J. Tidmus, A. Chalmers, and R. Miles. Distributed Monte Carlo techniques for interactive photo-realistic image synthesis. In *17th World Occam and Transputer Users Group*, 1994.

[176] P. C. Treleaven, D. R. Brownbridge, and R. P. Hopkins. Data driven and demand-driven computer architecture. *Communications of the ACM*, 14(1):95–143, March 1982.

[177] A. Trew and G. Wilson, editors. *Past, Present and Parallel: A survey of available parallel computer systems*. Springer-Verlag, London, 1991.

[178] L. W. Tucker and G. G. Robertson. Architecture and applications of the Connection Machine. *IEEE Computer*, 21(8):26–38, 1988.

[179] L. G. Valiant. A bridging model for parallel computation. *Communications of the ACM*, 33(8):103–111, Aug. 1990.

[180] C. von Conta. Torus and other networks as communication networks with up to some hundred points. *IEEE Transactions on Computers*, 33(7):657–666, 1983.

[181] D. H. D. Warren and S. Haridi. Data Diffusion Machine - a scalable shared virtual memory multiprocessor. In *International Conference on Fifth Generation Computer Systems*, pages 943–952, Tokyo, Dec. 1988.

[182] D. H. D. Warren and S. Haridi. The Data Diffusion Machine—a scalable shared virtual memory multiprocessor. In *Proceedings of the 1988 International Conference on Fifth Generation Computer Systems*, pages 943–952, Tokyo, Japan, Dec. 1988.

[183] R. P. Weicker. Dhrystone: A synthetic systems programming benchmark. *Communications of the ACM*, 27(10):1013–1030, 1984.

[184] H. Wettstein. The problem of nested monitor calls revisited. *ACM Operating Systems Review*, 12(1):19–23, Jan. 1978.

[185] L. D. Wittie. Communication structures for large networks of microcomputers. *IEEE Transactions on Computers*, 30(4):264–273, 1981.

Index